From Far Away™

Vol. 14

Story and Art by
Kyoko Hikawa

CONTENTS

Our Story So Far...

Eighteen-year-old high school student Noriko Tachiki has been transported to another world filled with magic, mystery, and a handsome but moody young warrior named Izark Kia Tarj. Now they are on the run from multiple enemies intent on destroying their partnership and harnessing the powerful energy that they possess.

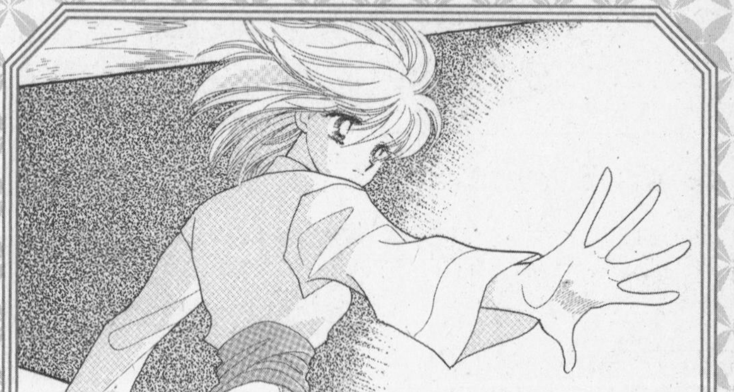

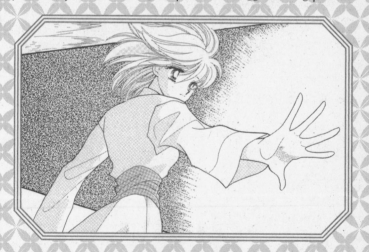

Noriko's life hangs in the balance as the final battle ensues between Izark and his foes. Keimos Lee Goda's dark new powers make him a formidable foe. And the rest of Noriko and Izark's enemies are gathering forces while the fight between Izark and Keimos rages on.

It's time for Noriko to use what she's learned in this magical land to become The Awakening and control The Sky Demon. The only hope for her friends and their entire universe is that the innocent young girl from our normal world really is as powerful as the prophecies say.

かなた
彼方から
FROM FAR AWAY

CAST OF CHARACTERS:

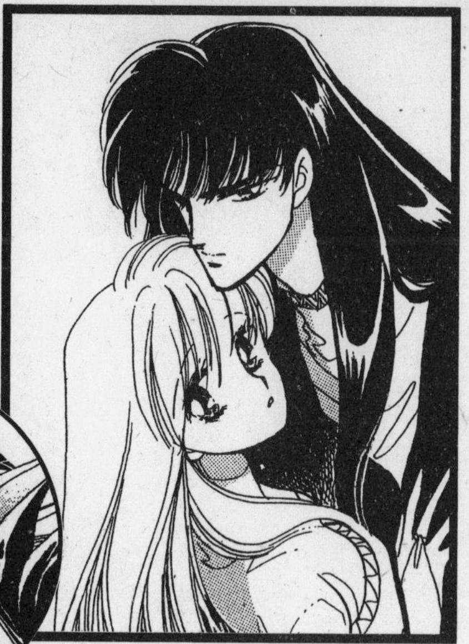

IZARK KIA TAJ
A TRAVELING WARRIOR WITH AMAZING POWERS. HE'S PROTECTED NORIKO DURING HER ENTIRE JOURNEY. BUT WILL THE DEMON WAITING INSIDE HIM ULTIMATELY DESTROY ALL HE LOVES?

DEEP IN THE RECESSES OF HIS MIND, IZARK HARBORS THE AWESOME POWER OF...

THE SKY DEMON

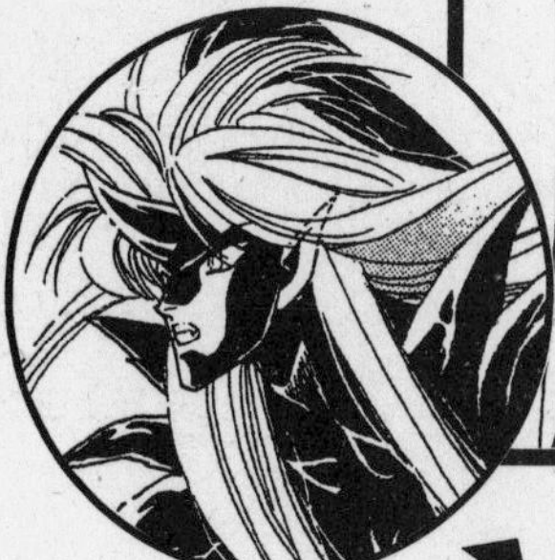

NORIKO TACHIKI
JUST AN ORDINARY TEEN FROM OUR WORLD UNTIL DESTINY WROTE HER INTO THE ROLE OF THE AWAKENING, DOOMED TO TURN THE YOUNG MAN SHE LOVES INTO A DEMON.

OUR SUPPORTING CAST:

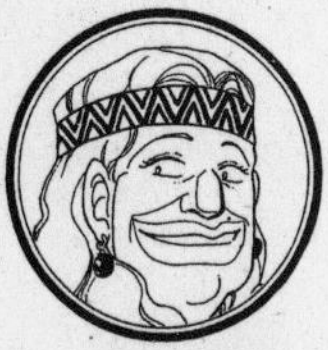

GAYA
POWERFUL MATRIARCH

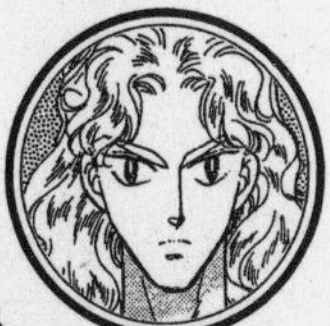

BANADAM
LOYAL ALLY

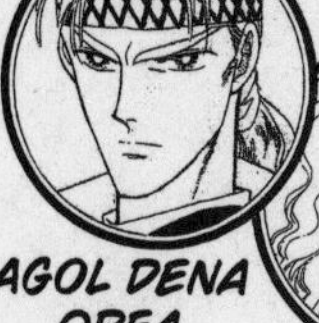

AGOL DENA ORFA
FIERCE DEFENDER

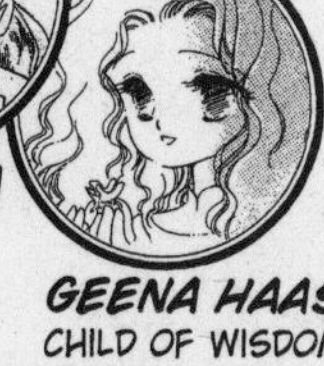

GEENA HAAS
CHILD OF WISDOM

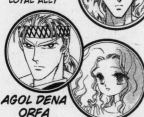

RACHEF
THE SHADOWY LEADER OF THE FREE CITY OF REINKA IS CLOSER THAN EVER TO HIS FINAL GOAL: HARNESSING THE POWER OF THE SKY DEMON FOR HIMSELF, EVEN IF IT MEANS KILLING IZARK TO PROCURE IT.

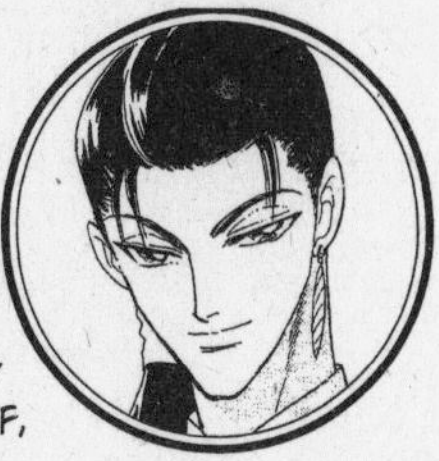

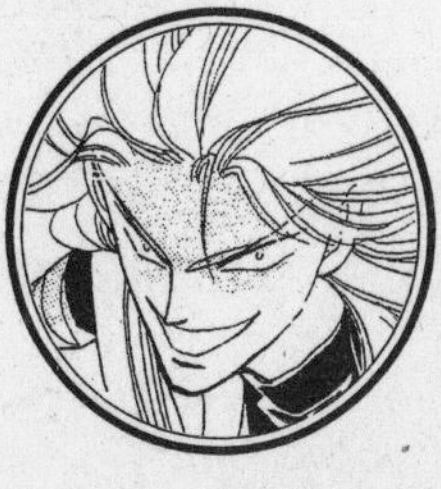

KEIMOS LEE GODA
HIS OBSESSION TO BEAT IZARK AT BATTLE HAS ALL BUT DESTROYE ANY SHRED OF HUMANIT THIS ONCE-PROMISING YOUNG WARRIOR HAD LEFT.

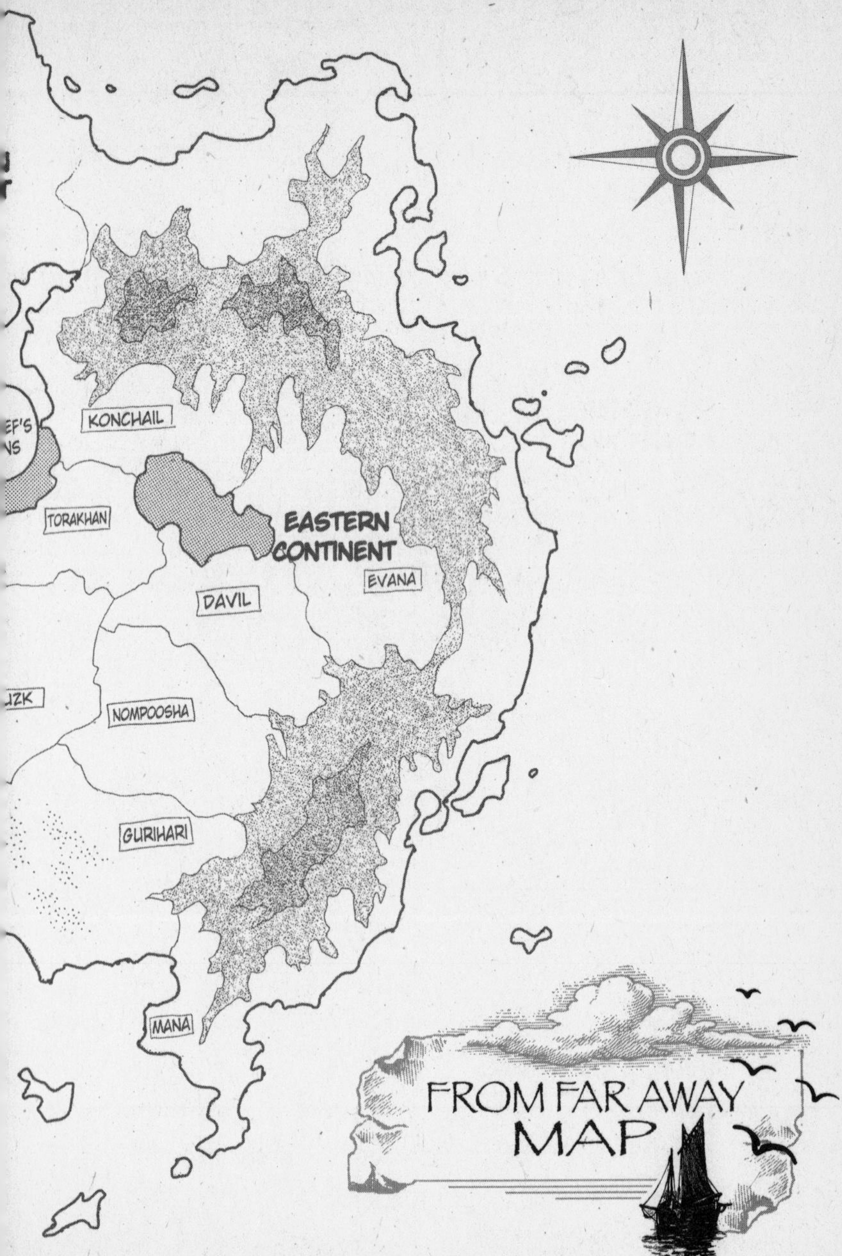
KONCHAIL
TORAKHAN
EASTERN CONTINENT
EVANA
DAVIL
NOMPOOSHA
GURIHARI
MANA
FROM FAR AWAY
MAP

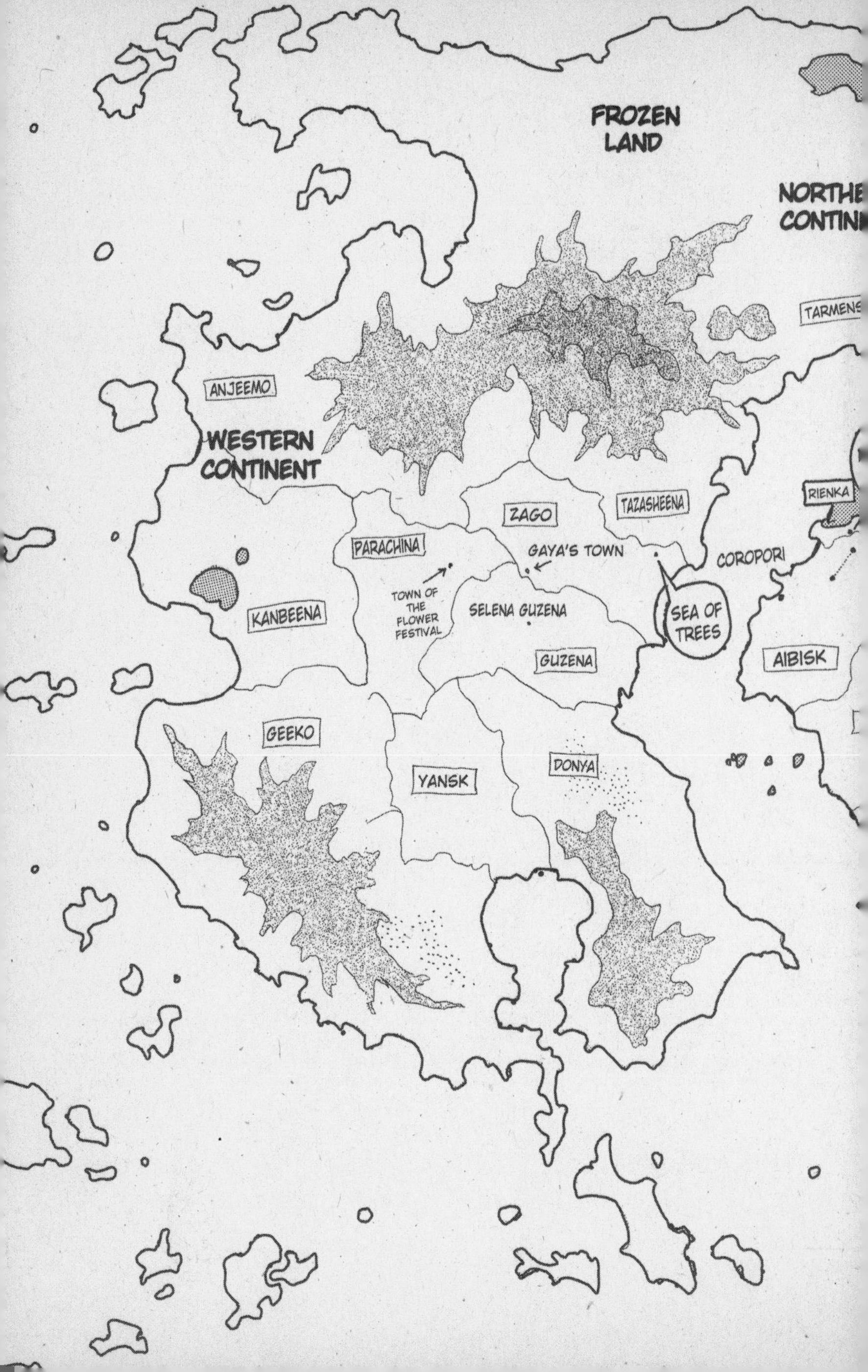
FROZEN LAND
NORTHE
CONTIN
TARMENS
ANJEEMO
WESTERN CONTINENT
RIENKA
ZAGO
TAZASHEENA
PARACHINA
GAYA'S TOWN
COROPORI
TOWN OF THE FLOWER FESTIVAL
SELENA GUZENA
SEA OF TREES
KANBEENA
GUZENA
AIBISK
GEEKO
YANSK
DONYA

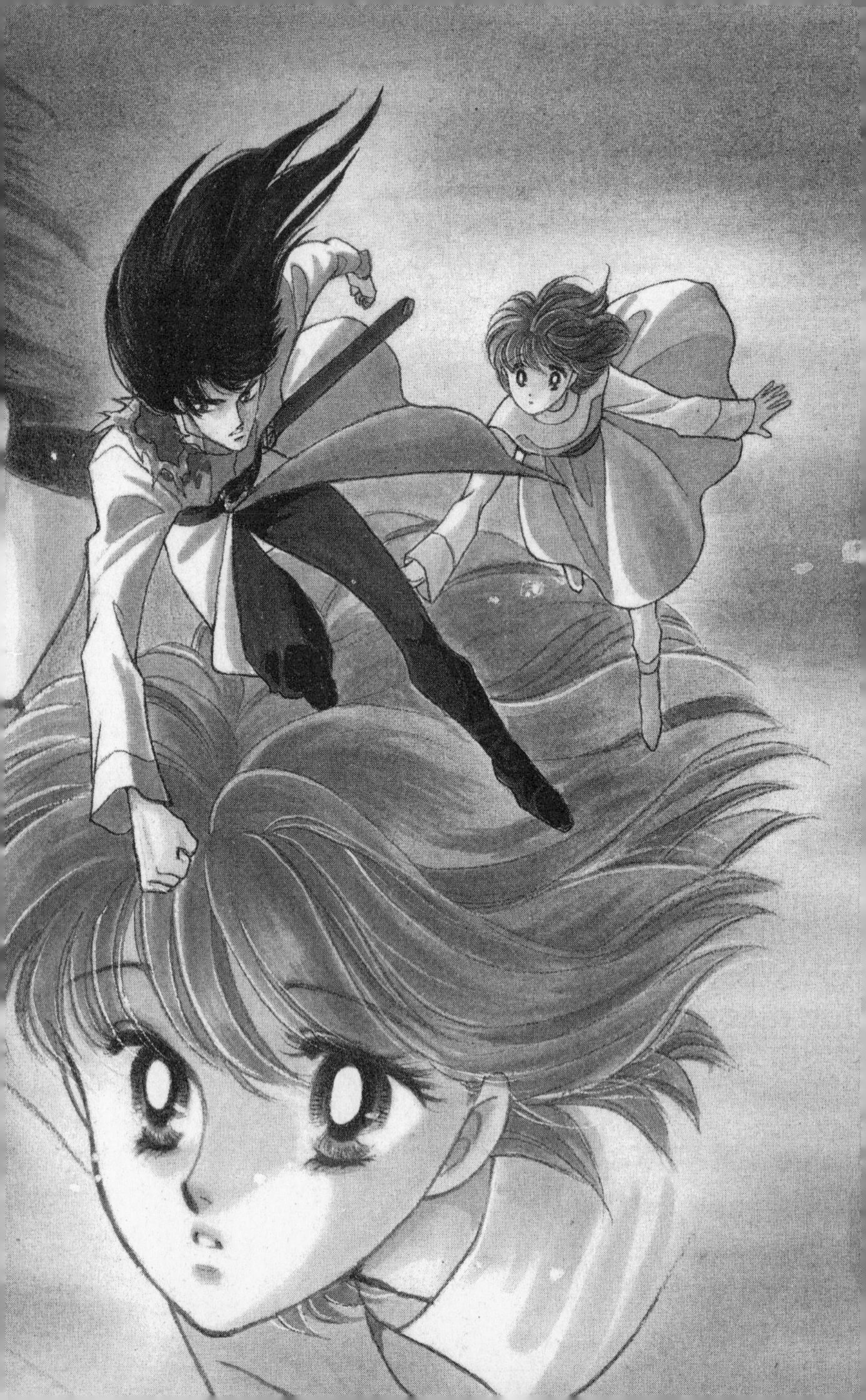

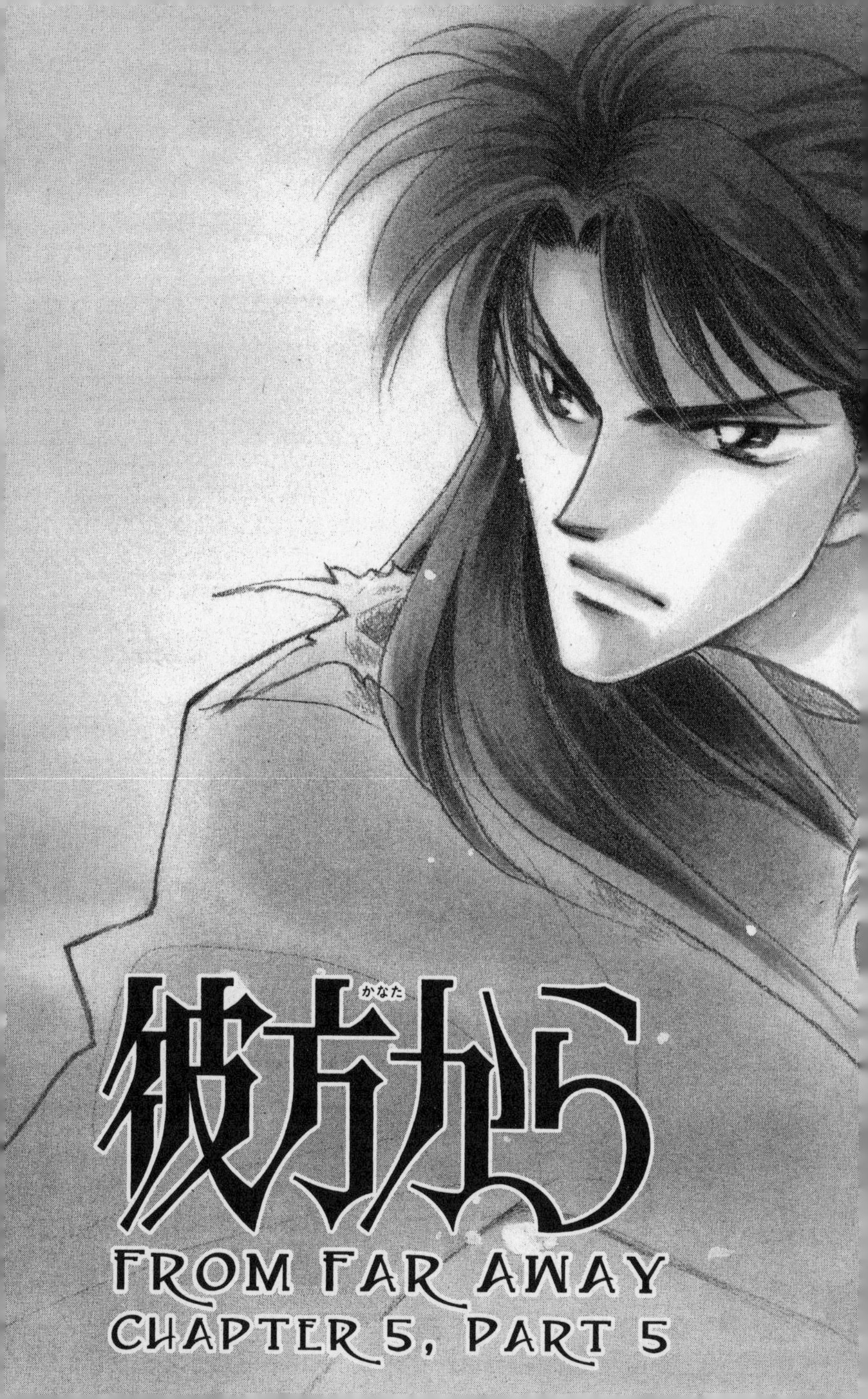

かなた
彼方から5
FROM FAR AWAY
CHAPTER 5, PART 5

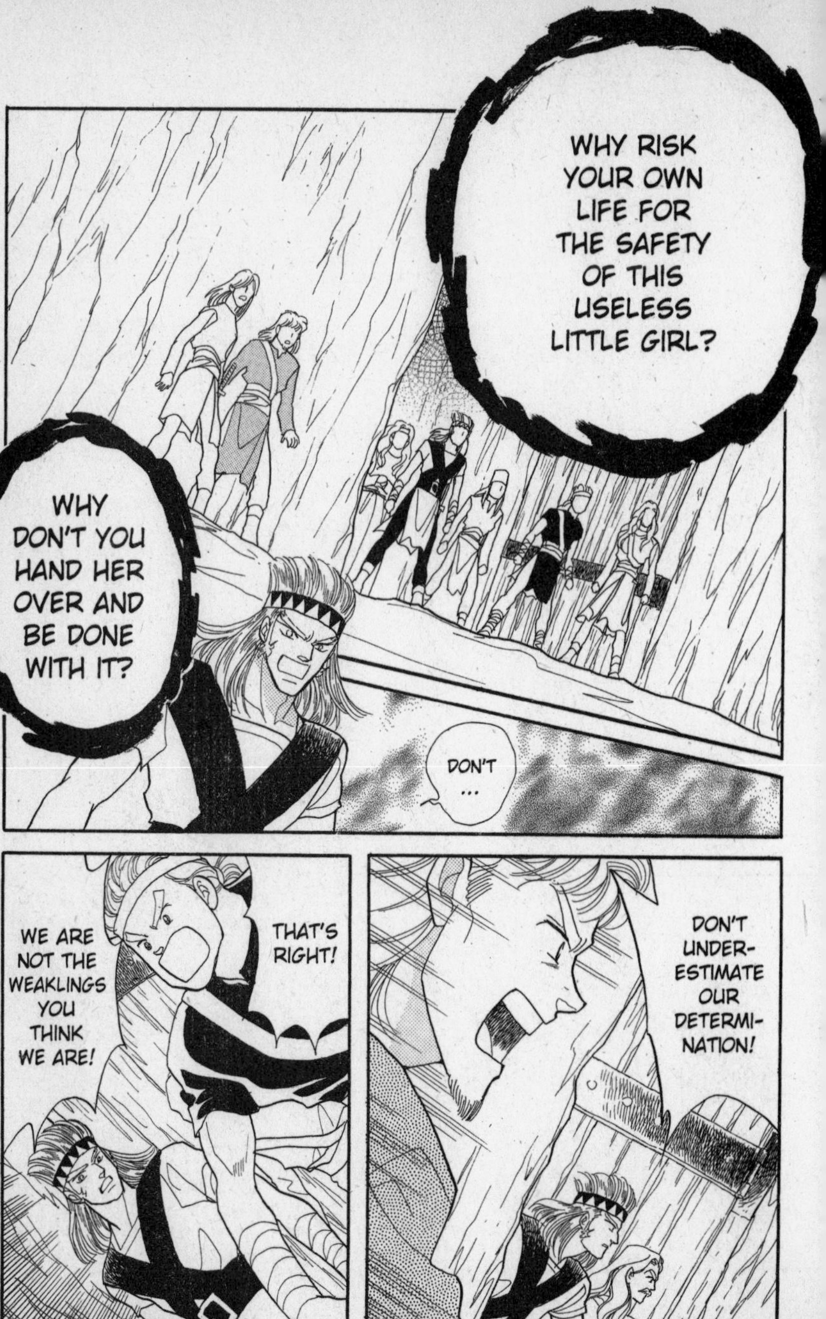
WHY RISK YOUR OWN LIFE FOR THE SAFETY OF THIS USELESS LITTLE GIRL?
WHY DON'T YOU HAND HER OVER AND BE DONE WITH IT?
DON'T ...
DON'T UNDER-ESTIMATE OUR DETERMI-NATION!
THAT'S RIGHT!
WE ARE NOT THE WEAKLINGS YOU THINK WE ARE!

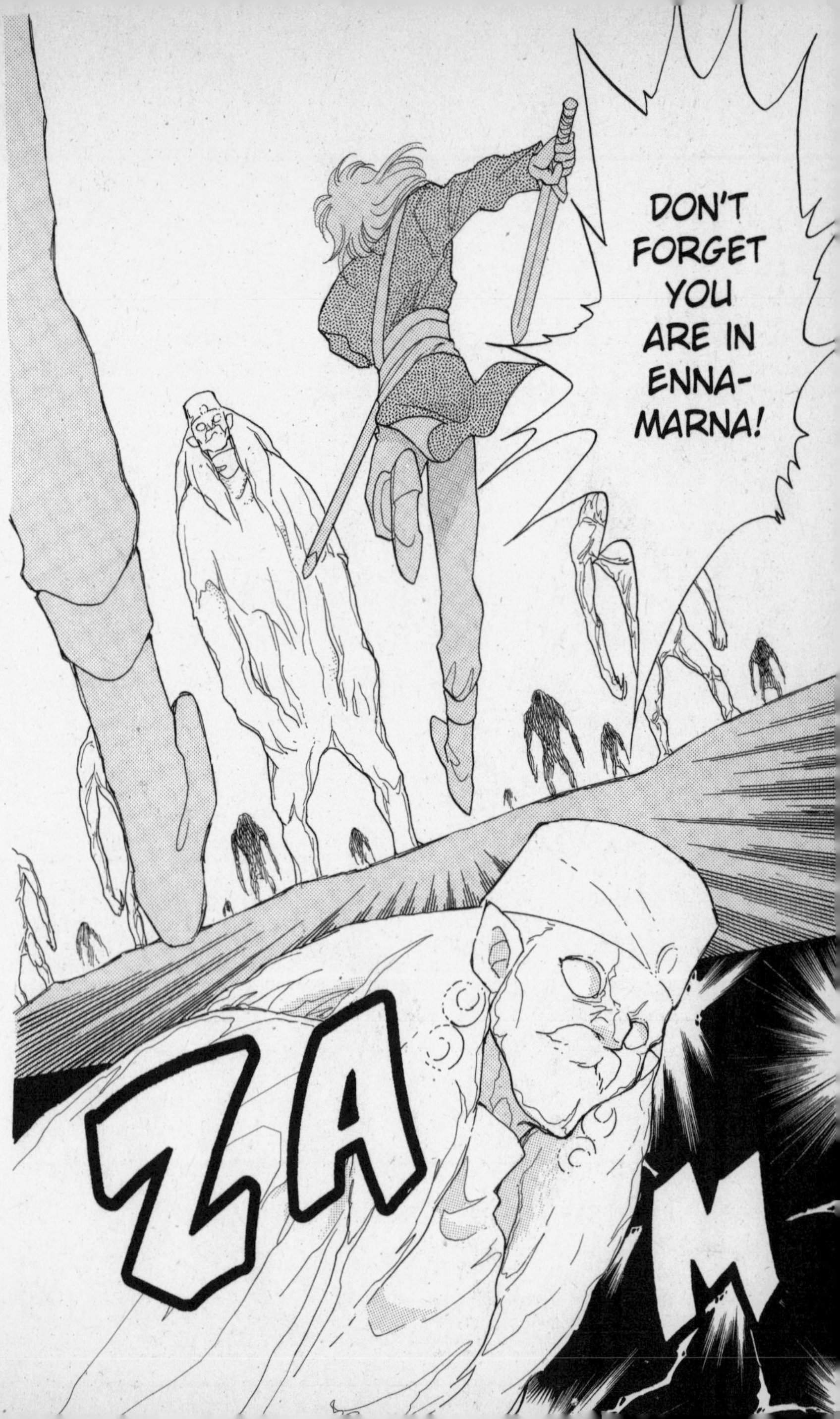
DON'T FORGET YOU ARE IN ENNA-MARNA!
ZAAM

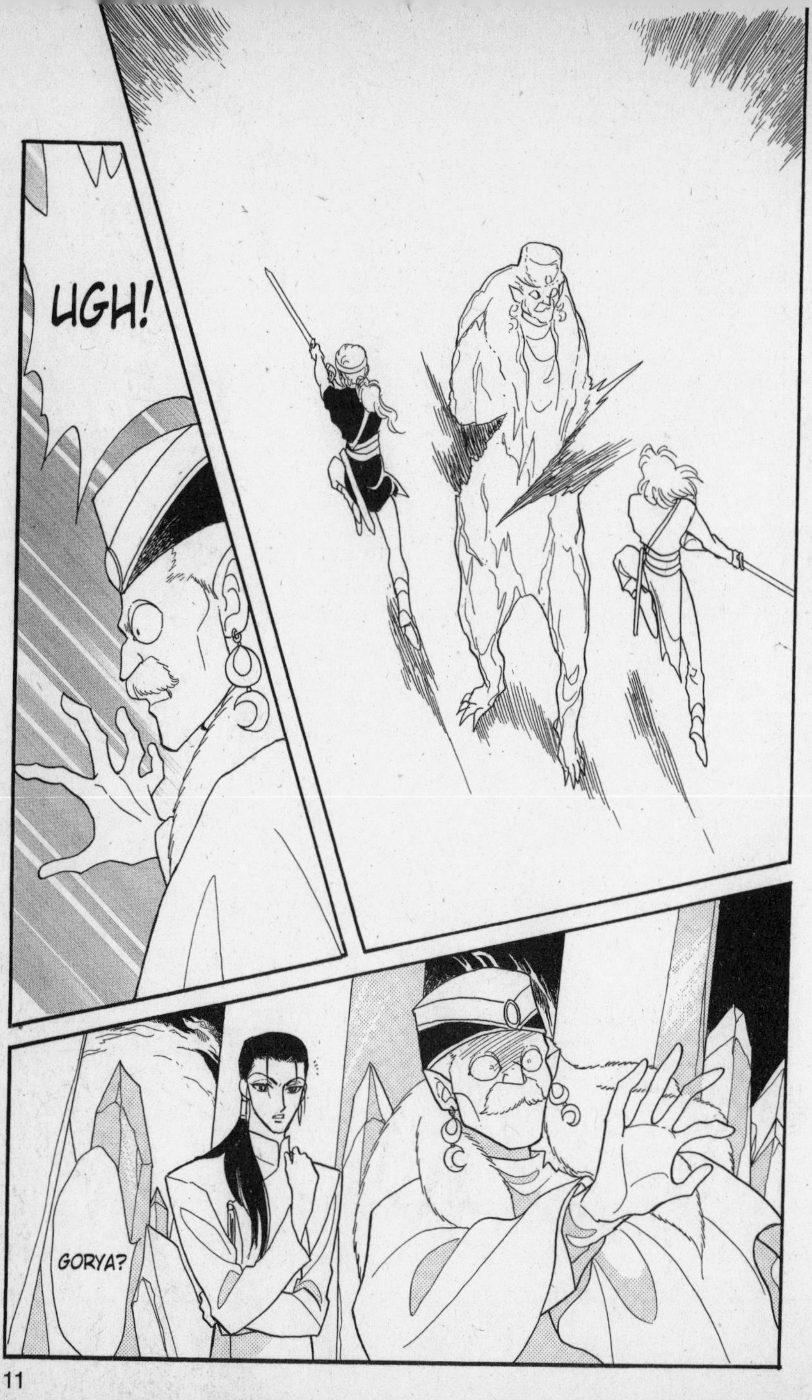
UGH!
GORYA?

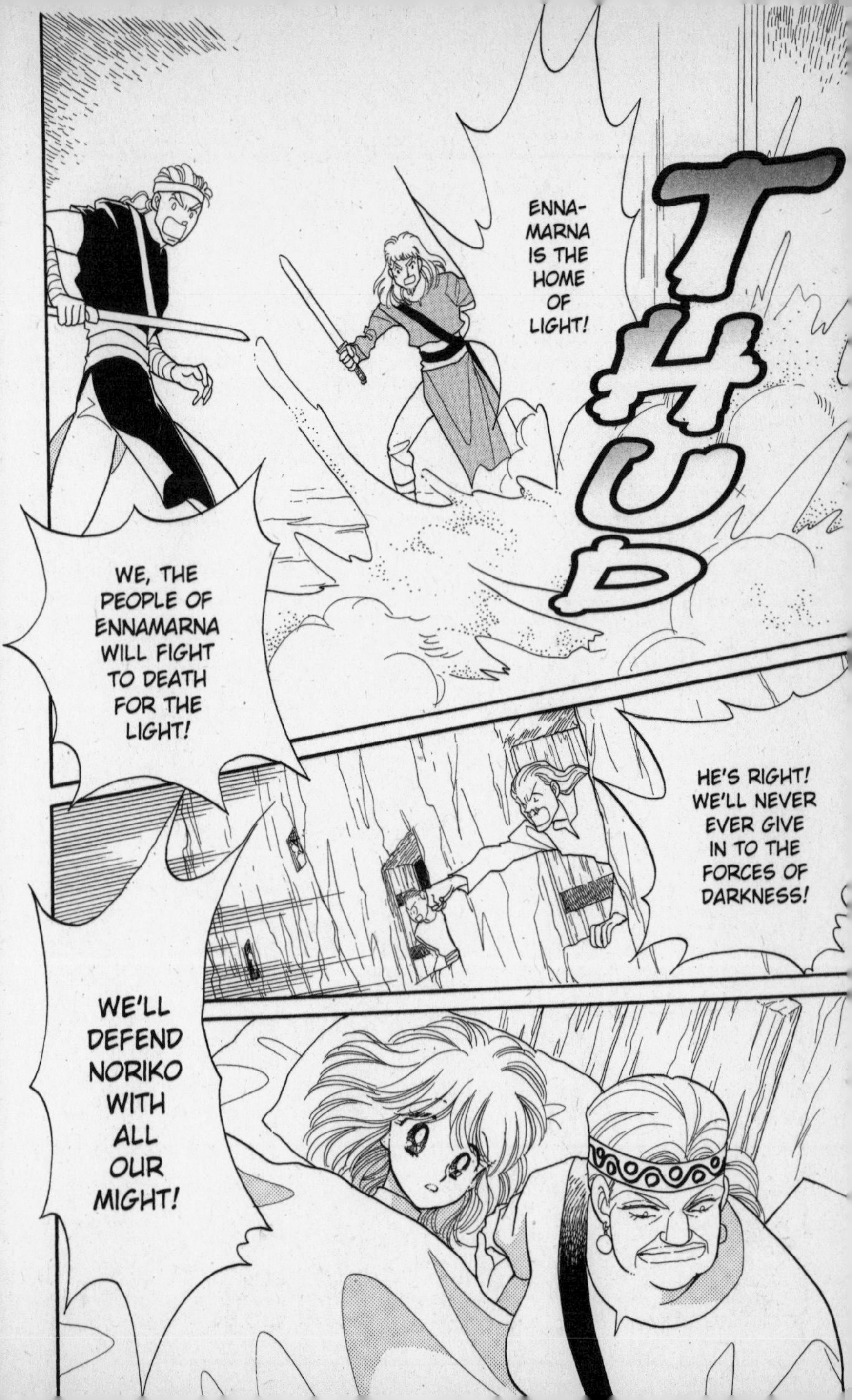
THUD
ENNA-MARNA IS THE HOME OF LIGHT!
WE, THE PEOPLE OF ENNAMARNA WILL FIGHT TO DEATH FOR THE LIGHT!
HE'S RIGHT! WE'LL NEVER EVER GIVE IN TO THE FORCES OF DARKNESS!
WE'LL DEFEND NORIKO WITH ALL OUR MIGHT!

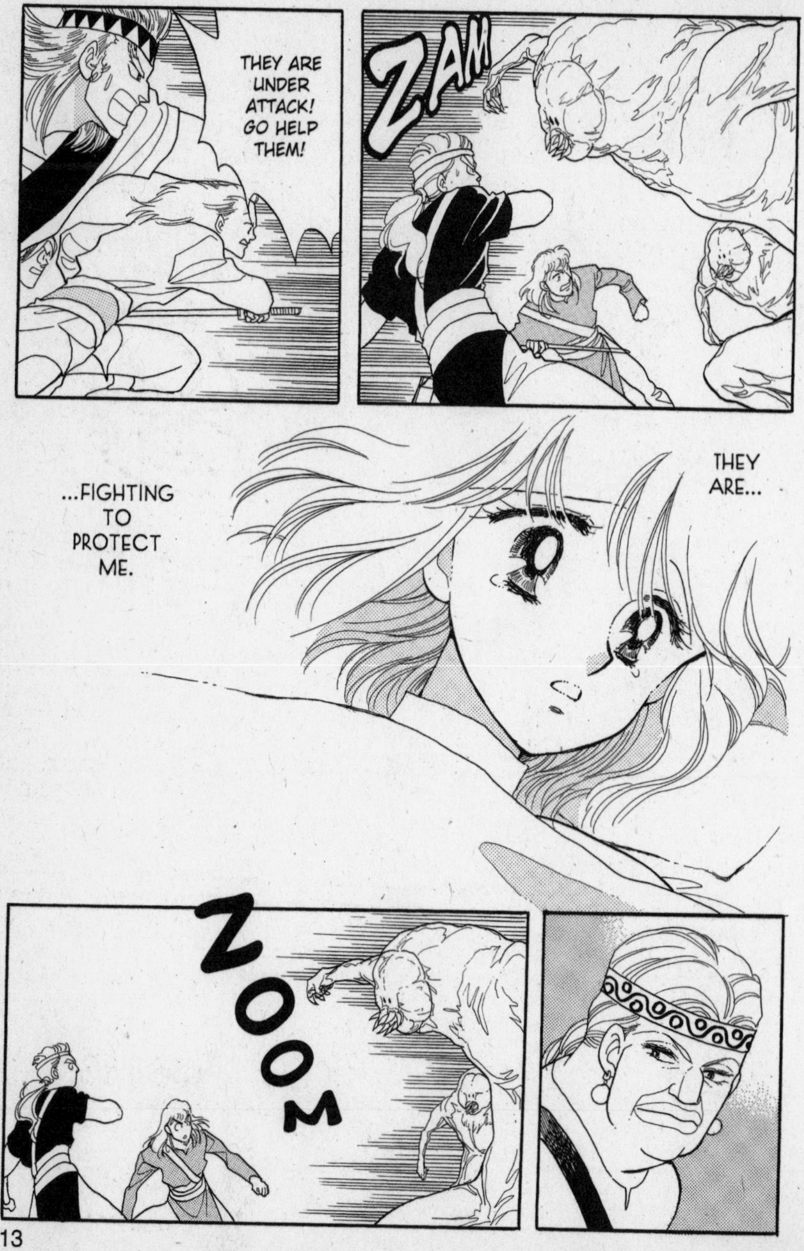
ZAM
THEY ARE UNDER ATTACK! GO HELP THEM!
THEY ARE...
...FIGHTING TO PROTECT ME.
ZOOM

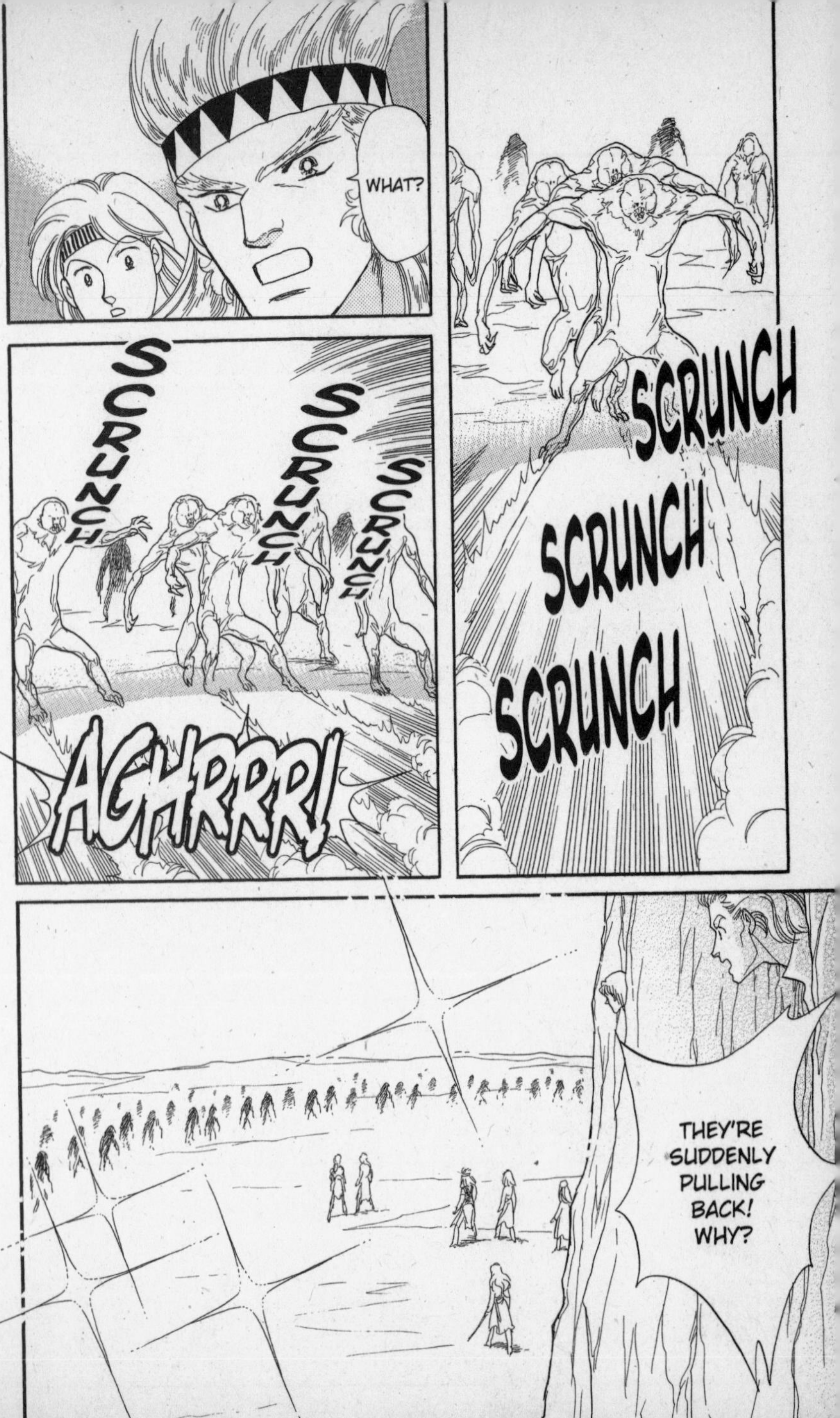
SCRUNCH
SCRUNCH
SCRUNCH
WHAT?
SCRUNCH
SCRUNCH
SCRUNCH
ACHRRR!
THEY'RE SUDDENLY PULLING BACK! WHY?

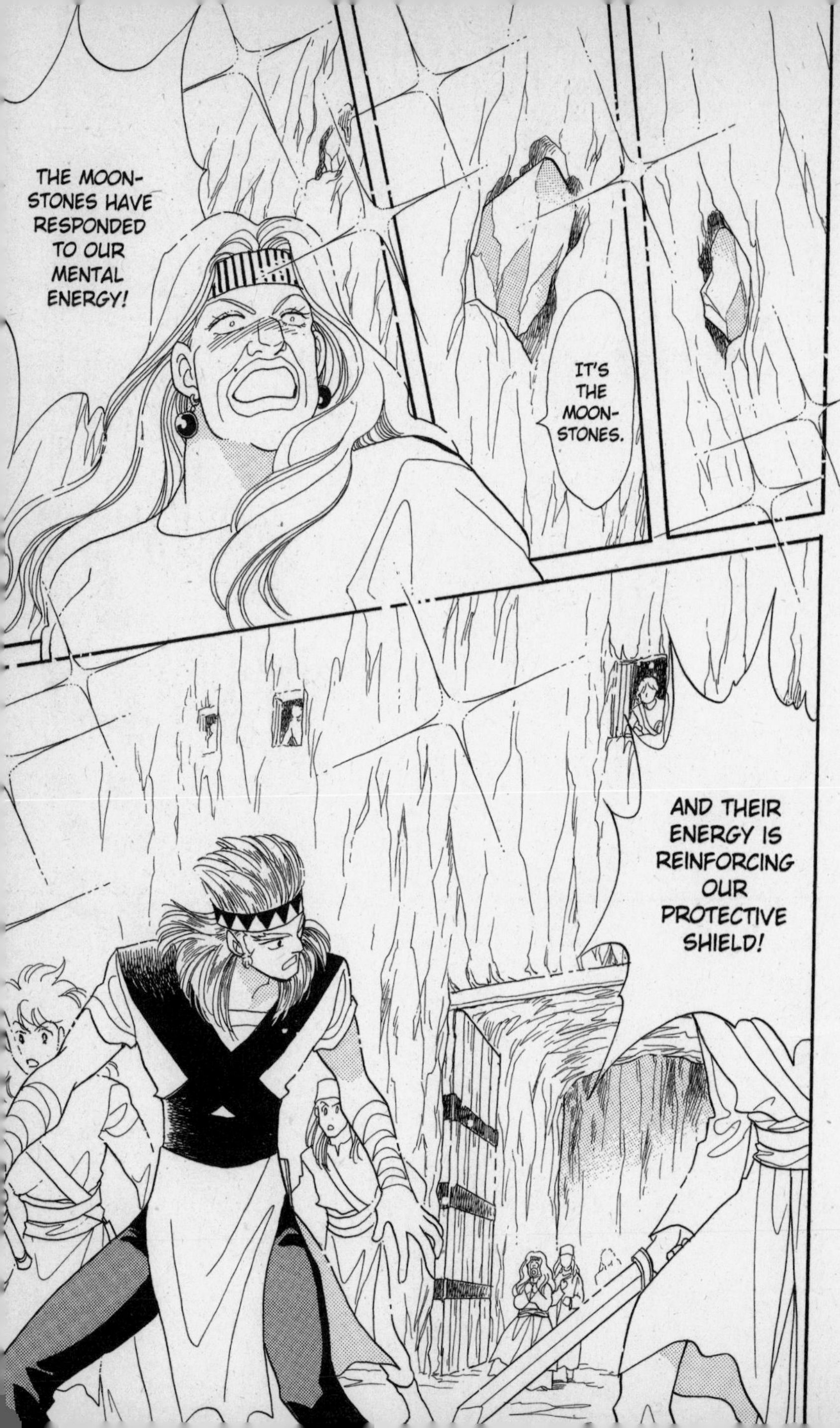
IT'S THE MOON-STONES.
THE MOON-STONES HAVE RESPONDED TO OUR MENTAL ENERGY!
AND THEIR ENERGY IS REINFORCING OUR PROTECTIVE SHIELD!

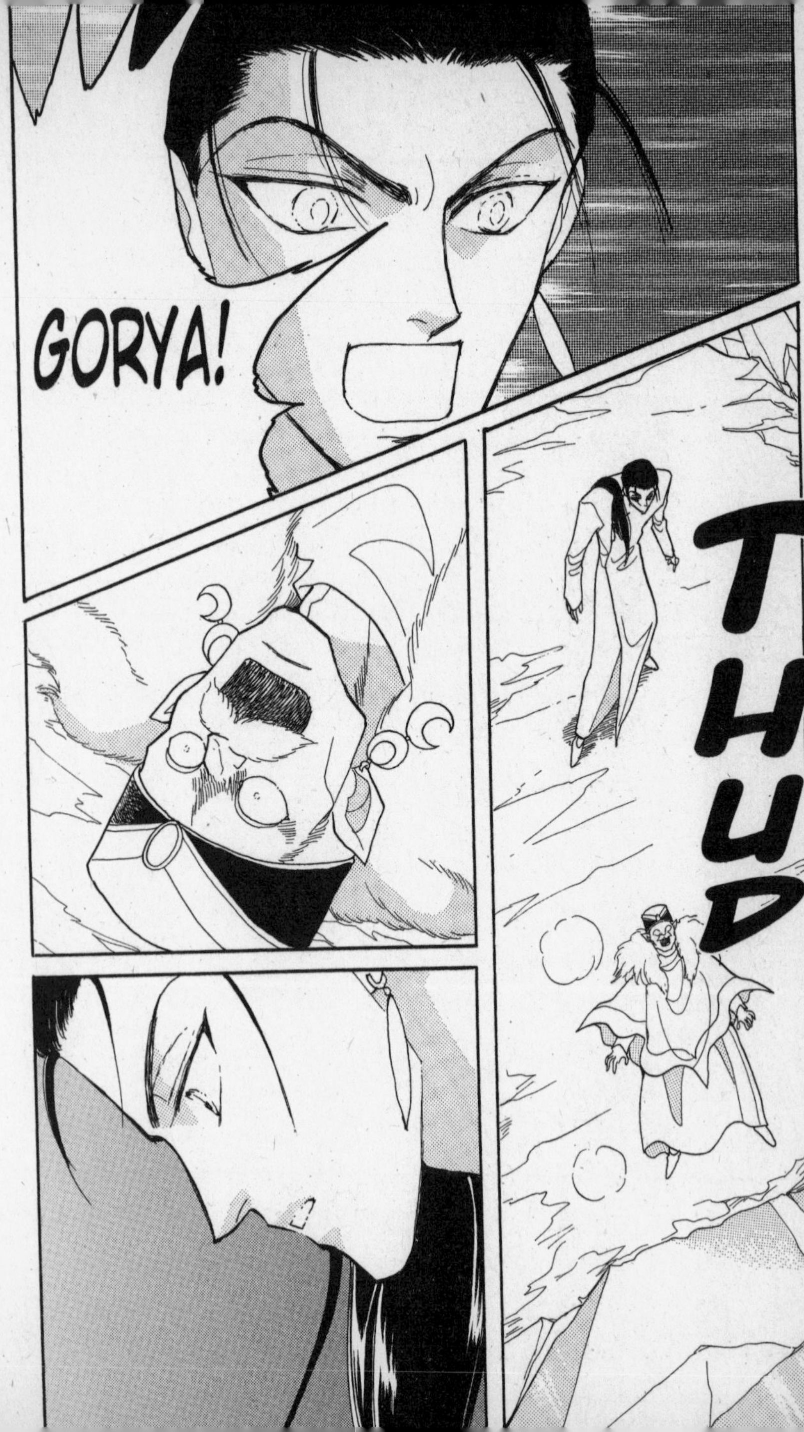
GORYA!
THUD

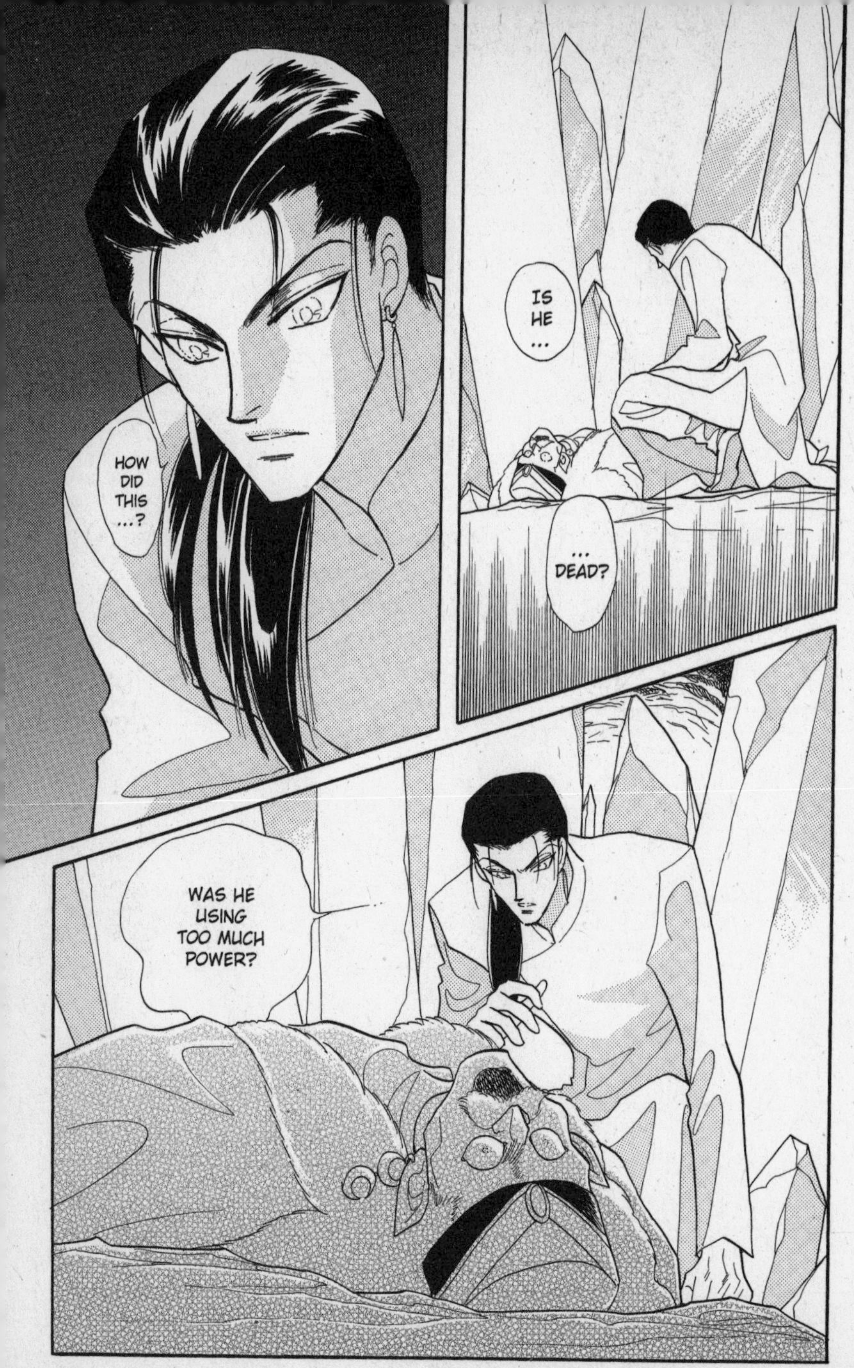
IS HE ...
... DEAD?
HOW DID THIS ...?
WAS HE USING TOO MUCH POWER?

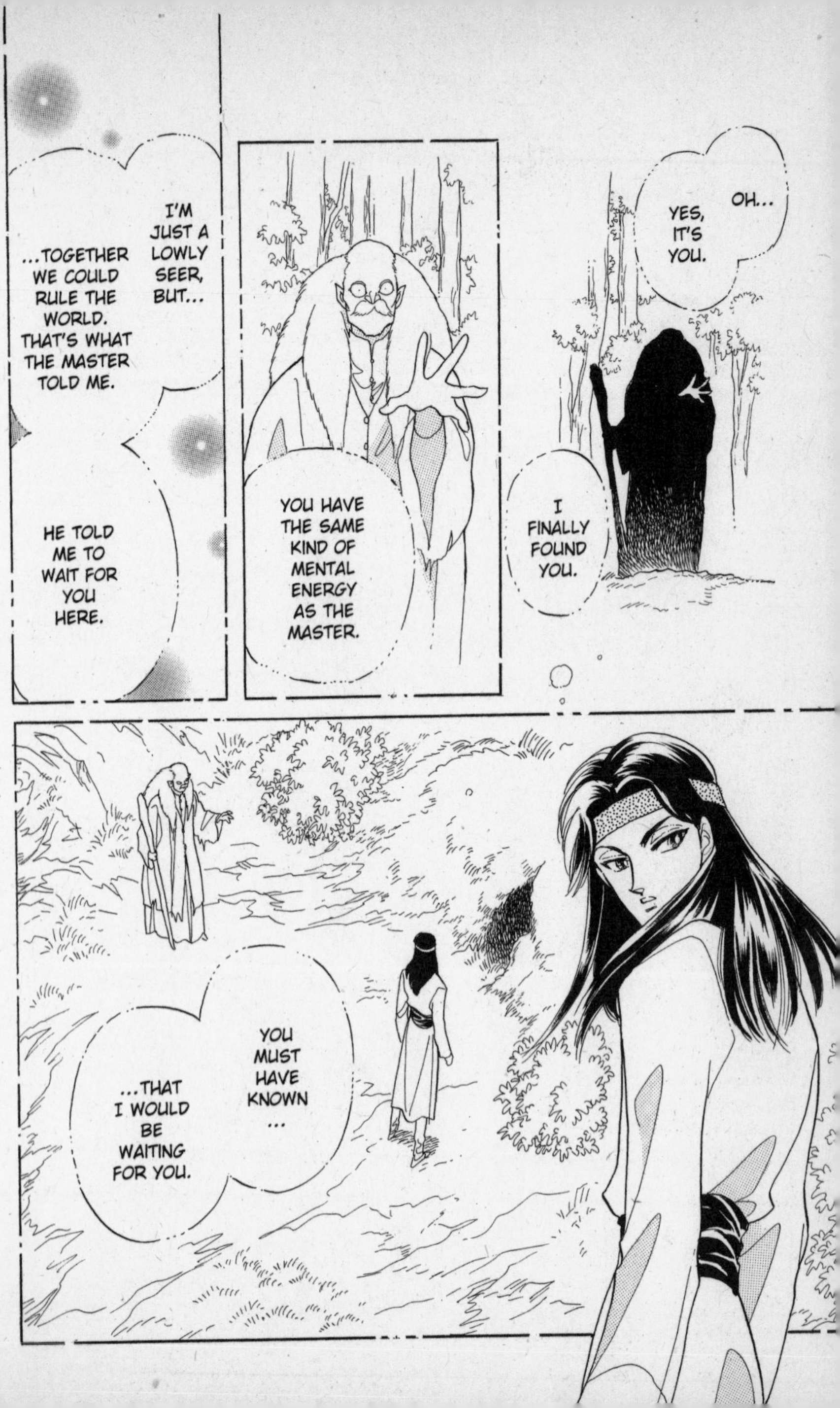
OH...
YES, IT'S YOU.
I FINALLY FOUND YOU.
YOU HAVE THE SAME KIND OF MENTAL ENERGY AS THE MASTER.
I'M JUST A LOWLY SEER, BUT...
...TOGETHER WE COULD RULE THE WORLD. THAT'S WHAT THE MASTER TOLD ME.
HE TOLD ME TO WAIT FOR YOU HERE.
YOU MUST HAVE KNOWN...
...THAT I WOULD BE WAITING FOR YOU.

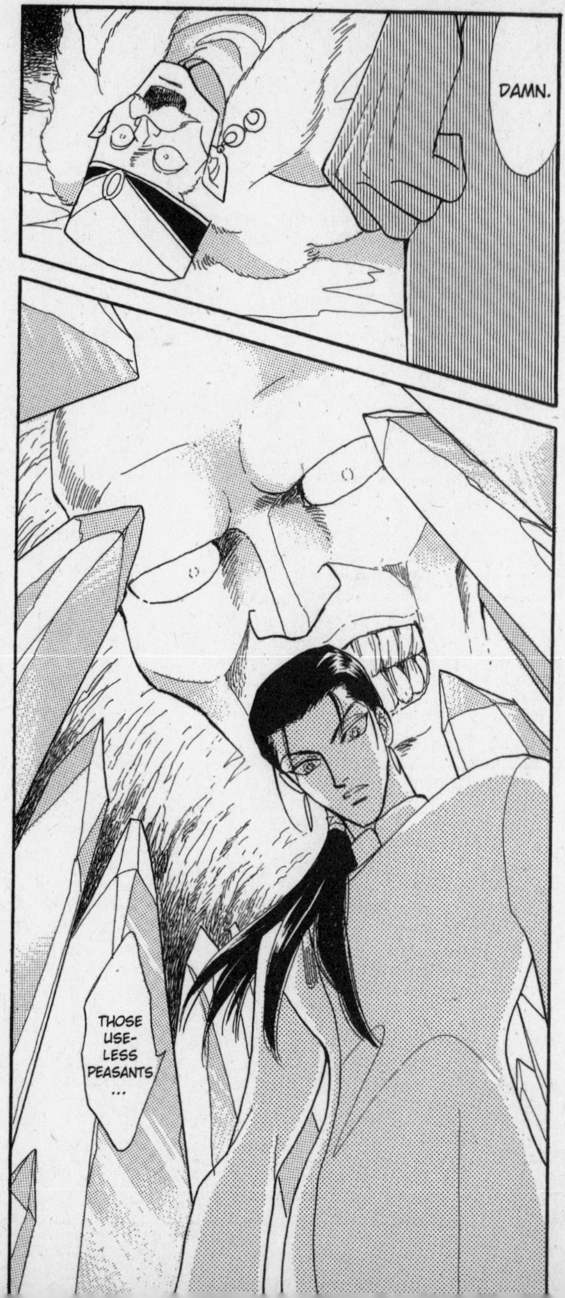
DAMN.
THOSE USE-LESS PEASANTS...

A Very Insignificant Story: Part 1

One day I was pushing my bicycle through a very narrow alley. Someone coming from the opposite direction, also pushing a bicycle, kindly yielded to me.

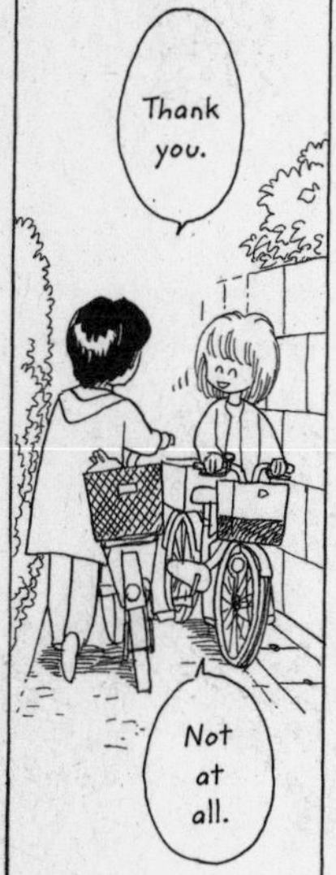
Thank you.
Not at all.

When she smiled at me as she said that, I felt that life is good.

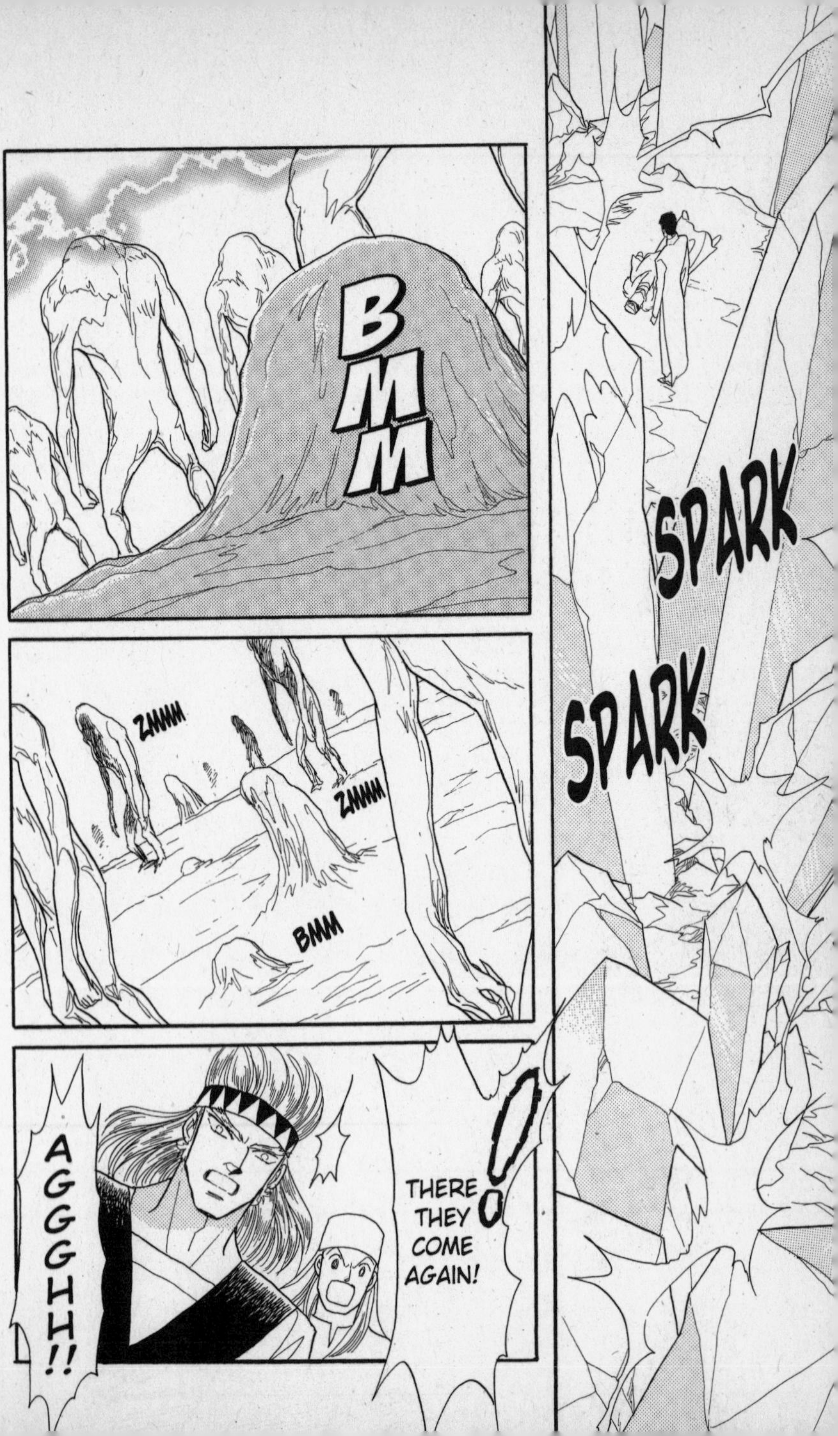
SPARK
SPARK
BMM
ZMMM
ZMMM
BMM
THERE THEY COME AGAIN!
AGGGHH!!

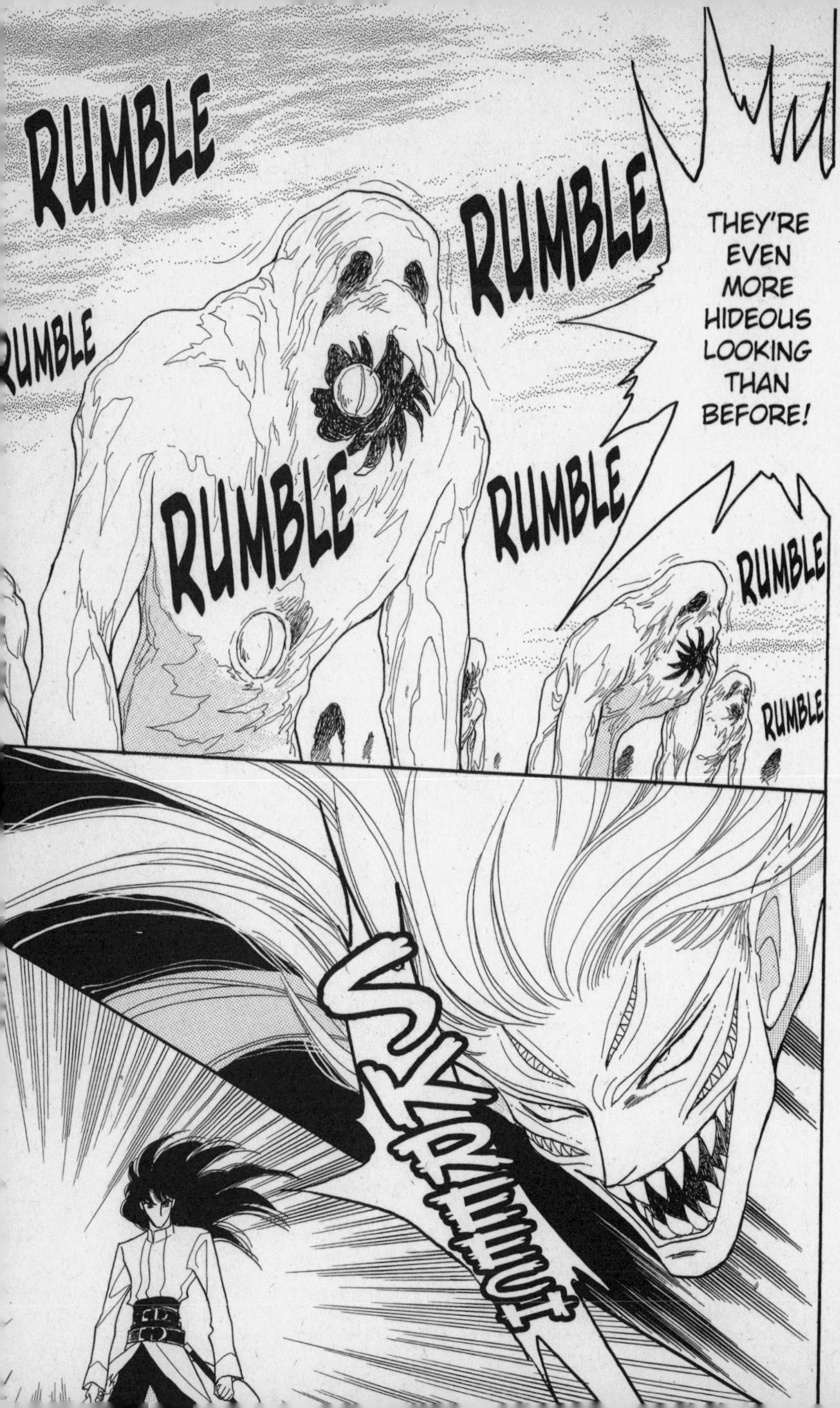
THEY'RE EVEN MORE HIDEOUS LOOKING THAN BEFORE!
RUMBLE
RUMBLE
RUMBLE
RUMBLE
RUMBLE
RUMBLE
RUMBLE
SKREEUT!

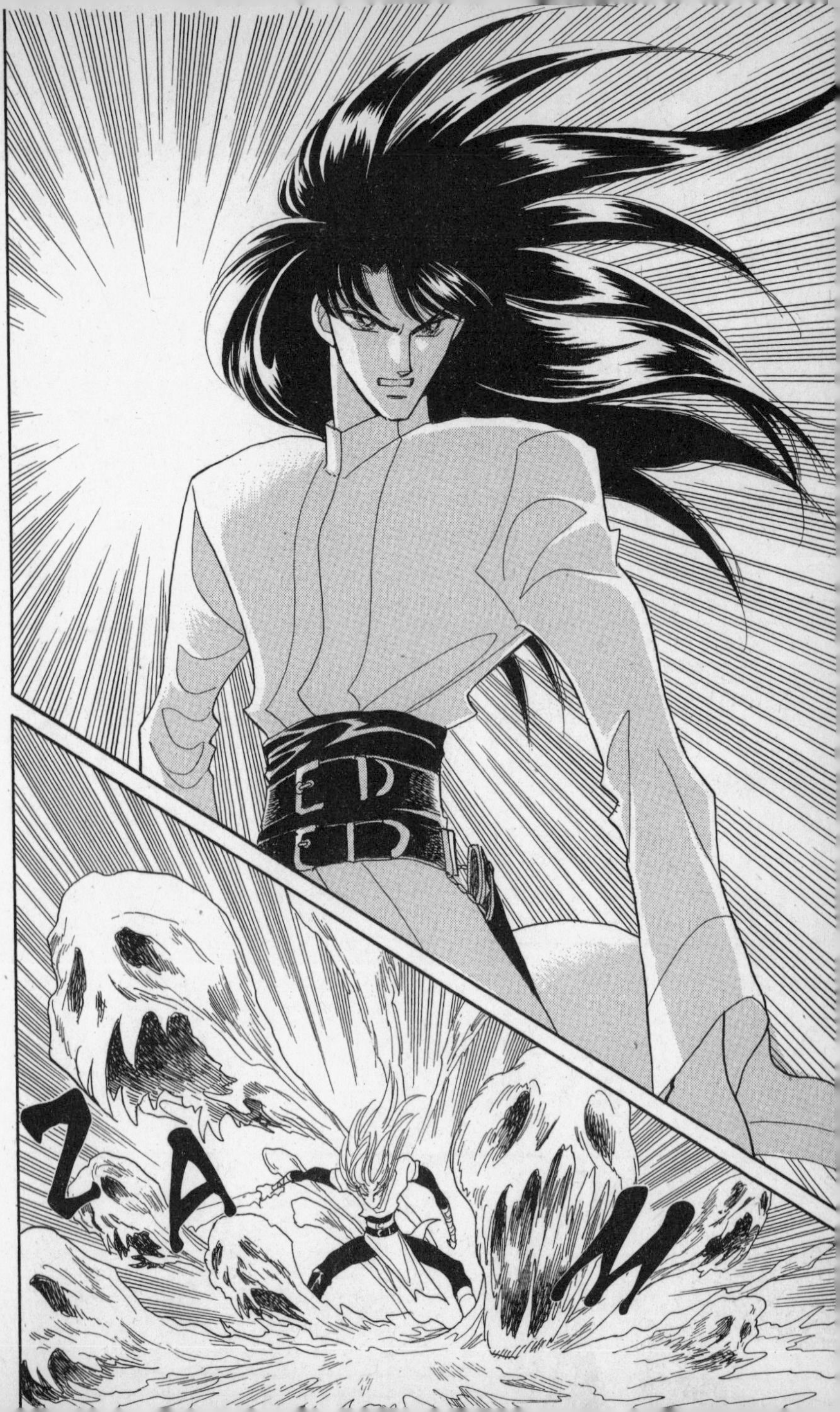
ZAM

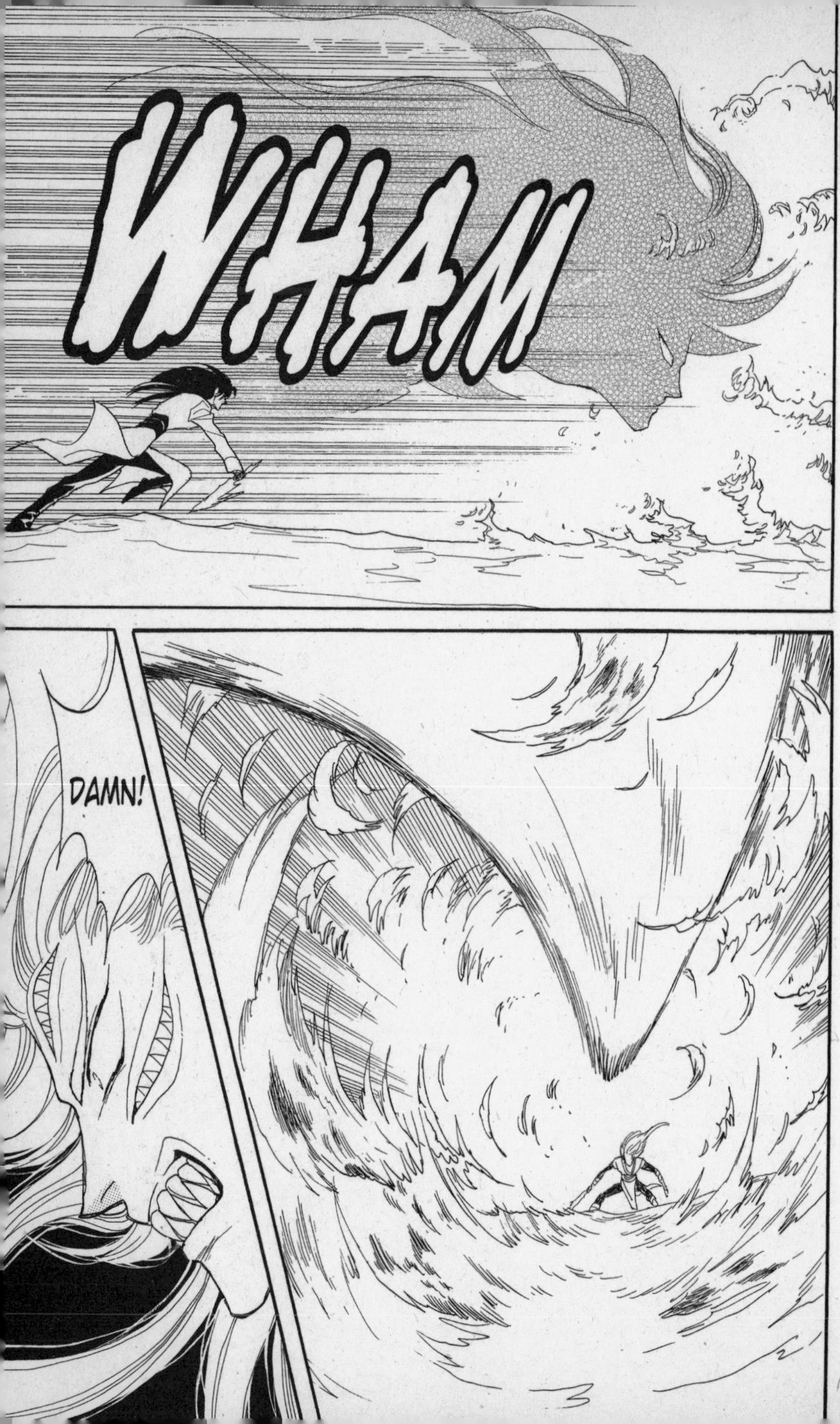
WHAM
DAMN!

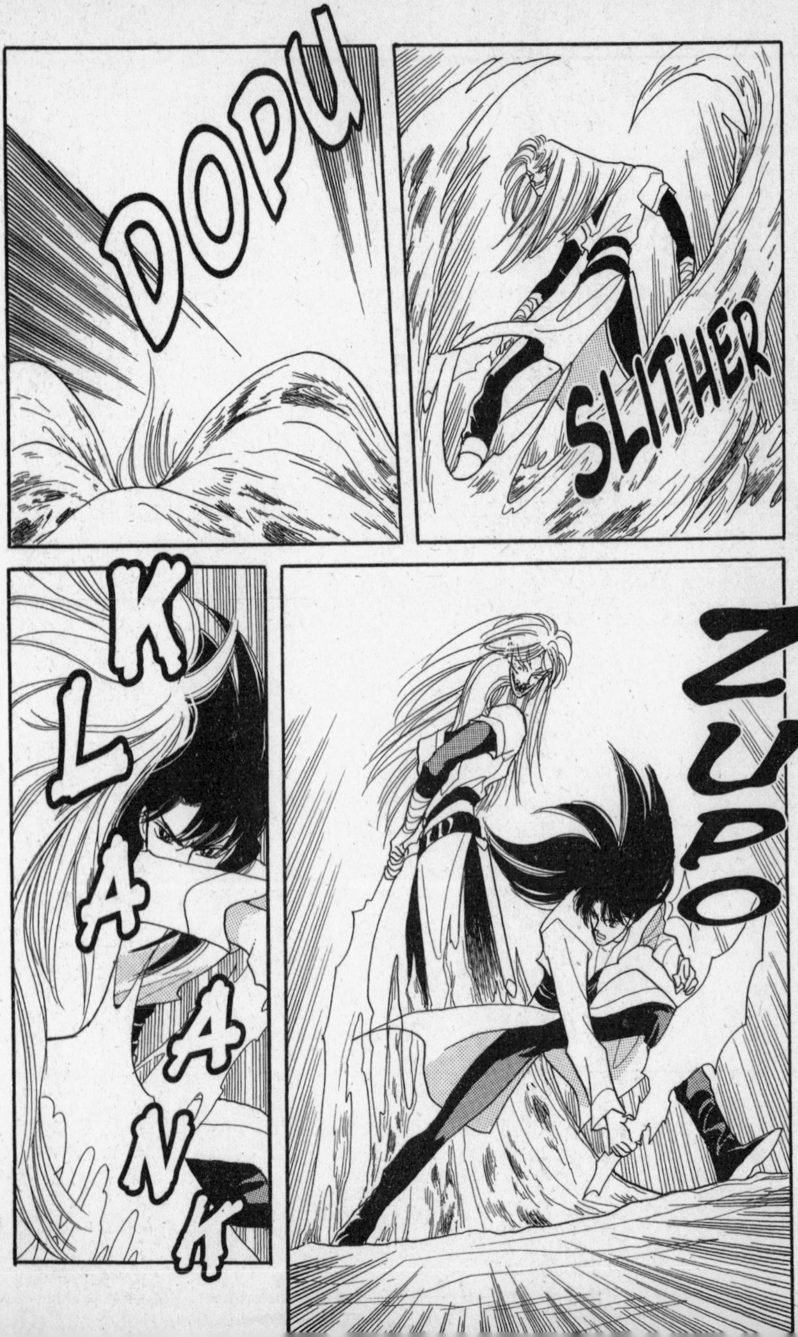
SLITHER
DOPU
ZUPO
KLAANK

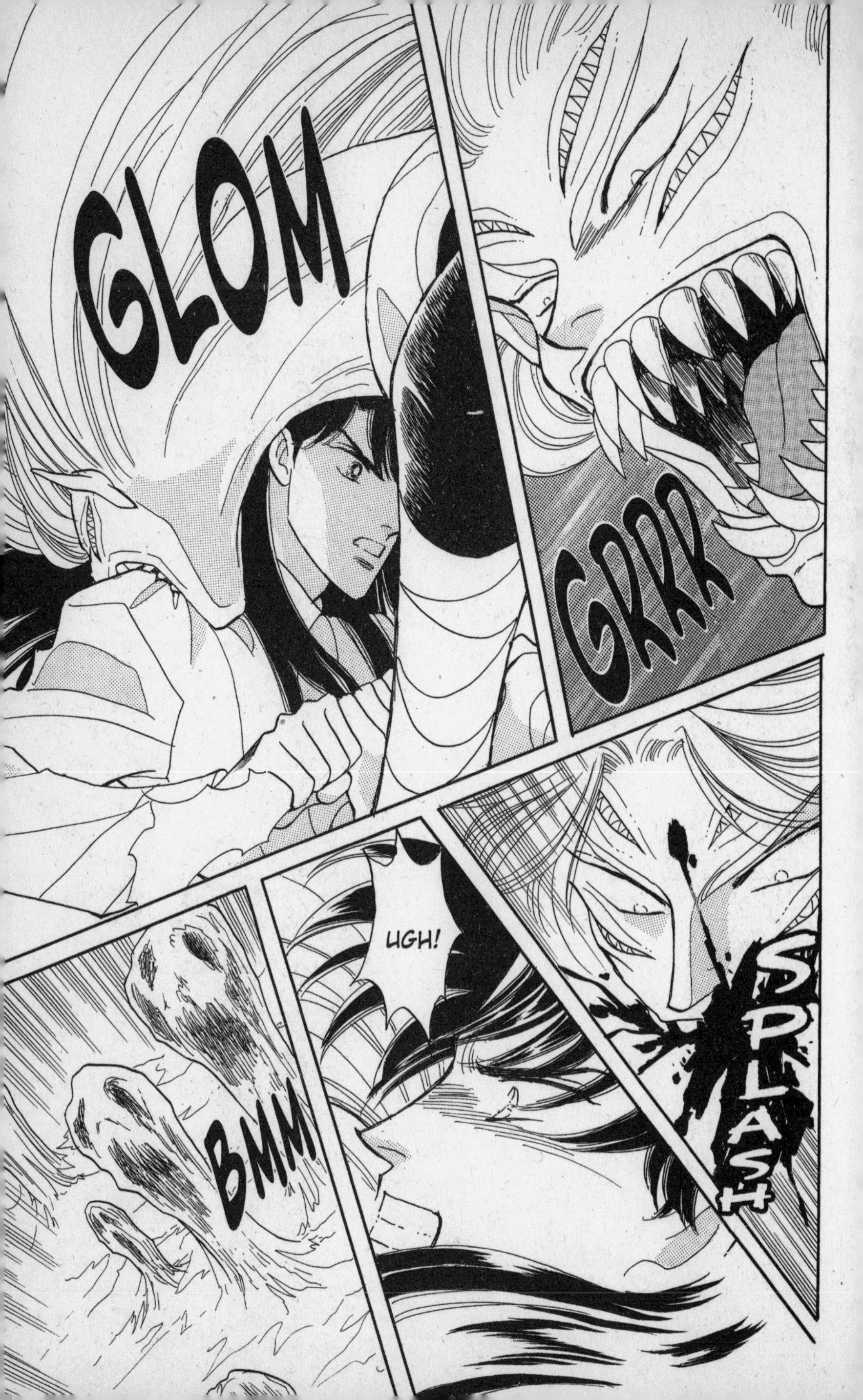
GRRR
GLOM
SPLASH
UGH!
BMM

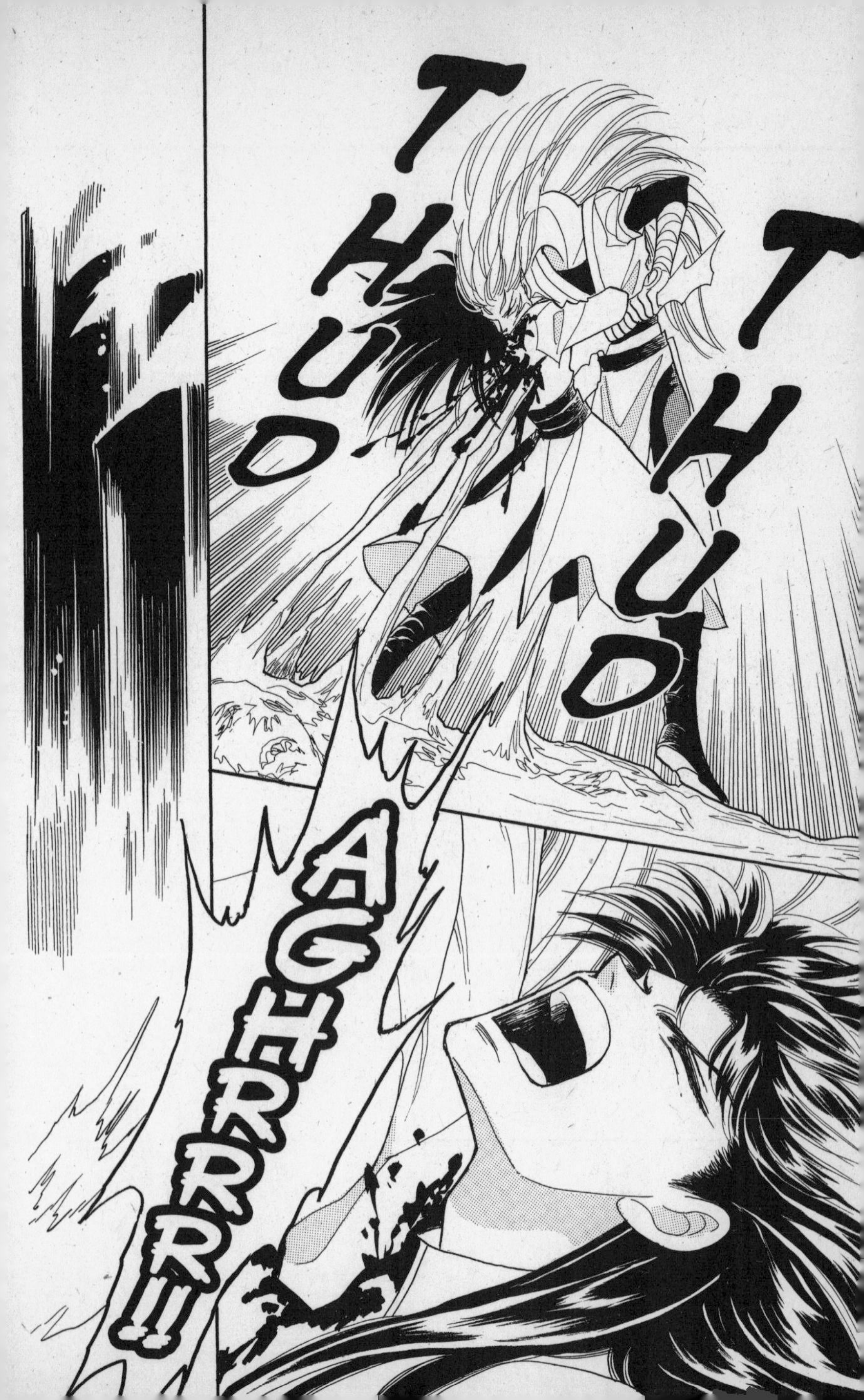
THUD
THUD
AGHRRR!!

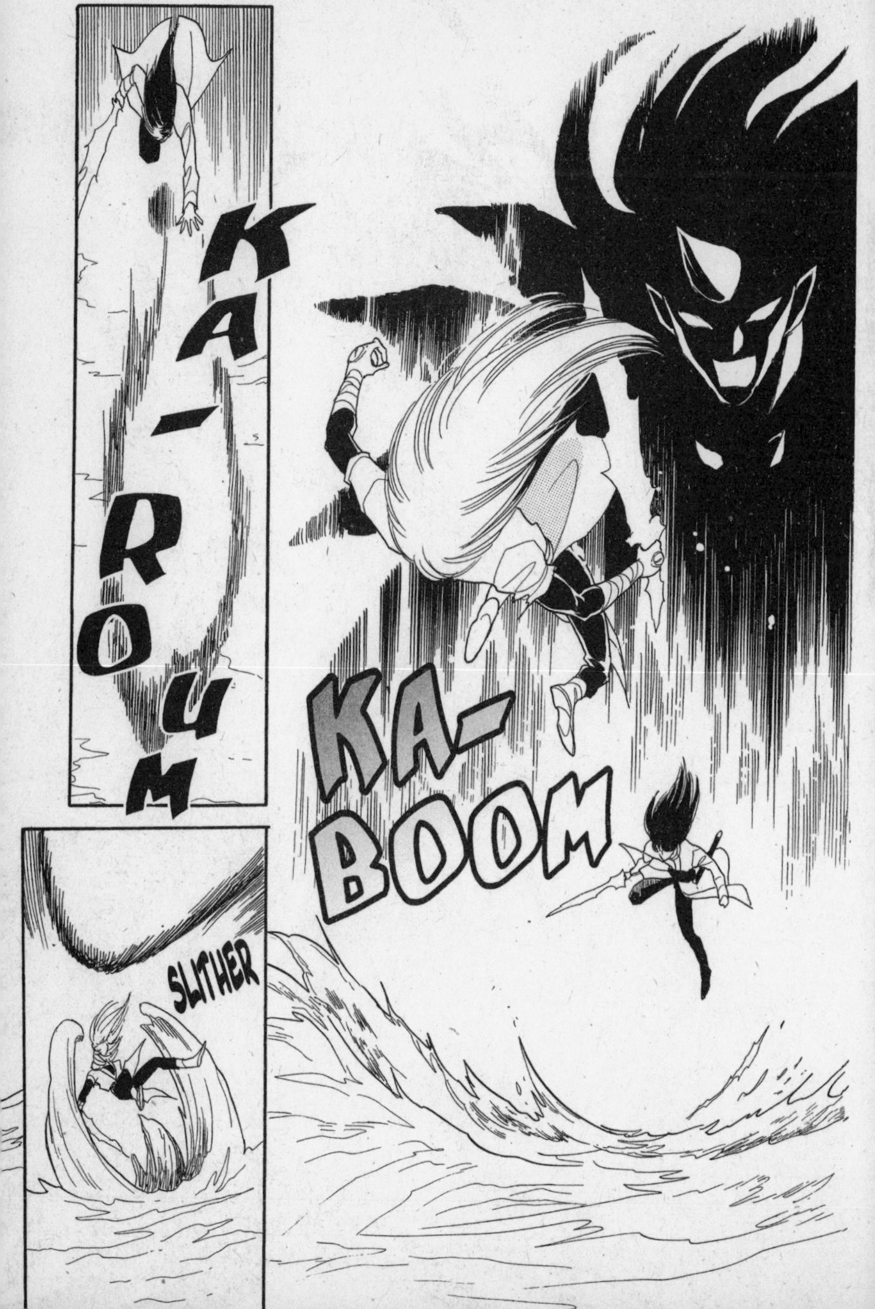
KA-BOOM
KA-ROUM
SLITHER

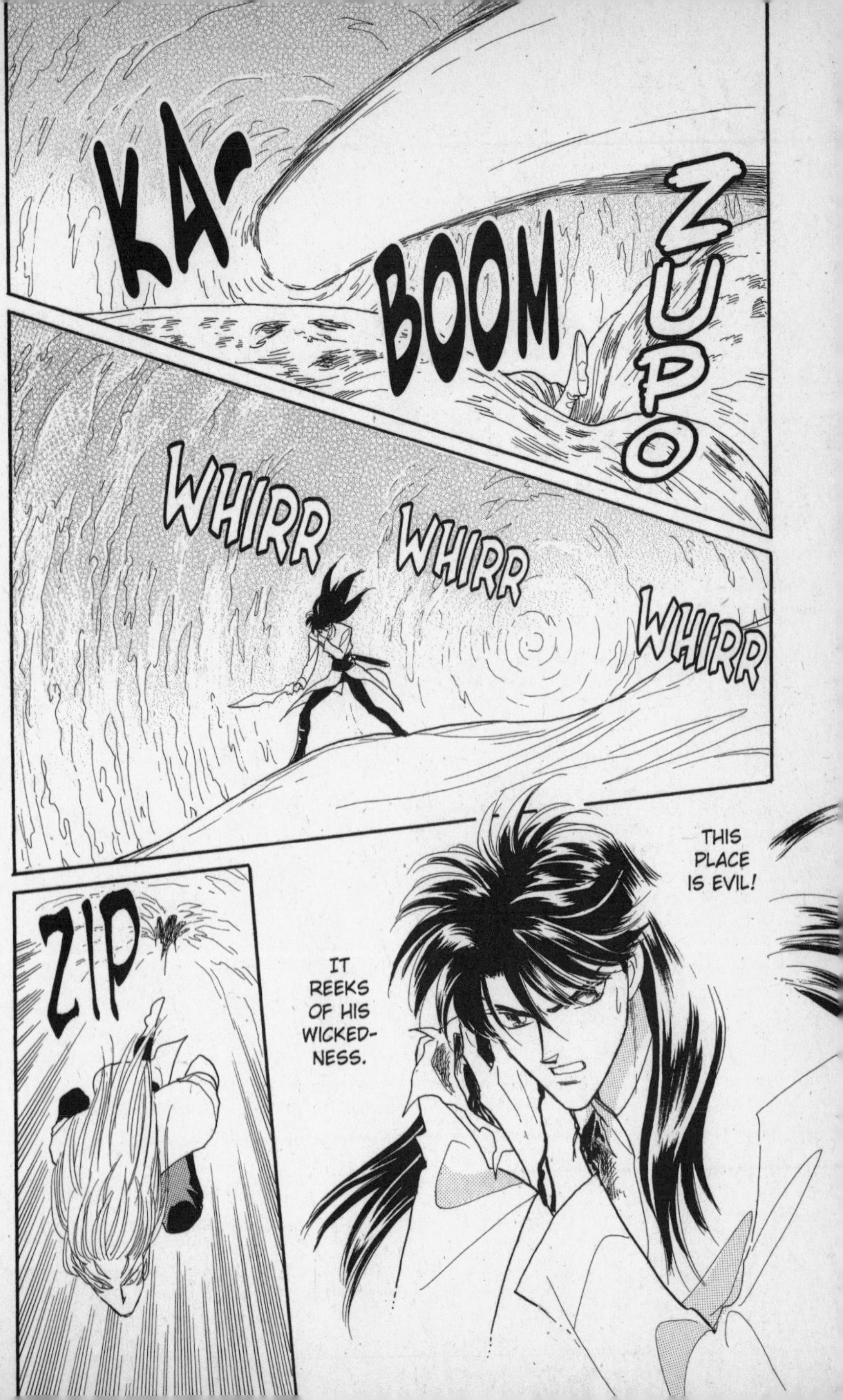

ZUPO
KA-
BOOM
WHIRR
WHIRR
WHIRR
THIS PLACE IS EVIL!
IT REEKS OF HIS WICKED-NESS.
ZIP

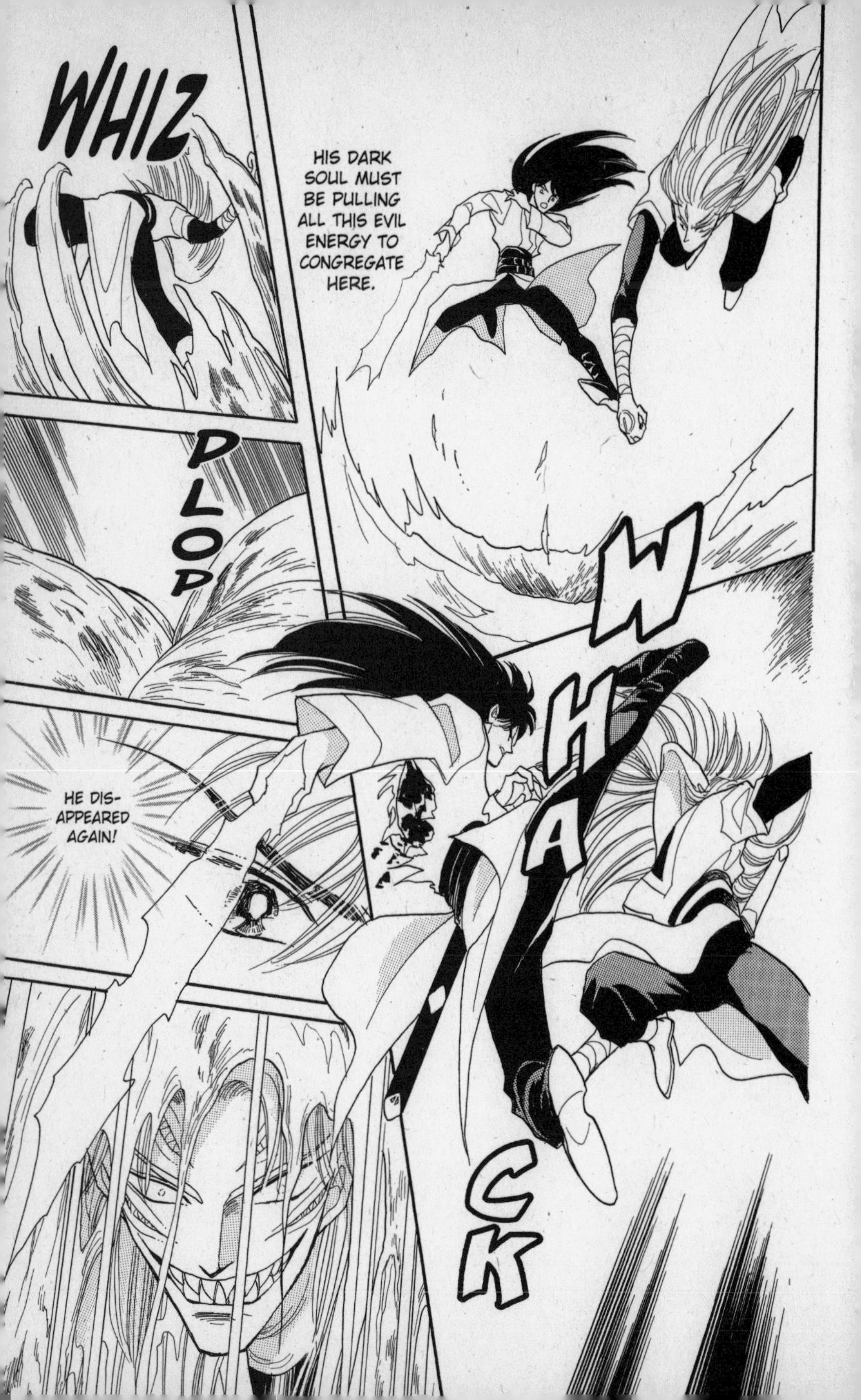
HIS DARK SOUL MUST BE PULLING ALL THIS EVIL ENERGY TO CONGREGATE HERE.
WHIZ
WHACK
DLOP
HE DIS-APPEARED AGAIN!

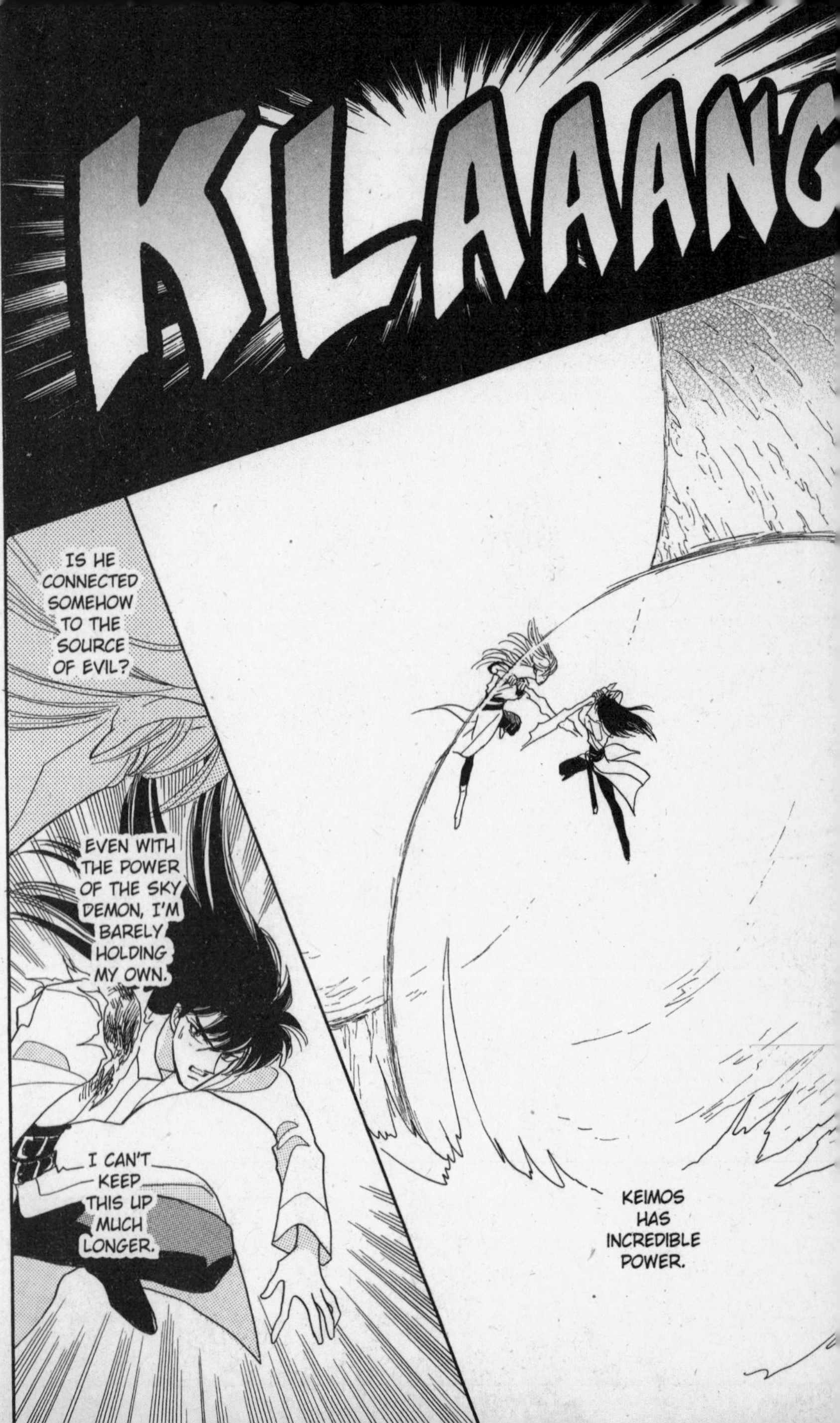
KLAAANG
KEIMOS HAS INCREDIBLE POWER.
IS HE CONNECTED SOMEHOW TO THE SOURCE OF EVIL?
EVEN WITH THE POWER OF THE SKY DEMON, I'M BARELY HOLDING MY OWN.
I CAN'T KEEP THIS UP MUCH LONGER.

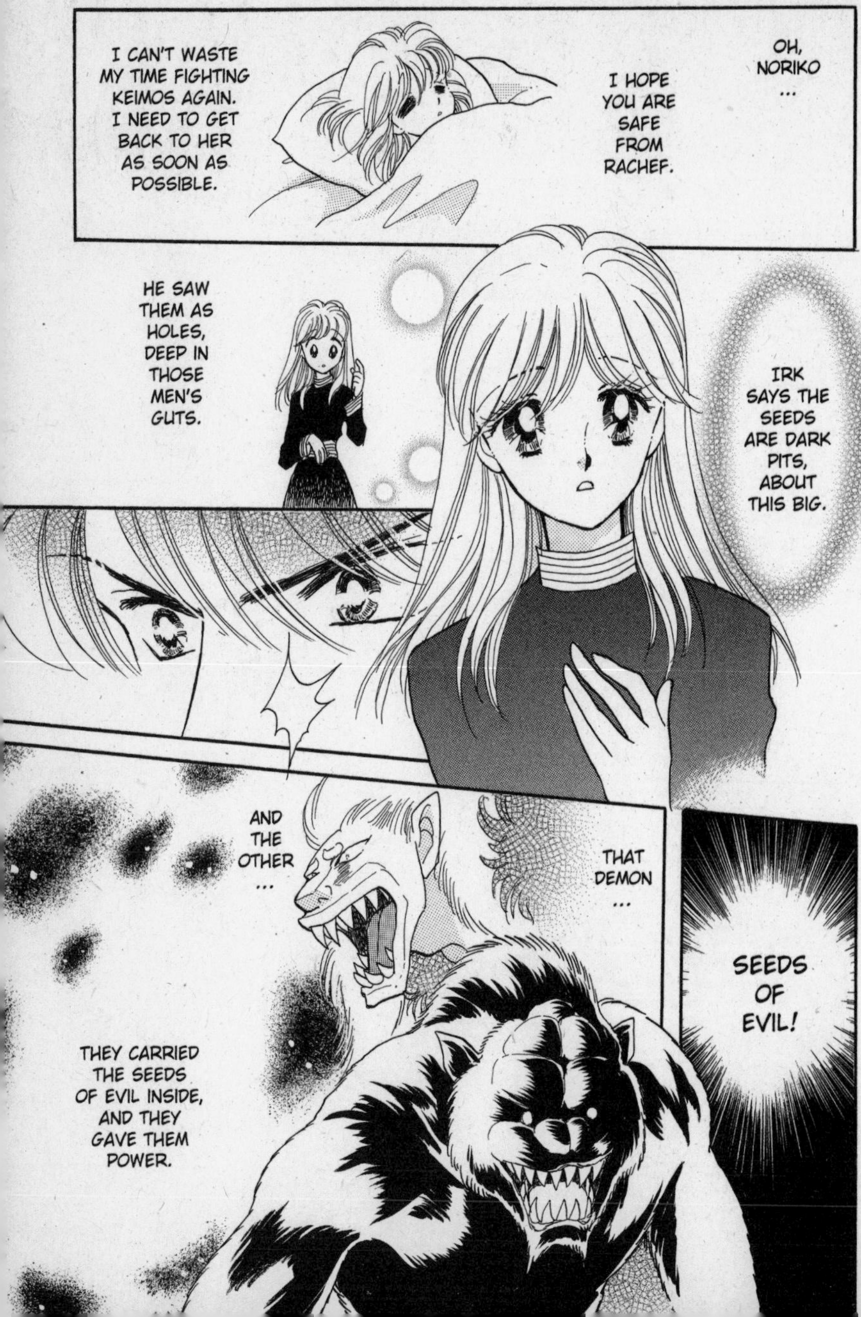
OH, NORIKO ...
I HOPE YOU ARE SAFE FROM RACHEF.
I CAN'T WASTE MY TIME FIGHTING KEIMOS AGAIN. I NEED TO GET BACK TO HER AS SOON AS POSSIBLE.
IRK SAYS THE SEEDS ARE DARK PITS, ABOUT THIS BIG.
HE SAW THEM AS HOLES, DEEP IN THOSE MEN'S GUTS.
SEEDS OF EVIL!
THAT DEMON ...
AND THE OTHER ...
THEY CARRIED THE SEEDS OF EVIL INSIDE, AND THEY GAVE THEM POWER.

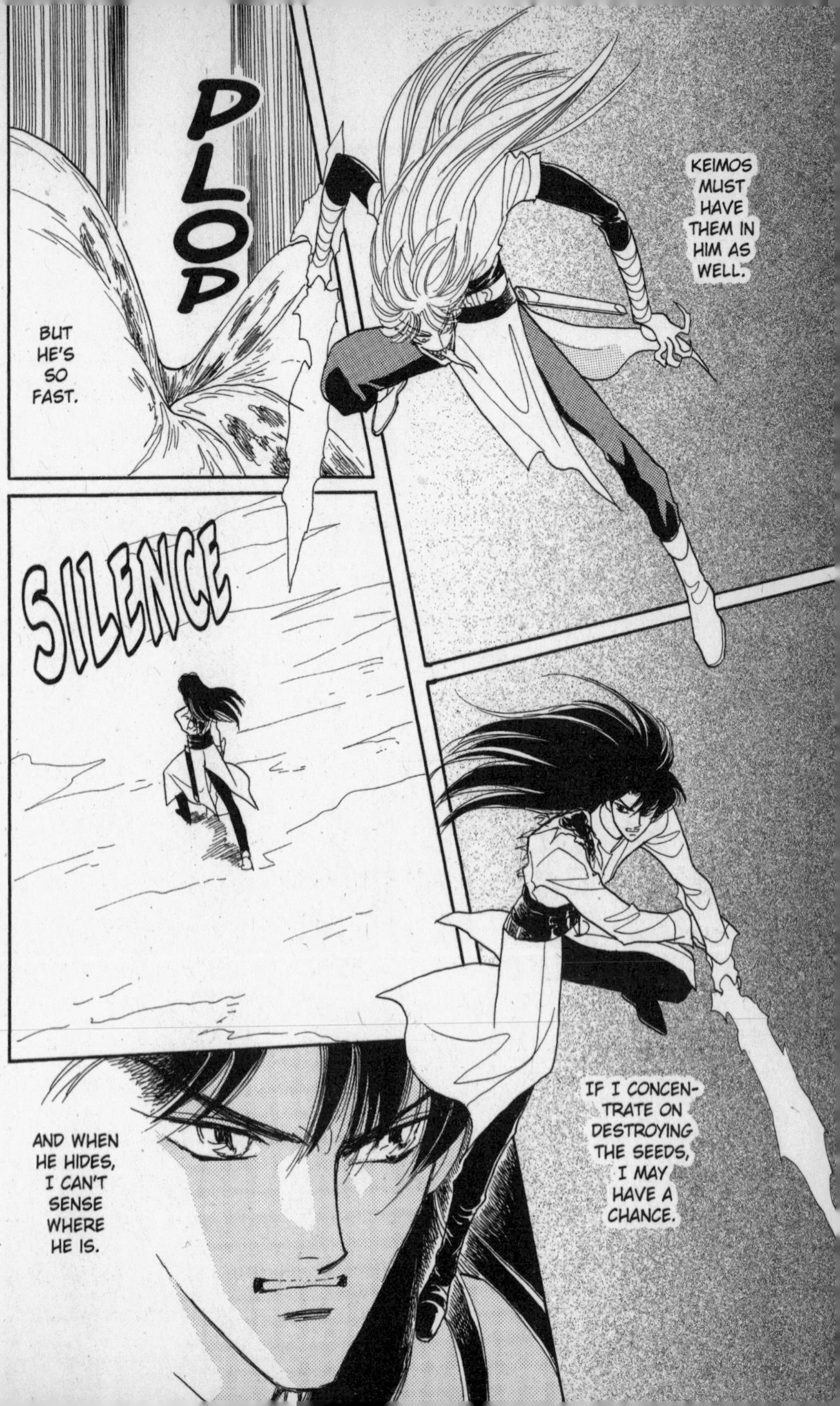
KEIMOS MUST HAVE THEM IN HIM AS WELL.
PLOP
BUT HE'S SO FAST.
SILENCE
AND WHEN HE HIDES, I CAN'T SENSE WHERE HE IS.
IF I CONCENTRATE ON DESTROYING THE SEEDS, I MAY HAVE A CHANCE.

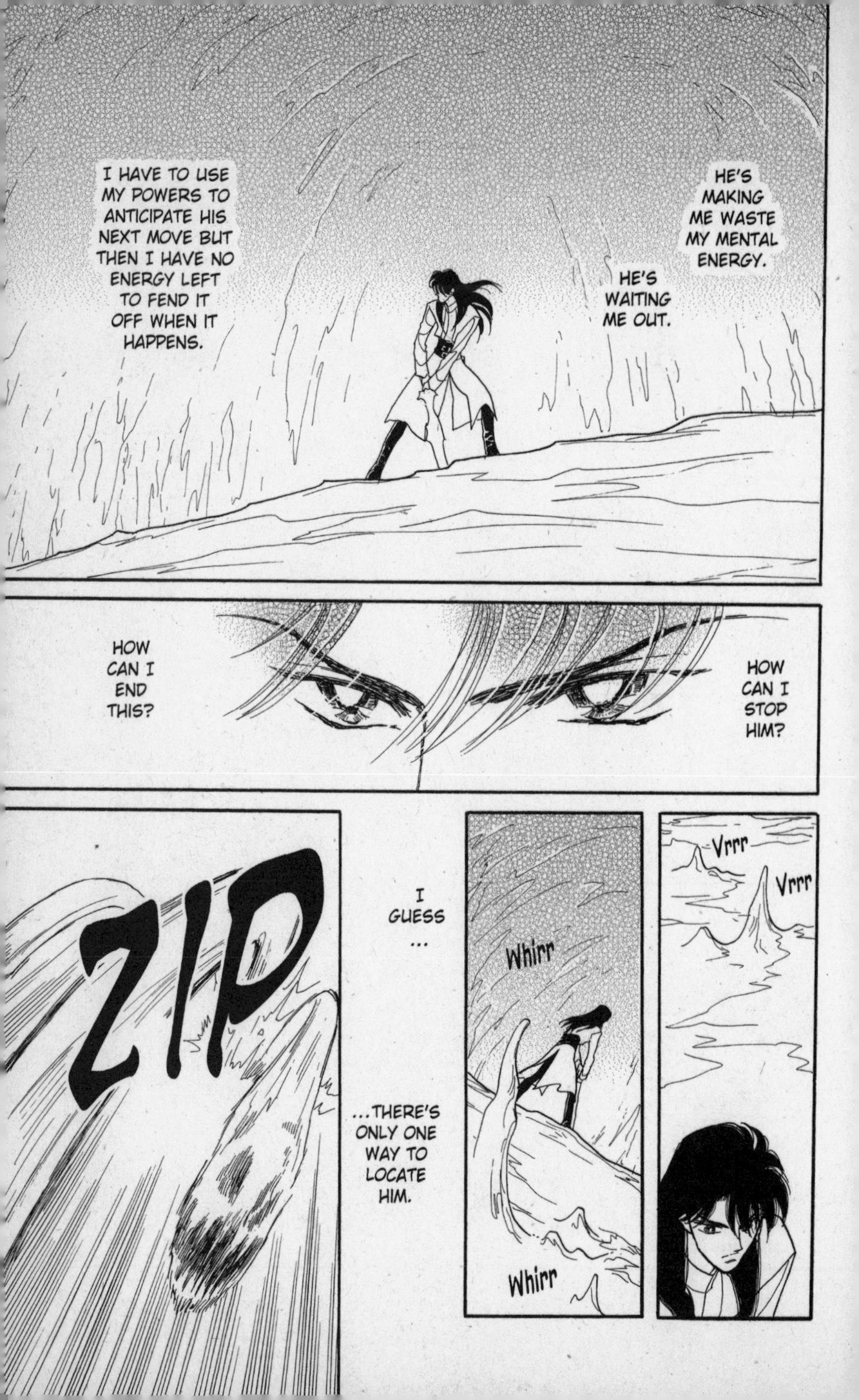
HE'S MAKING ME WASTE MY MENTAL ENERGY.
HE'S WAITING ME OUT.
I HAVE TO USE MY POWERS TO ANTICIPATE HIS NEXT MOVE BUT THEN I HAVE NO ENERGY LEFT TO FEND IT OFF WHEN IT HAPPENS.
HOW CAN I STOP HIM?
HOW CAN I END THIS?
Vrrr
Vrrr
Whirr
Whirr
I GUESS ...
...THERE'S ONLY ONE WAY TO LOCATE HIM.
ZIP

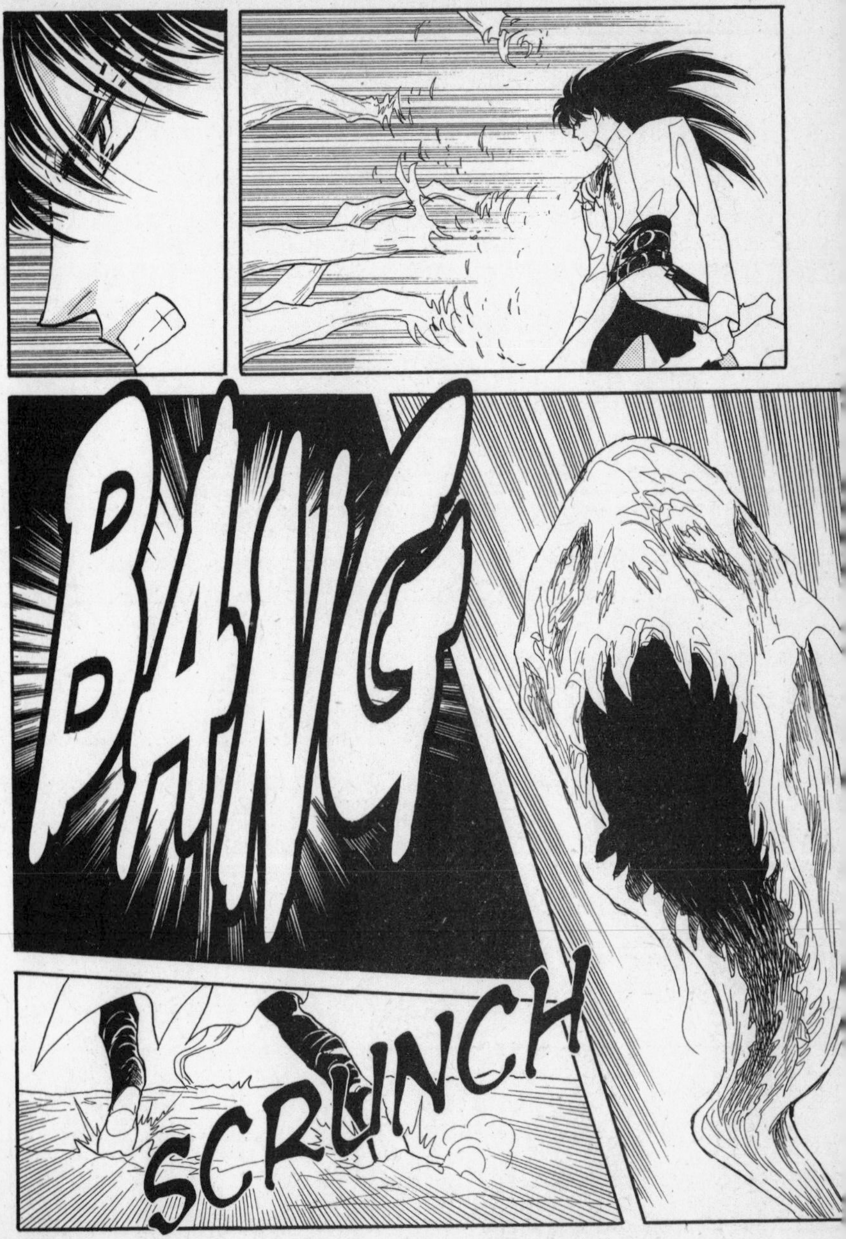
BANG
SCRUNCH

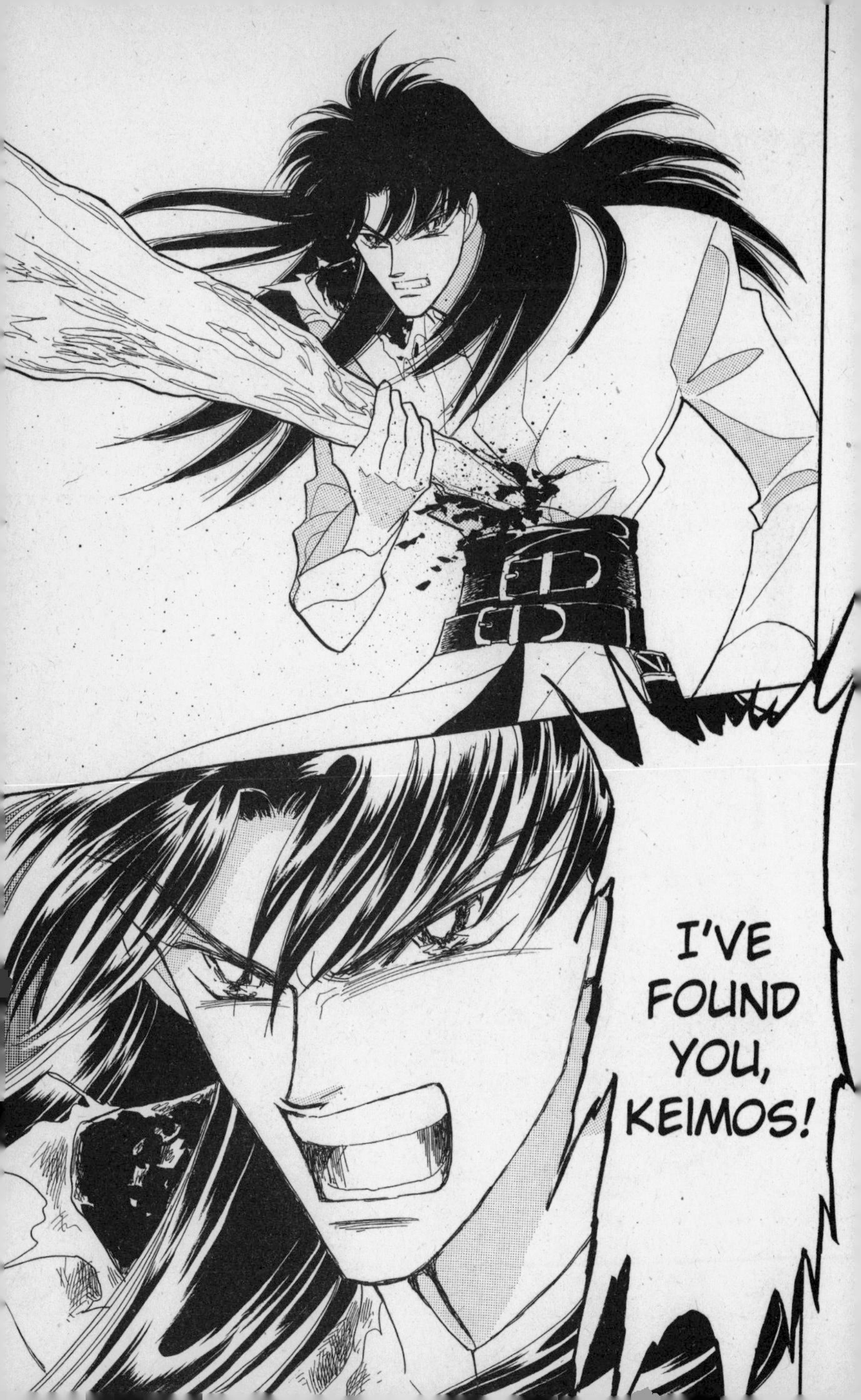
I'VE FOUND YOU, KEIMOS!

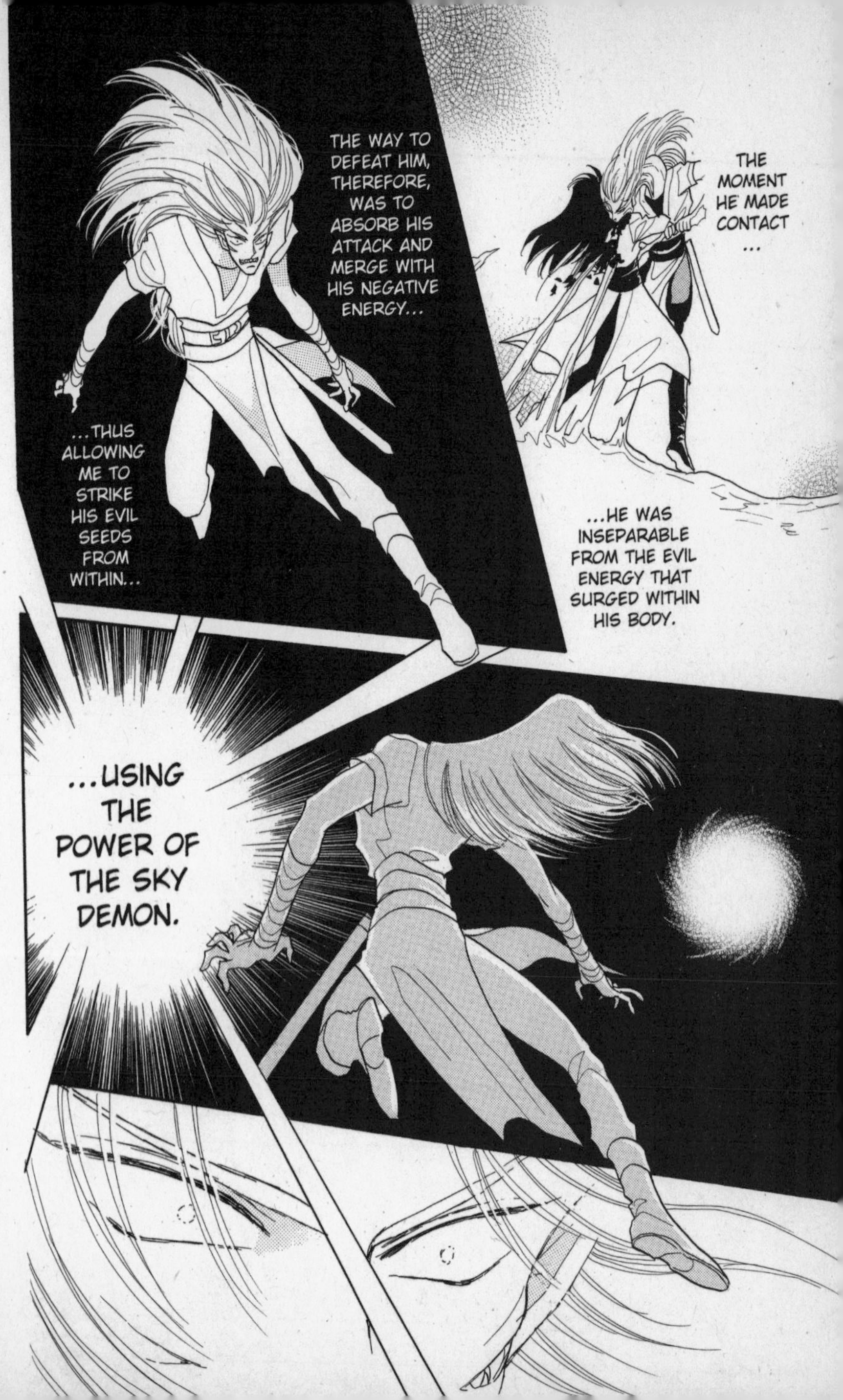
THE MOMENT HE MADE CONTACT ...
...HE WAS INSEPARABLE FROM THE EVIL ENERGY THAT SURGED WITHIN HIS BODY.
THE WAY TO DEFEAT HIM, THEREFORE, WAS TO ABSORB HIS ATTACK AND MERGE WITH HIS NEGATIVE ENERGY...
...THUS ALLOWING ME TO STRIKE HIS EVIL SEEDS FROM WITHIN...
...USING THE POWER OF THE SKY DEMON.

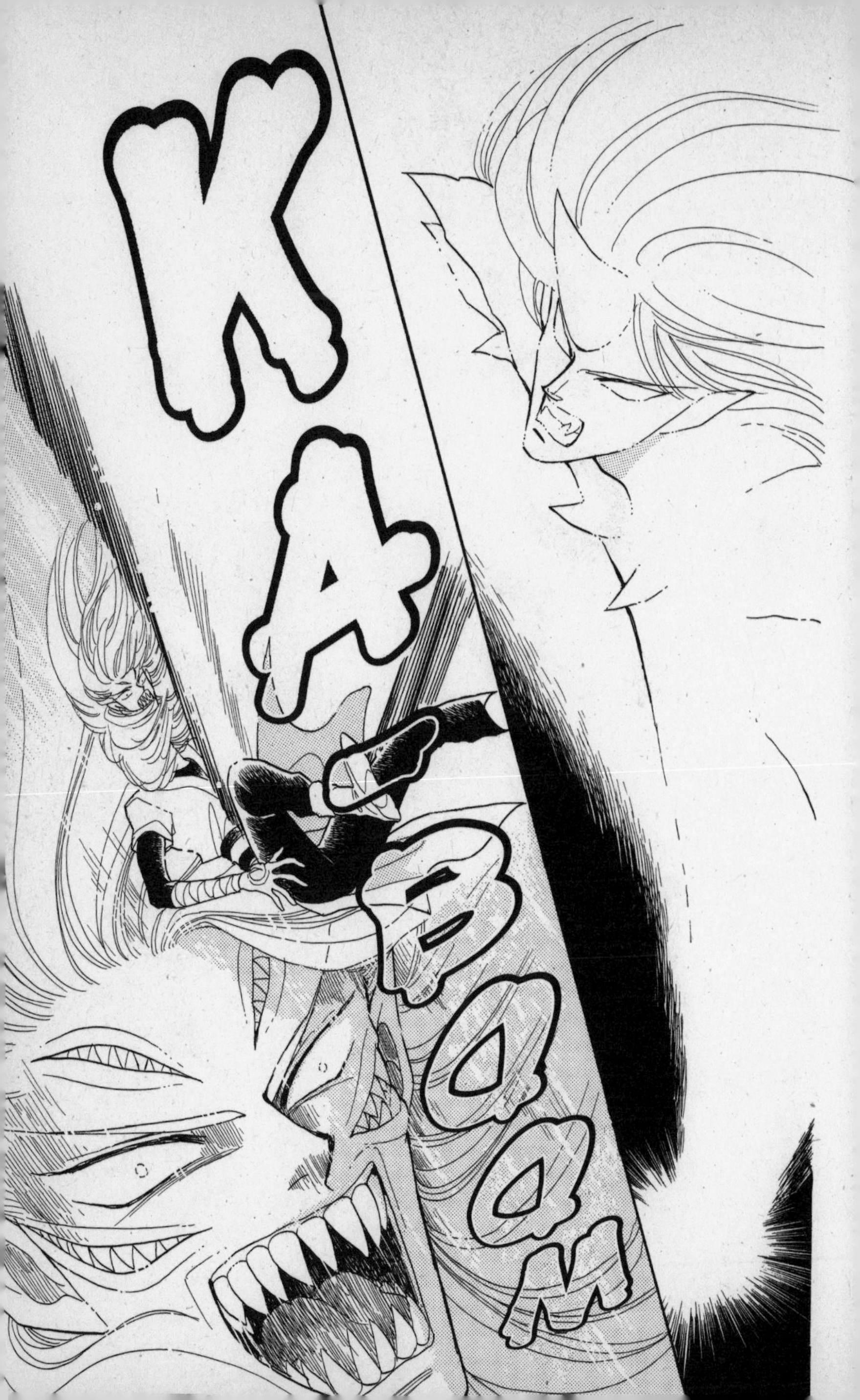
KABOOM

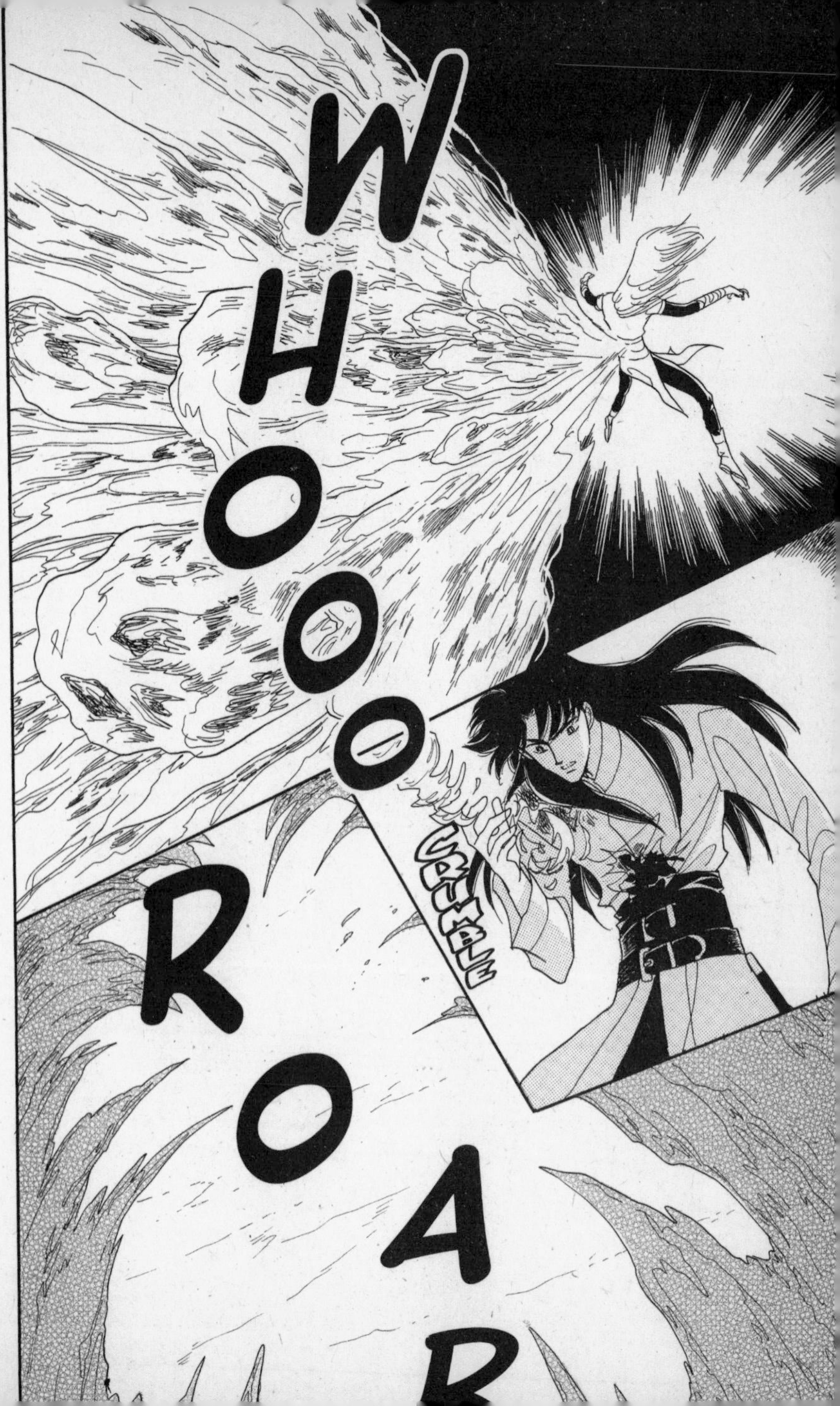
WHOOOROAR
CRUMBLE

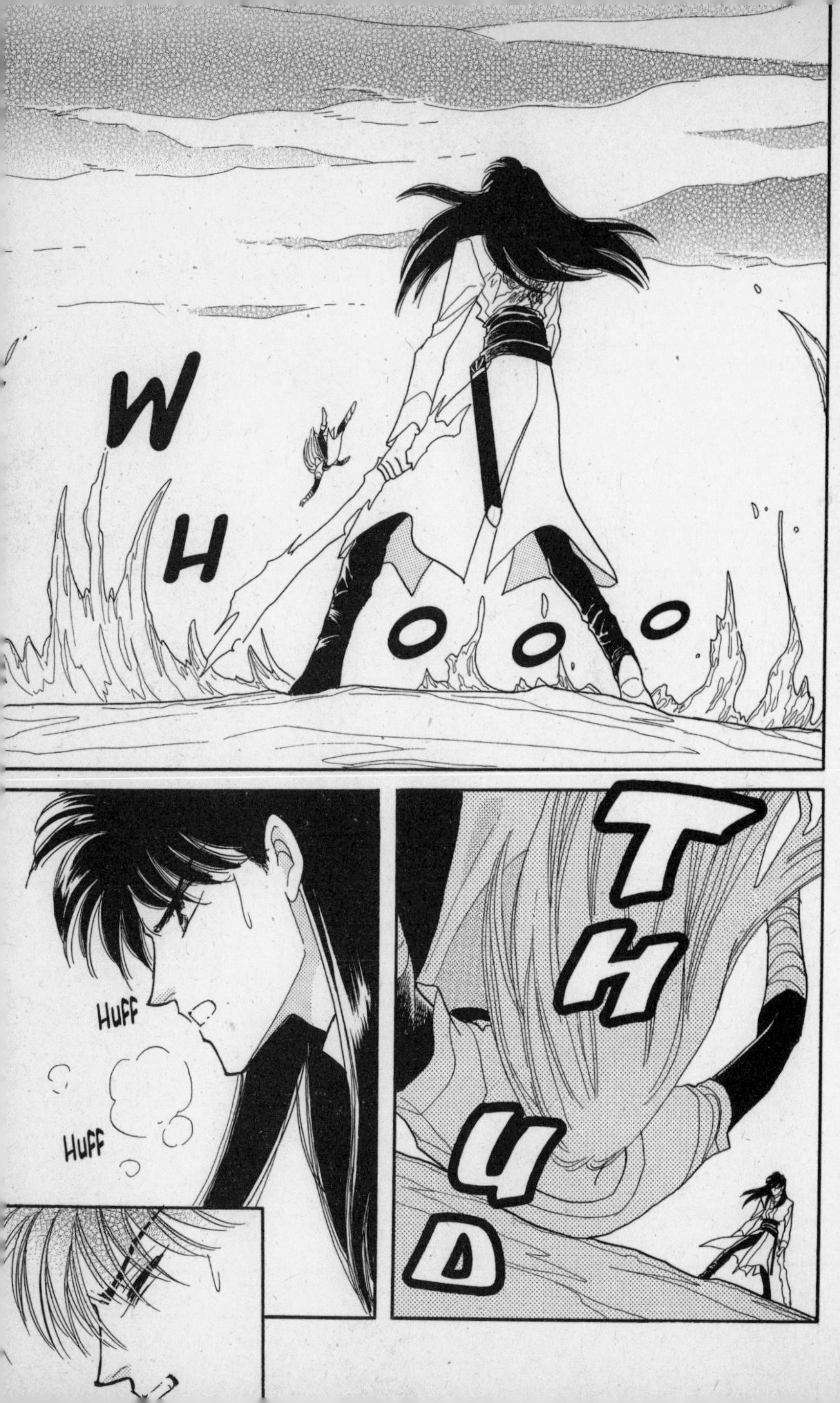
WHOOOO
THUD
Huff
Huff

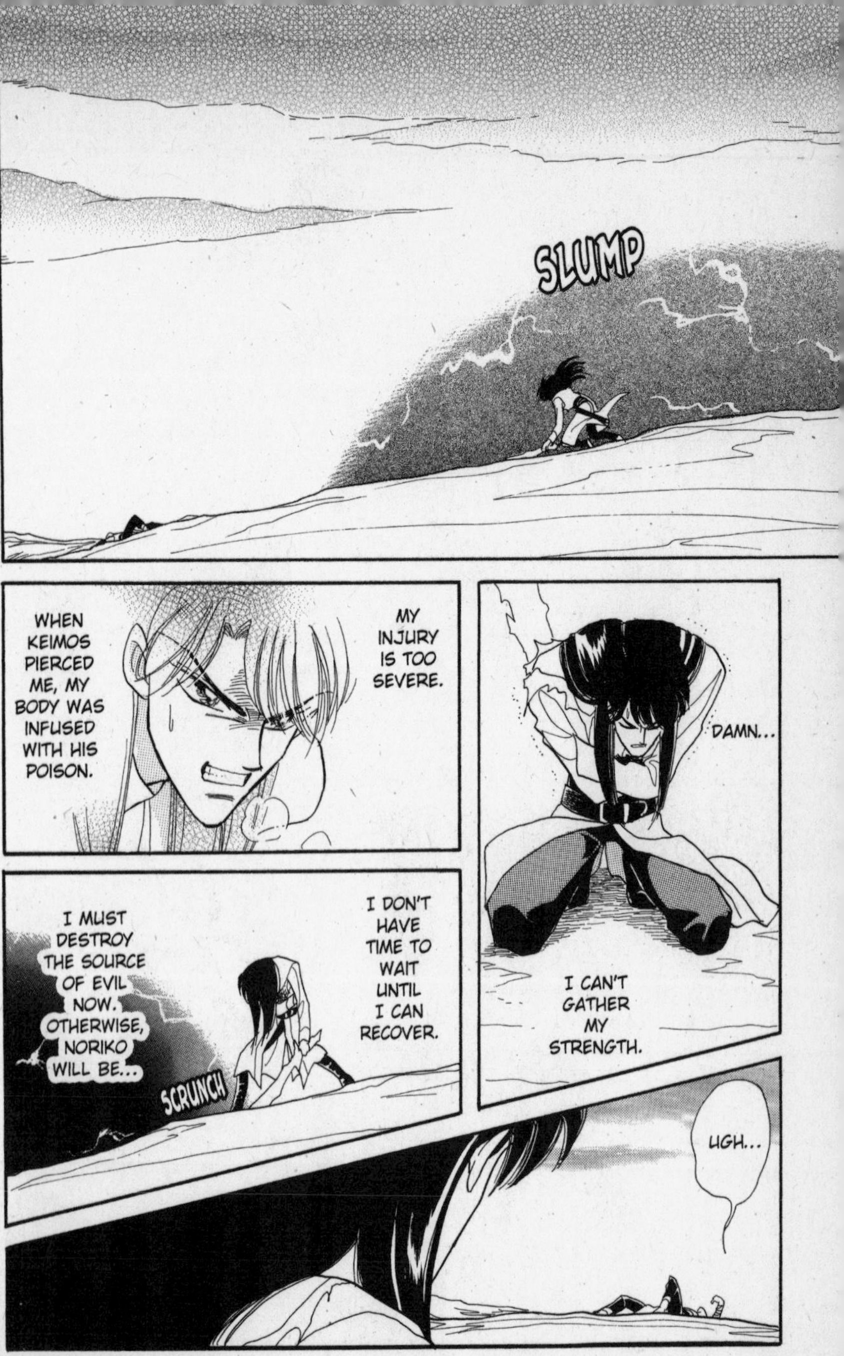
SLUMP
DAMN...
I CAN'T GATHER MY STRENGTH.
MY INJURY IS TOO SEVERE.
WHEN KEIMOS PIERCED ME, MY BODY WAS INFUSED WITH HIS POISON.
I DON'T HAVE TIME TO WAIT UNTIL I CAN RECOVER.
I MUST DESTROY THE SOURCE OF EVIL NOW. OTHERWISE, NORIKO WILL BE...
SCRUNCH
UGH...

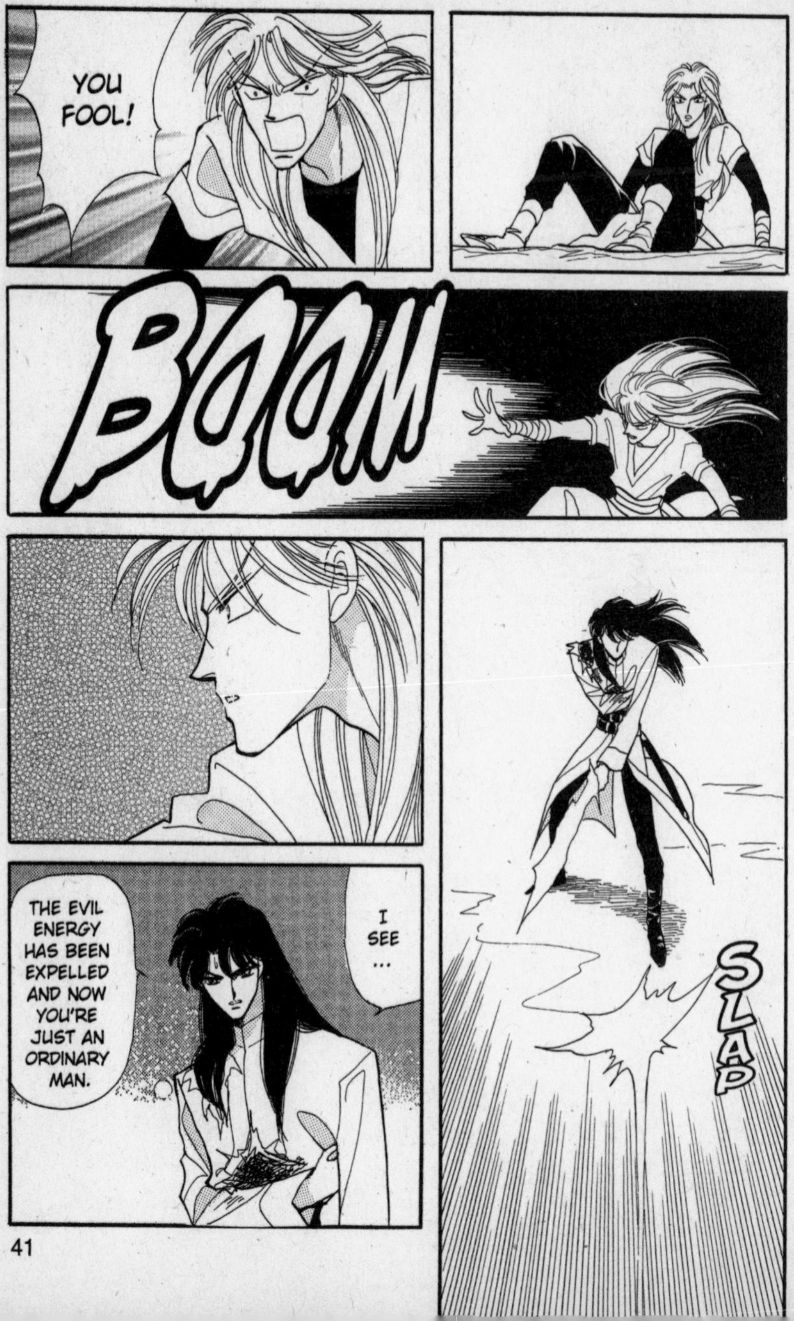
YOU FOOL!
BOOM
SLAP
I SEE ...
THE EVIL ENERGY HAS BEEN EXPELLED AND NOW YOU'RE JUST AN ORDINARY MAN.

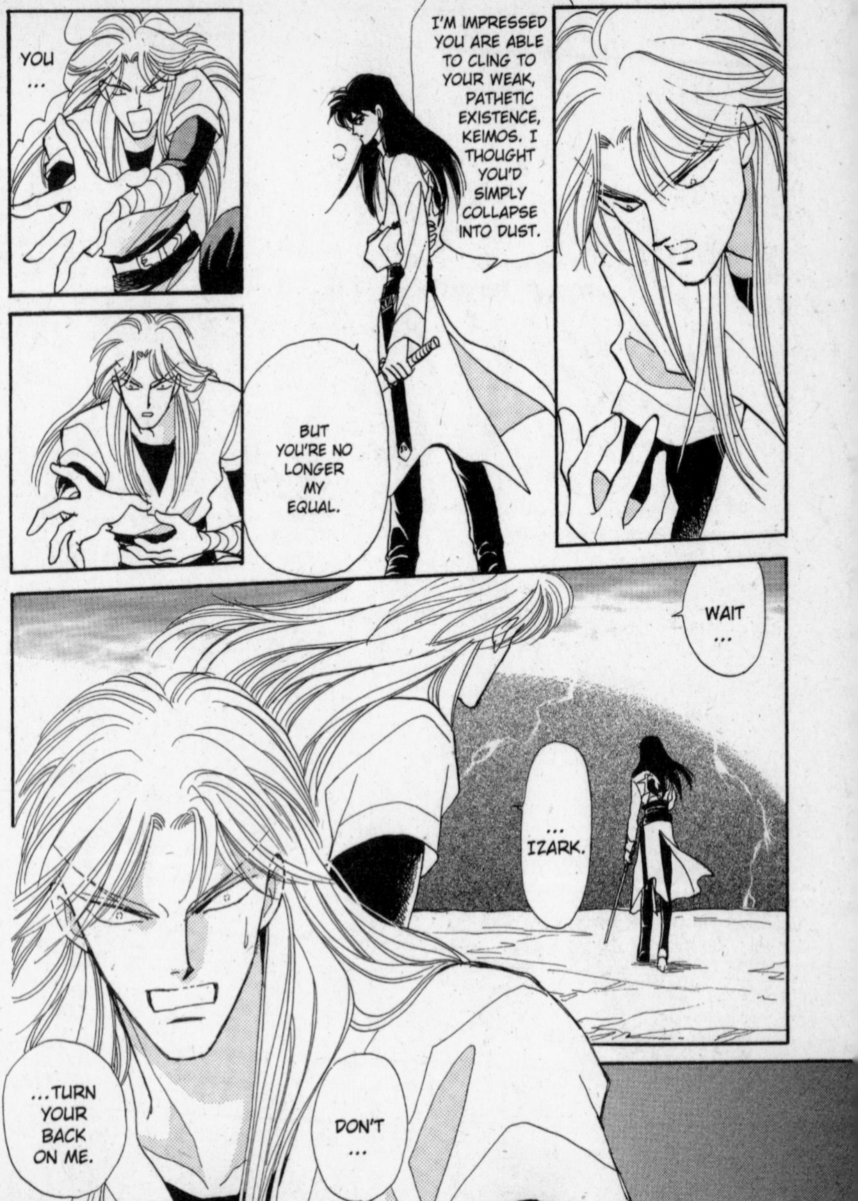
I'M IMPRESSED YOU ARE ABLE TO CLING TO YOUR WEAK, PATHETIC EXISTENCE, KEIMOS. I THOUGHT YOU'D SIMPLY COLLAPSE INTO DUST.
YOU ...
BUT YOU'RE NO LONGER MY EQUAL.
WAIT ...
... IZARK.
DON'T ...
...TURN YOUR BACK ON ME.

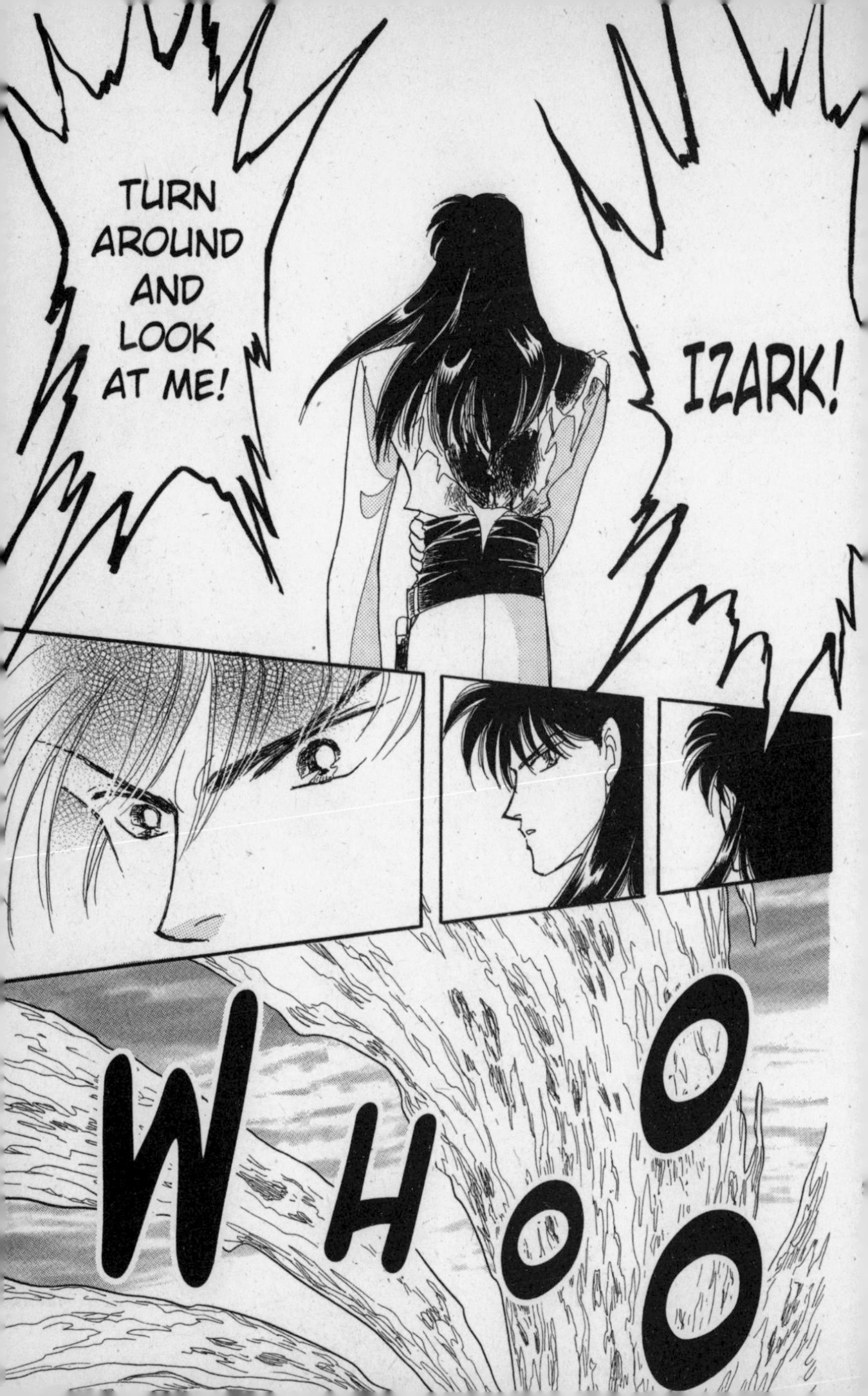
IZARK!
TURN AROUND AND LOOK AT ME!
WHOOOO

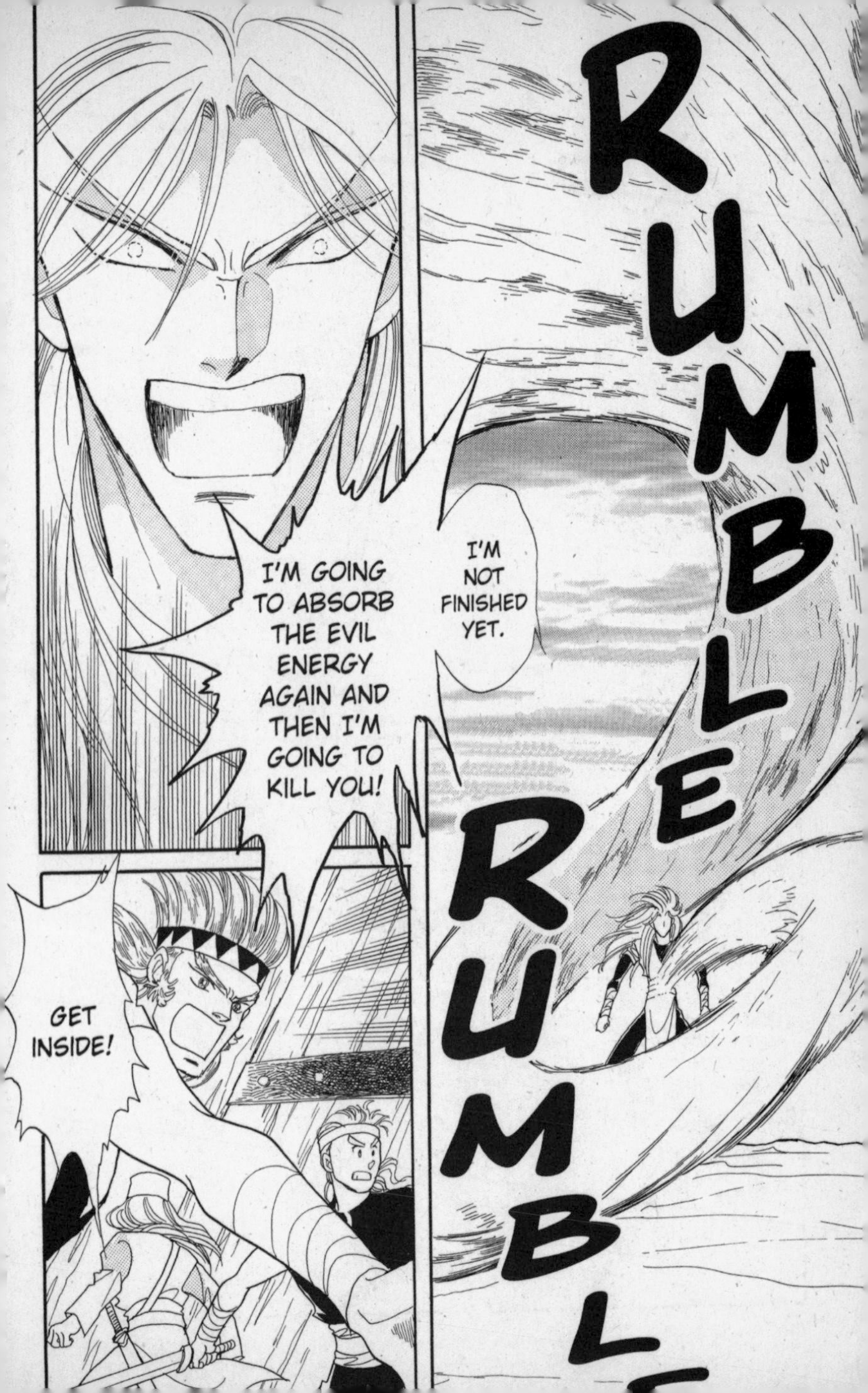
RUMBLE
I'M NOT FINISHED YET.
RUMBL
I'M GOING TO ABSORB THE EVIL ENERGY AGAIN AND THEN I'M GOING TO KILL YOU!
GET INSIDE!

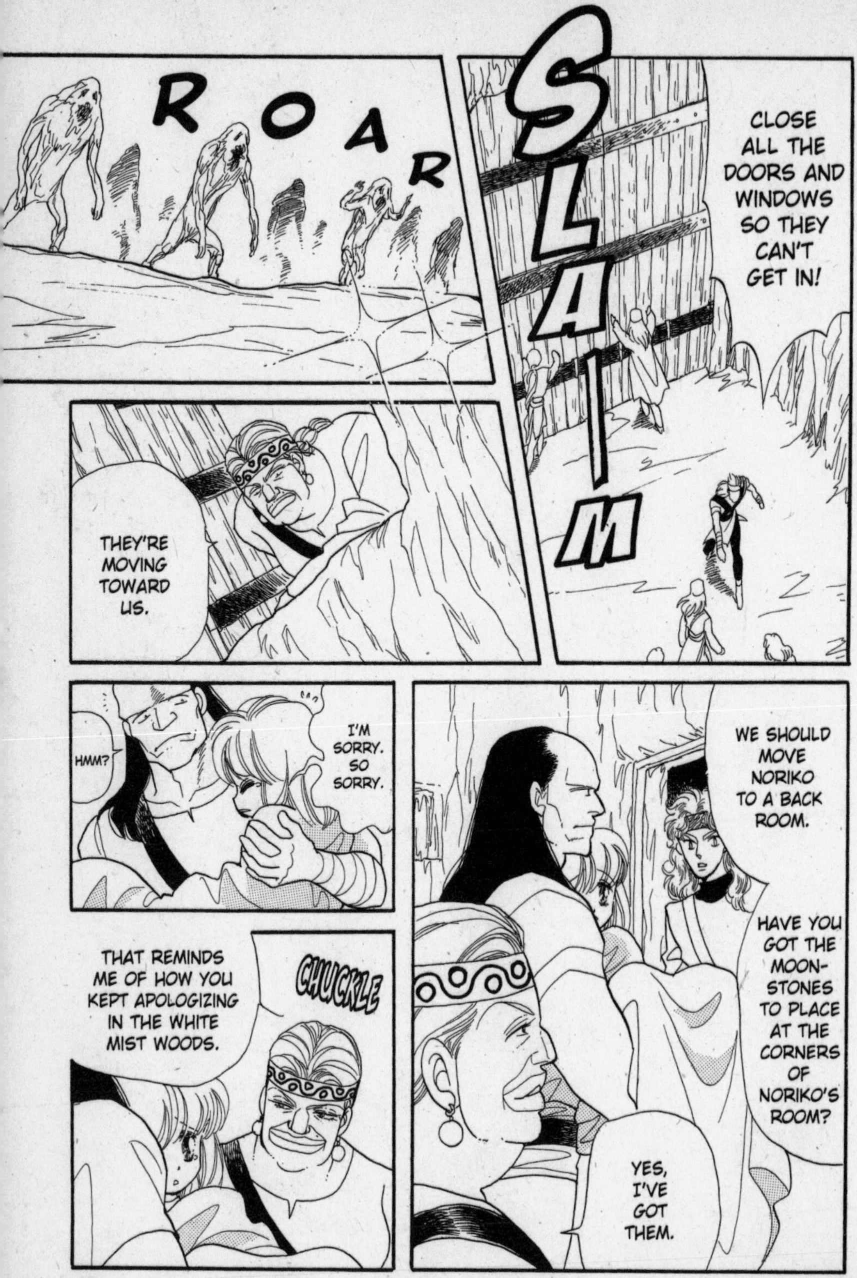
SLAM
CLOSE ALL THE DOORS AND WINDOWS SO THEY CAN'T GET IN!
ROAR
THEY'RE MOVING TOWARD US.
WE SHOULD MOVE NORIKO TO A BACK ROOM.
HAVE YOU GOT THE MOON-STONES TO PLACE AT THE CORNERS OF NORIKO'S ROOM?
YES, I'VE GOT THEM.
I'M SORRY. SO SORRY.
HMM?
CHUCKLE
THAT REMINDS ME OF HOW YOU KEPT APOLOGIZING IN THE WHITE MIST WOODS.

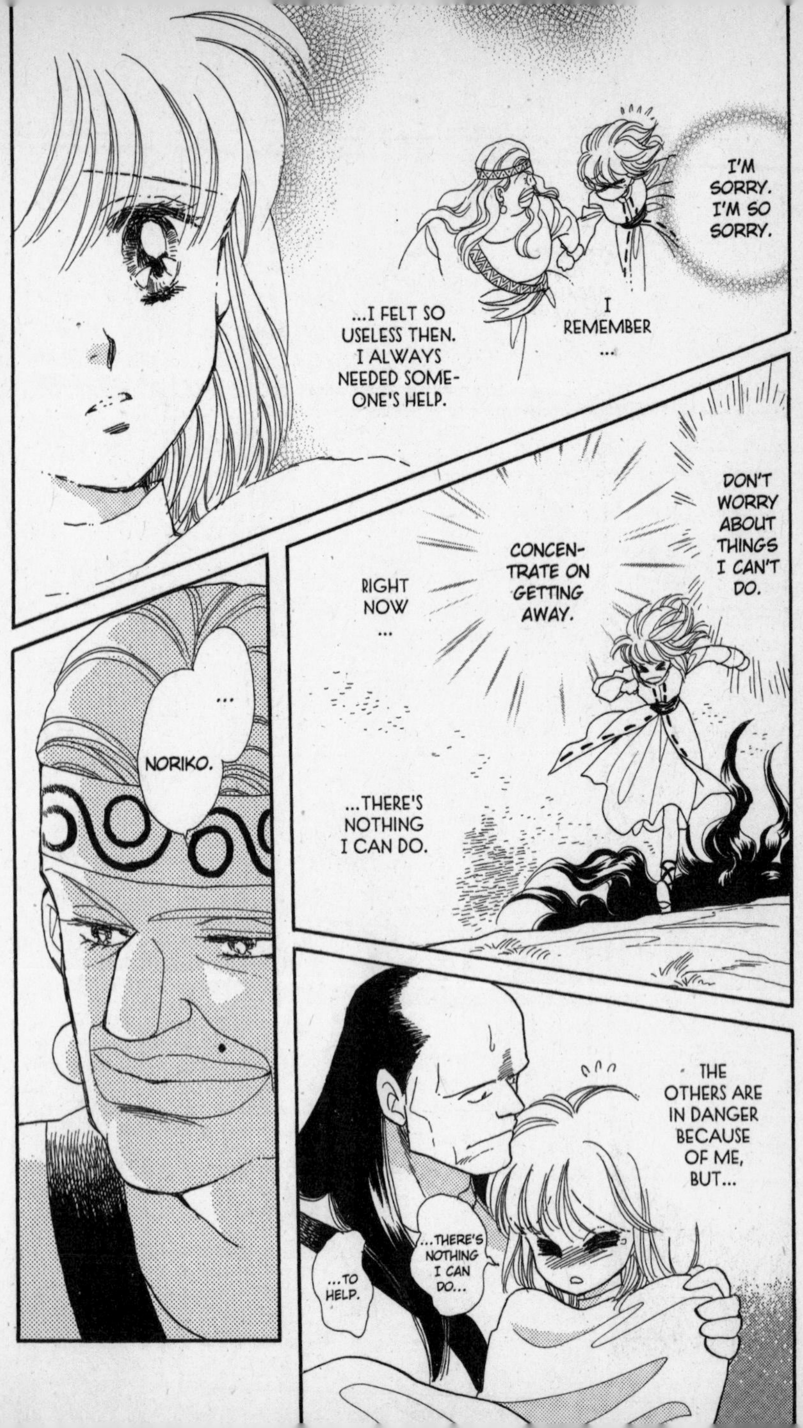
I'M SORRY. I'M SO SORRY.
I REMEMBER ...
...I FELT SO USELESS THEN. I ALWAYS NEEDED SOMEONE'S HELP.
DON'T WORRY ABOUT THINGS I CAN'T DO.
CONCENTRATE ON GETTING AWAY.
RIGHT NOW ...
...THERE'S NOTHING I CAN DO.
THE OTHERS ARE IN DANGER BECAUSE OF ME, BUT...
...THERE'S NOTHING I CAN DO...
...TO HELP.
...
NORIKO.

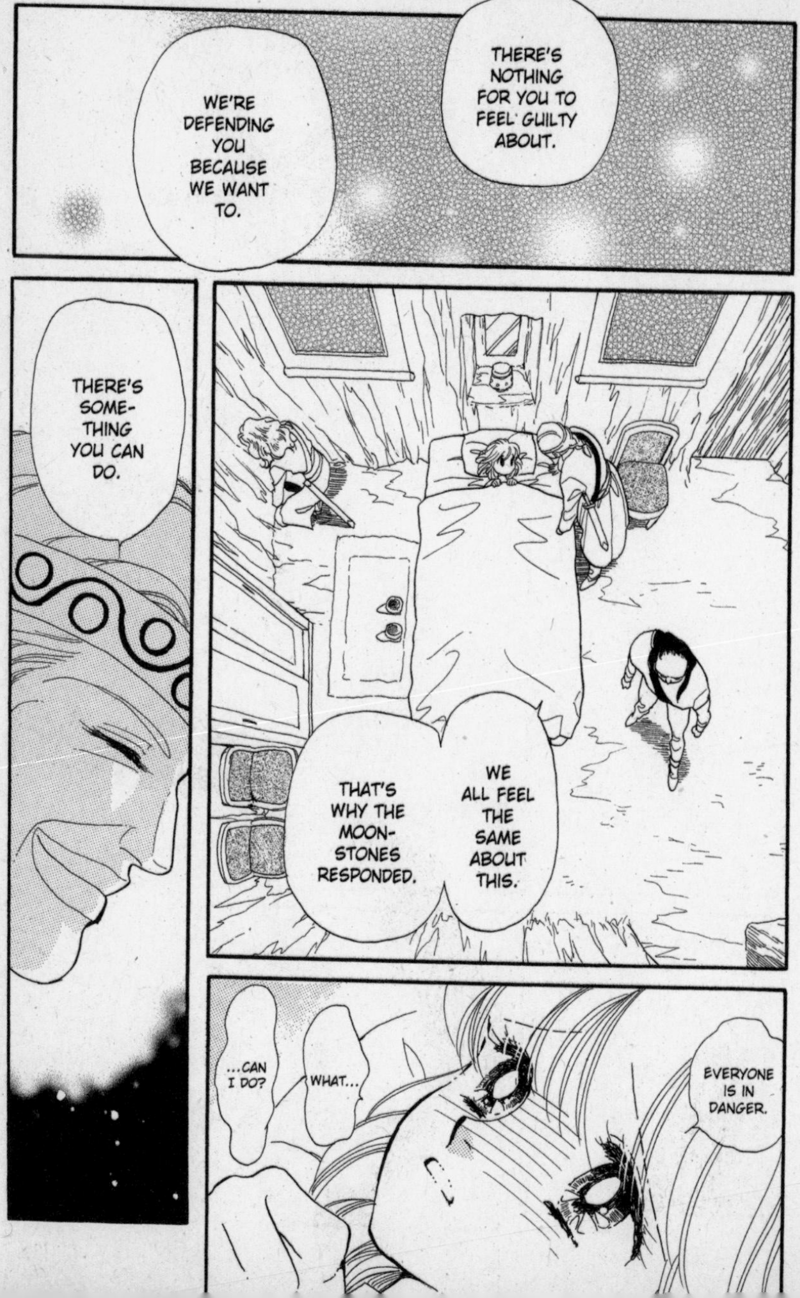
THERE'S NOTHING FOR YOU TO FEEL GUILTY ABOUT.
WE'RE DEFENDING YOU BECAUSE WE WANT TO.
WE ALL FEEL THE SAME ABOUT THIS.
THAT'S WHY THE MOON-STONES RESPONDED.
EVERYONE IS IN DANGER.
WHAT...
...CAN I DO?
THERE'S SOME-THING YOU CAN DO.

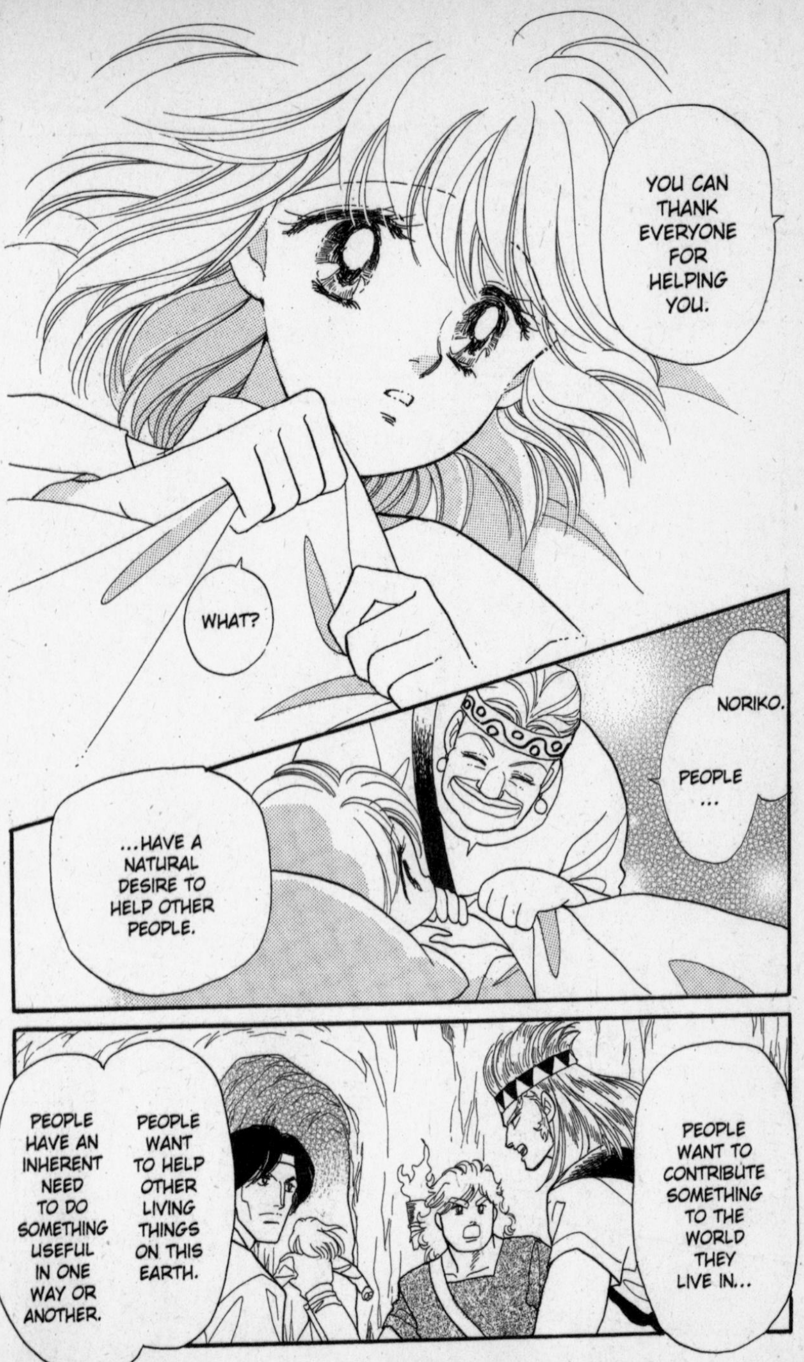
YOU CAN THANK EVERYONE FOR HELPING YOU.
WHAT?
NORIKO.
PEOPLE ...
...HAVE A NATURAL DESIRE TO HELP OTHER PEOPLE.
PEOPLE WANT TO CONTRIBUTE SOMETHING TO THE WORLD THEY LIVE IN...
PEOPLE WANT TO HELP OTHER LIVING THINGS ON THIS EARTH.
PEOPLE HAVE AN INHERENT NEED TO DO SOMETHING USEFUL IN ONE WAY OR ANOTHER.

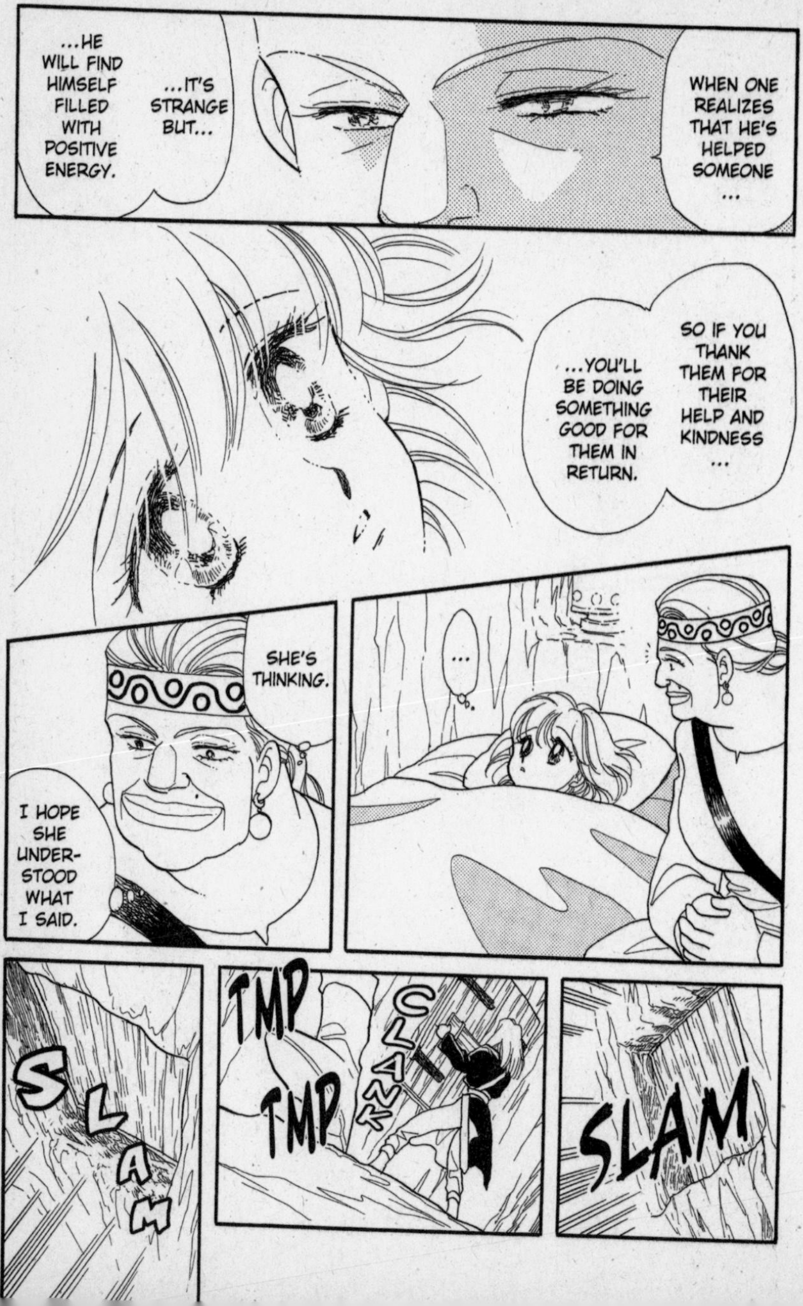
WHEN ONE REALIZES THAT HE'S HELPED SOMEONE ...
...IT'S STRANGE BUT...
...HE WILL FIND HIMSELF FILLED WITH POSITIVE ENERGY.
SO IF YOU THANK THEM FOR THEIR HELP AND KINDNESS ...
...YOU'LL BE DOING SOMETHING GOOD FOR THEM IN RETURN.
...
SHE'S THINKING.
I HOPE SHE UNDER-STOOD WHAT I SAID.
SLAM
TMP
TMP
CLANK
SLAM

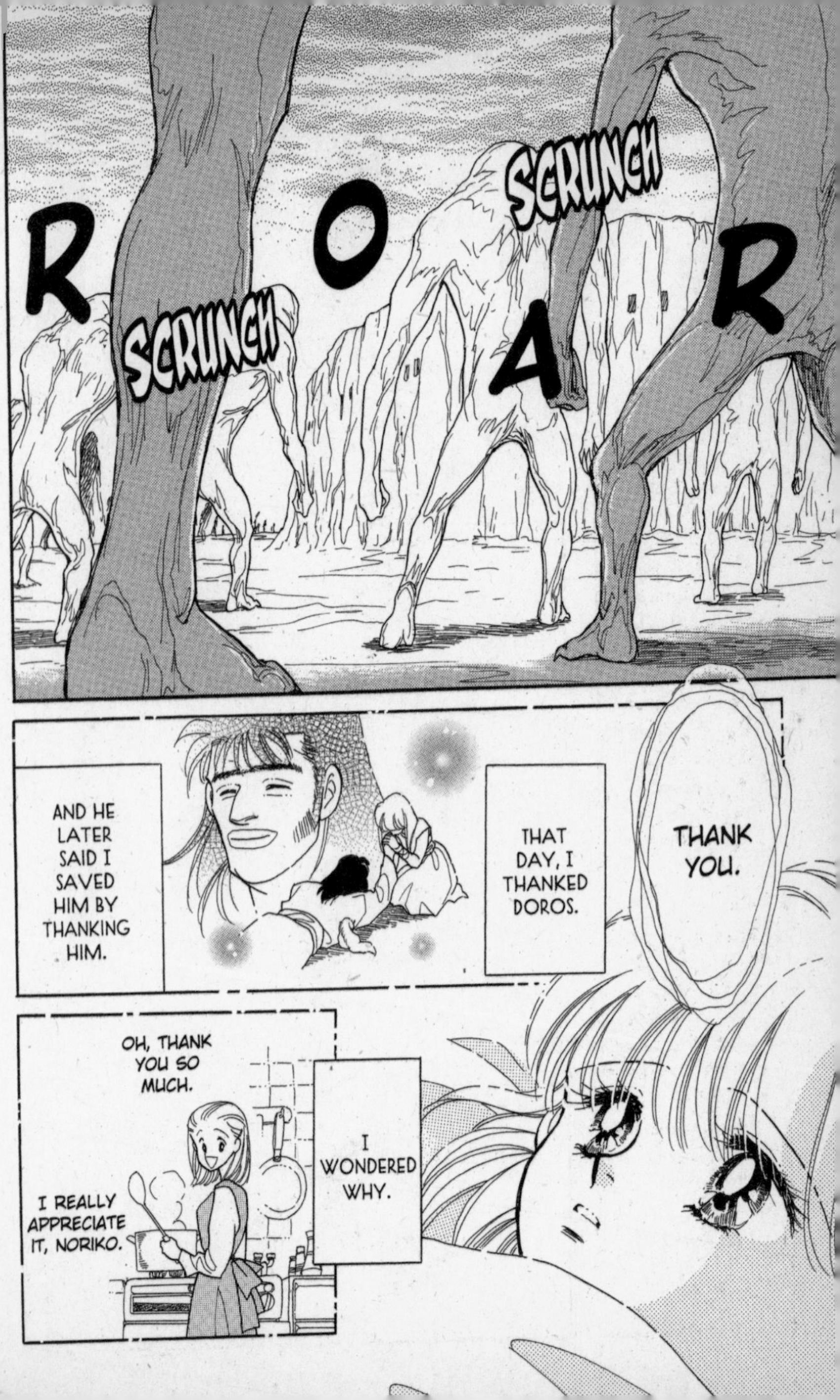
ROAR
SCRUNCH
SCRUNCH
THANK YOU.
THAT DAY, I THANKED DOROS.
AND HE LATER SAID I SAVED HIM BY THANKING HIM.
I WONDERED WHY.
OH, THANK YOU SO MUCH.
I REALLY APPRECIATE IT, NORIKO.

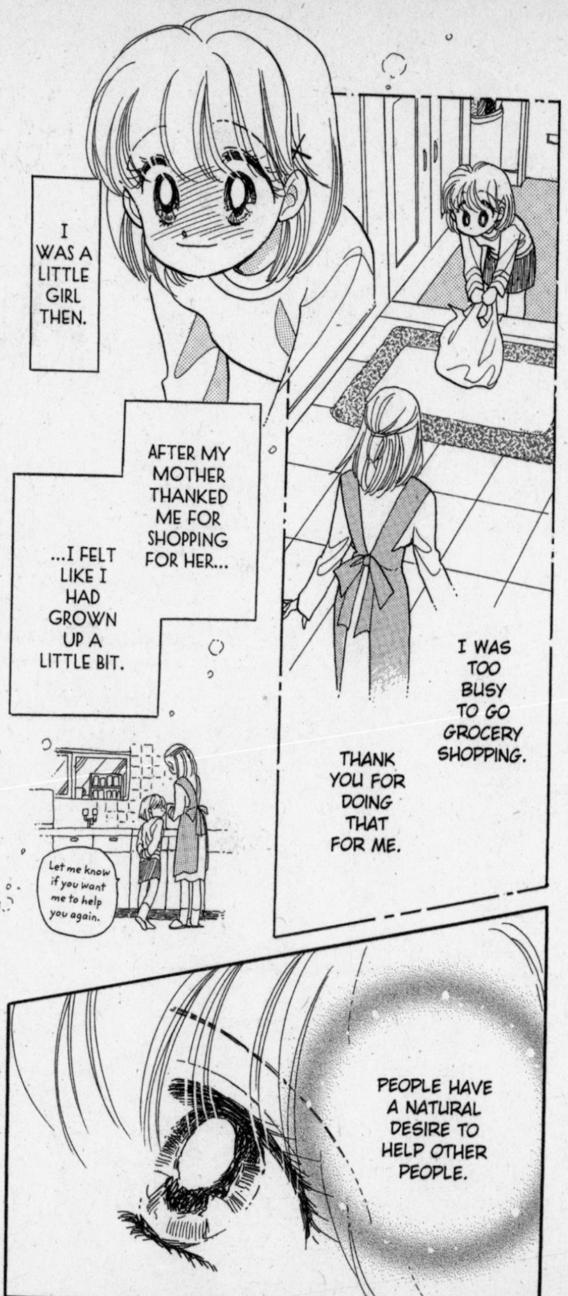
I WAS A LITTLE GIRL THEN.
I WAS TOO BUSY TO GO GROCERY SHOPPING.
THANK YOU FOR DOING THAT FOR ME.
AFTER MY MOTHER THANKED ME FOR SHOPPING FOR HER...
...I FELT LIKE I HAD GROWN UP A LITTLE BIT.
Let me know if you want me to help you again.
PEOPLE HAVE A NATURAL DESIRE TO HELP OTHER PEOPLE.

A Very Insignificant Story: Part 2

One day an old man and an old woman were chatting on the street. A car drove by and honked at them. Perhaps the driver wanted them to make way for his car. When the car passed, the old man cursed at it. Perhaps he felt that the driver had been very rude to honk like that.

I thought, if the driver had said, "Excuse me", or "Thank you for moving" as he drove by, instead of honking, the old man wouldn't have been offended.

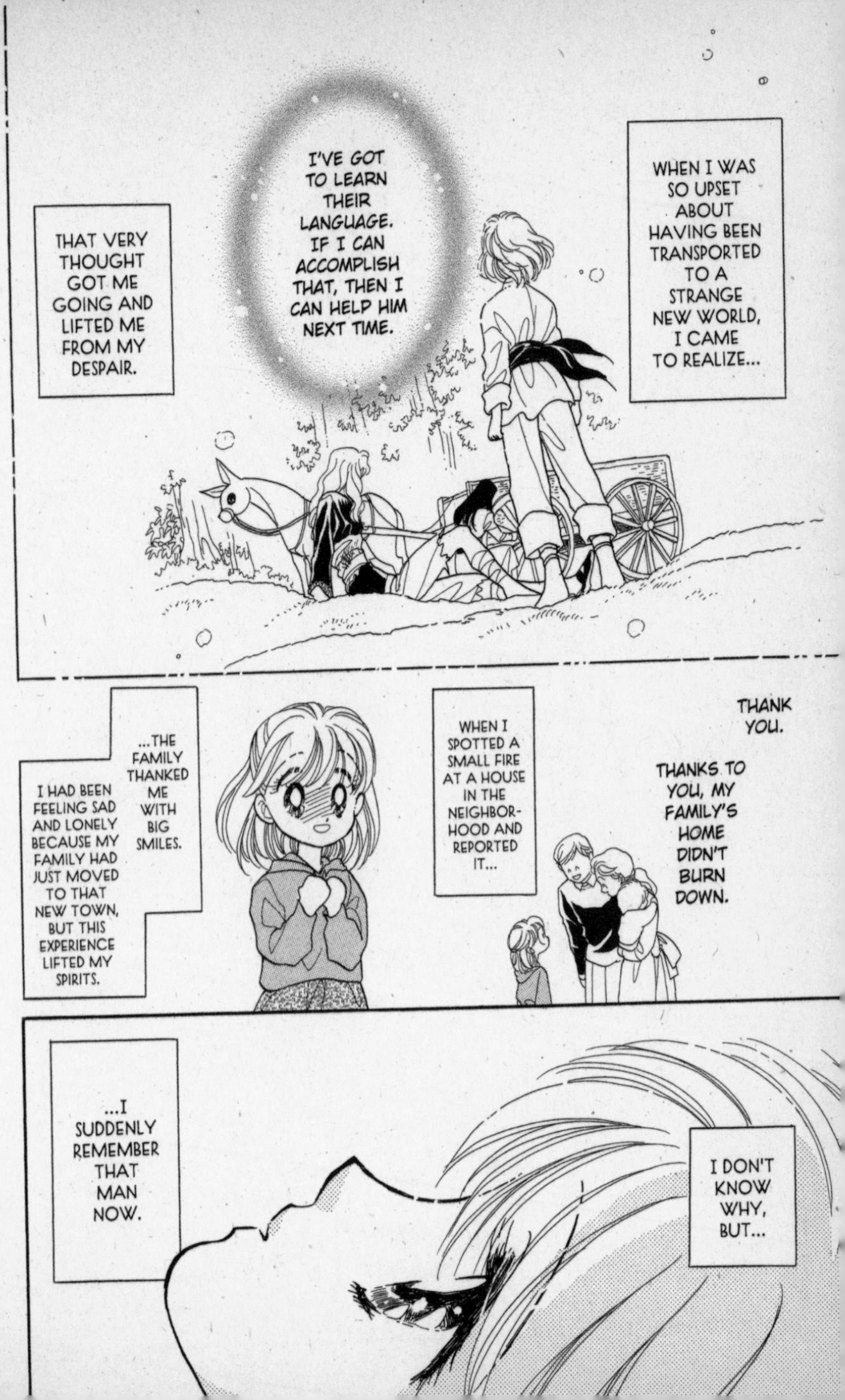
WHEN I WAS SO UPSET ABOUT HAVING BEEN TRANSPORTED TO A STRANGE NEW WORLD, I CAME TO REALIZE...
I'VE GOT TO LEARN THEIR LANGUAGE. IF I CAN ACCOMPLISH THAT, THEN I CAN HELP HIM NEXT TIME.
THAT VERY THOUGHT GOT ME GOING AND LIFTED ME FROM MY DESPAIR.
THANK YOU.
THANKS TO YOU, MY FAMILY'S HOME DIDN'T BURN DOWN.
WHEN I SPOTTED A SMALL FIRE AT A HOUSE IN THE NEIGHBOR-HOOD AND REPORTED IT...
...THE FAMILY THANKED ME WITH BIG SMILES.
I HAD BEEN FEELING SAD AND LONELY BECAUSE MY FAMILY HAD JUST MOVED TO THAT NEW TOWN, BUT THIS EXPERIENCE LIFTED MY SPIRITS.
I DON'T KNOW WHY, BUT...
...I SUDDENLY REMEMBER THAT MAN NOW.

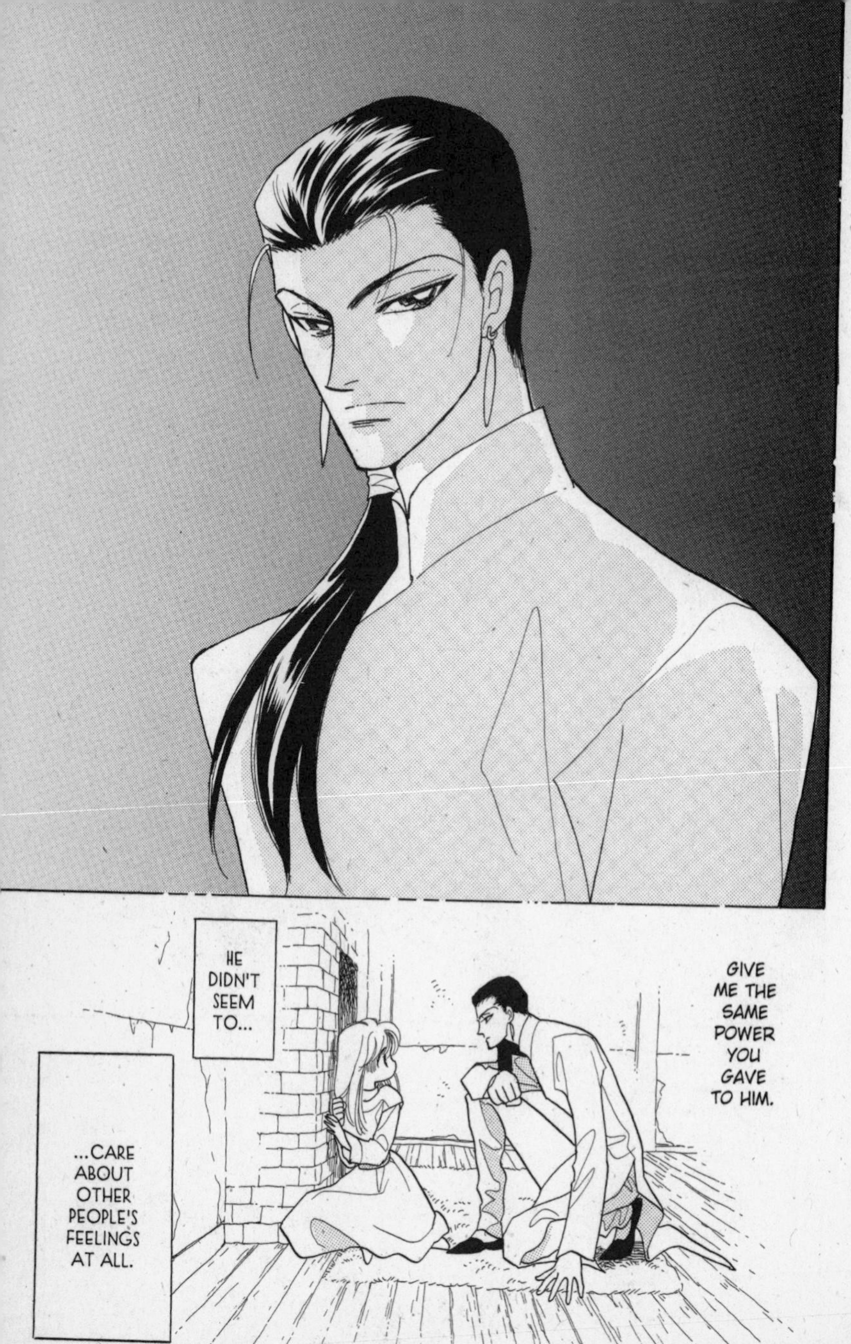
GIVE ME THE SAME POWER YOU GAVE TO HIM.
HE DIDN'T SEEM TO...
...CARE ABOUT OTHER PEOPLE'S FEELINGS AT ALL.

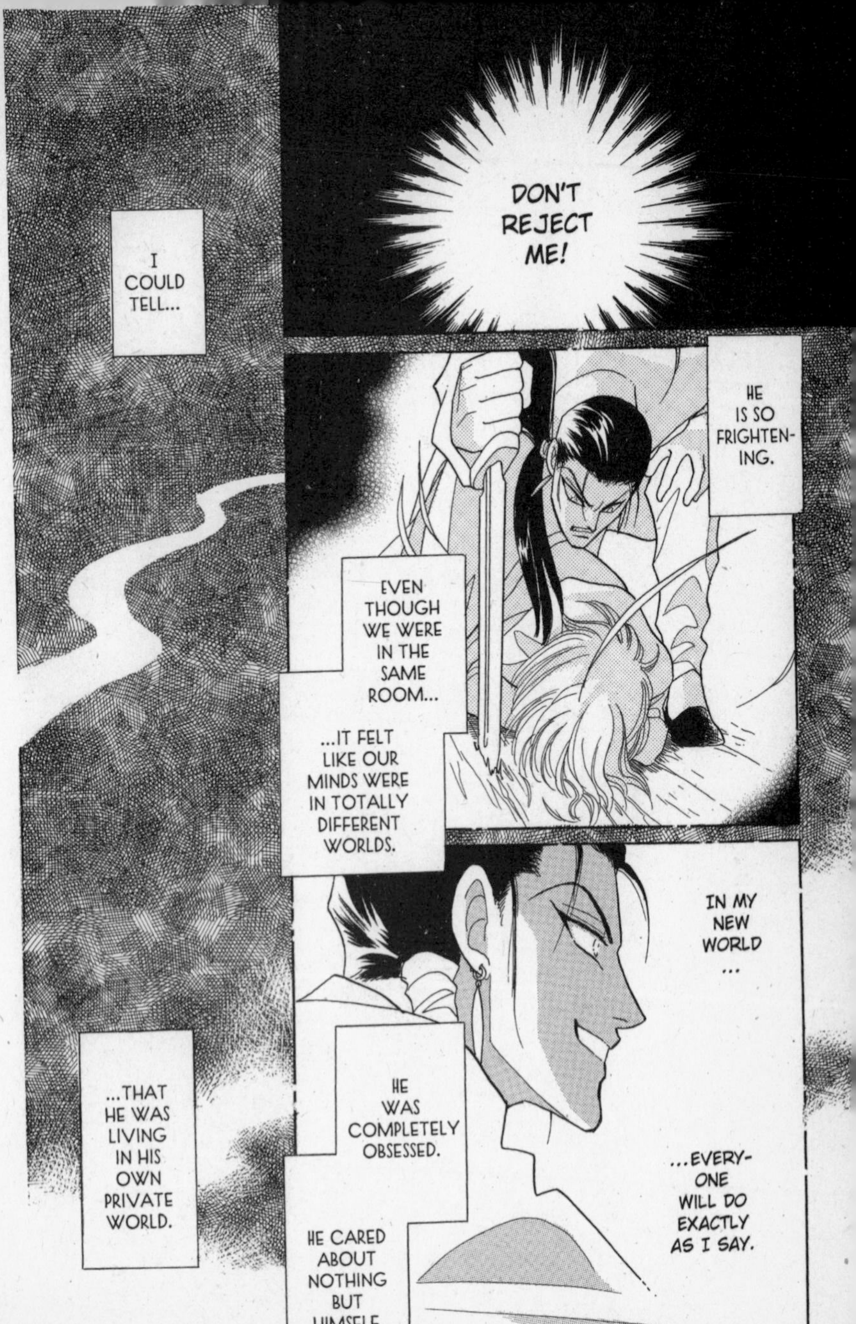
DON'T REJECT ME!
HE IS SO FRIGHTENING.
EVEN THOUGH WE WERE IN THE SAME ROOM...
...IT FELT LIKE OUR MINDS WERE IN TOTALLY DIFFERENT WORLDS.
I COULD TELL...
...THAT HE WAS LIVING IN HIS OWN PRIVATE WORLD.
IN MY NEW WORLD...
...EVERYONE WILL DO EXACTLY AS I SAY.
HE WAS COMPLETELY OBSESSED.
HE CARED ABOUT NOTHING BUT HIMSELF.

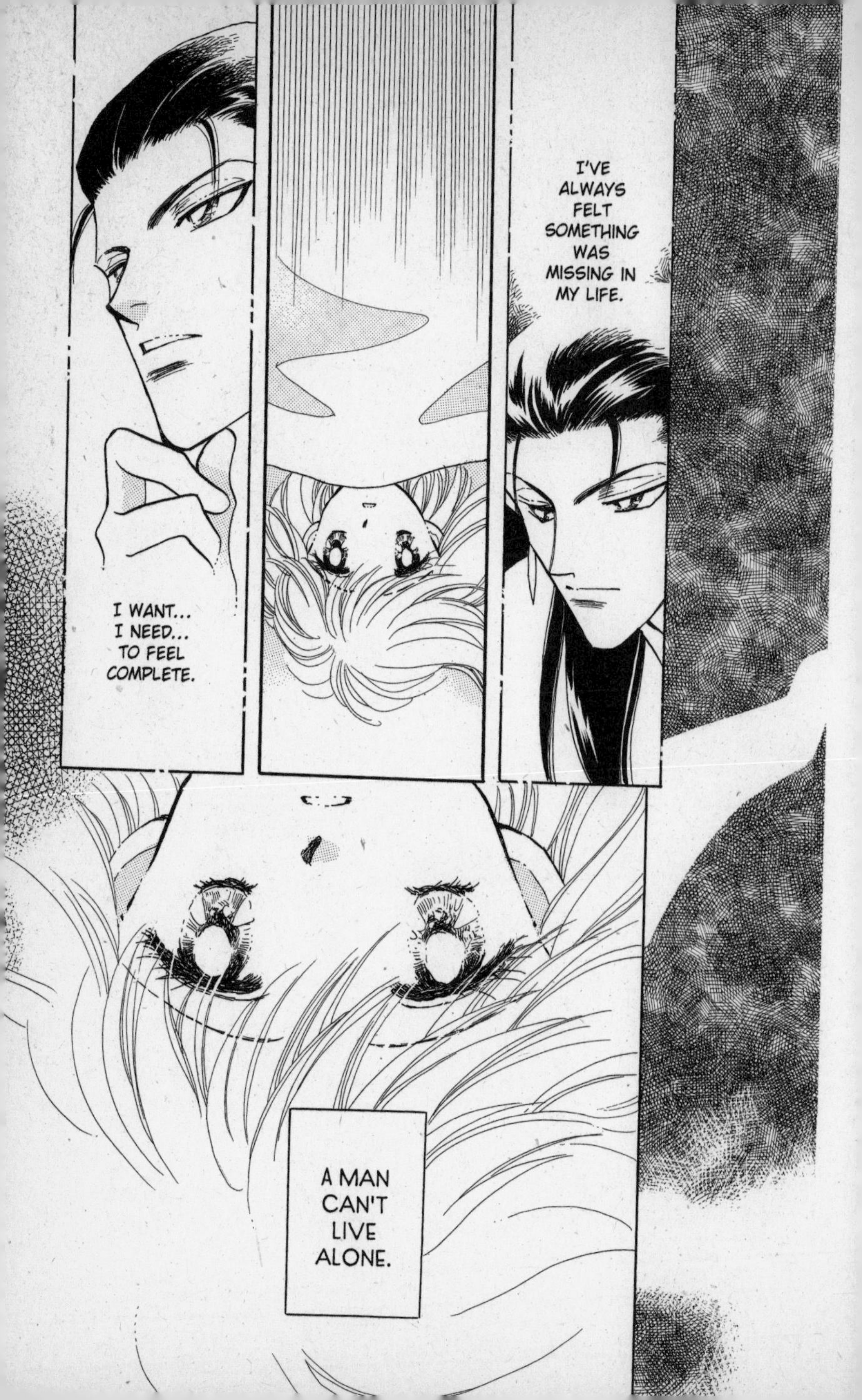
I'VE ALWAYS FELT SOMETHING WAS MISSING IN MY LIFE.
I WANT... I NEED... TO FEEL COMPLETE.
A MAN CAN'T LIVE ALONE.

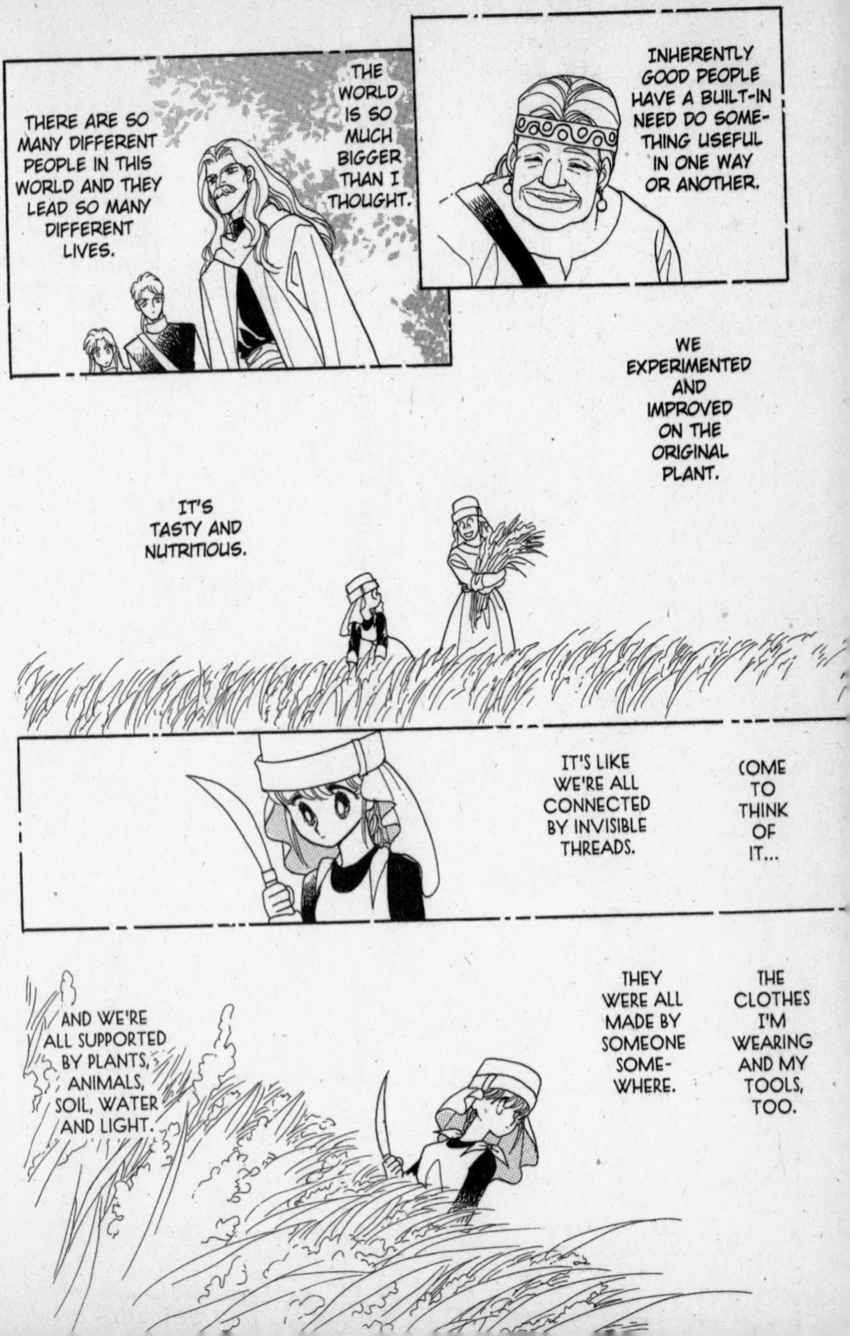
INHERENTLY GOOD PEOPLE HAVE A BUILT-IN NEED DO SOME-THING USEFUL IN ONE WAY OR ANOTHER.
THE WORLD IS SO MUCH BIGGER THAN I THOUGHT.
THERE ARE SO MANY DIFFERENT PEOPLE IN THIS WORLD AND THEY LEAD SO MANY DIFFERENT LIVES.
WE EXPERIMENTED AND IMPROVED ON THE ORIGINAL PLANT.
IT'S TASTY AND NUTRITIOUS.
COME TO THINK OF IT...
IT'S LIKE WE'RE ALL CONNECTED BY INVISIBLE THREADS.
THE CLOTHES I'M WEARING AND MY TOOLS, TOO.
THEY WERE ALL MADE BY SOMEONE SOME-WHERE.
AND WE'RE ALL SUPPORTED BY PLANTS, ANIMALS, SOIL, WATER AND LIGHT.

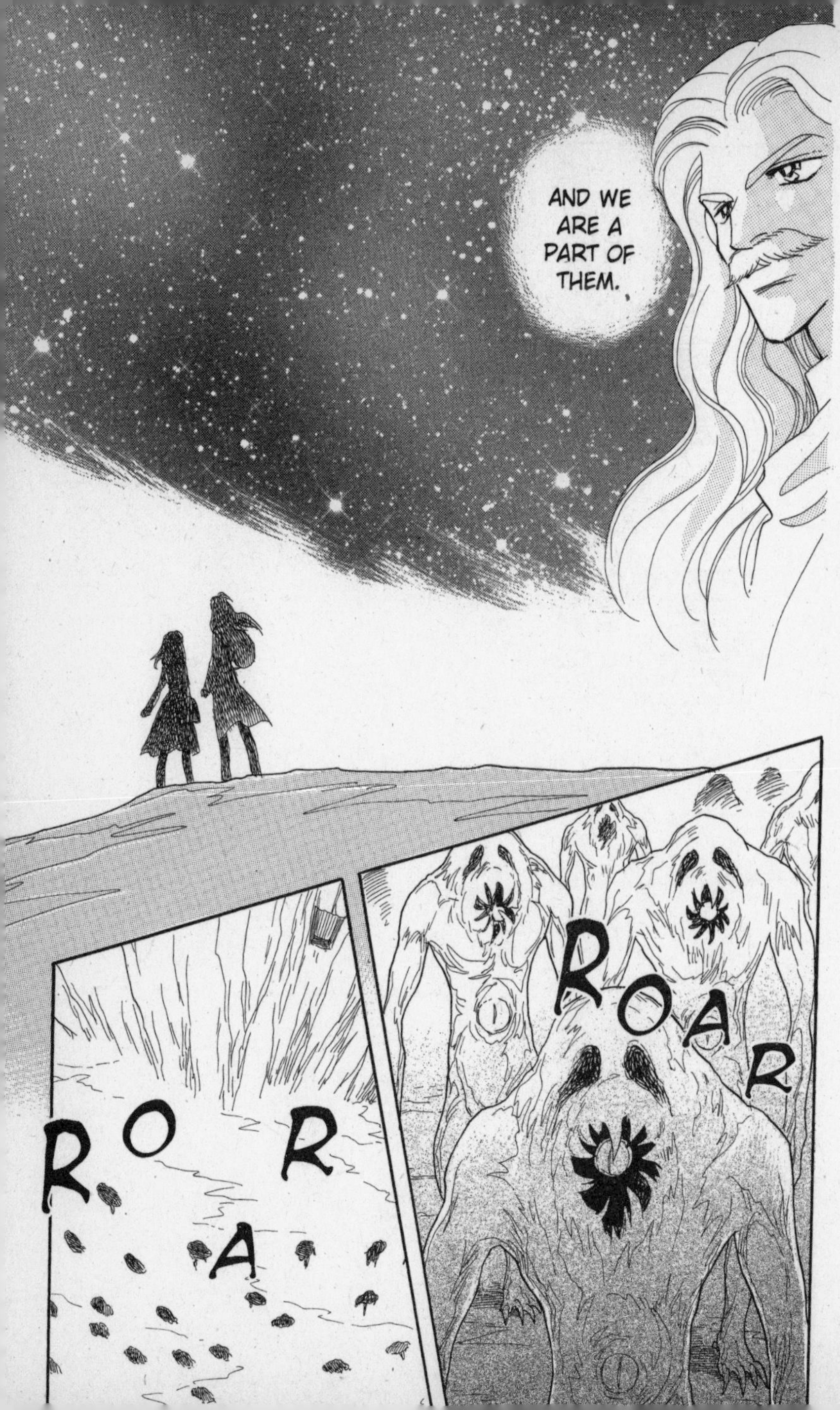
AND WE ARE A PART OF THEM.
ROAR
ROAR

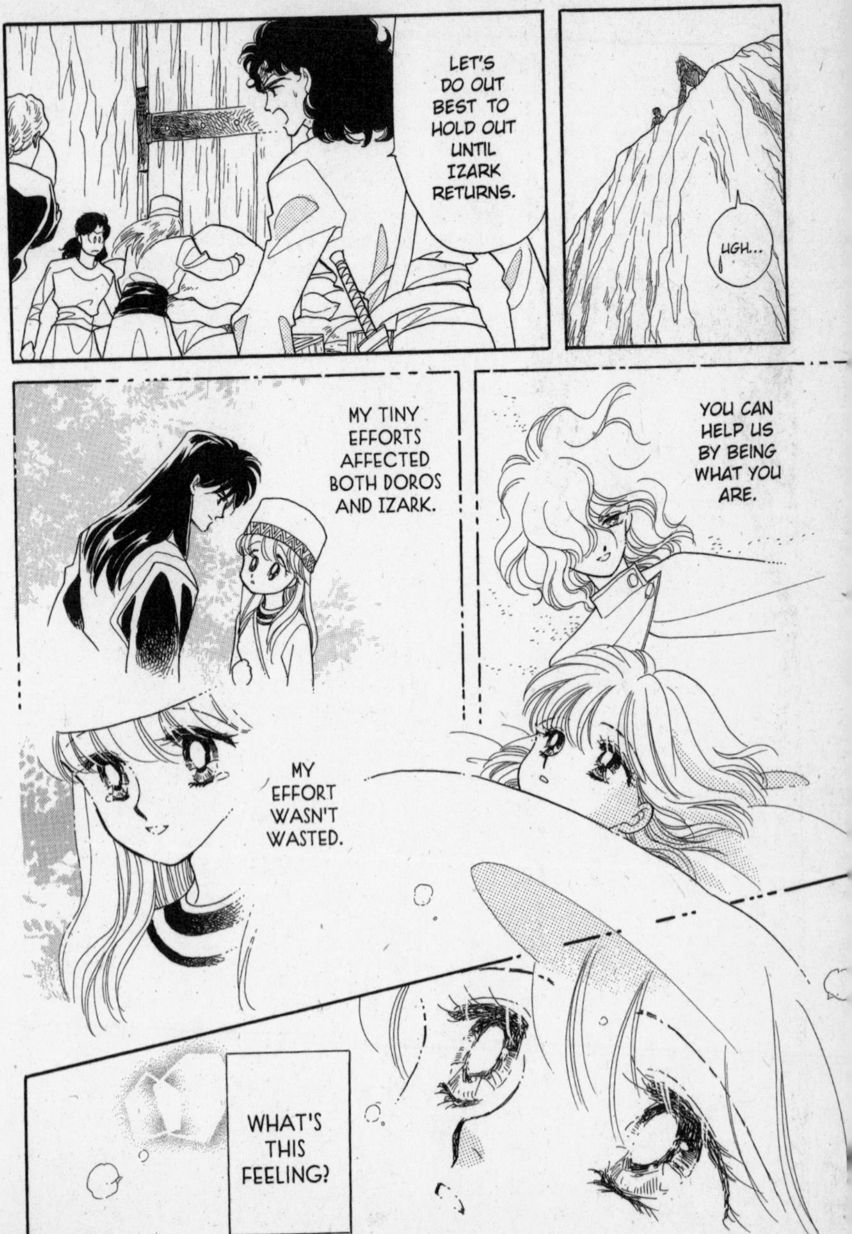
UGH...
LET'S DO OUT BEST TO HOLD OUT UNTIL IZARK RETURNS.
YOU CAN HELP US BY BEING WHAT YOU ARE.
MY TINY EFFORTS AFFECTED BOTH DOROS AND IZARK.
MY EFFORT WASN'T WASTED.
WHAT'S THIS FEELING?

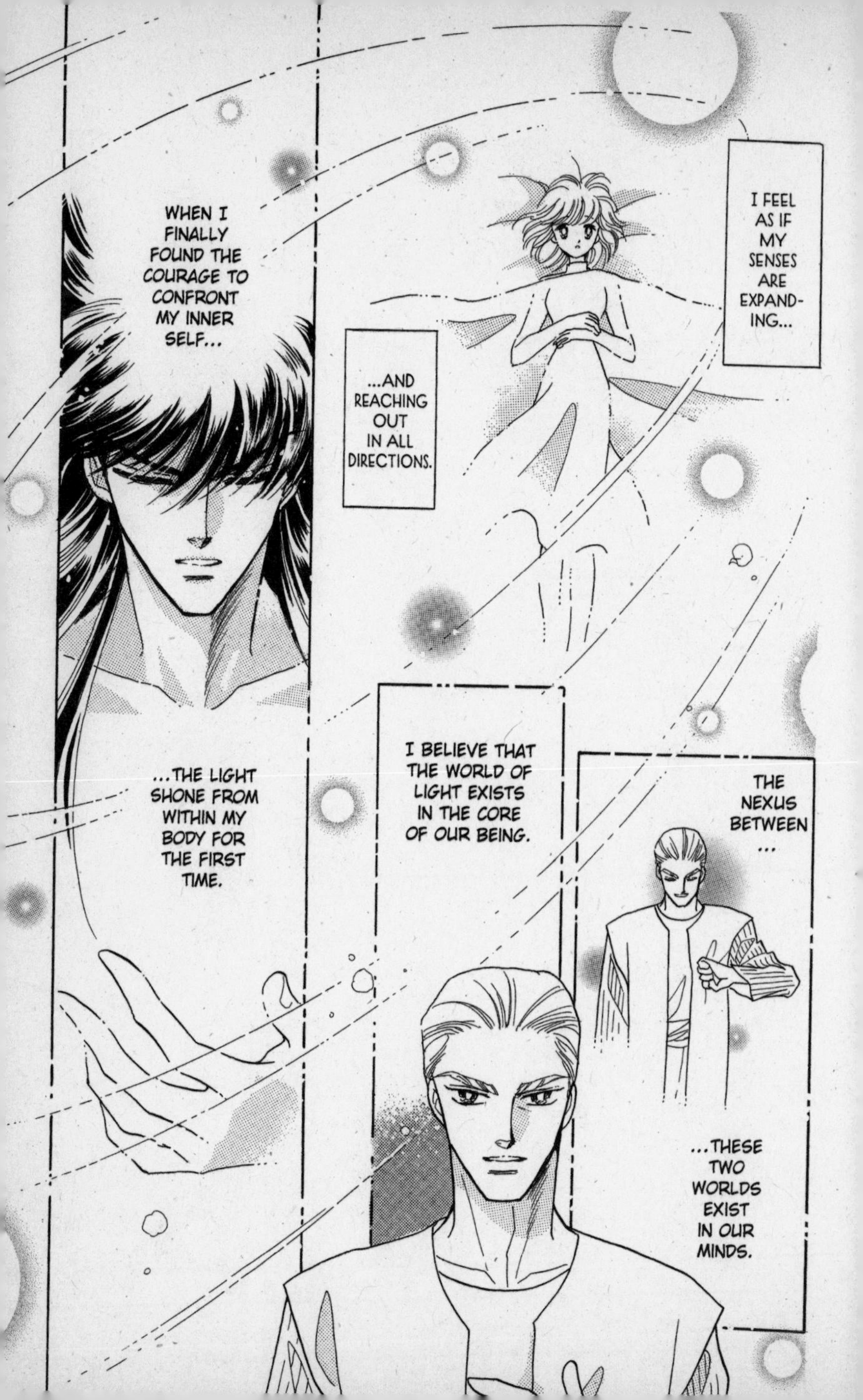
I FEEL AS IF MY SENSES ARE EXPAND-ING...
...AND REACHING OUT IN ALL DIRECTIONS.
THE NEXUS BETWEEN...
...THESE TWO WORLDS EXIST IN OUR MINDS.
I BELIEVE THAT THE WORLD OF LIGHT EXISTS IN THE CORE OF OUR BEING.
WHEN I FINALLY FOUND THE COURAGE TO CONFRONT MY INNER SELF...
...THE LIGHT SHONE FROM WITHIN MY BODY FOR THE FIRST TIME.

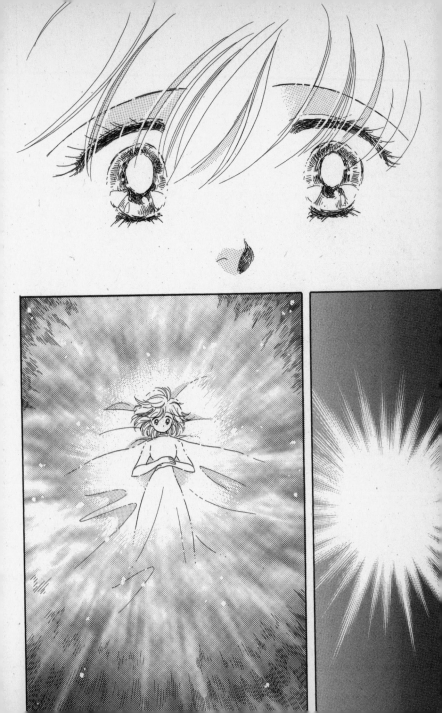

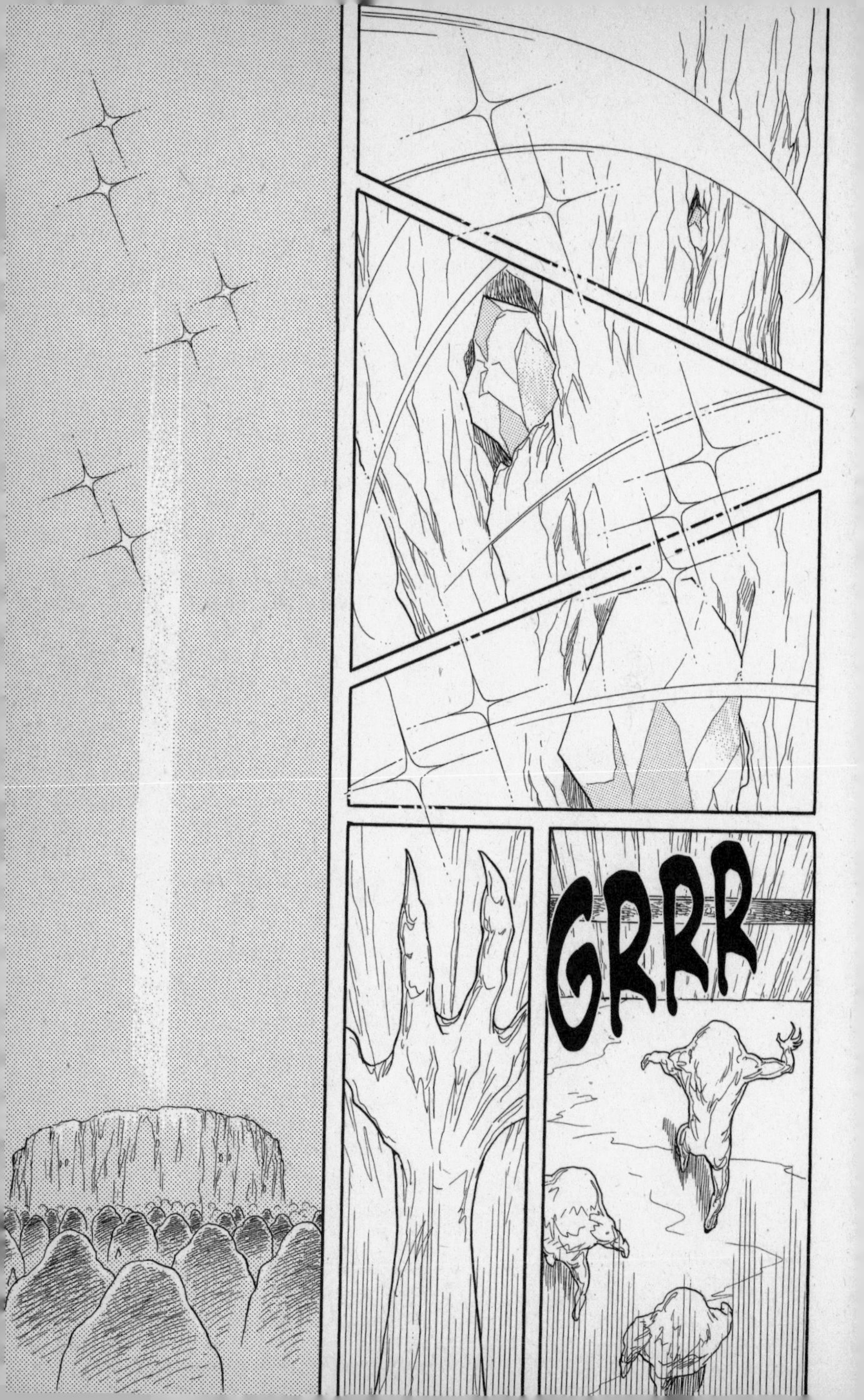
GRRR

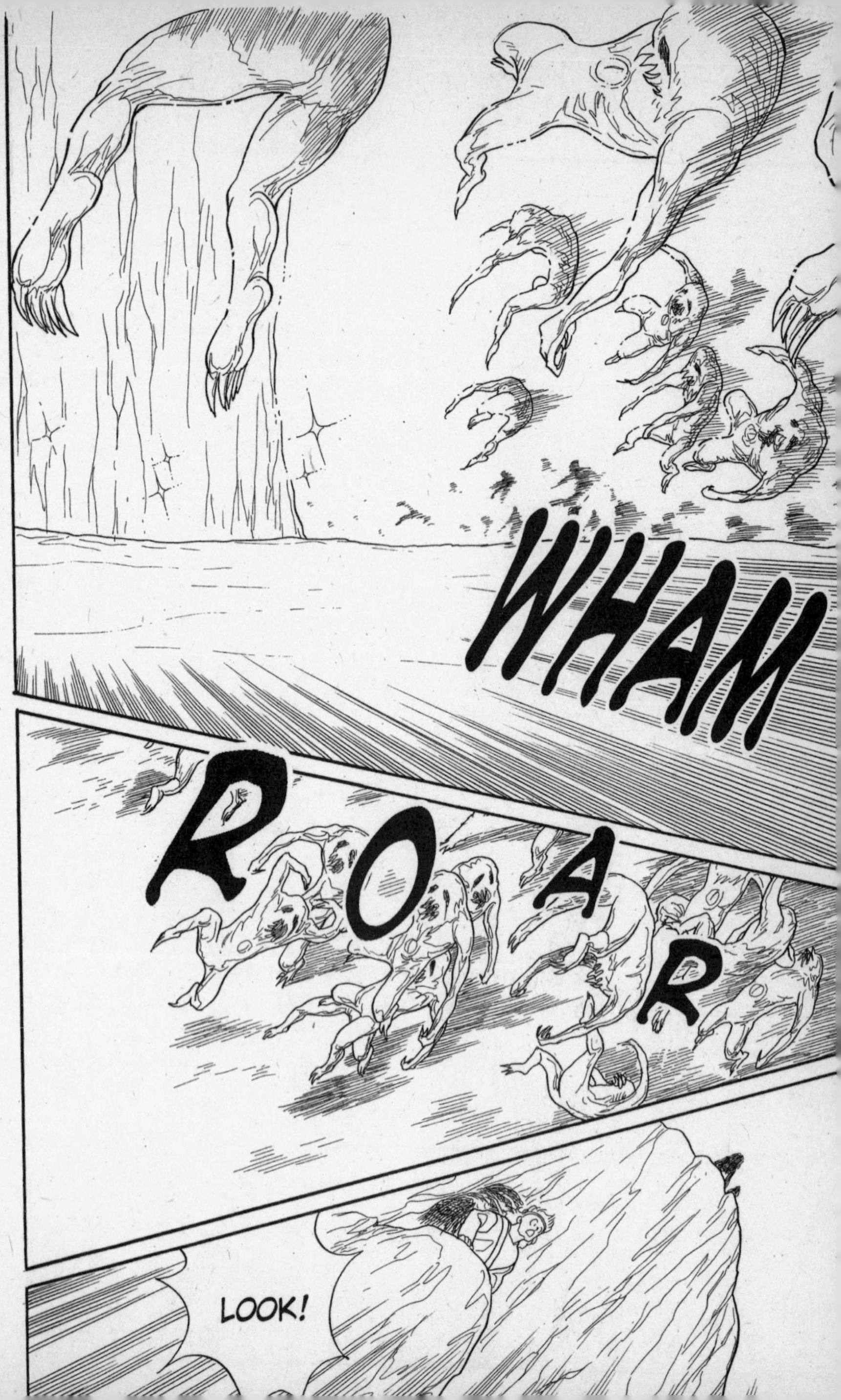
WHAM
ROAR
LOOK!

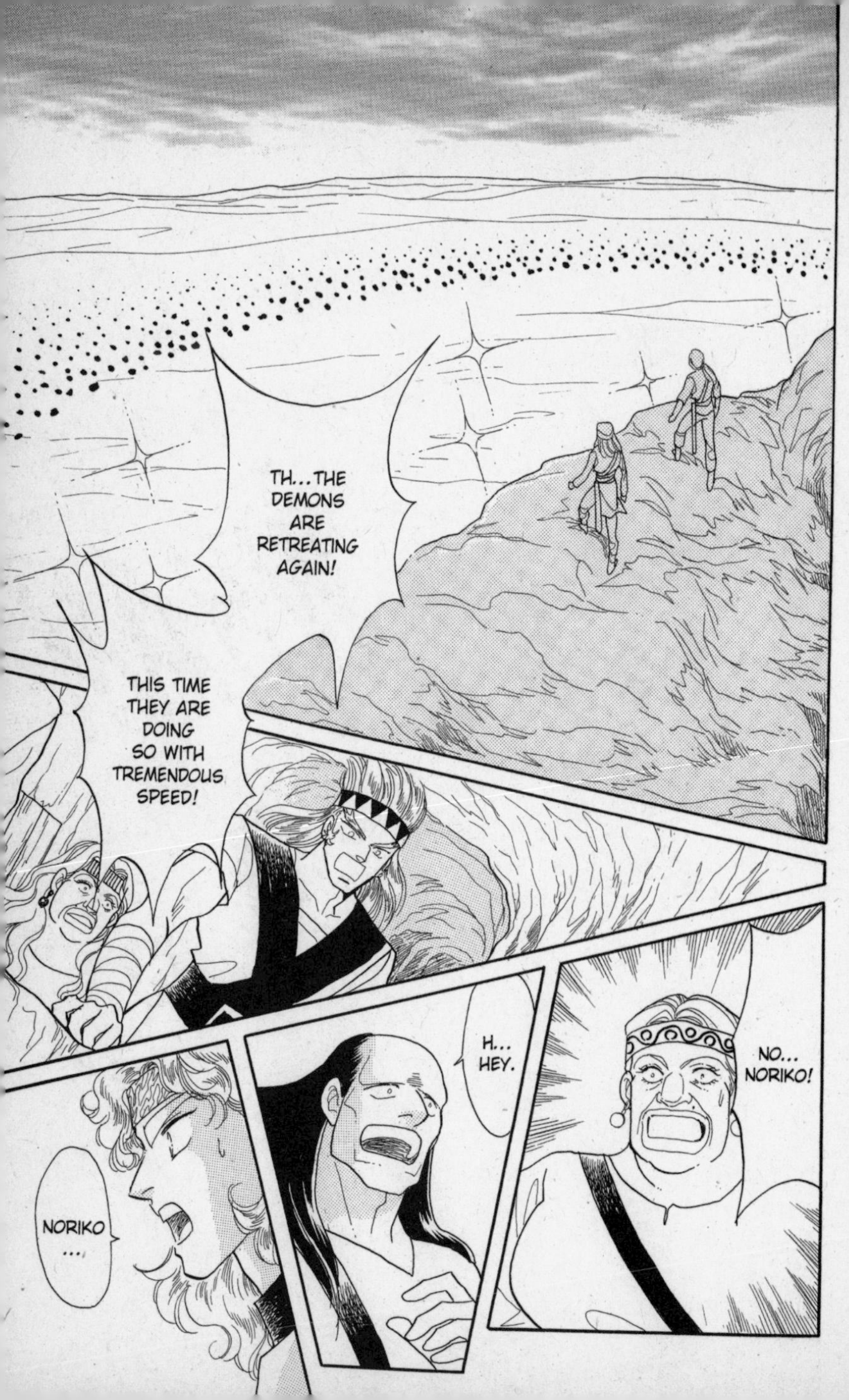
TH...THE DEMONS ARE RETREATING AGAIN!
THIS TIME THEY ARE DOING SO WITH TREMENDOUS SPEED!
NO... NORIKO!
H... HEY.
NORIKO ...!

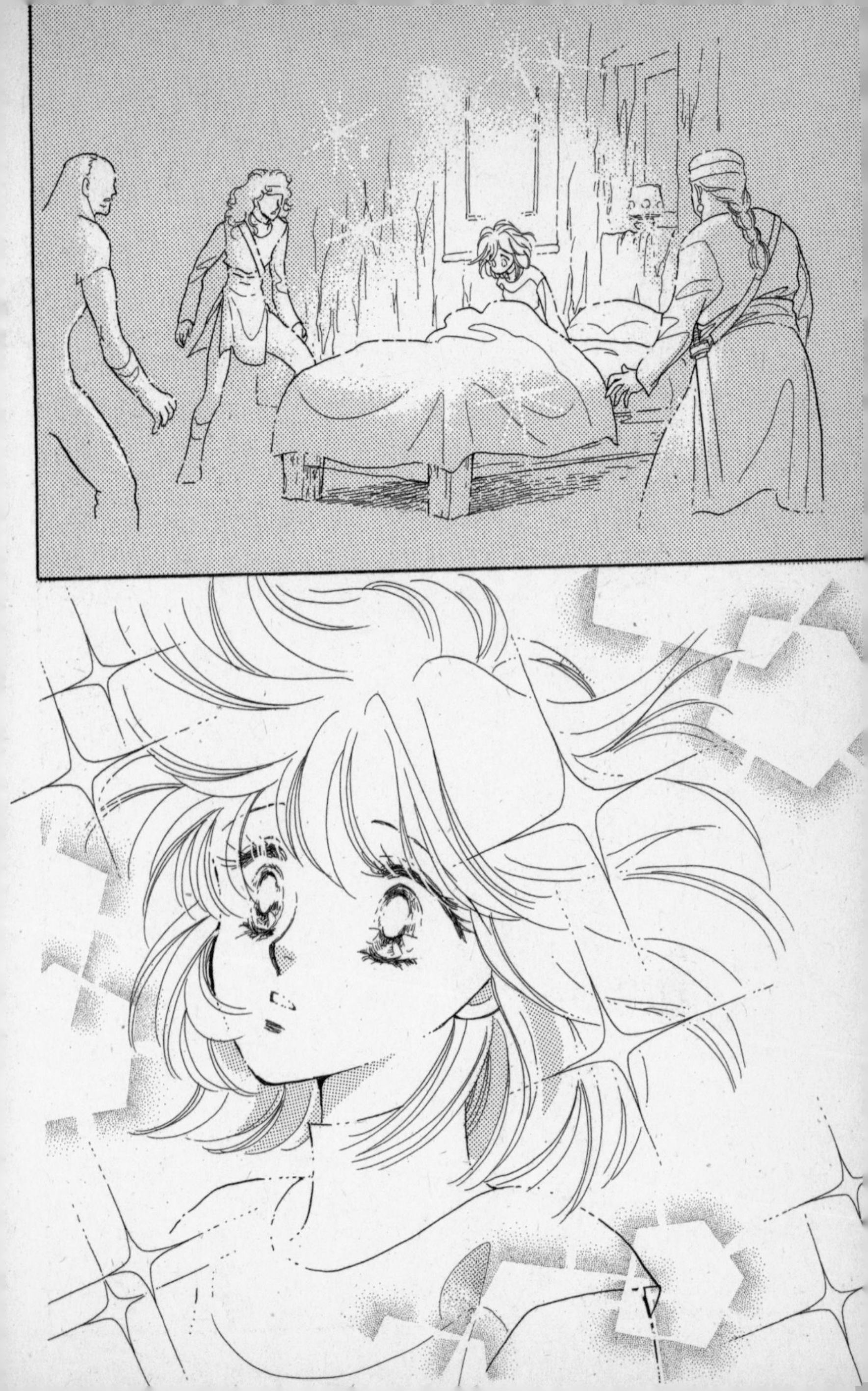

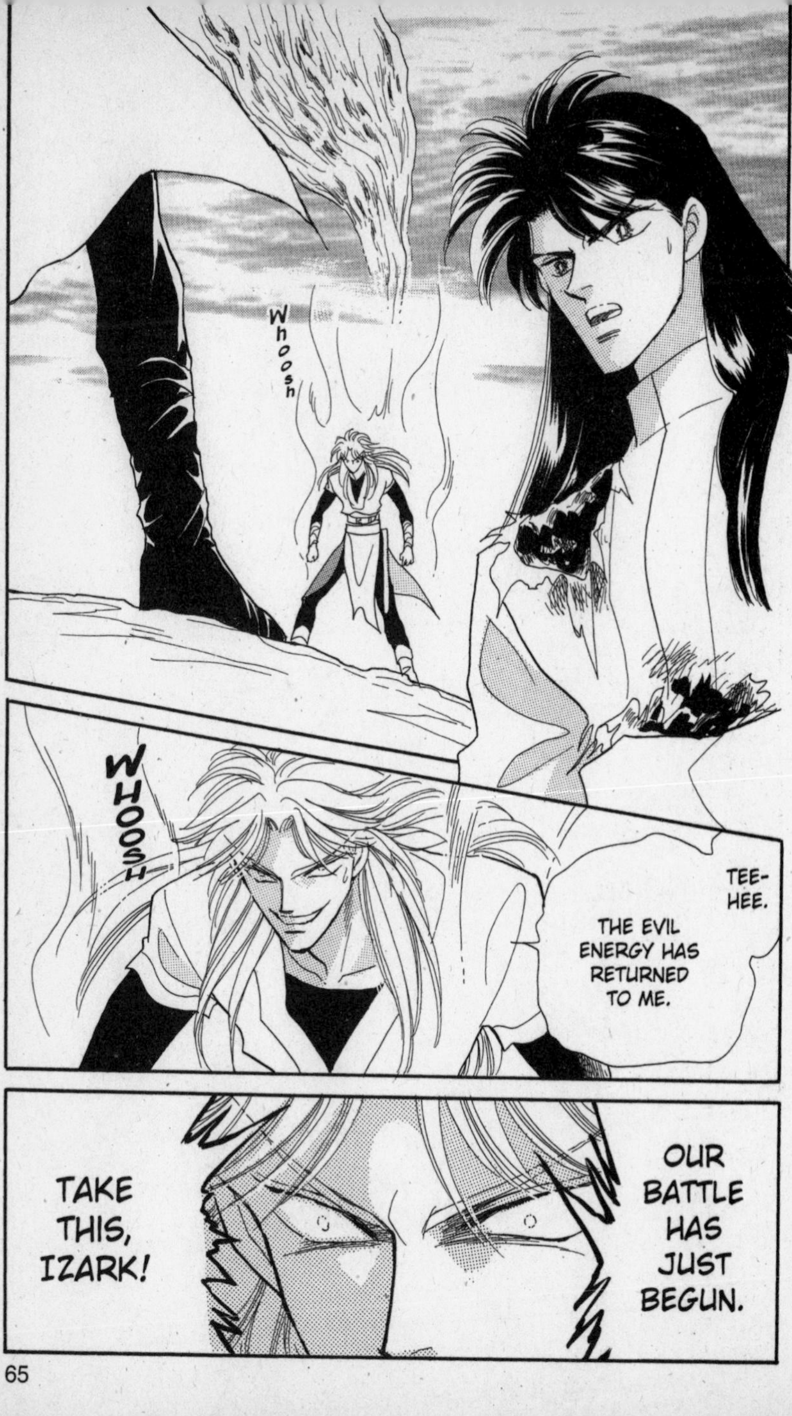
Whoosh
WHOOSH
TEE-HEE.
THE EVIL ENERGY HAS RETURNED TO ME.
OUR BATTLE HAS JUST BEGUN.
TAKE THIS, IZARK!

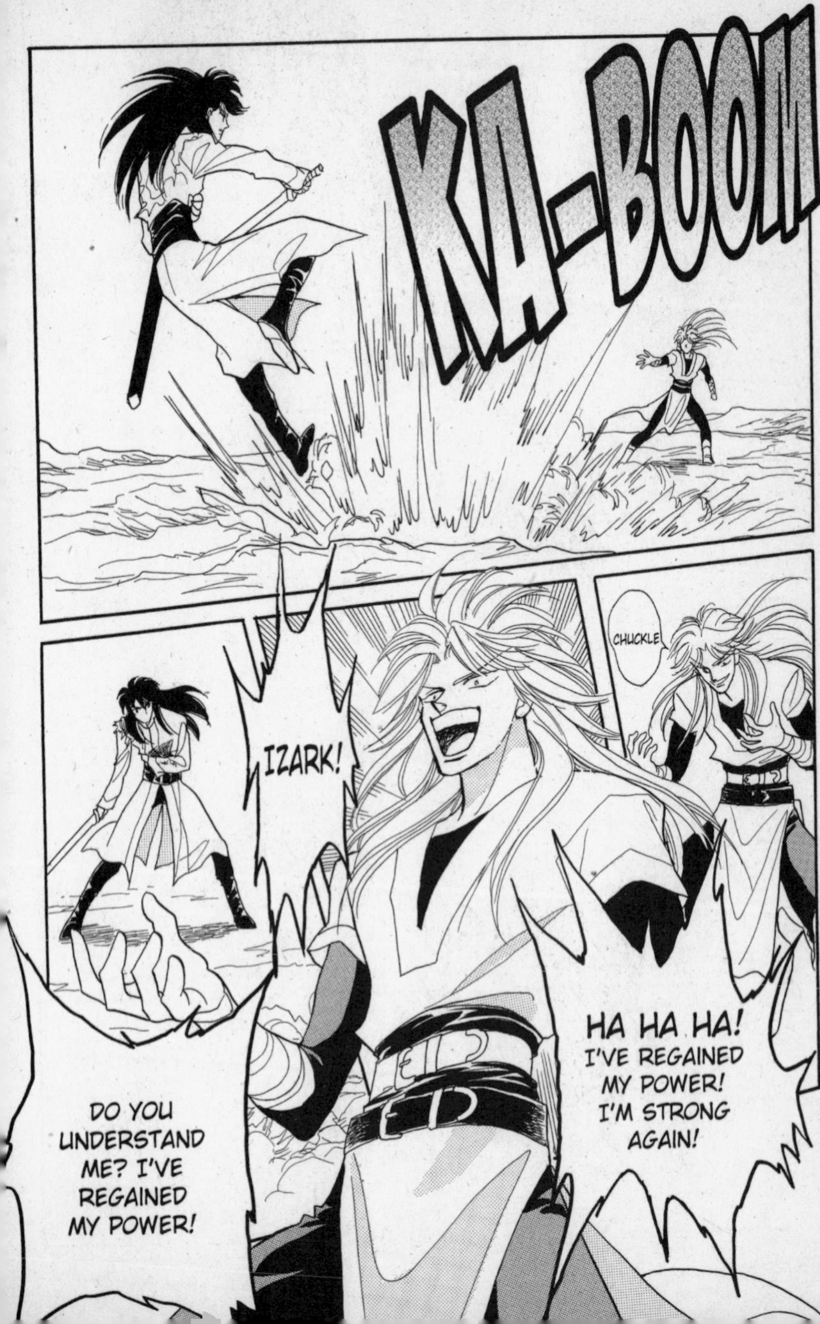
KA-BOOM
CHUCKLE
IZARK!
HA HA HA! I'VE REGAINED MY POWER! I'M STRONG AGAIN!
DO YOU UNDERSTAND ME? I'VE REGAINED MY POWER!

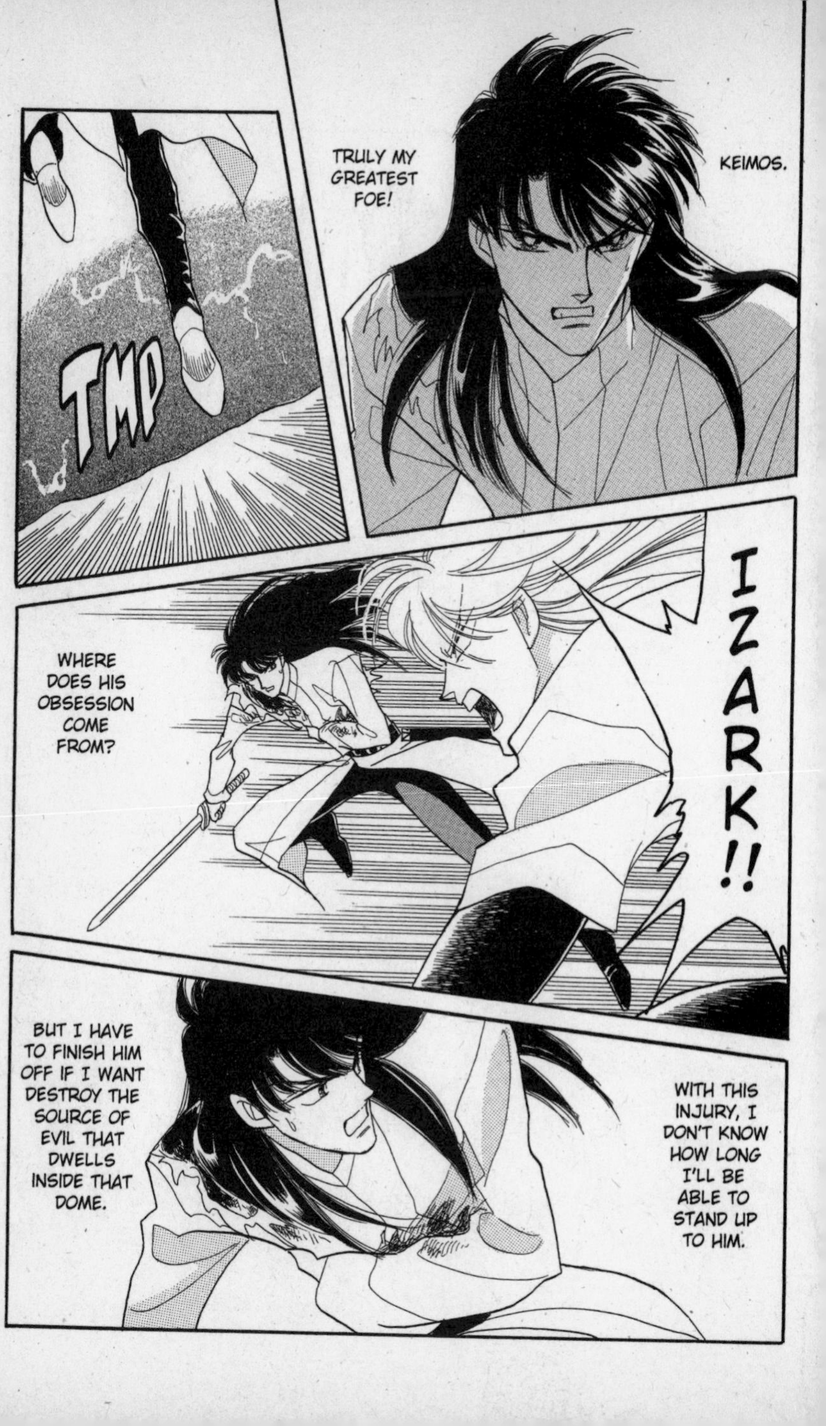
KEIMOS.
TRULY MY GREATEST FOE!
TMP
IZARK!!
WHERE DOES HIS OBSESSION COME FROM?
WITH THIS INJURY, I DON'T KNOW HOW LONG I'LL BE ABLE TO STAND UP TO HIM.
BUT I HAVE TO FINISH HIM OFF IF I WANT DESTROY THE SOURCE OF EVIL THAT DWELLS INSIDE THAT DOME.

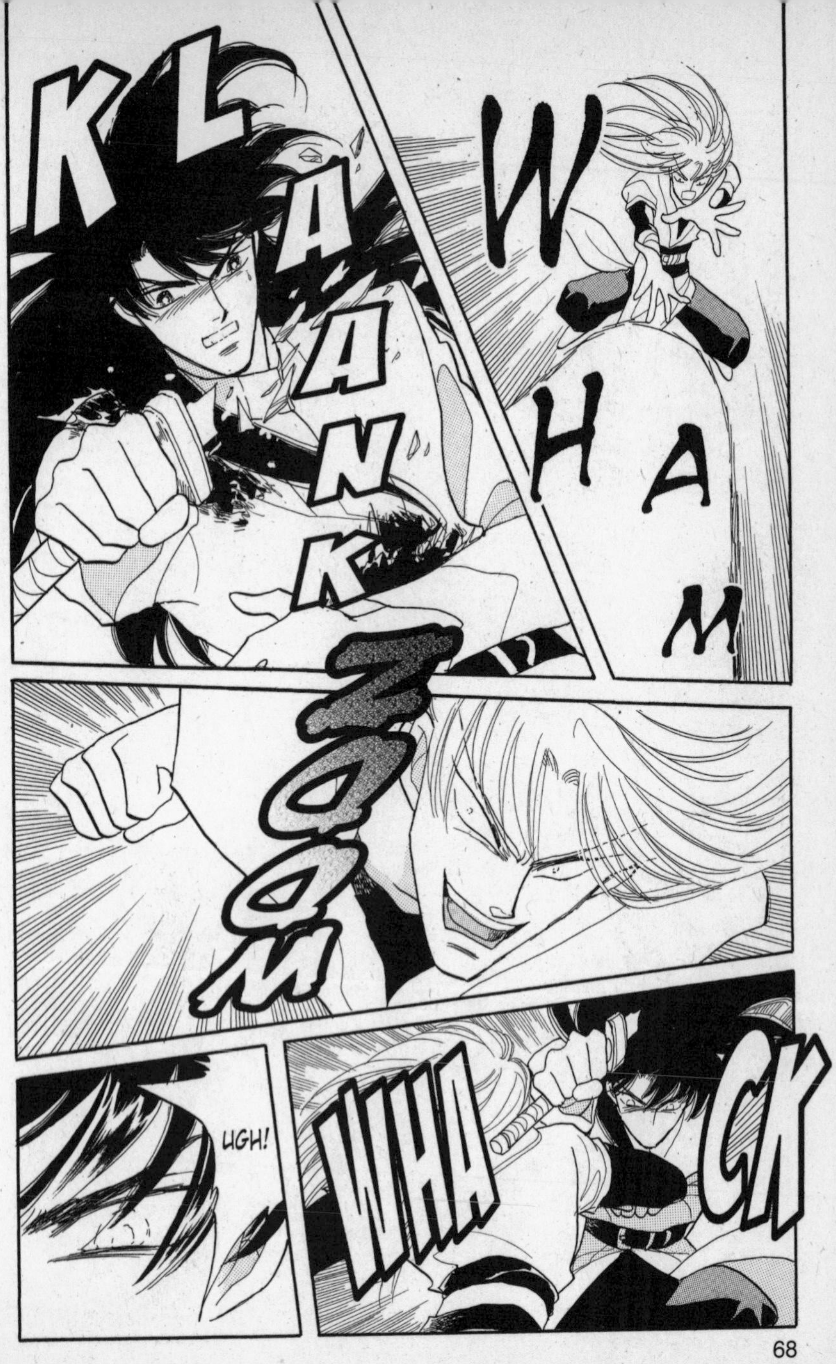
WHAM
KLAANK
ZOOM
WHACK
UGH!

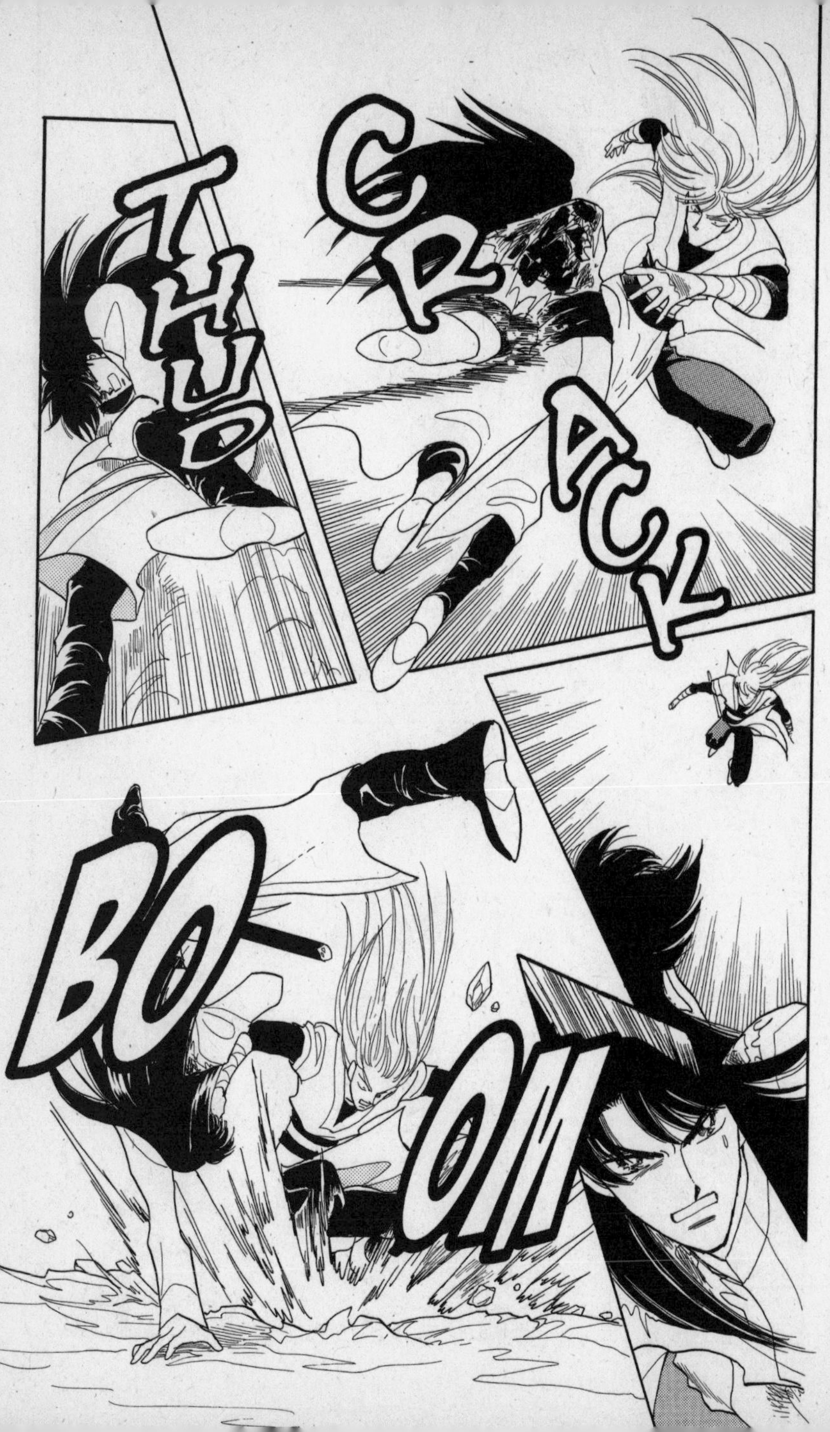
CRACK
THUD
BOOM

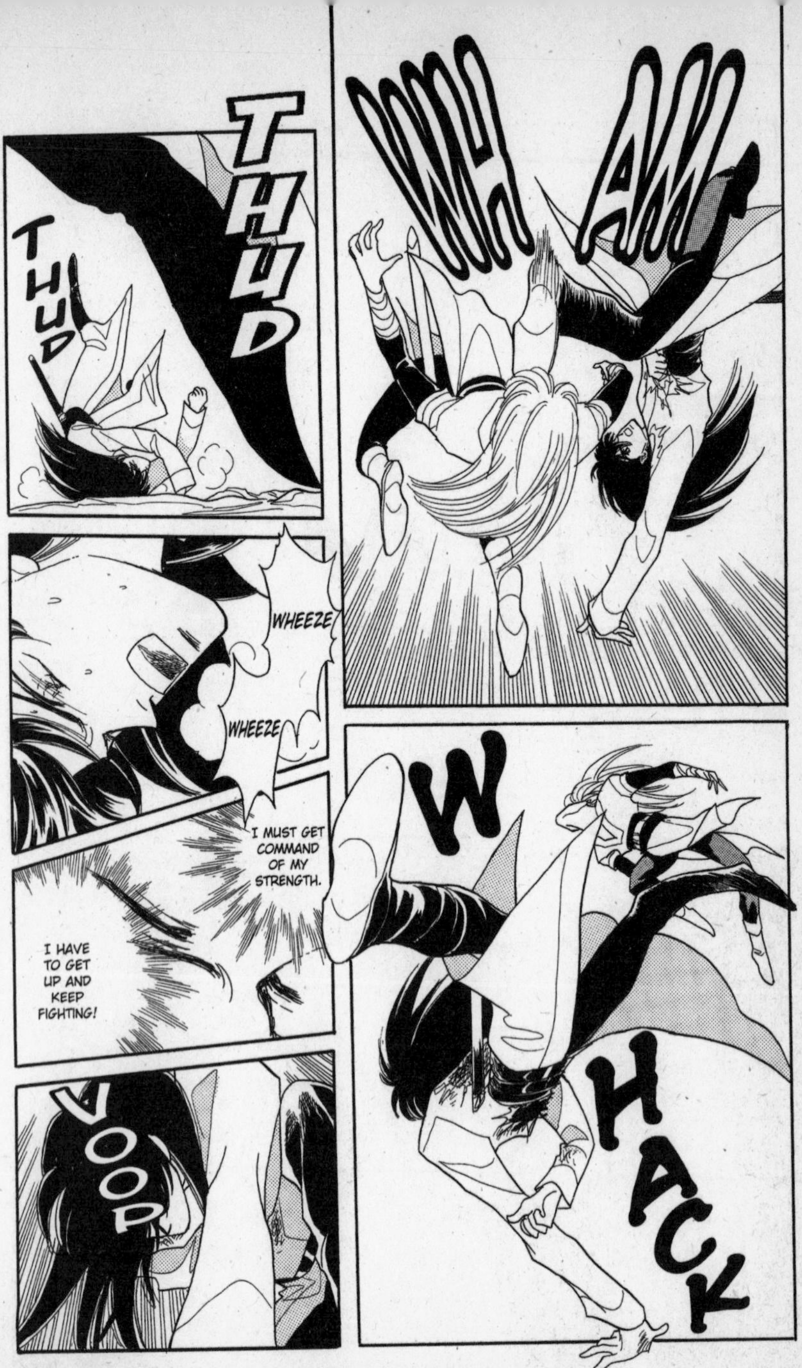
THUD
THUD
WHEEZE
WHEEZE
WHACK
I MUST GET COMMAND OF MY STRENGTH.
I HAVE TO GET UP AND KEEP FIGHTING!
VOOP

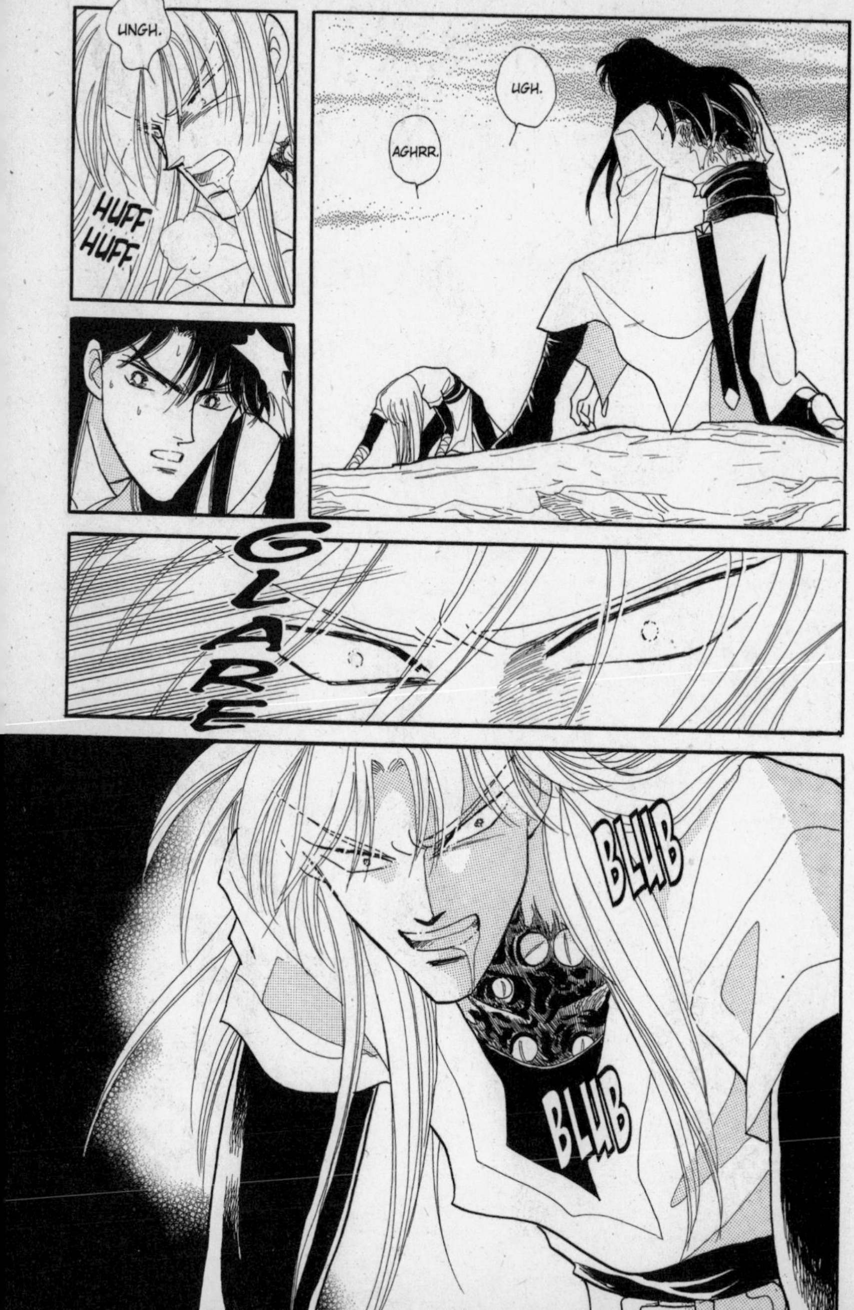
UGH.
AGHRR.
UNGH.
HUFF HUFF
GLARE
BLUB
BLUB

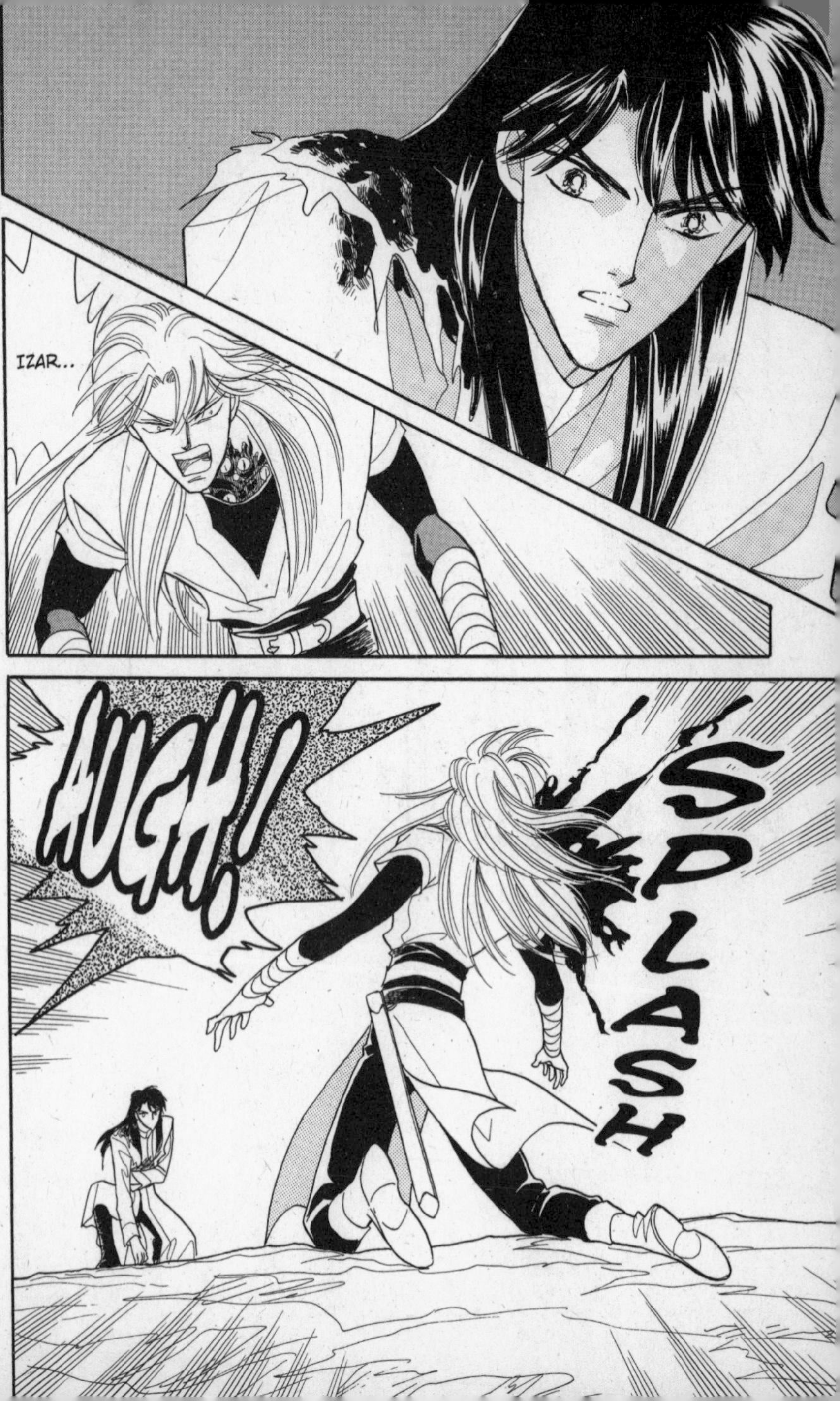

IZAR...
SPLASH
AUGH!

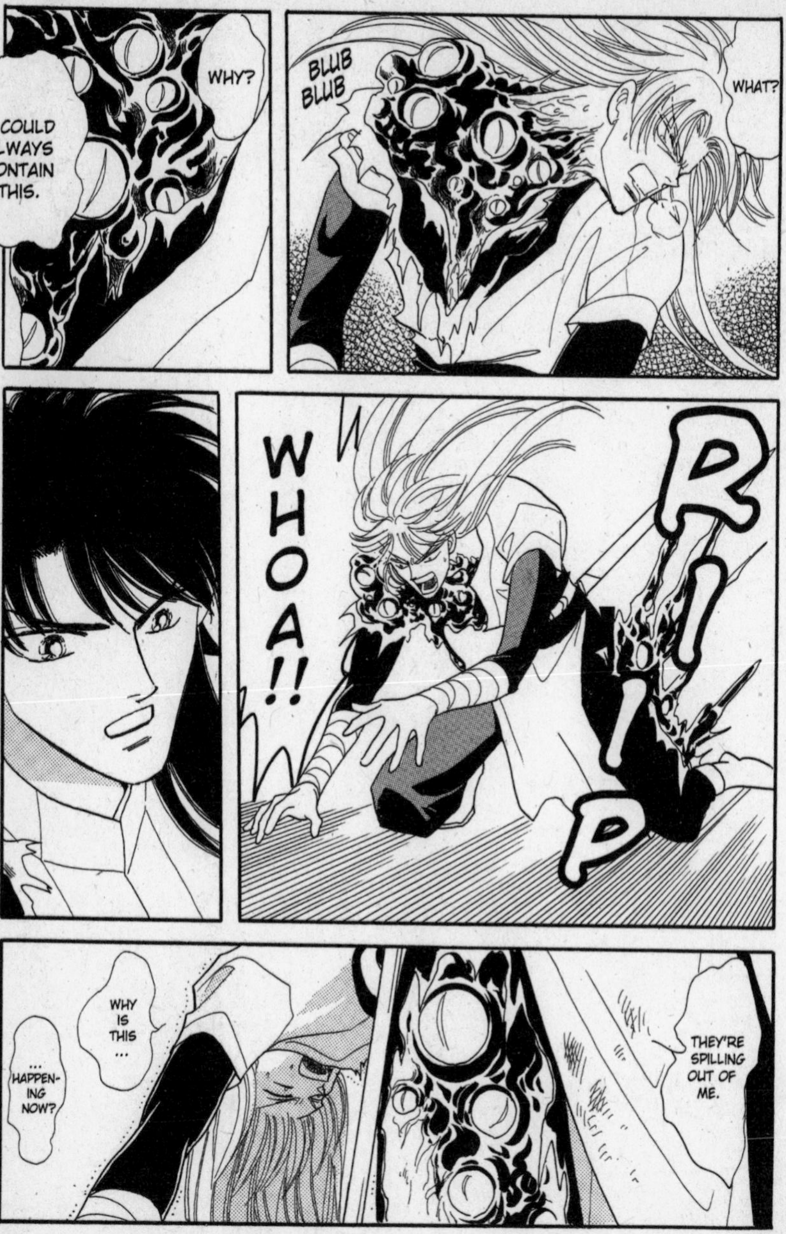
WHAT?
BLUB BLUB
WHY?
I COULD ALWAYS CONTAIN THIS.
RIP
WHOA!!
THEY'RE SPILLING OUT OF ME.
WHY IS THIS ...
... HAPPENING NOW?

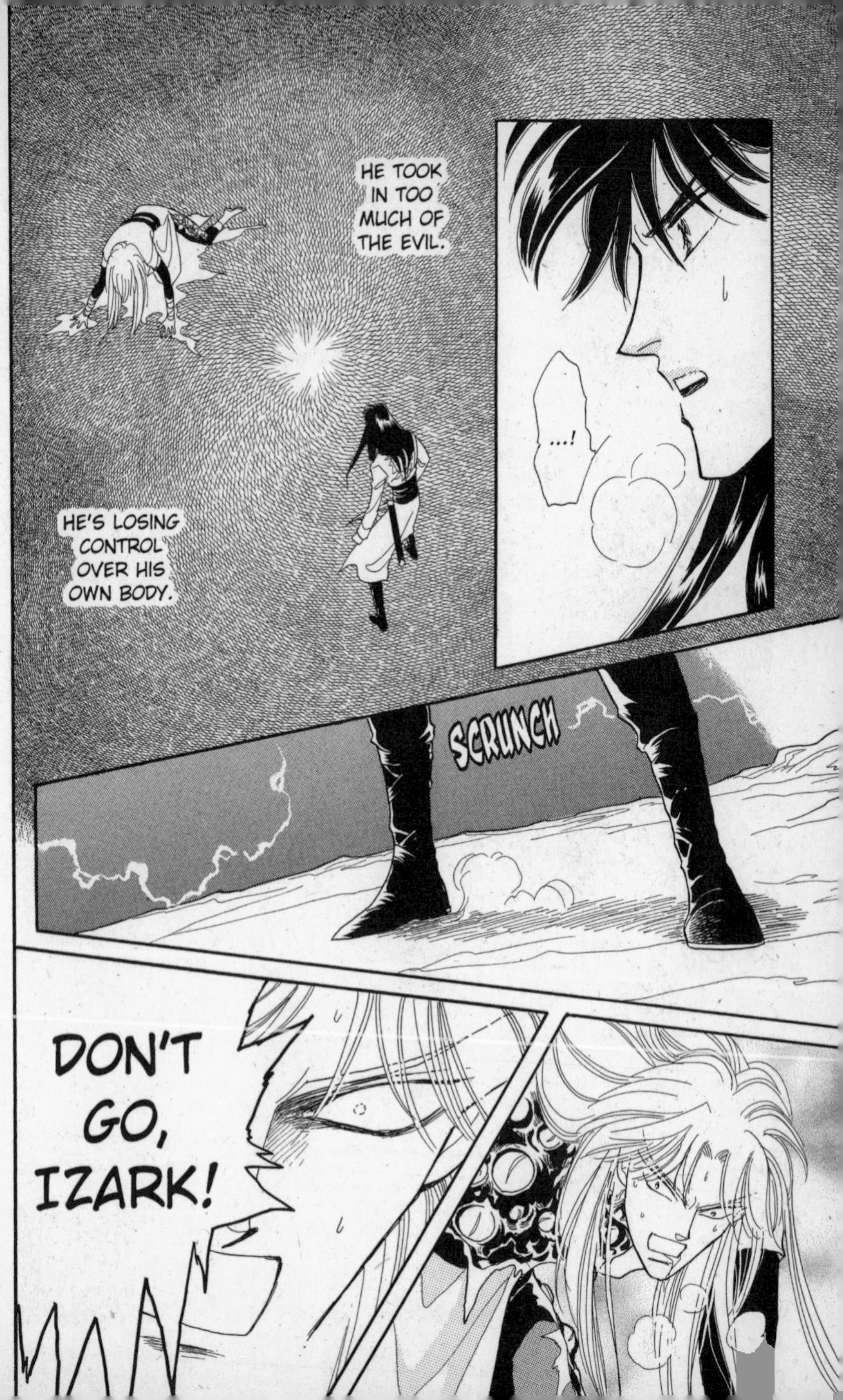
...!
HE TOOK IN TOO MUCH OF THE EVIL.
HE'S LOSING CONTROL OVER HIS OWN BODY.
SCRUNCH
DON'T GO, IZARK!

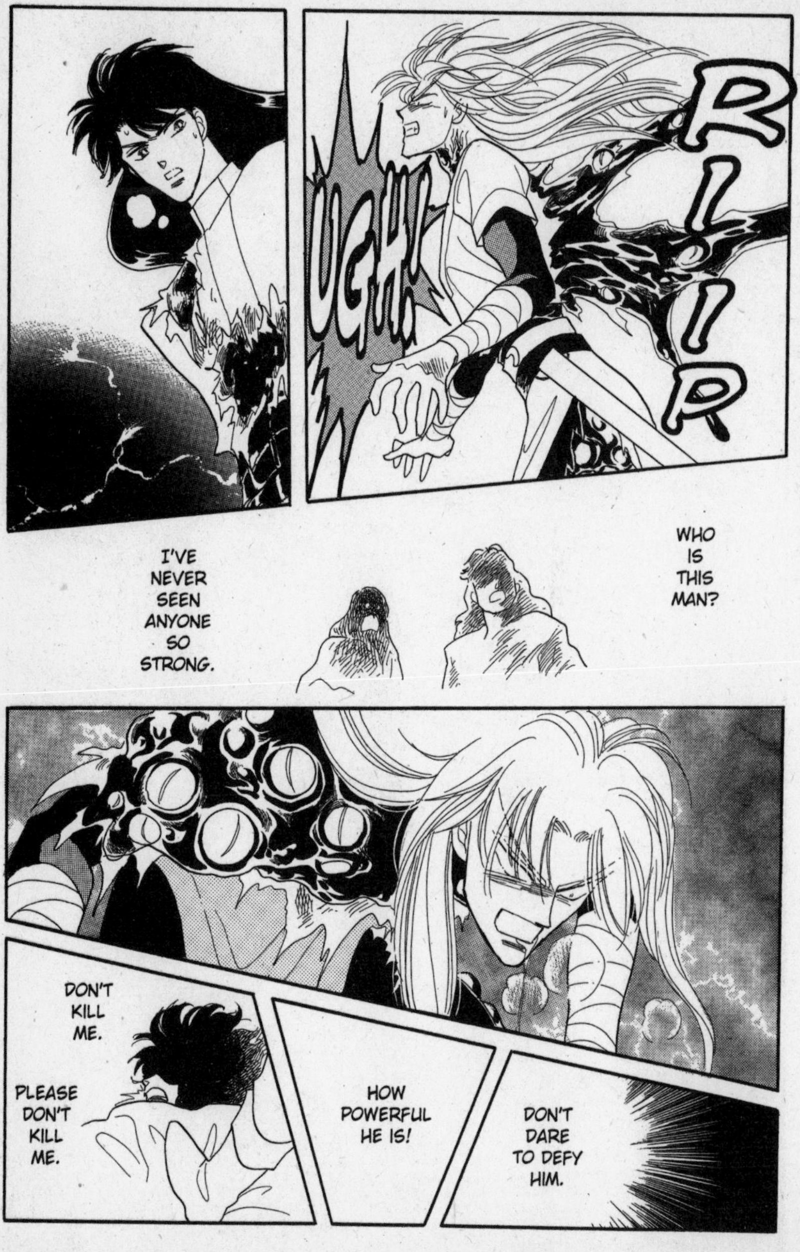
RIIP
UGH!
WHO IS THIS MAN?
I'VE NEVER SEEN ANYONE SO STRONG.
DON'T DARE TO DEFY HIM.
HOW POWERFUL HE IS!
DON'T KILL ME.
PLEASE DON'T KILL ME.

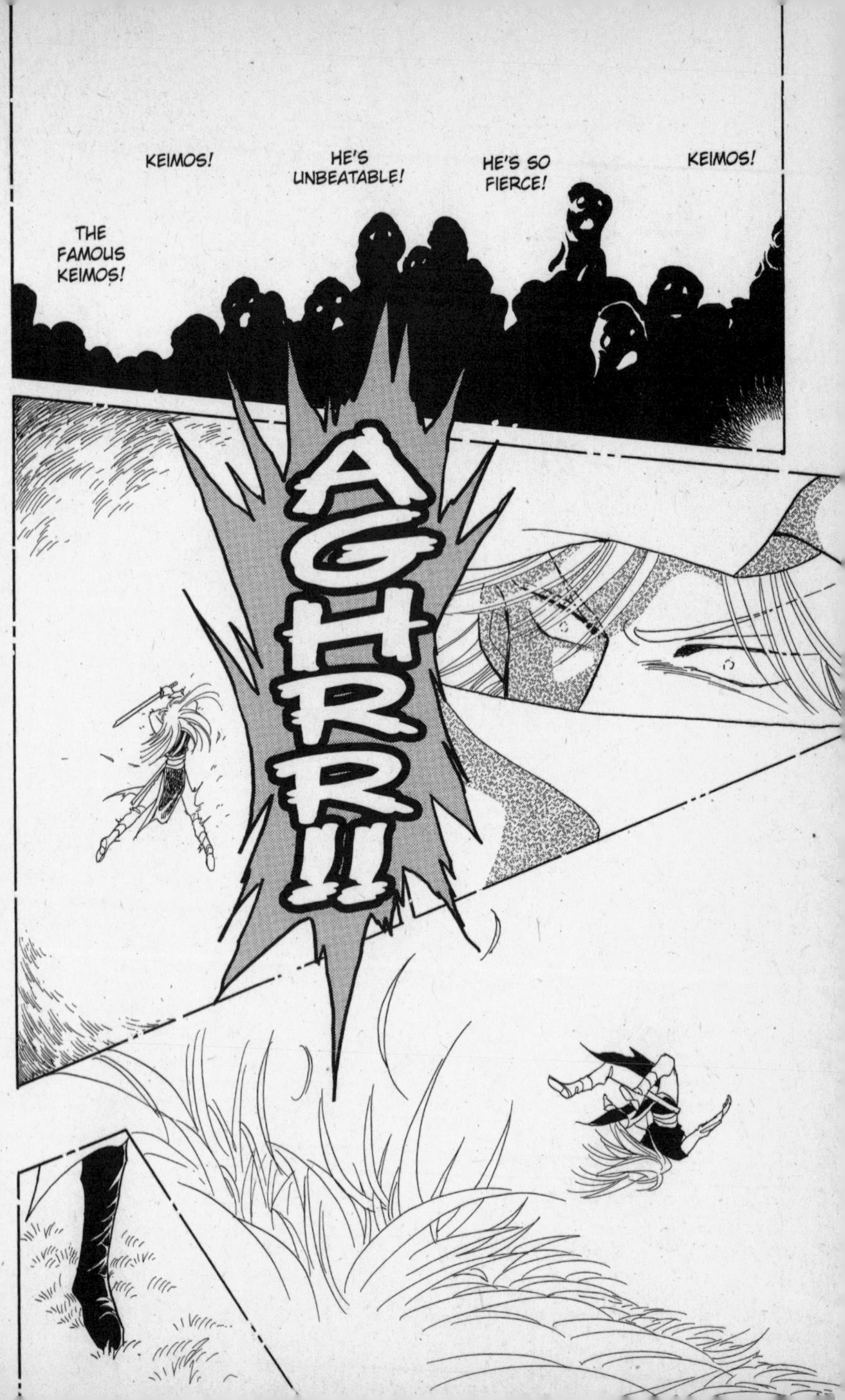
KEIMOS!
HE'S SO FIERCE!
HE'S UNBEATABLE!
KEIMOS!
THE FAMOUS KEIMOS!
AGHRR!!

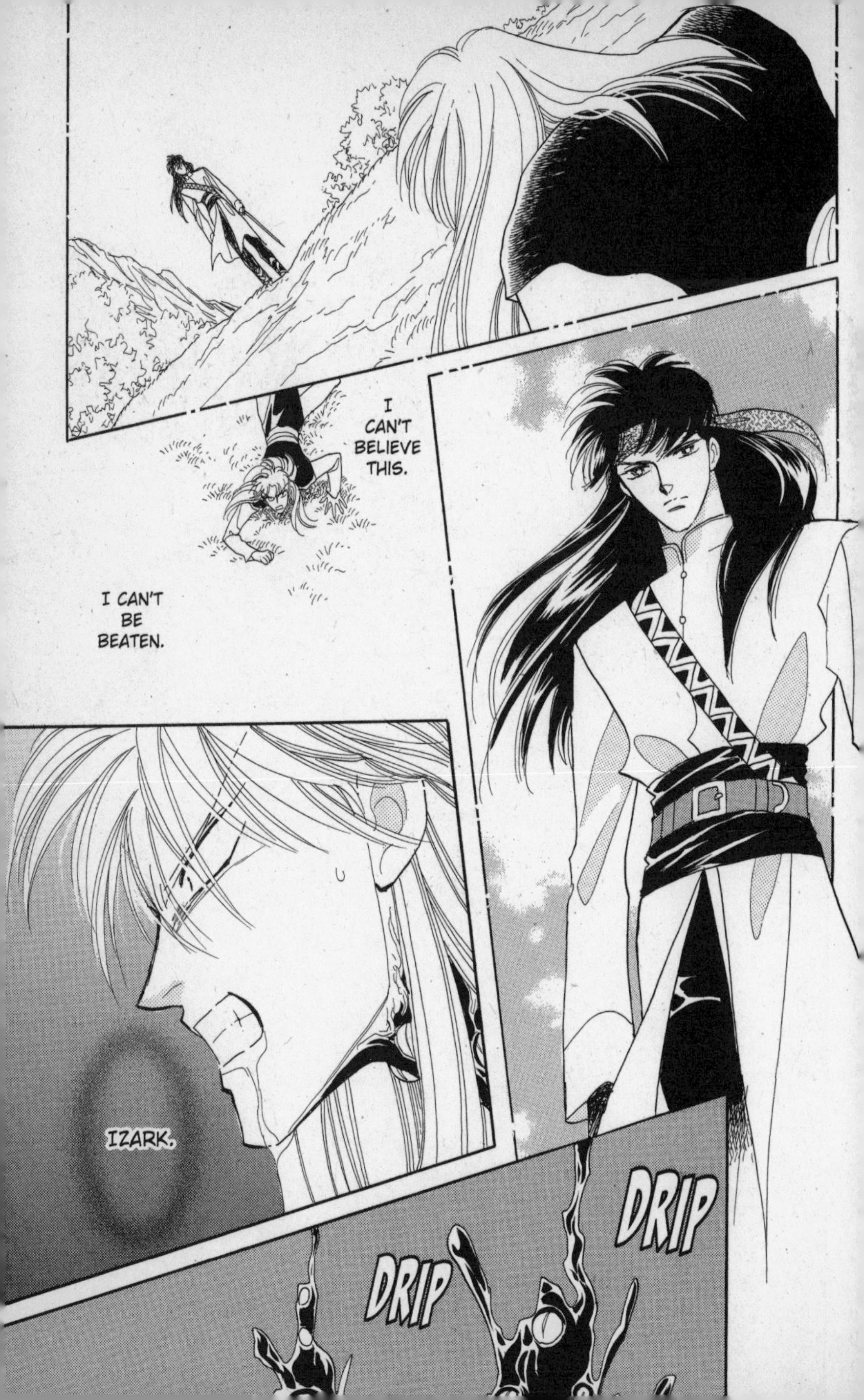
I CAN'T BELIEVE THIS.
I CAN'T BE BEATEN.
IZARK.
DRIP
DRIP

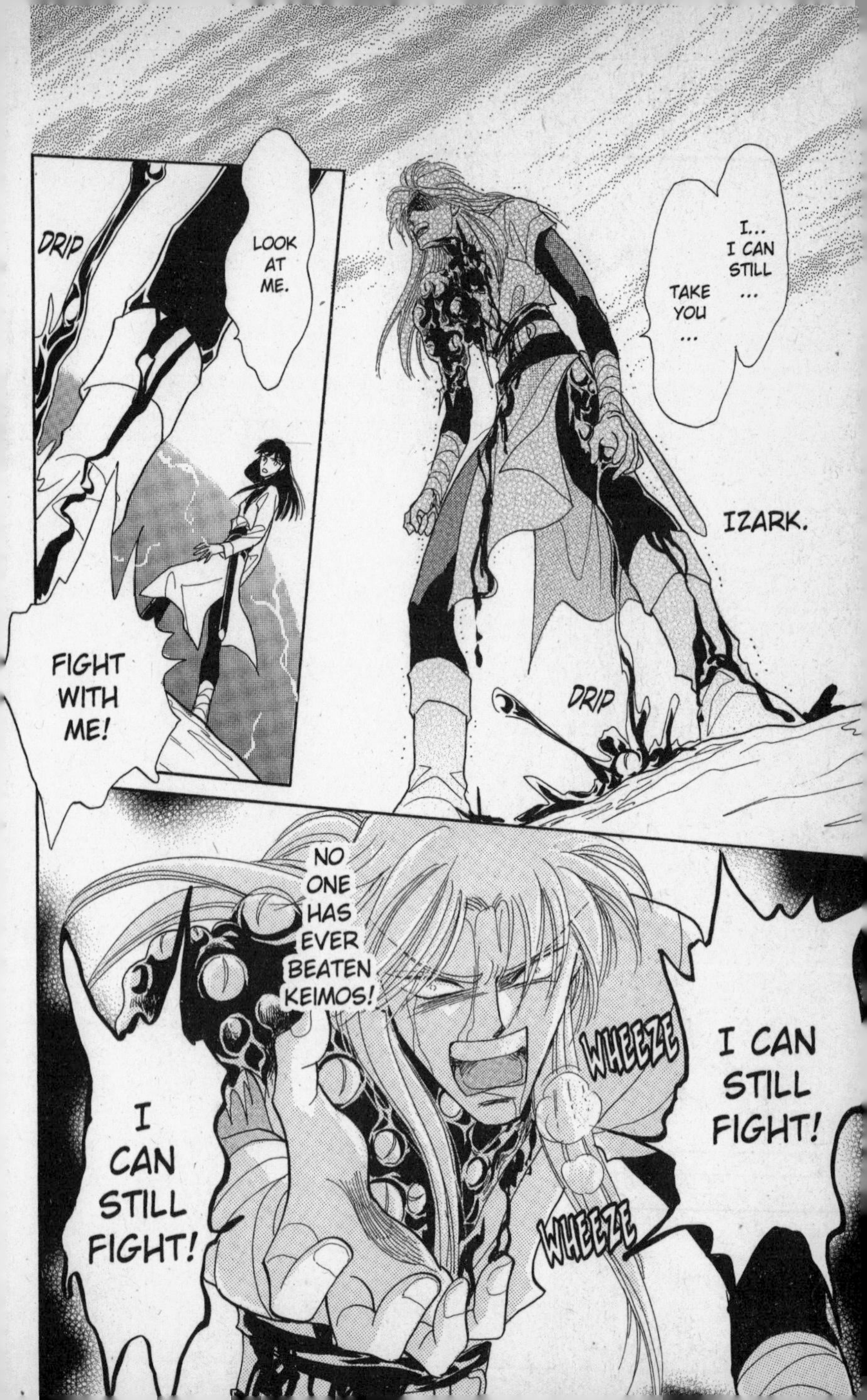
I... I CAN STILL ...
TAKE YOU ...
IZARK.
DRIP
DRIP
LOOK AT ME.
FIGHT WITH ME!
I CAN STILL FIGHT!
WHEEZE
NO ONE HAS EVER BEATEN KEIMOS!
WHEEZE
I CAN STILL FIGHT!

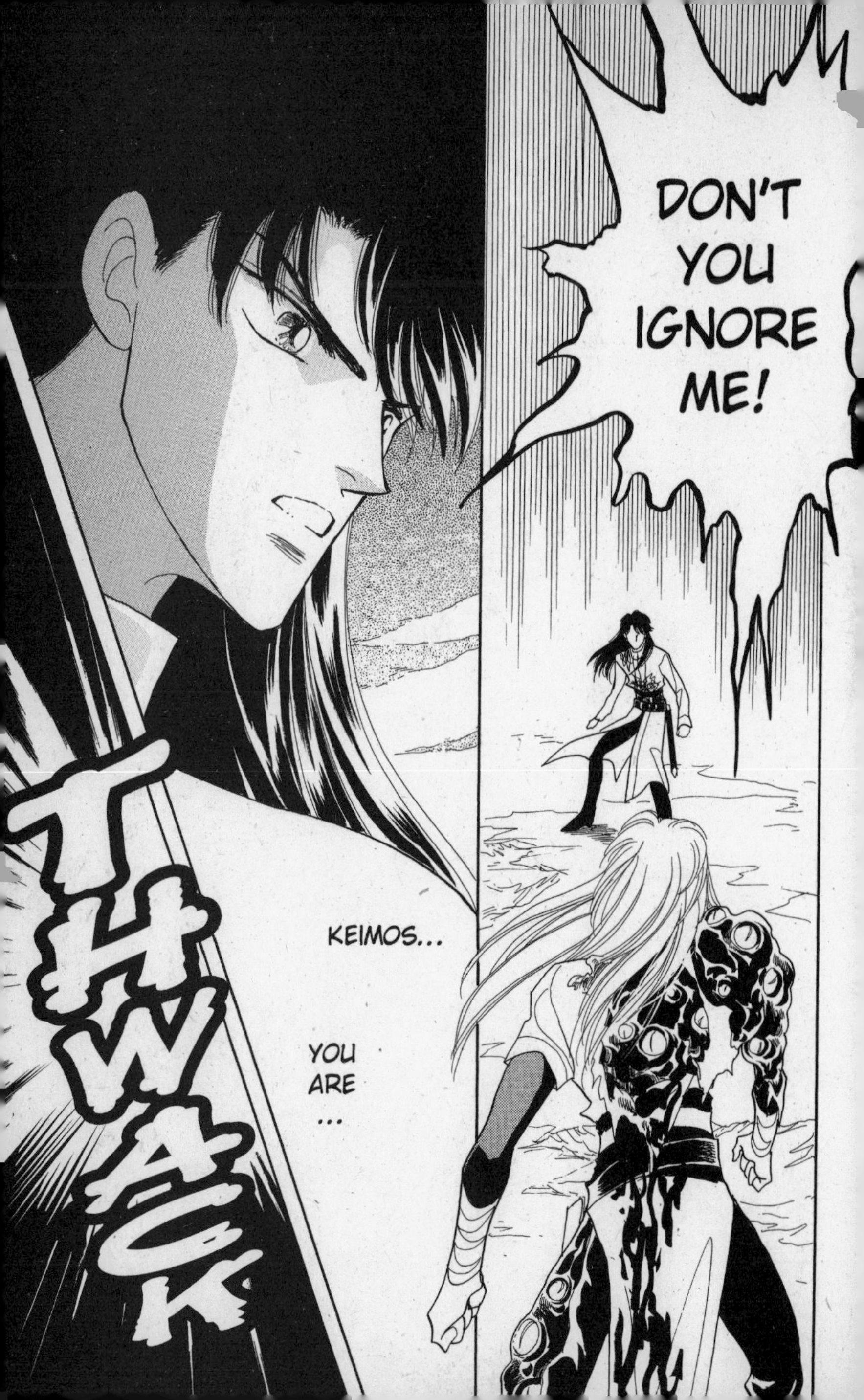
DON'T YOU IGNORE ME!
KEIMOS...
YOU ARE ...
THWACK

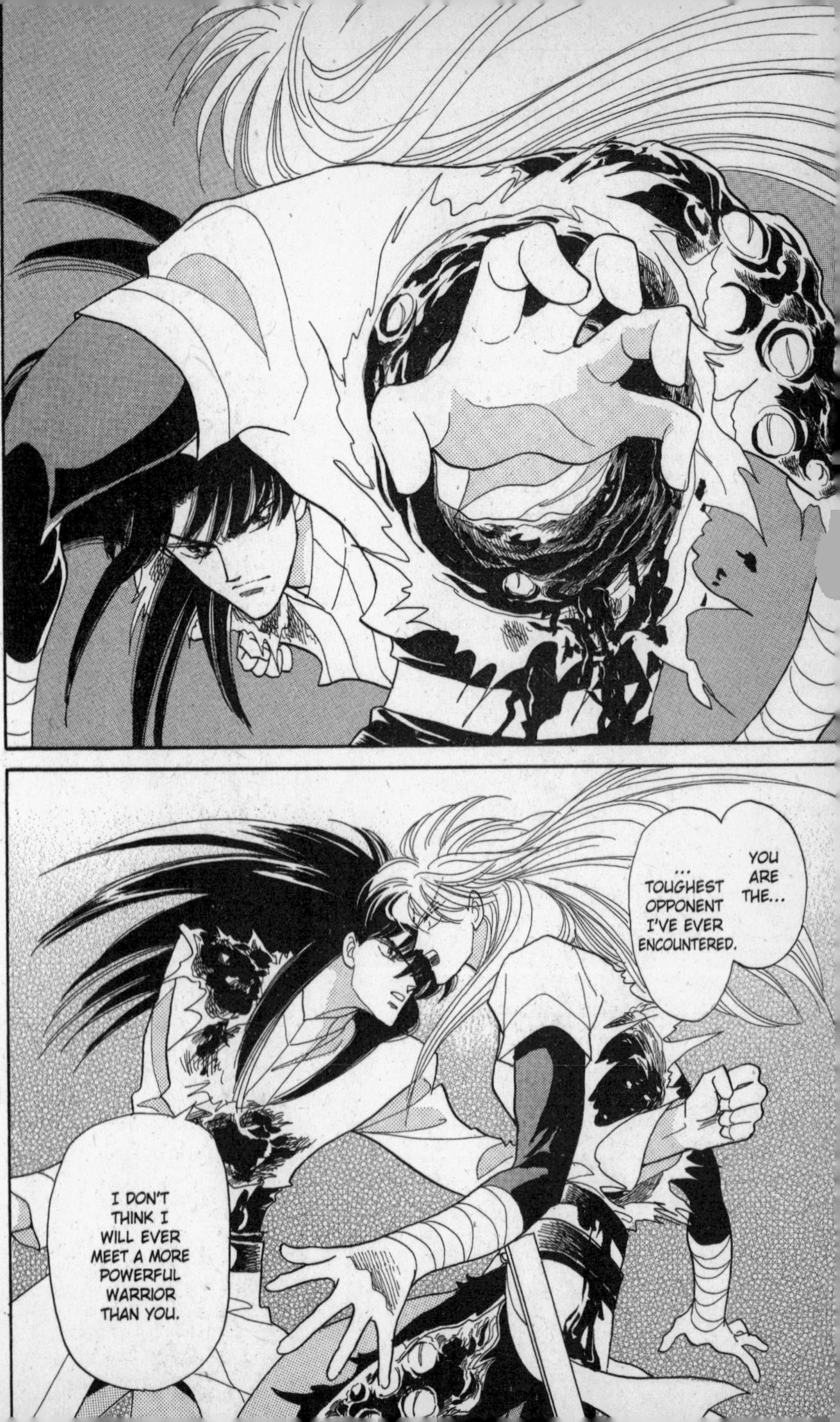
YOU ARE THE...
...TOUGHEST OPPONENT I'VE EVER ENCOUNTERED.
I DON'T THINK I WILL EVER MEET A MORE POWERFUL WARRIOR THAN YOU.

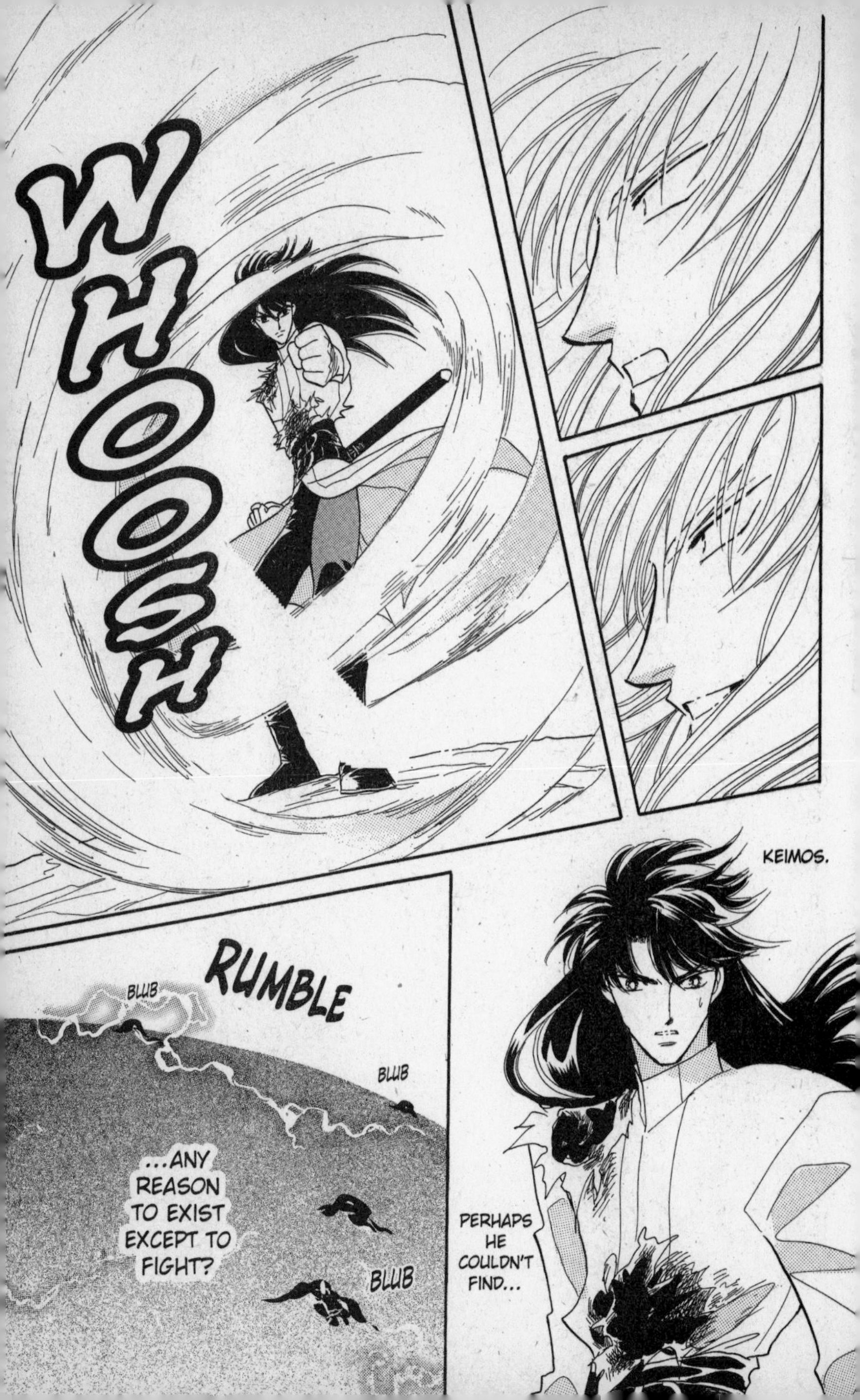
WHOOSH
KEIMOS.
PERHAPS HE COULDN'T FIND...
RUMBLE
BLUB
BLUB
...ANY REASON TO EXIST EXCEPT TO FIGHT?
BLUB

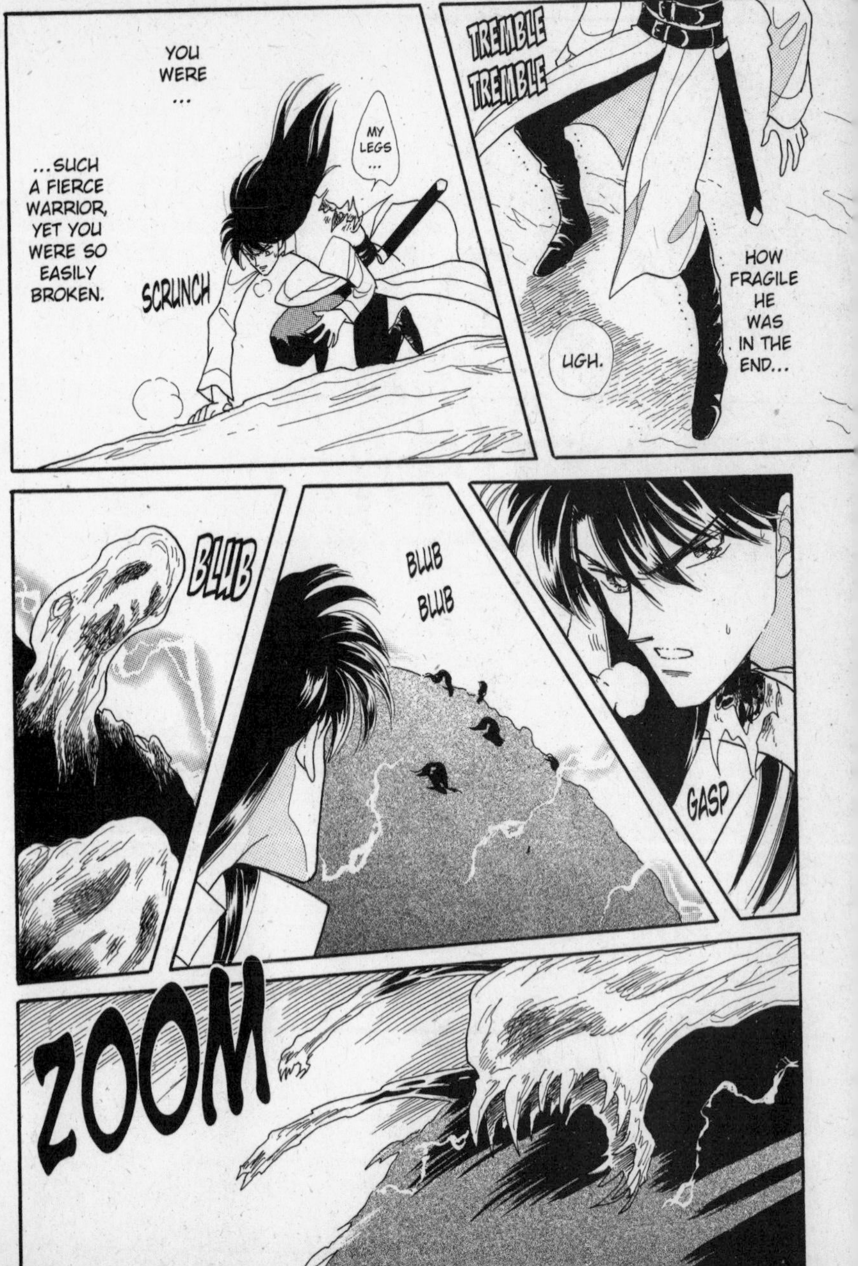
TREMBLE
TREMBLE
HOW FRAGILE HE WAS IN THE END...
UGH.
YOU WERE ...
MY LEGS ...
...SUCH A FIERCE WARRIOR, YET YOU WERE SO EASILY BROKEN.
SCRUNCH
GASP
BLUB BLUB
BLUB
ZOOM

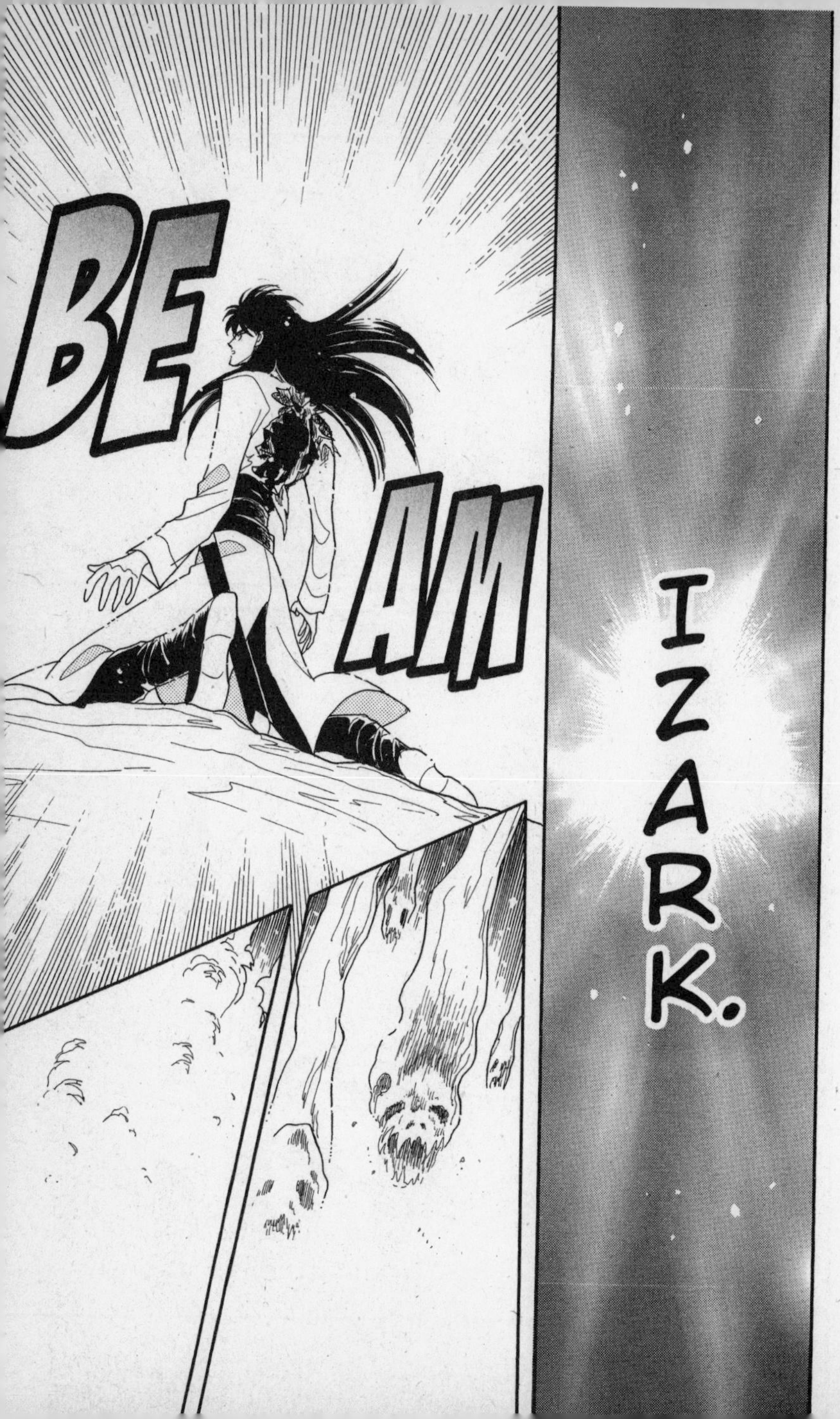
IZARK.
BEAM

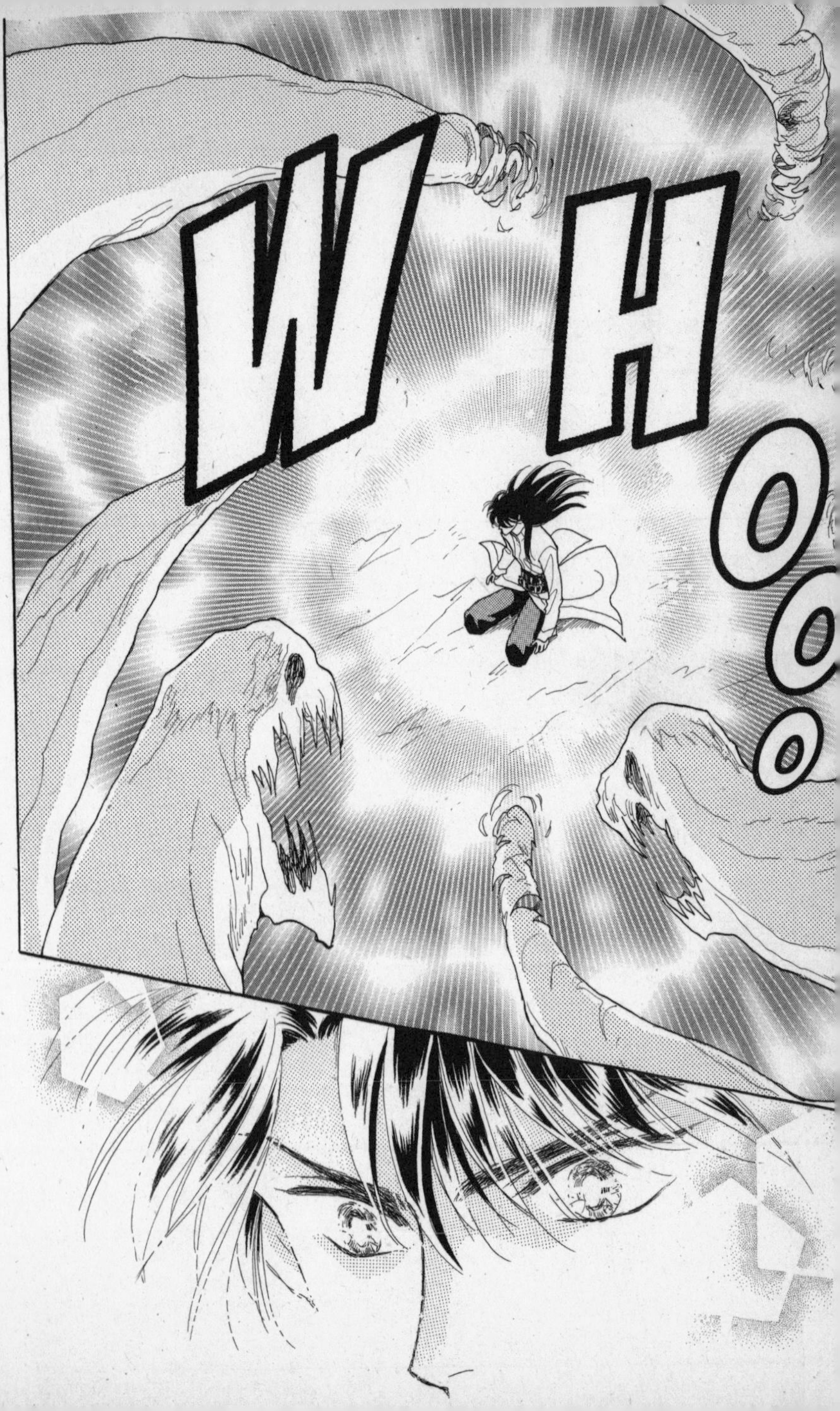
WHOOOO

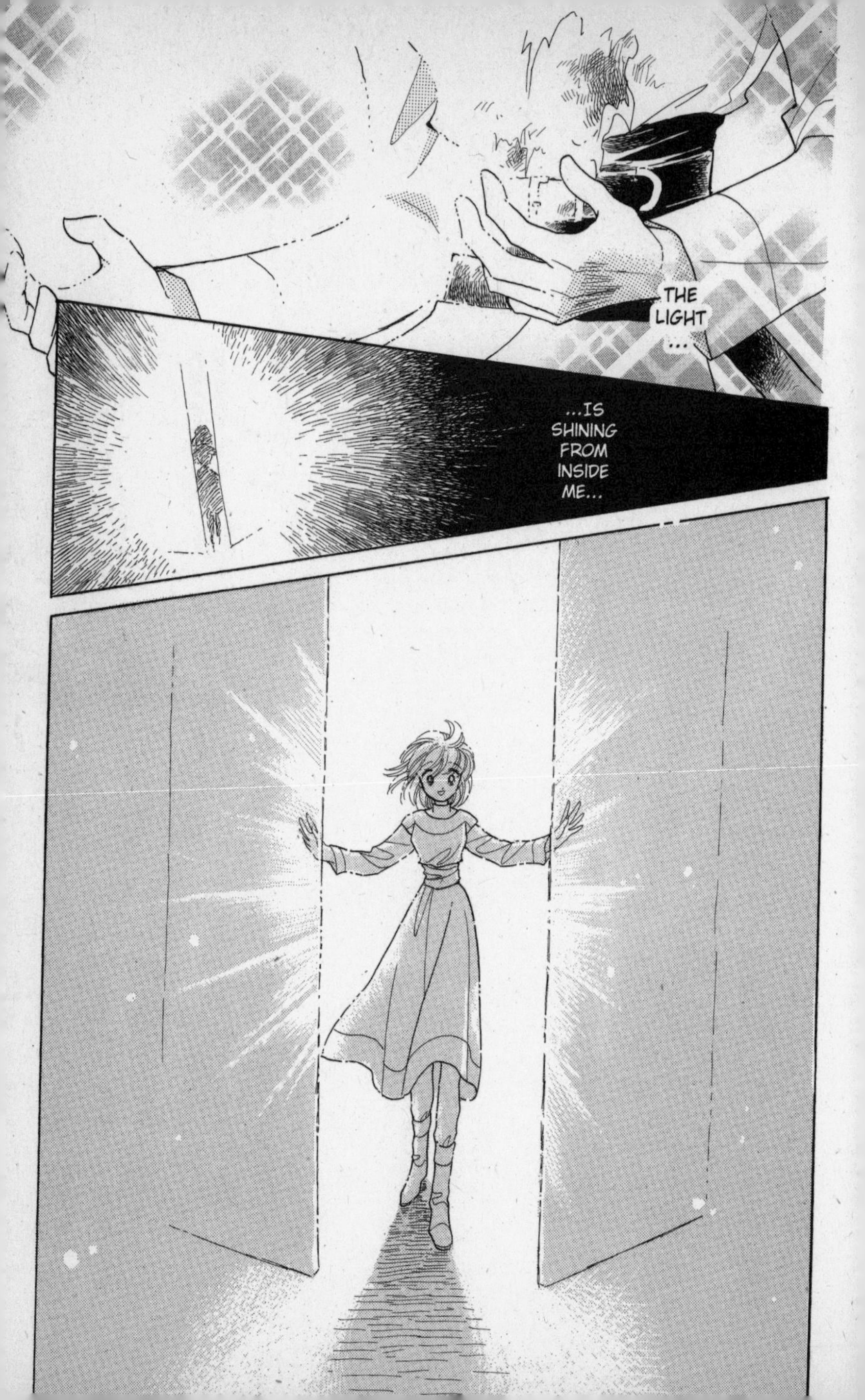
THE LIGHT ...
...IS SHINING FROM INSIDE ME...

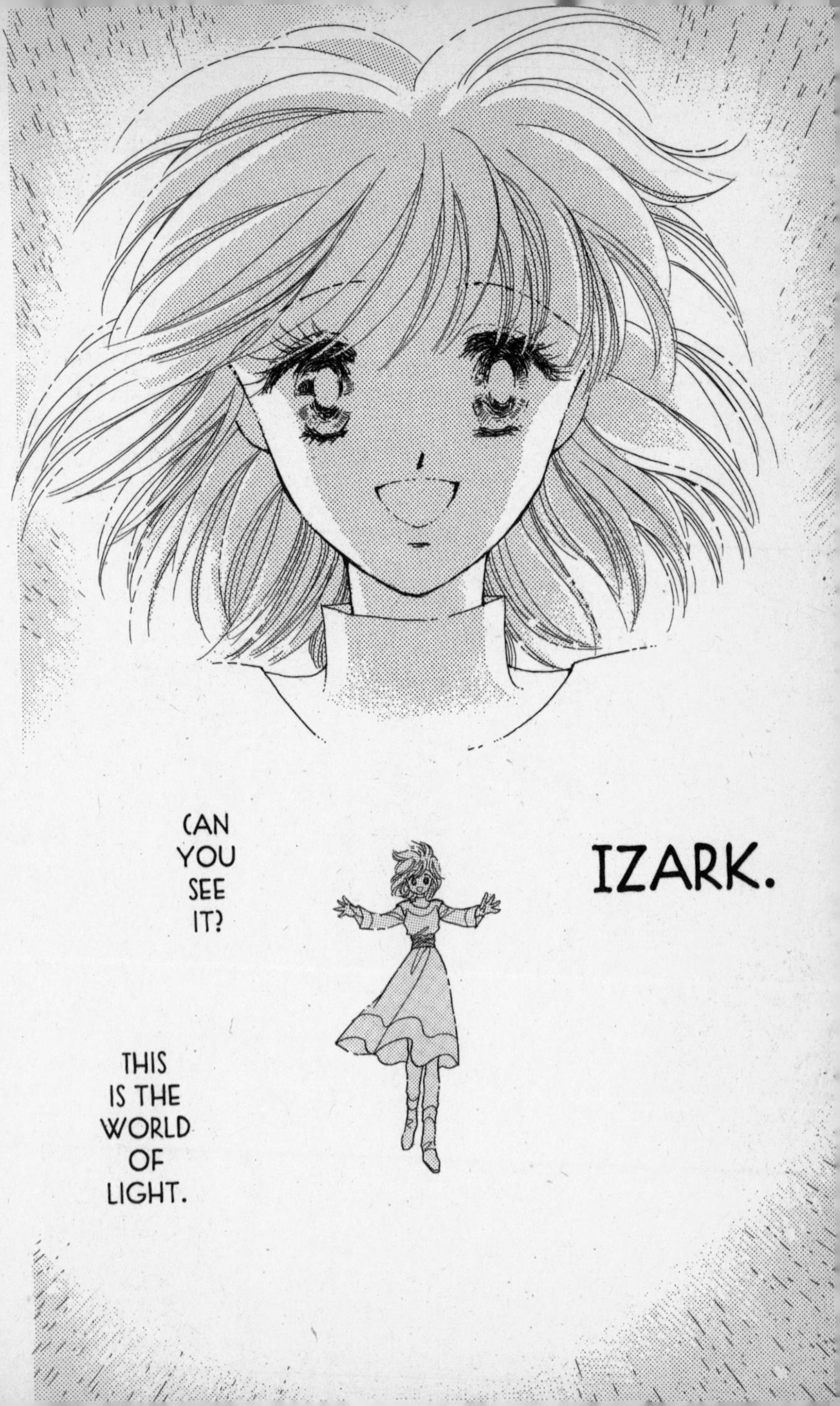
IZARK.
CAN YOU SEE IT?
THIS IS THE WORLD OF LIGHT.

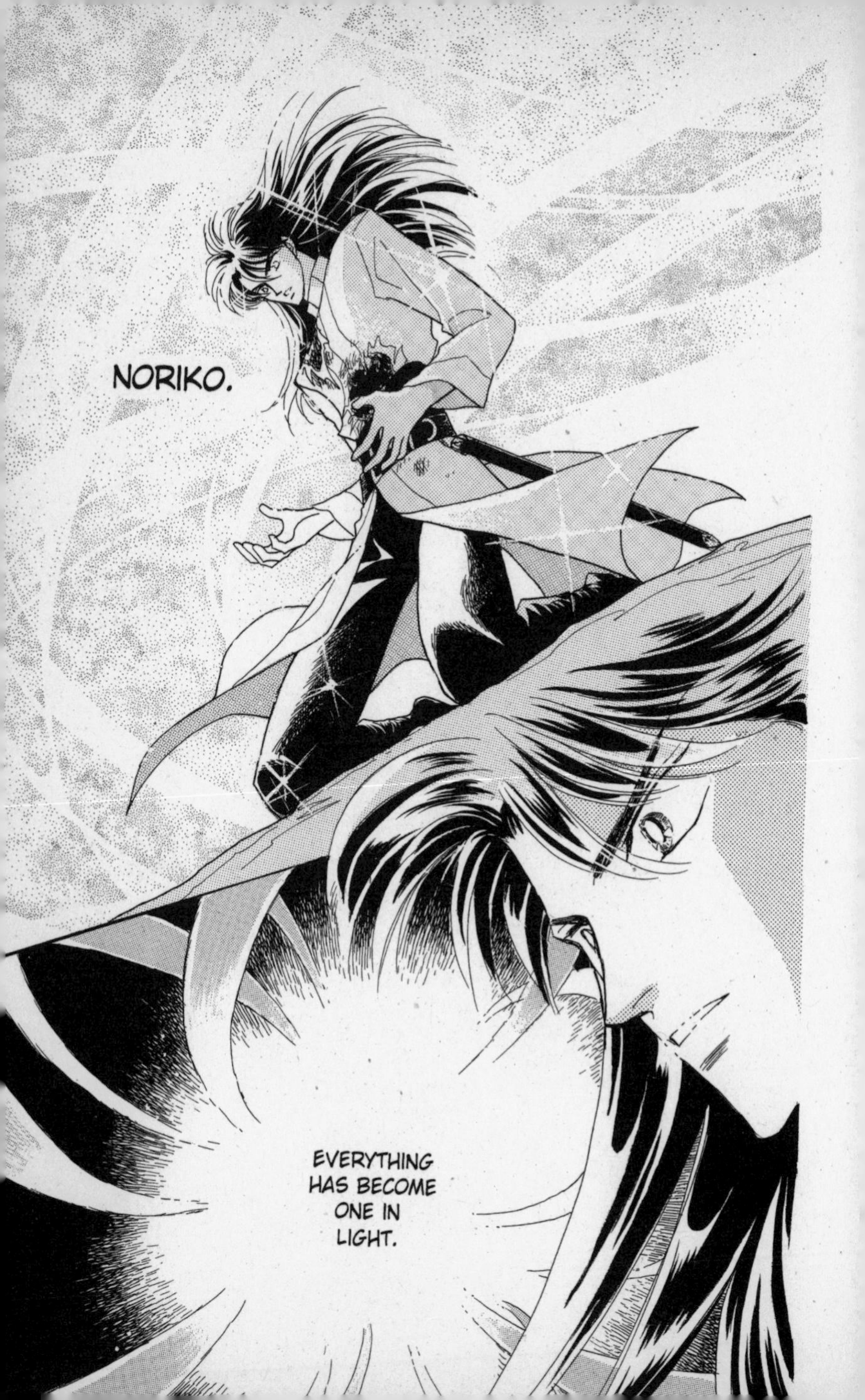
NORIKO.
EVERYTHING HAS BECOME ONE IN LIGHT.

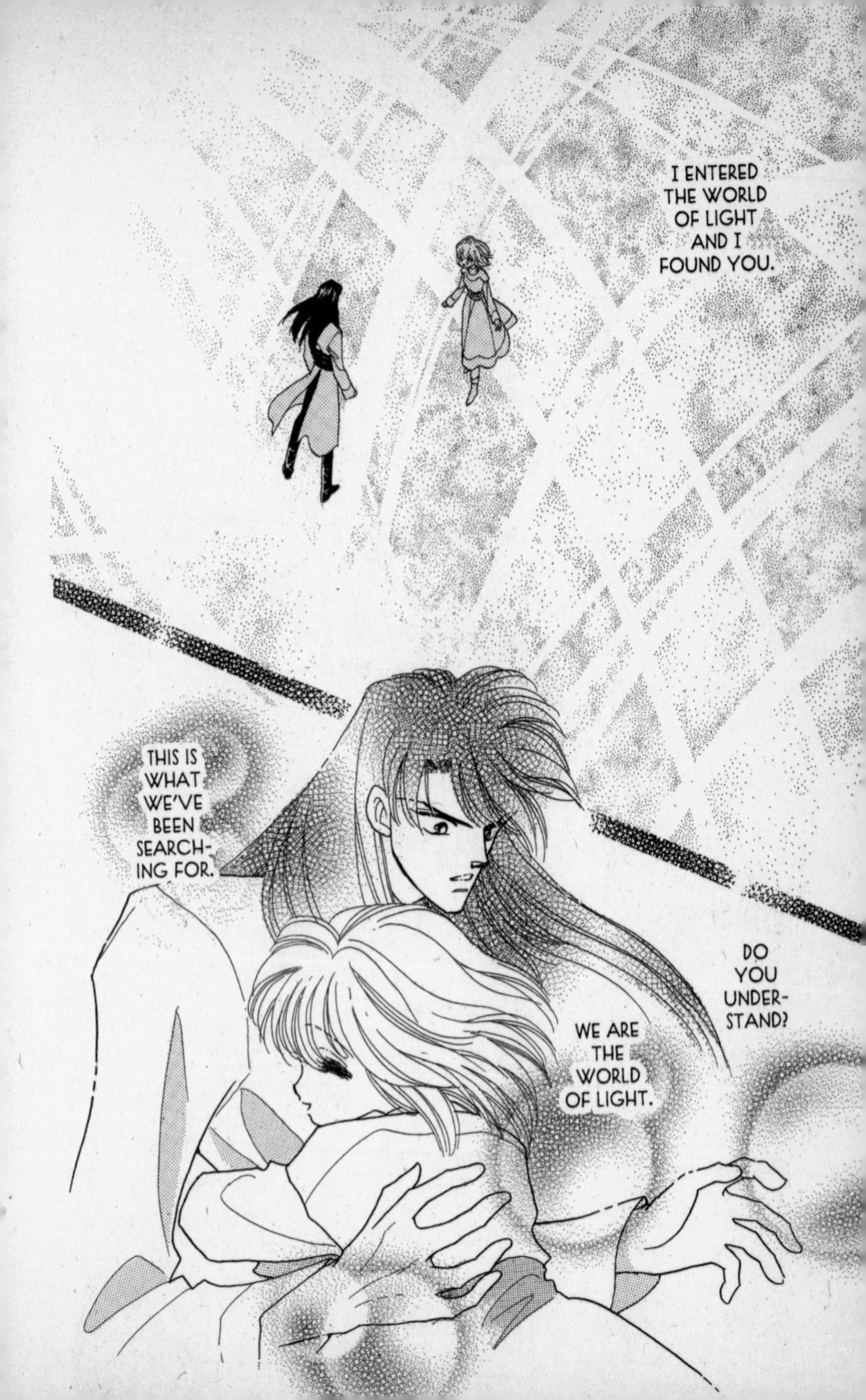
I ENTERED THE WORLD OF LIGHT AND I FOUND YOU.
THIS IS WHAT WE'VE BEEN SEARCHING FOR.
WE ARE THE WORLD OF LIGHT.
DO YOU UNDERSTAND?

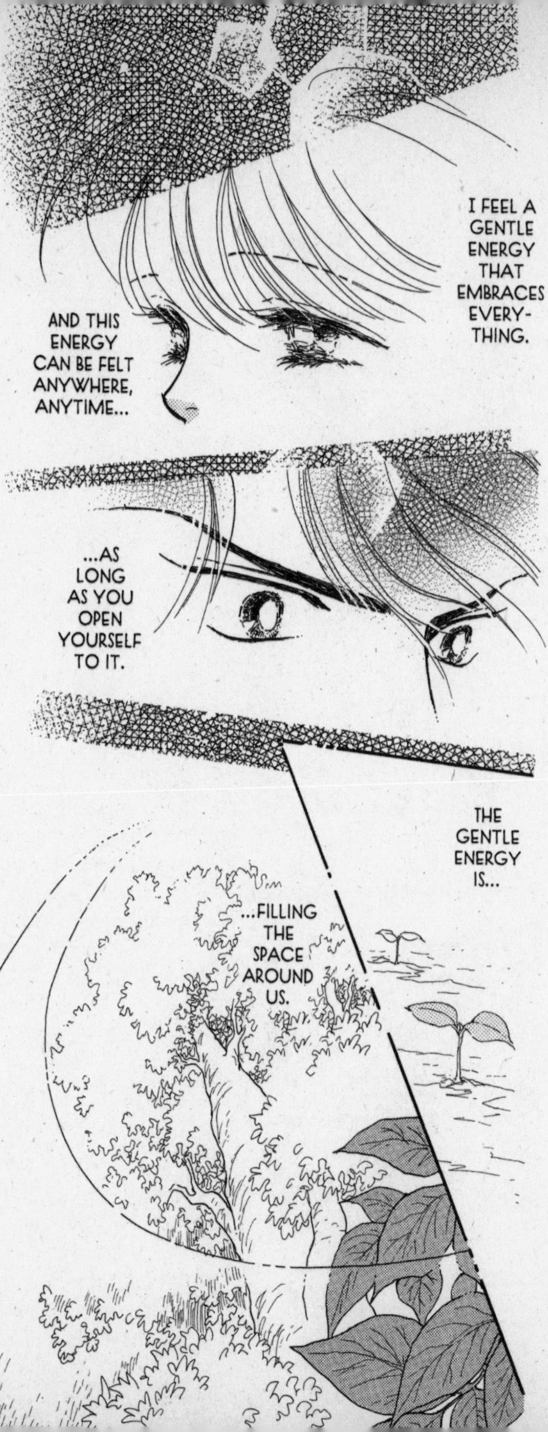
I FEEL A GENTLE ENERGY THAT EMBRACES EVERY-THING.
AND THIS ENERGY CAN BE FELT ANYWHERE, ANYTIME...
...AS LONG AS YOU OPEN YOURSELF TO IT.
THE GENTLE ENERGY IS...
...FILLING THE SPACE AROUND US.

A Very Insignificant Story: Part 3

Every time I go to the supermarket in my neighborhood, the cashier cheerfully greets me saying, "Hello, how are you?"

I always wonder whether it is better for a customer to respond to her or to say nothing.

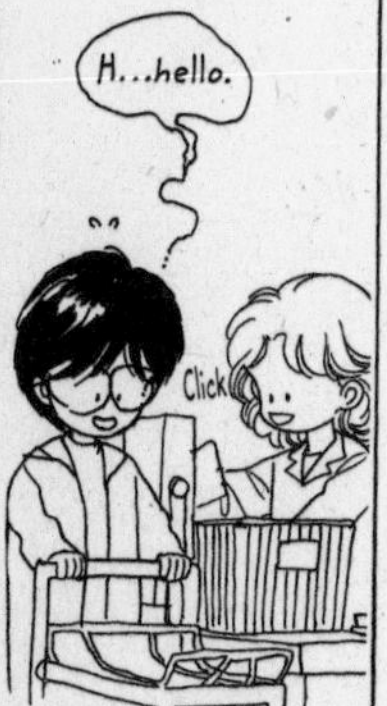
H...hello.
Click

Then I always end up responding to her in an almost inaudible voice.

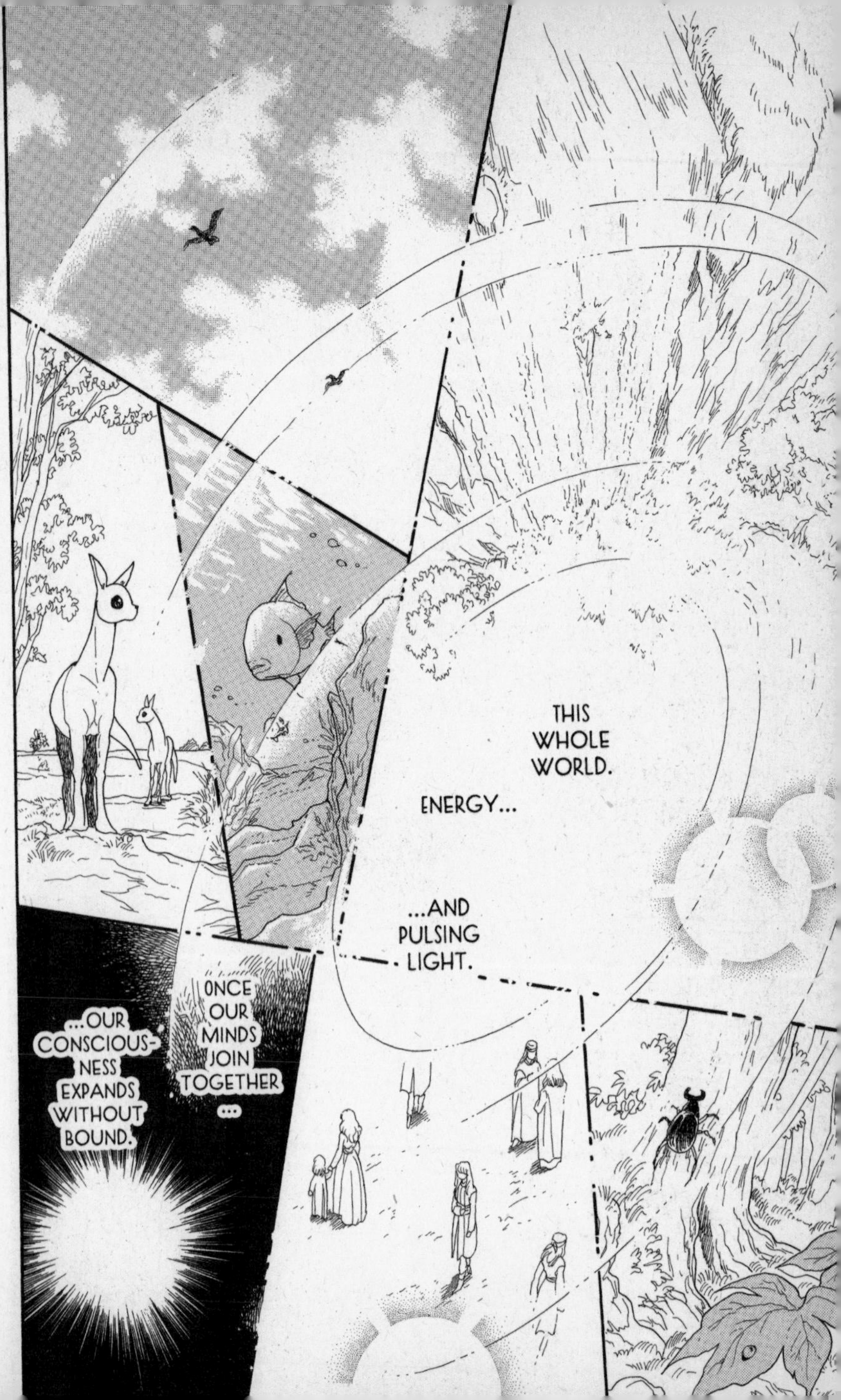
THIS WHOLE WORLD.
ENERGY...
...AND PULSING LIGHT.
ONCE OUR MINDS JOIN TOGETHER...
...OUR CONSCIOUS-NESS EXPANDS WITHOUT BOUND.

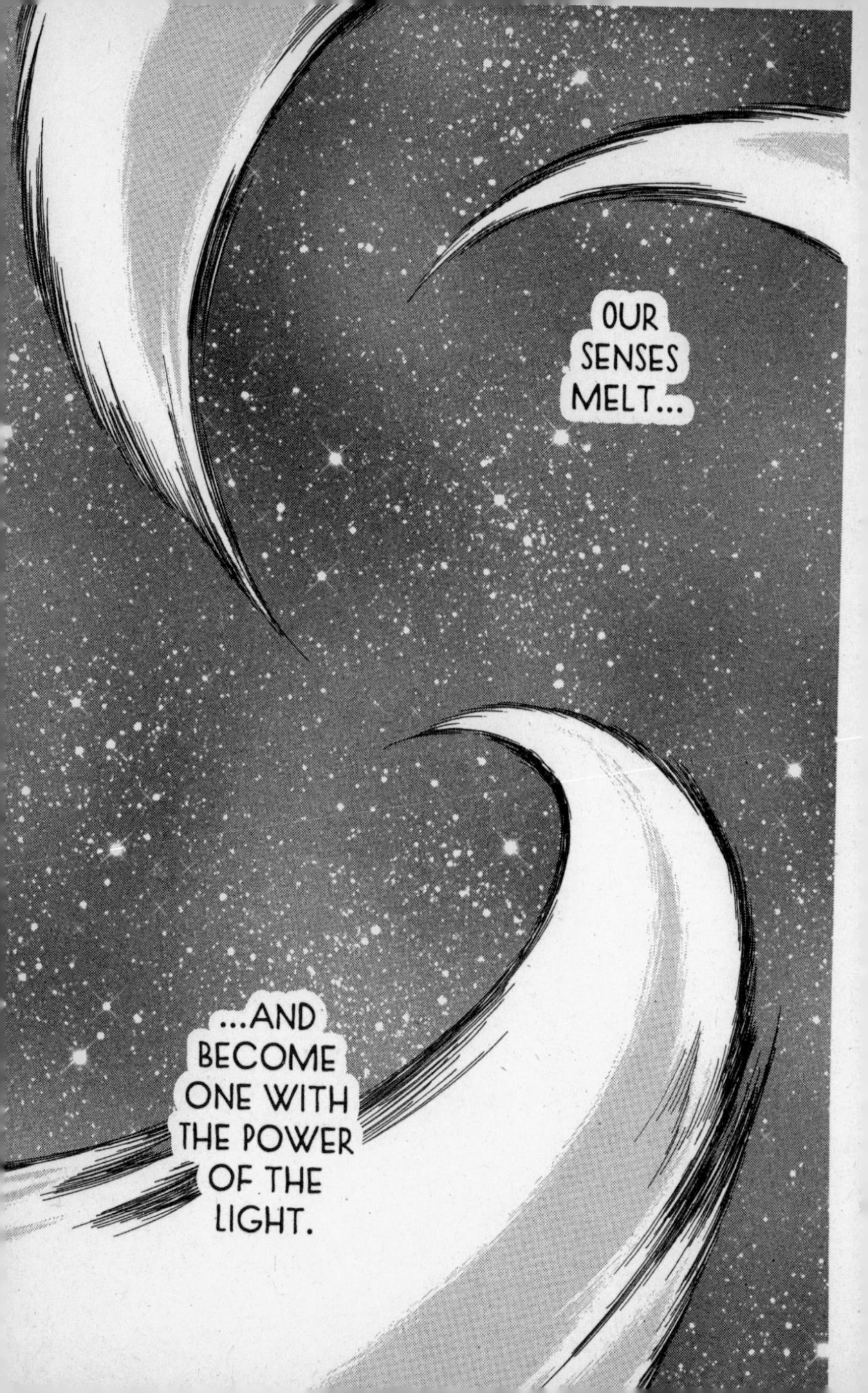
OUR SENSES MELT...
...AND BECOME ONE WITH THE POWER OF THE LIGHT.

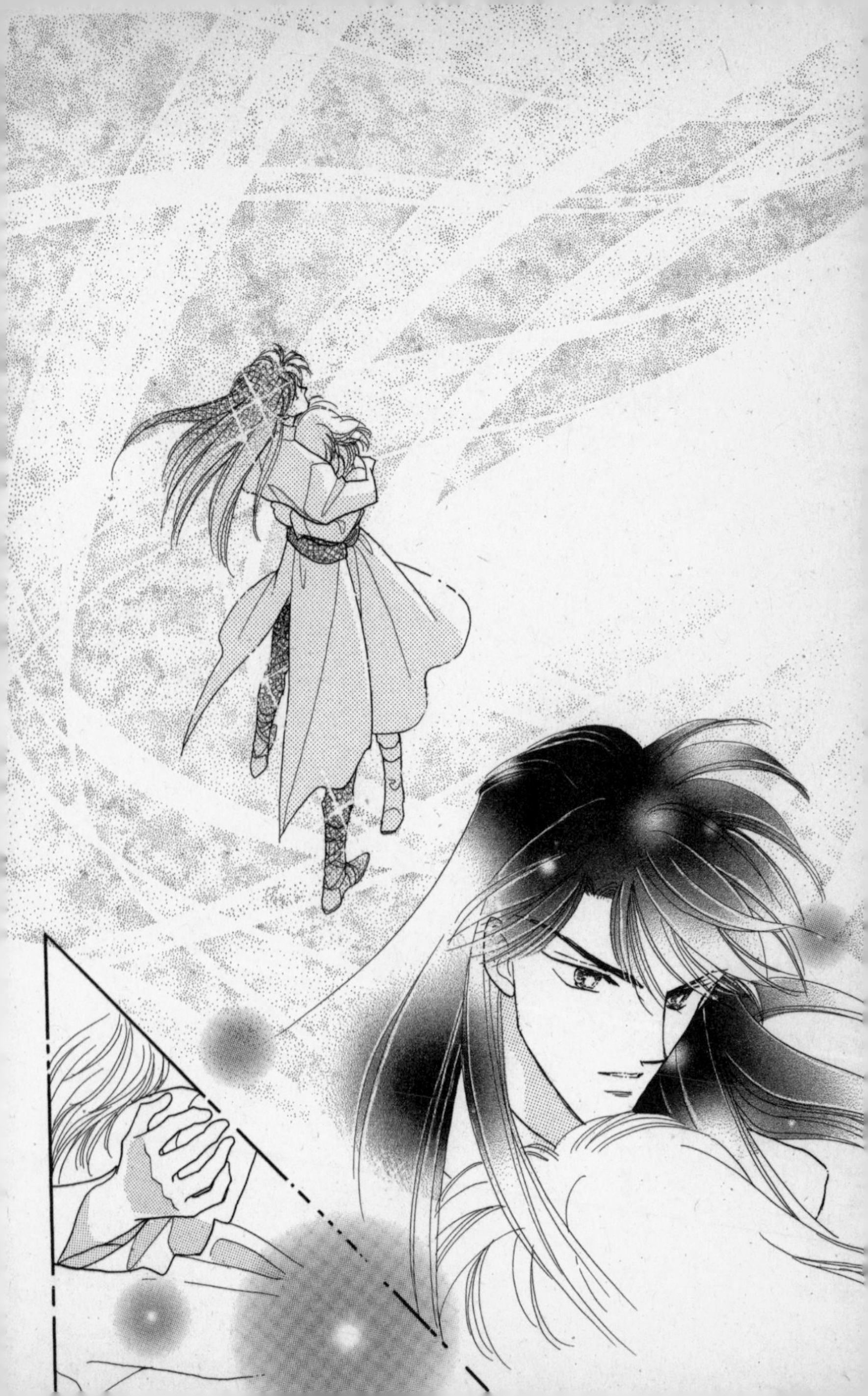

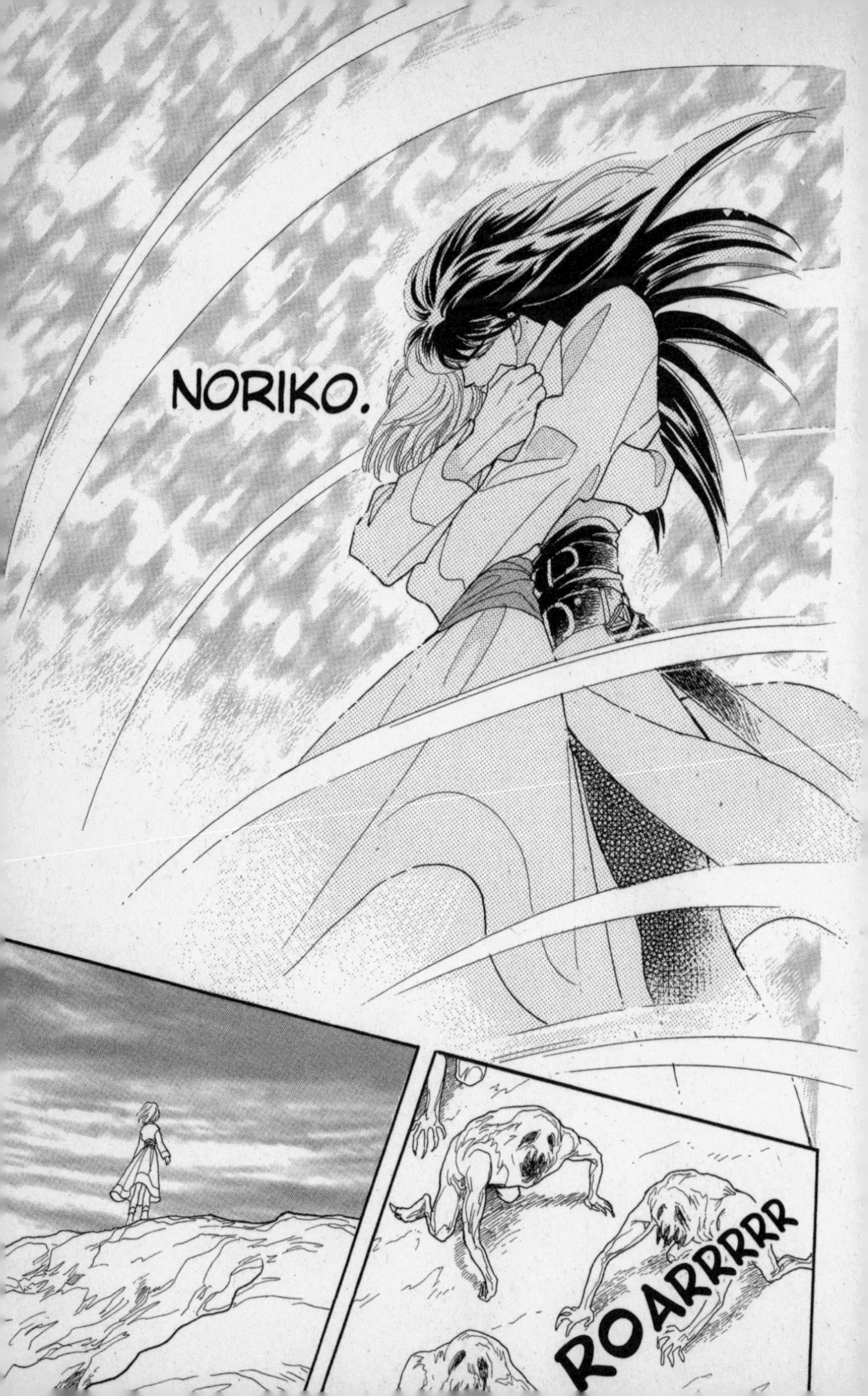
NORIKO.
ROARRRRR

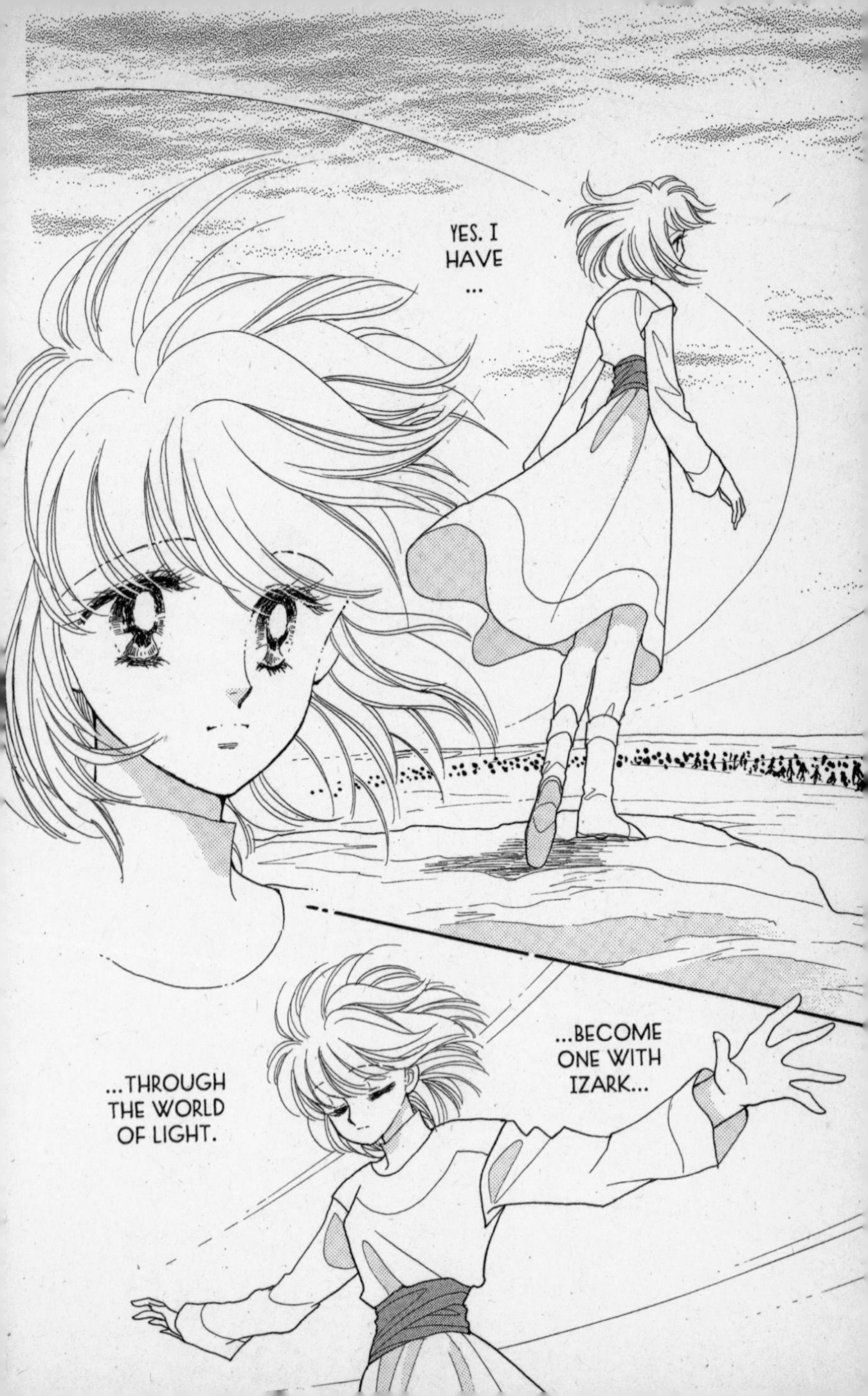
YES. I HAVE ...
...BECOME ONE WITH IZARK...
...THROUGH THE WORLD OF LIGHT.

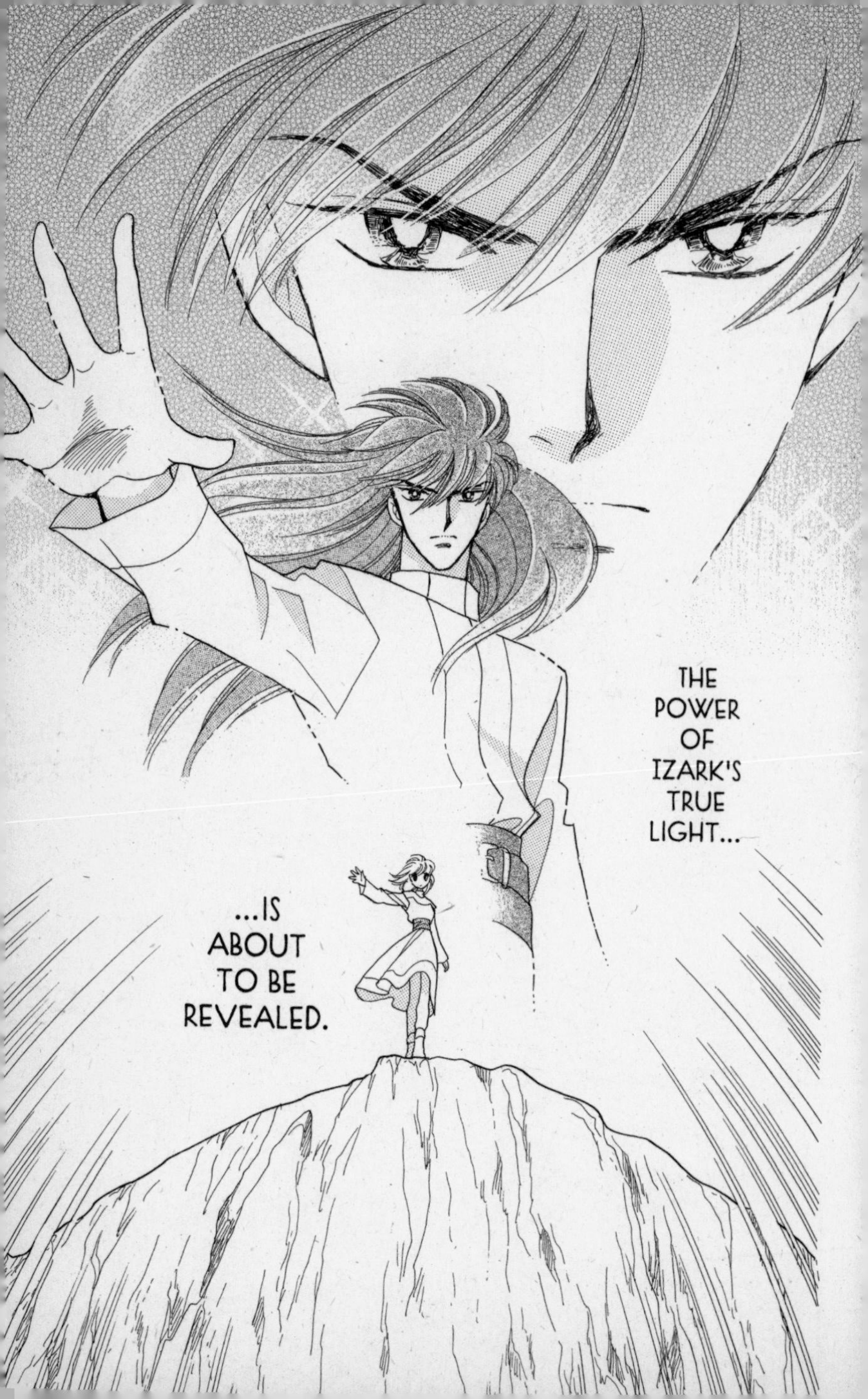
THE POWER OF IZARK'S TRUE LIGHT...
...IS ABOUT TO BE REVEALED.

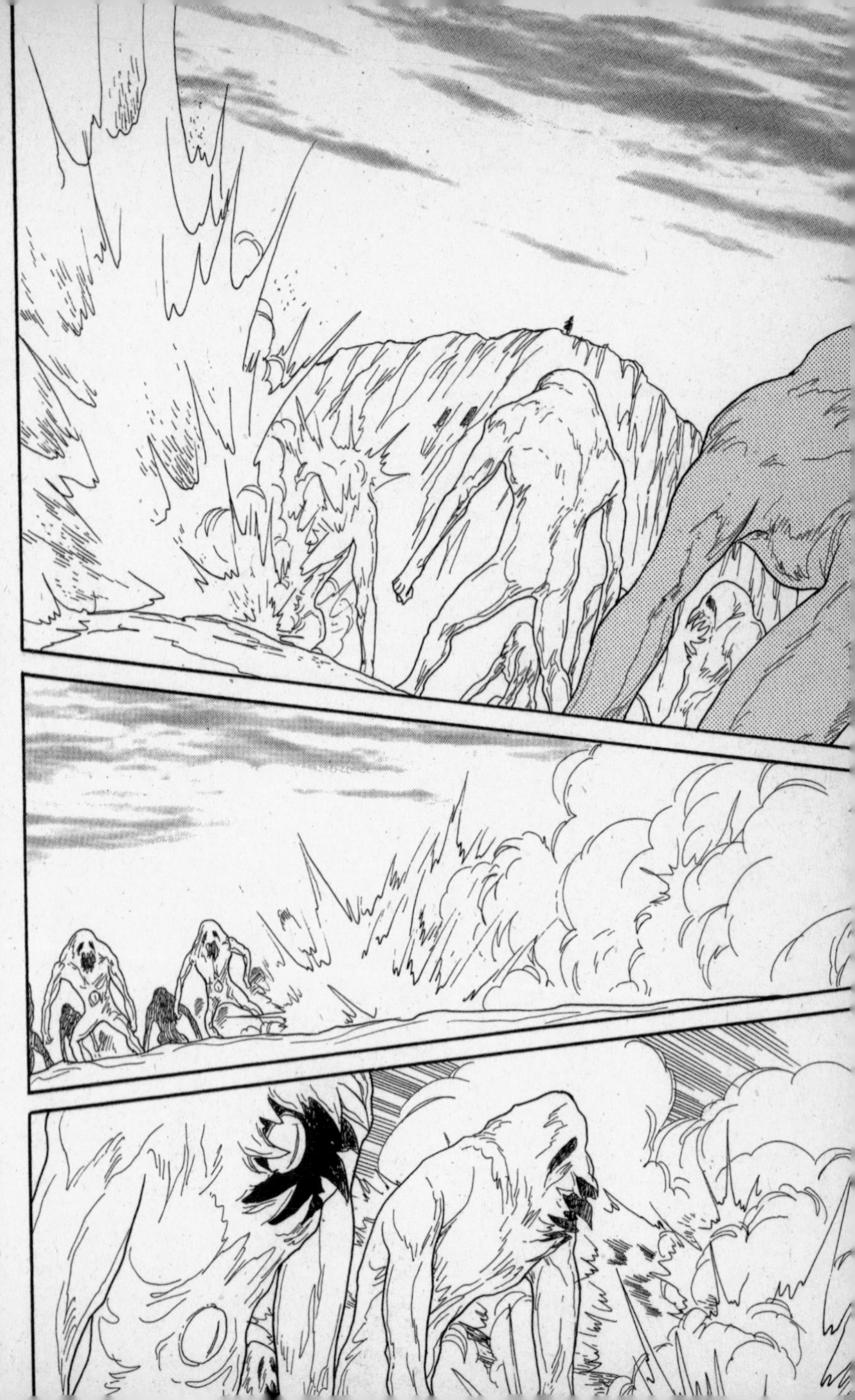

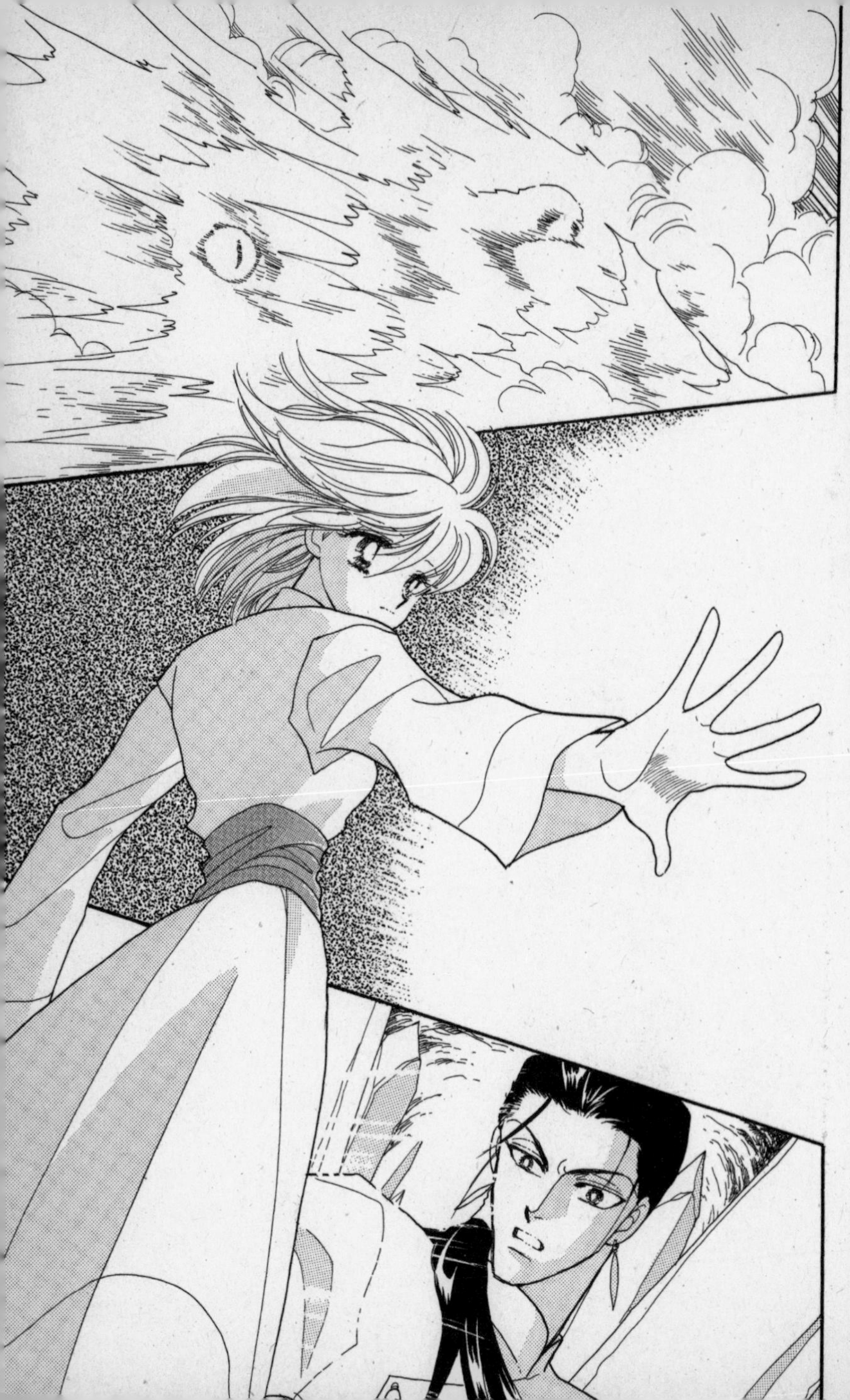

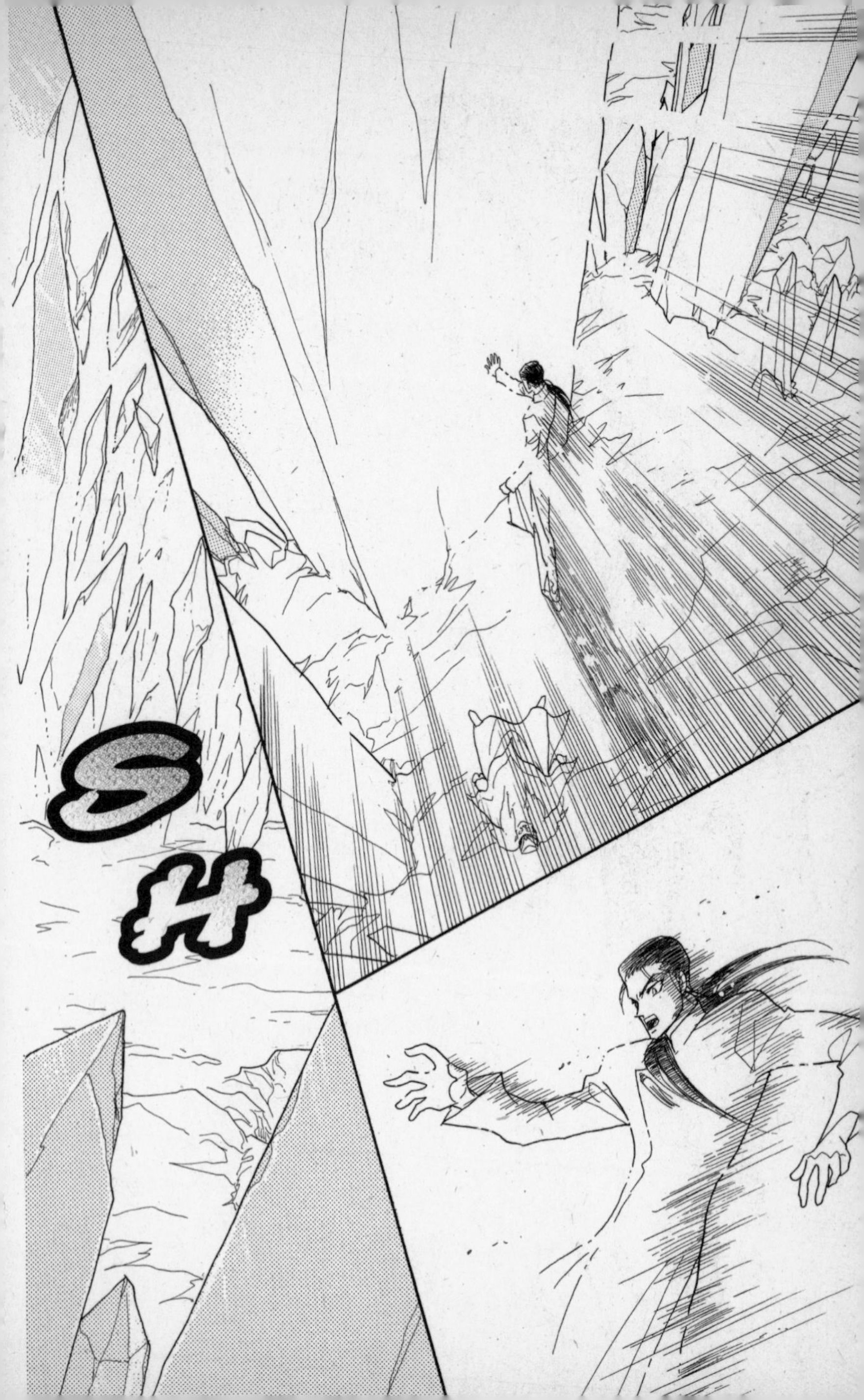
SH

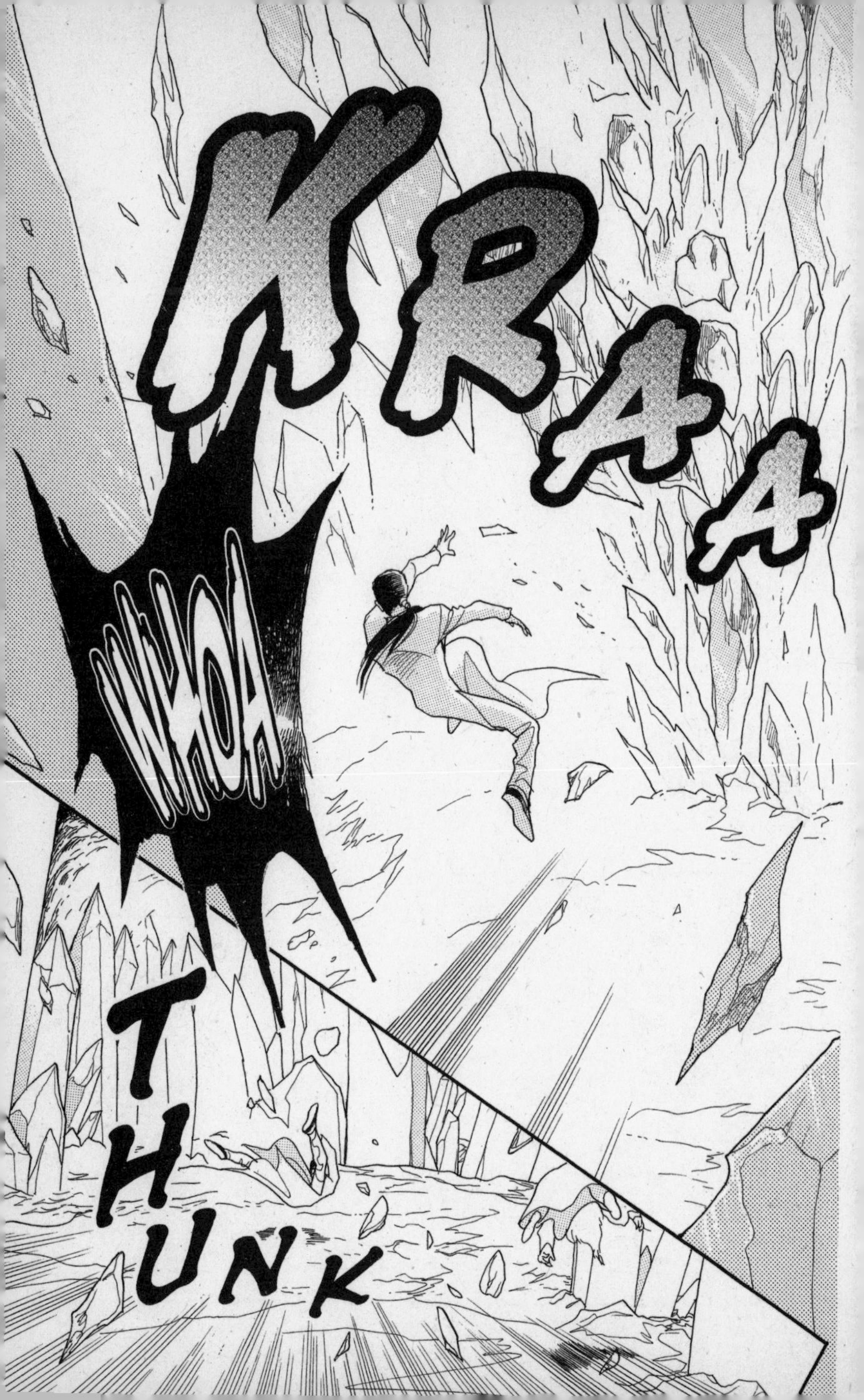
KRAAA
WHOA!
THUNK

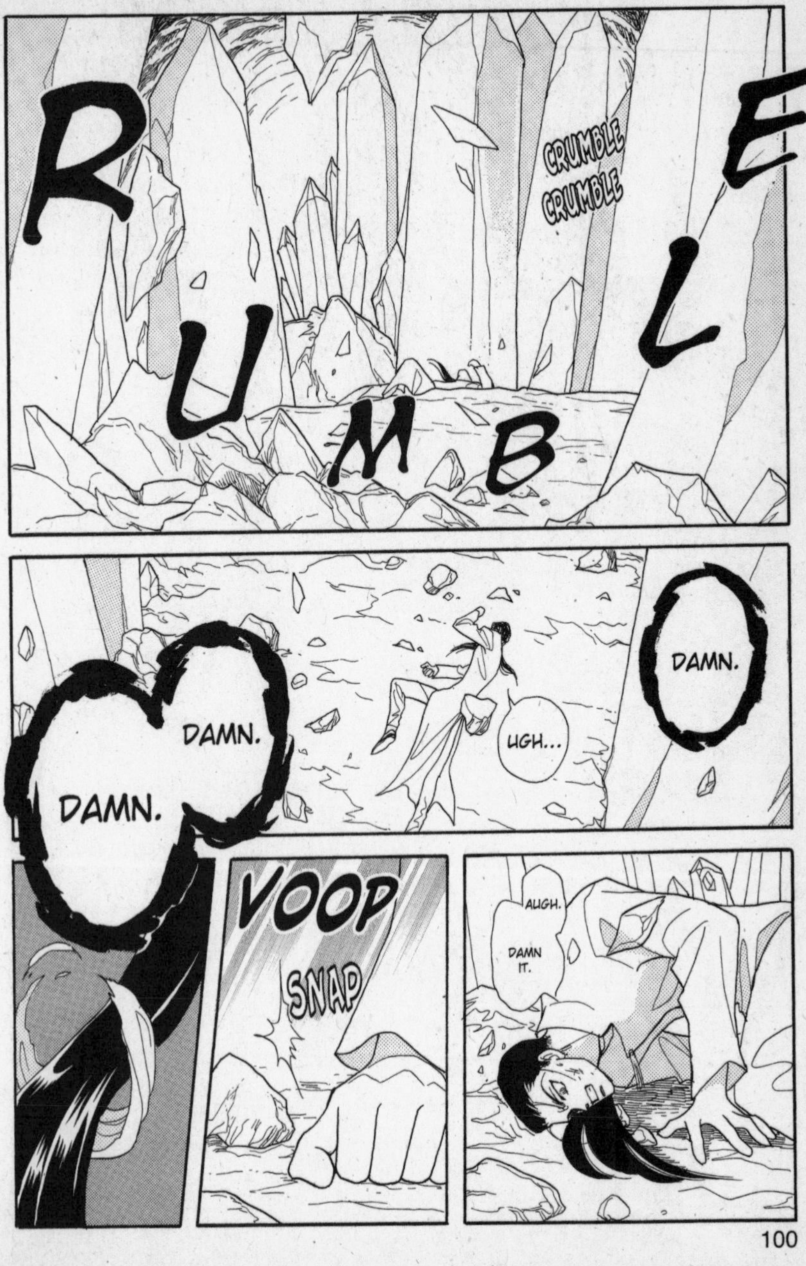
RUMBLE
CRUMBLE CRUMBLE
DAMN.
UGH...
DAMN.
DAMN.
AUGH.
DAMN IT.
VOOP
SNAP

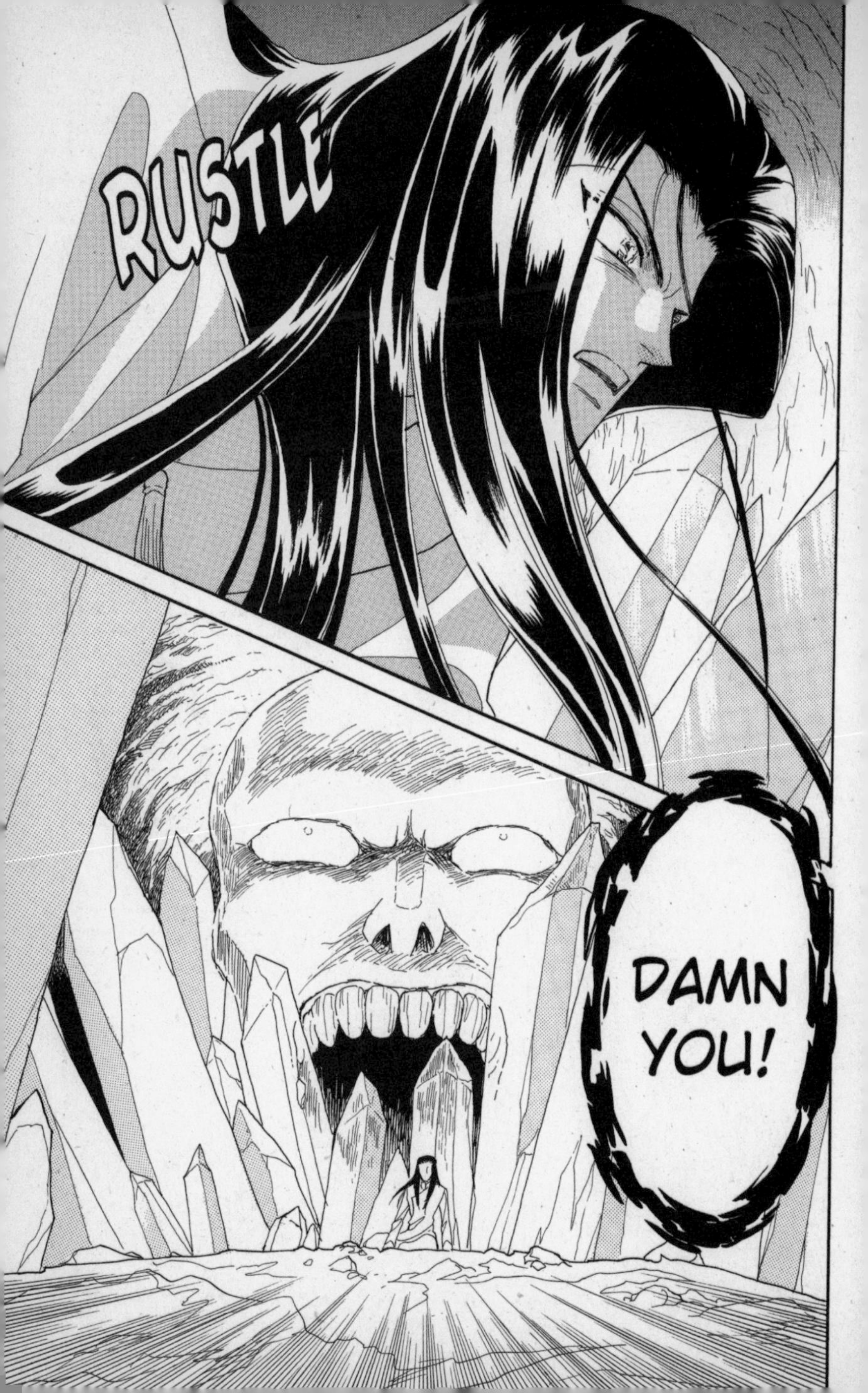
RUSTLE
DAMN YOU!

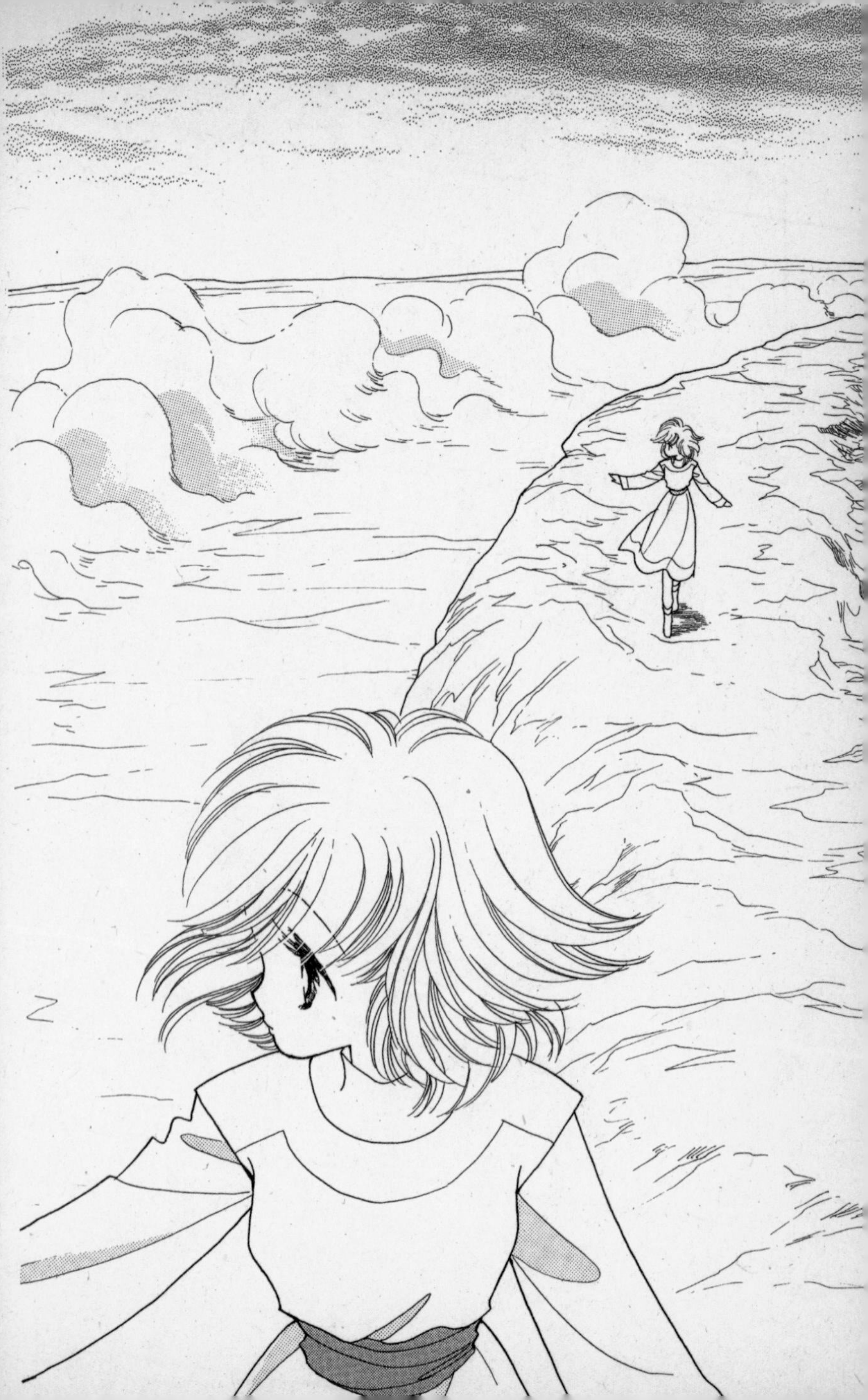

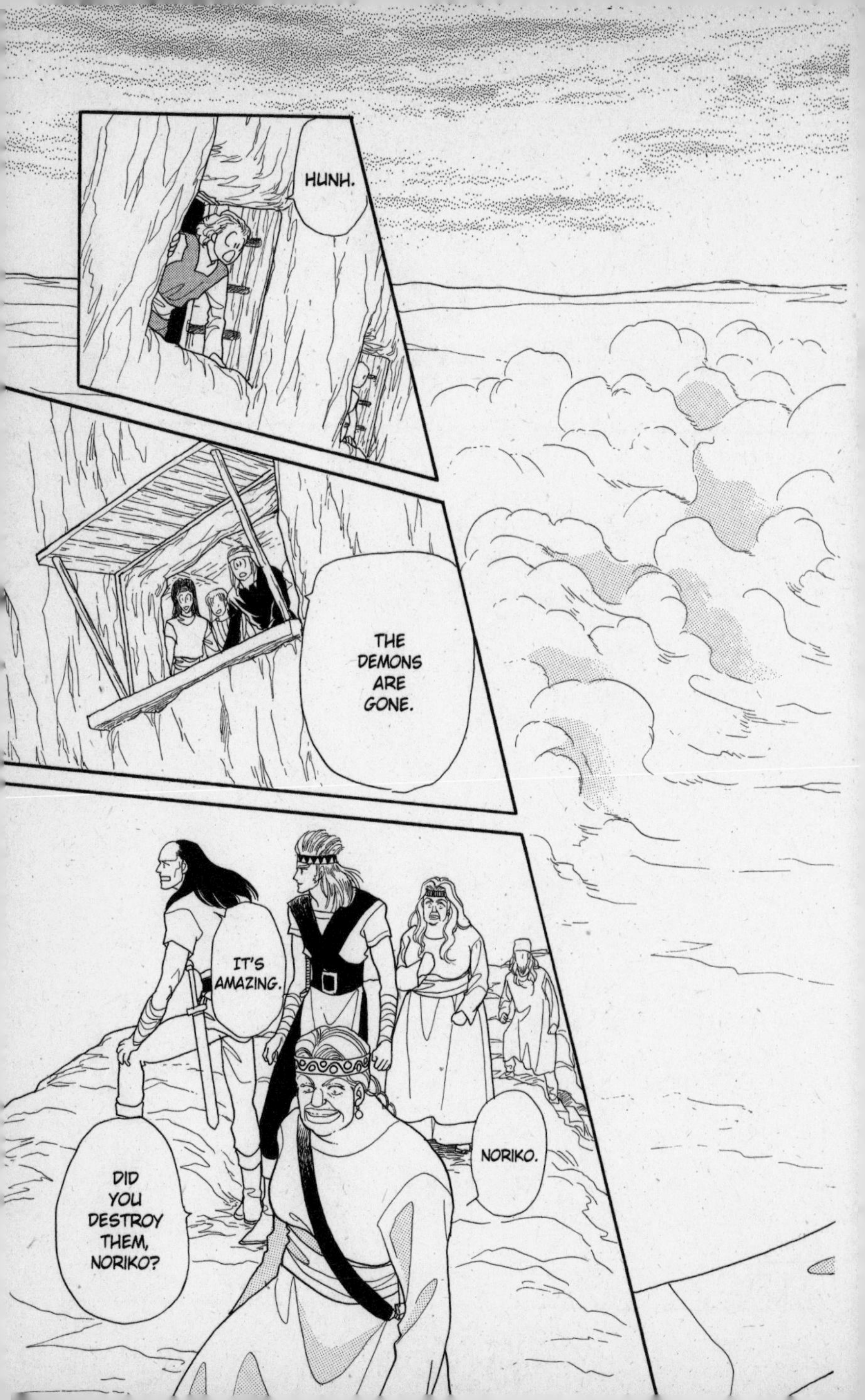
HUNH.
THE DEMONS ARE GONE.
IT'S AMAZING.
NORIKO.
DID YOU DESTROY THEM, NORIKO?

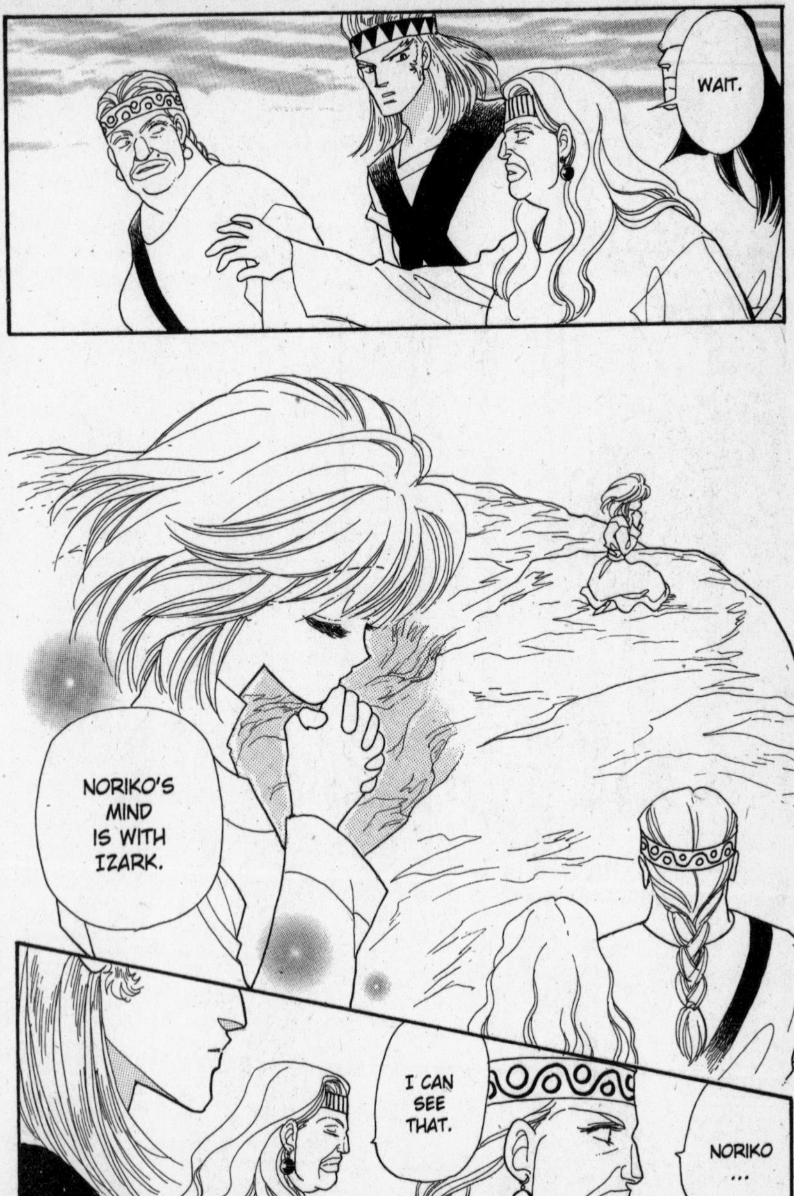
WAIT.
NORIKO'S MIND IS WITH IZARK.
NORIKO ...
I CAN SEE THAT.

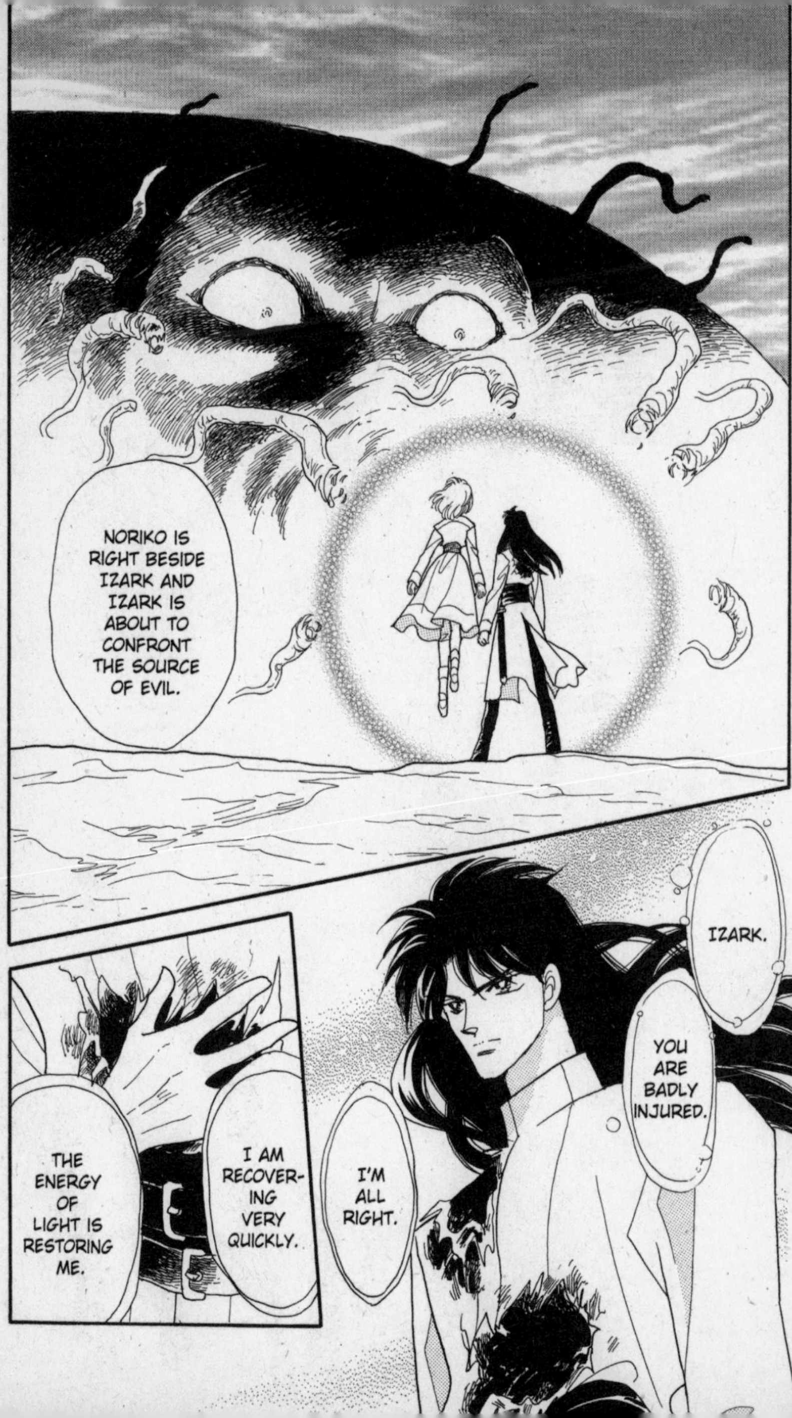
NORIKO IS RIGHT BESIDE IZARK AND IZARK IS ABOUT TO CONFRONT THE SOURCE OF EVIL.
IZARK.
YOU ARE BADLY INJURED.
I'M ALL RIGHT.
I AM RECOVER-ING VERY QUICKLY.
THE ENERGY OF LIGHT IS RESTORING ME.

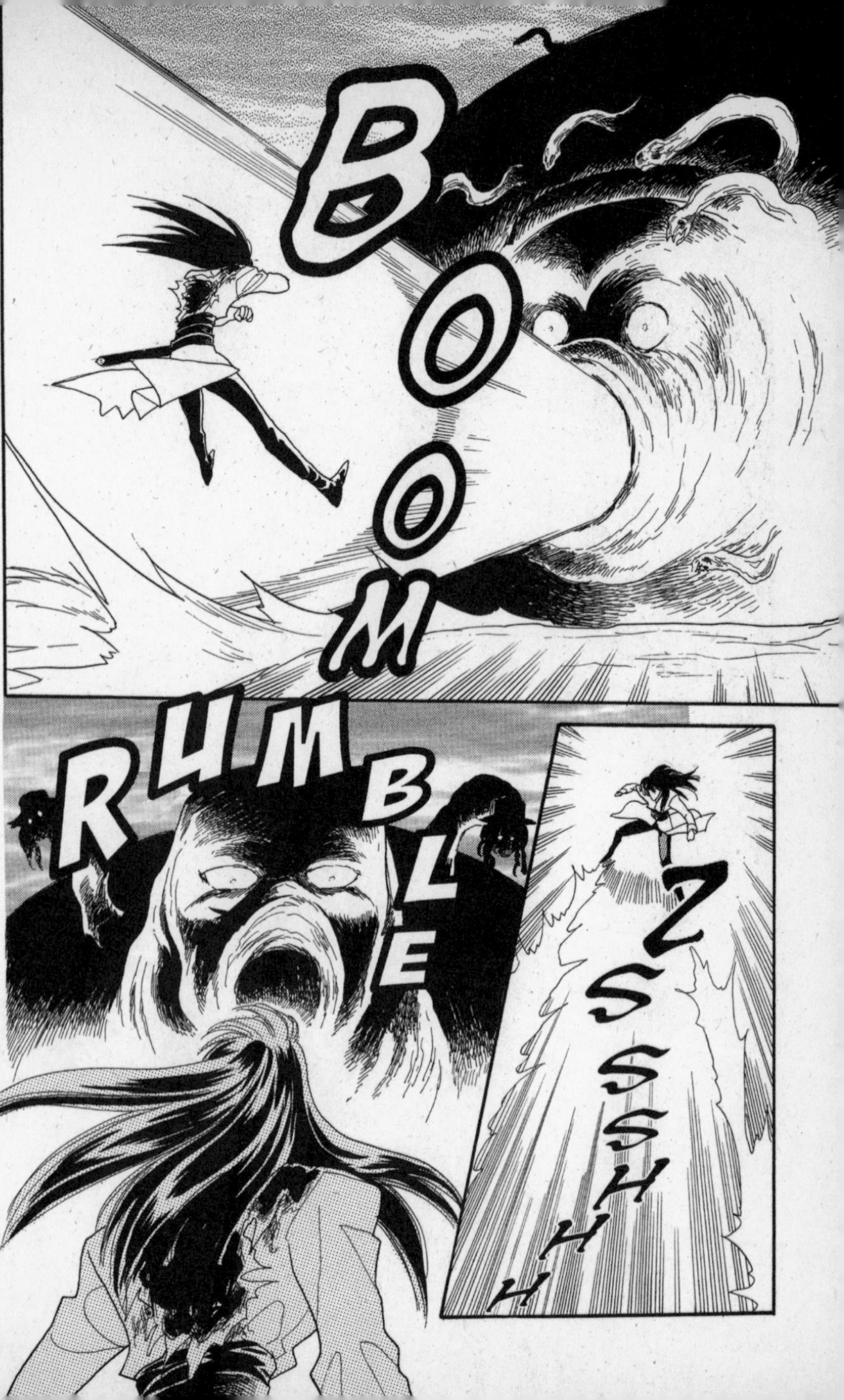
BOOOM
ZSSSHHH
RUMBLE

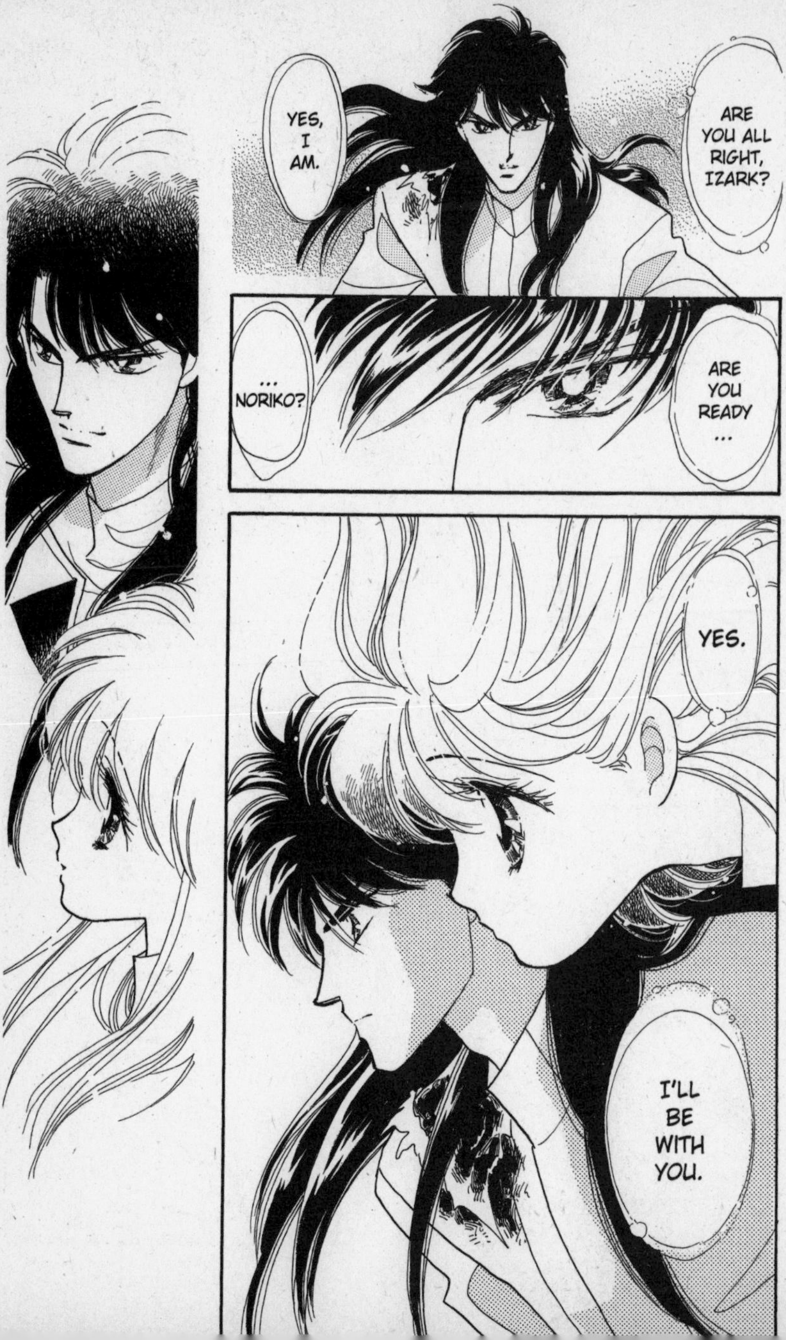
ARE YOU ALL RIGHT, IZARK?
YES, I AM.
ARE YOU READY ...
... NORIKO?
YES.
I'LL BE WITH YOU.

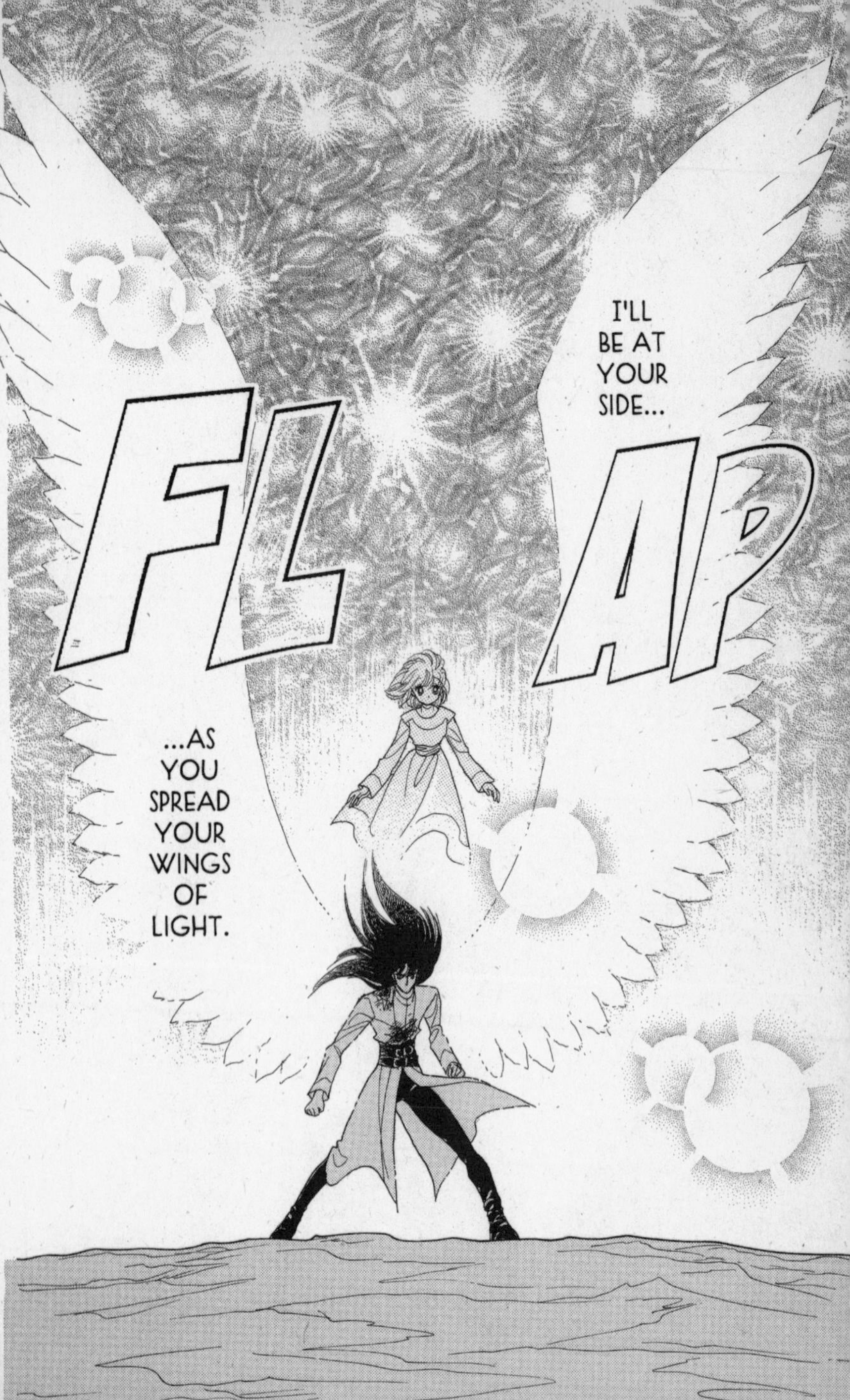
I'LL BE AT YOUR SIDE...
FLAP
...AS YOU SPREAD YOUR WINGS OF LIGHT.

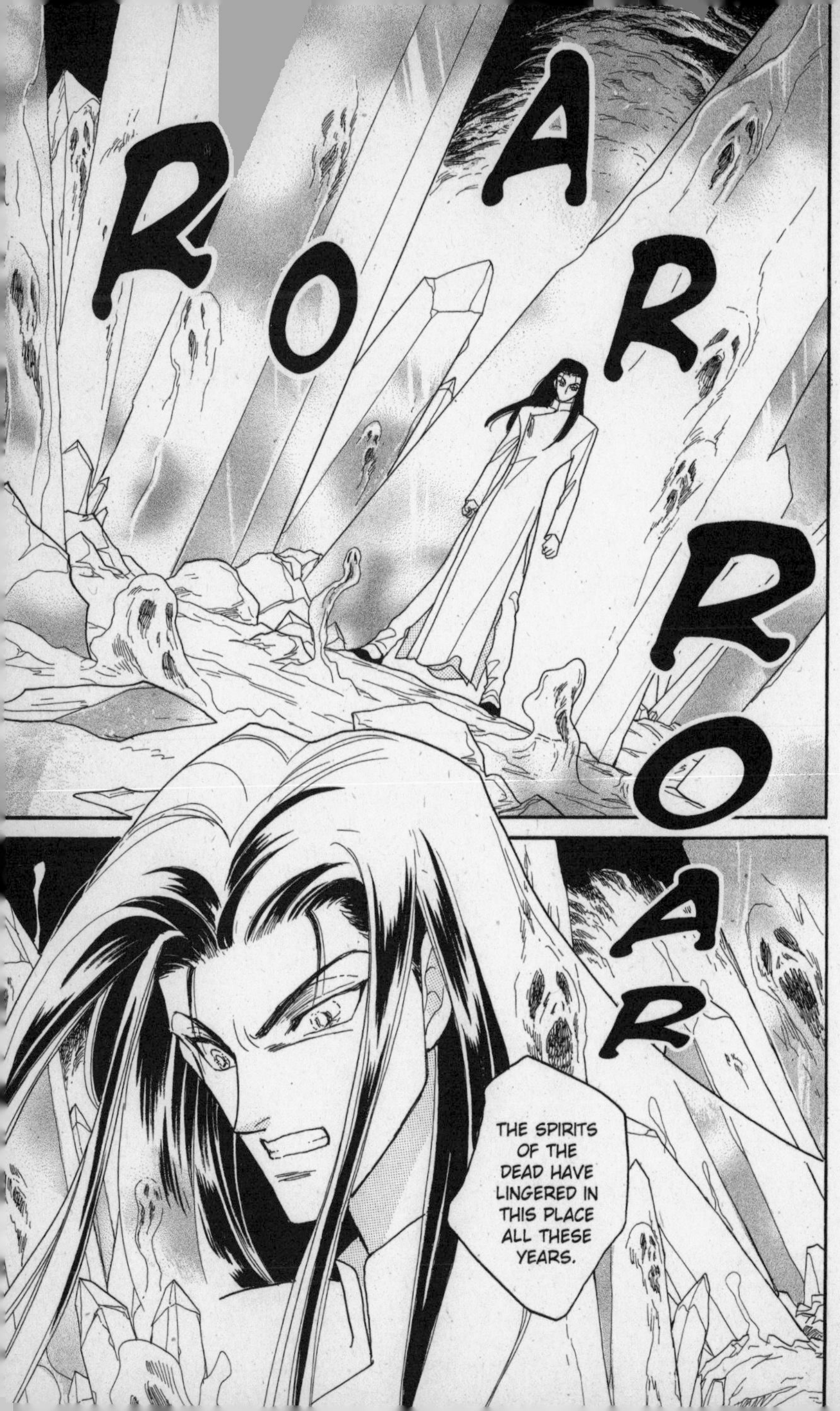
ROAR
ROARROAR
THE SPIRITS OF THE DEAD HAVE LINGERED IN THIS PLACE ALL THESE YEARS.

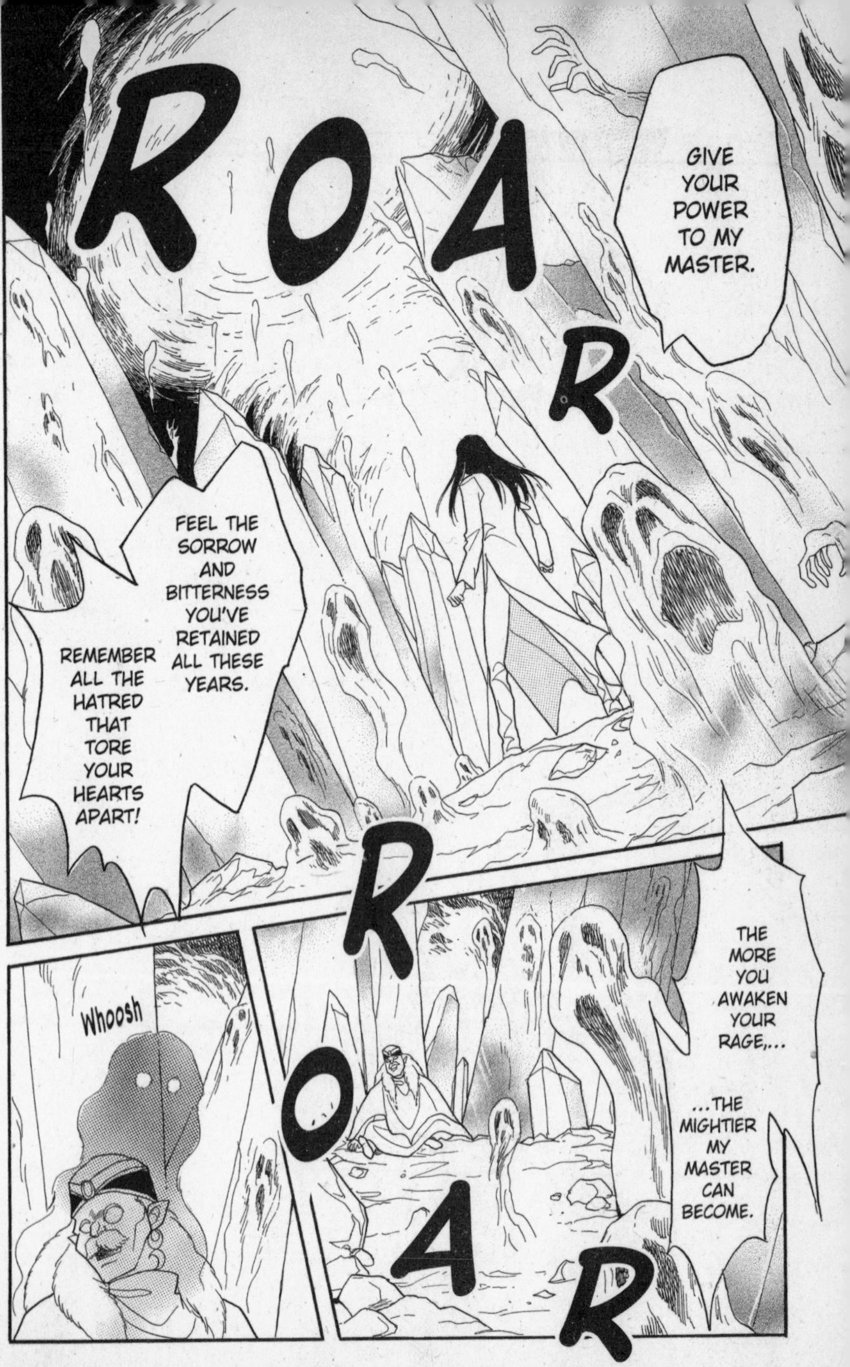
GIVE YOUR POWER TO MY MASTER.
ROAR
FEEL THE SORROW AND BITTERNESS YOU'VE RETAINED ALL THESE YEARS.
REMEMBER ALL THE HATRED THAT TORE YOUR HEARTS APART!
THE MORE YOU AWAKEN YOUR RAGE,...
...THE MIGHTIER MY MASTER CAN BECOME.
ROAR
Whoosh

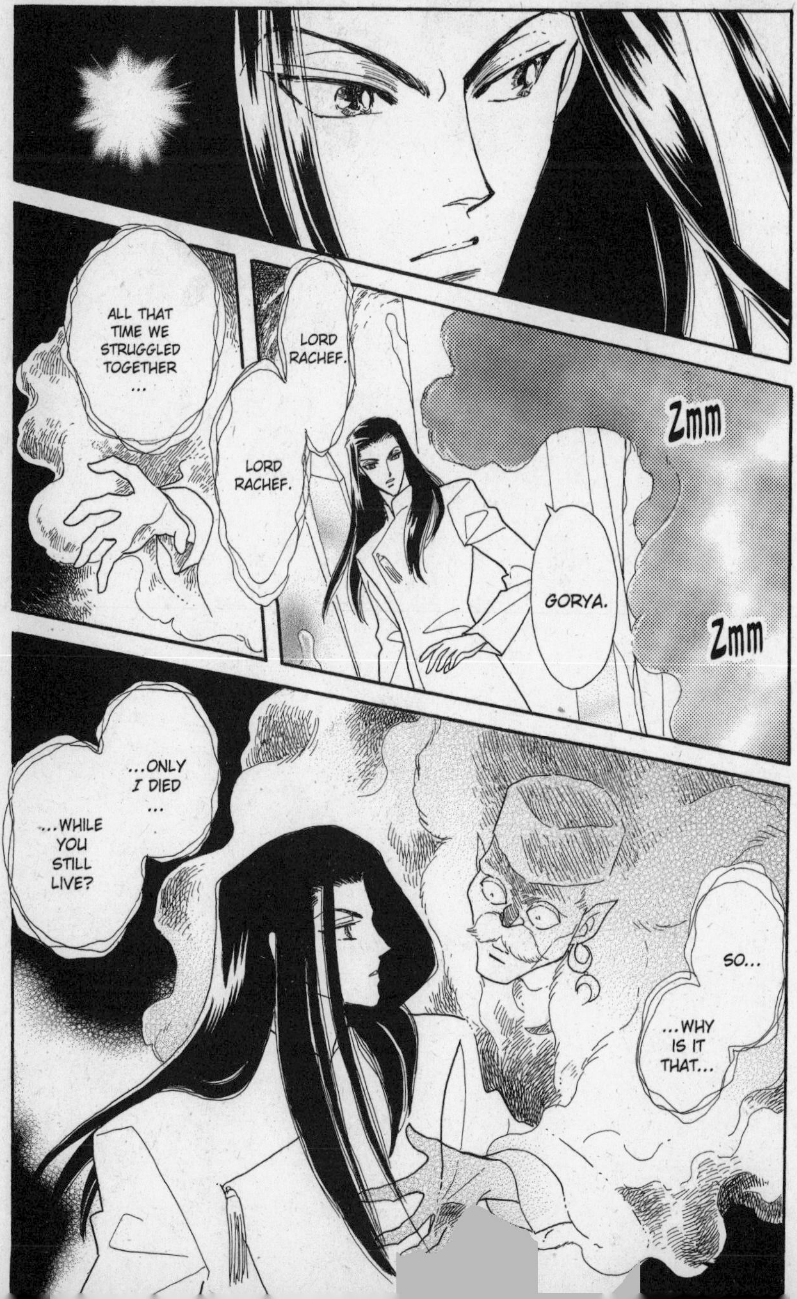
Zmm
LORD RACHEF.
LORD RACHEF.
GORYA.
Zmm
ALL THAT TIME WE STRUGGLED TOGETHER ...
SO...
...WHY IS IT THAT...
...ONLY I DIED ...
...WHILE YOU STILL LIVE?

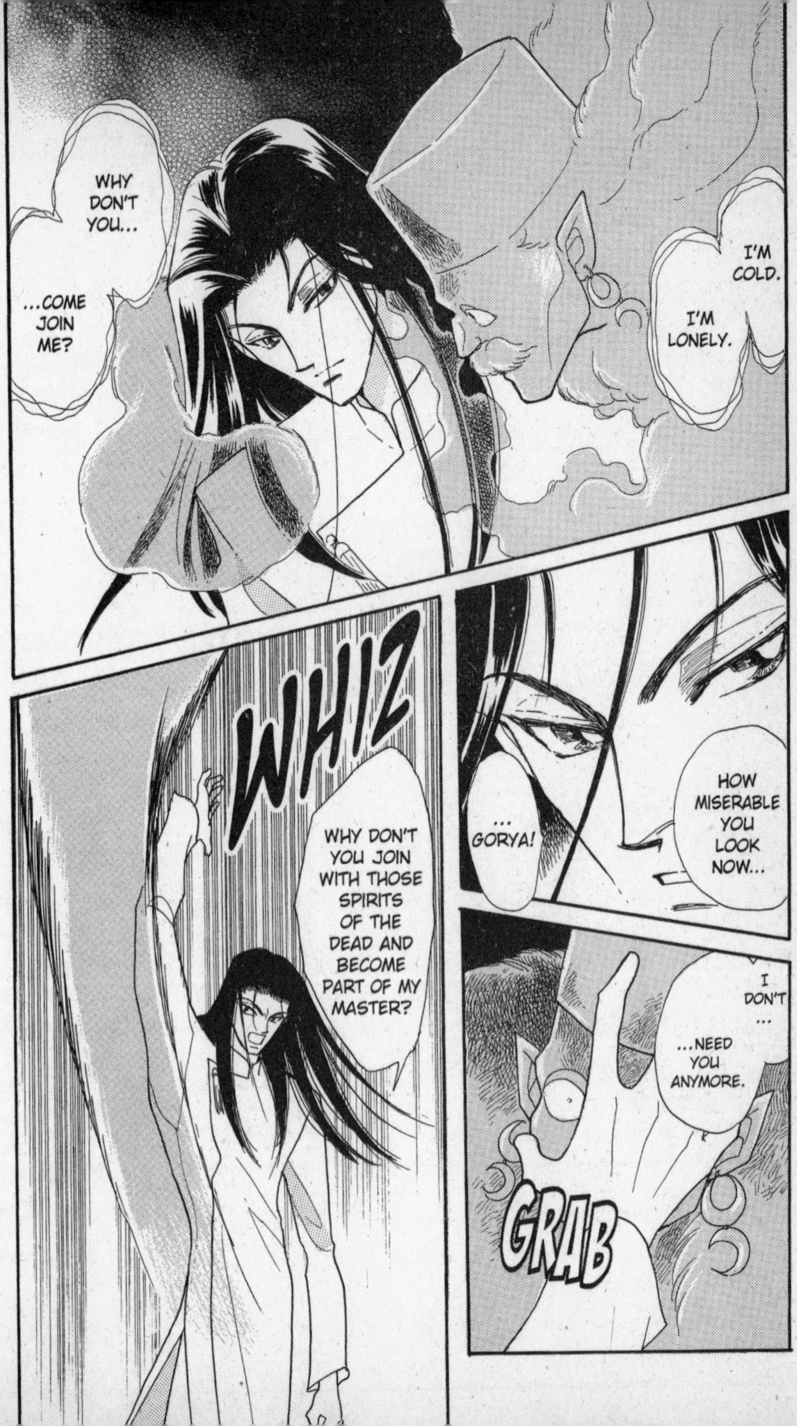
I'M COLD.
I'M LONELY.
WHY DON'T YOU...
...COME JOIN ME?
HOW MISERABLE YOU LOOK NOW...
... GORYA!
I DON'T ...
...NEED YOU ANYMORE.
GRAB
WHIZ
WHY DON'T YOU JOIN WITH THOSE SPIRITS OF THE DEAD AND BECOME PART OF MY MASTER?

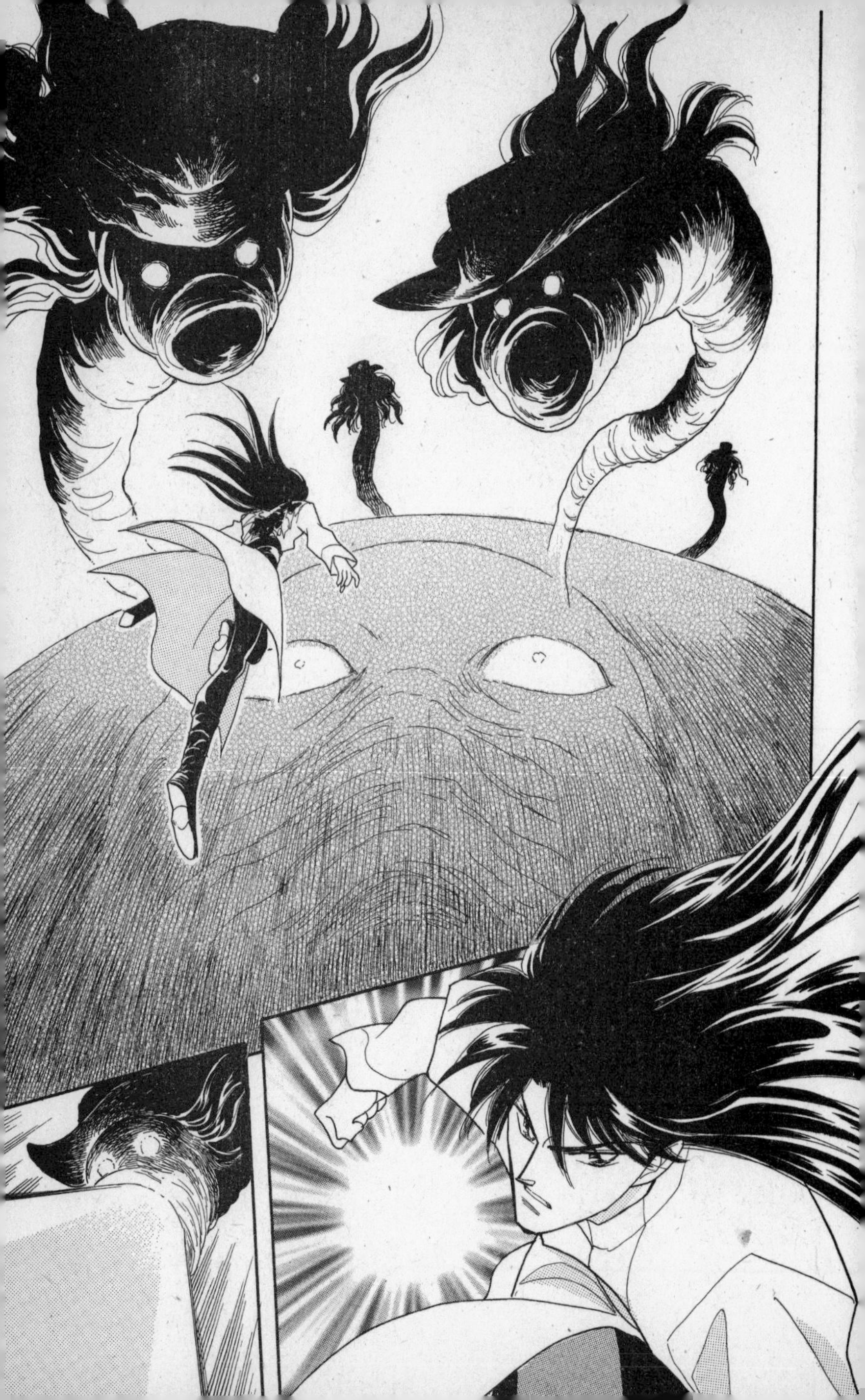

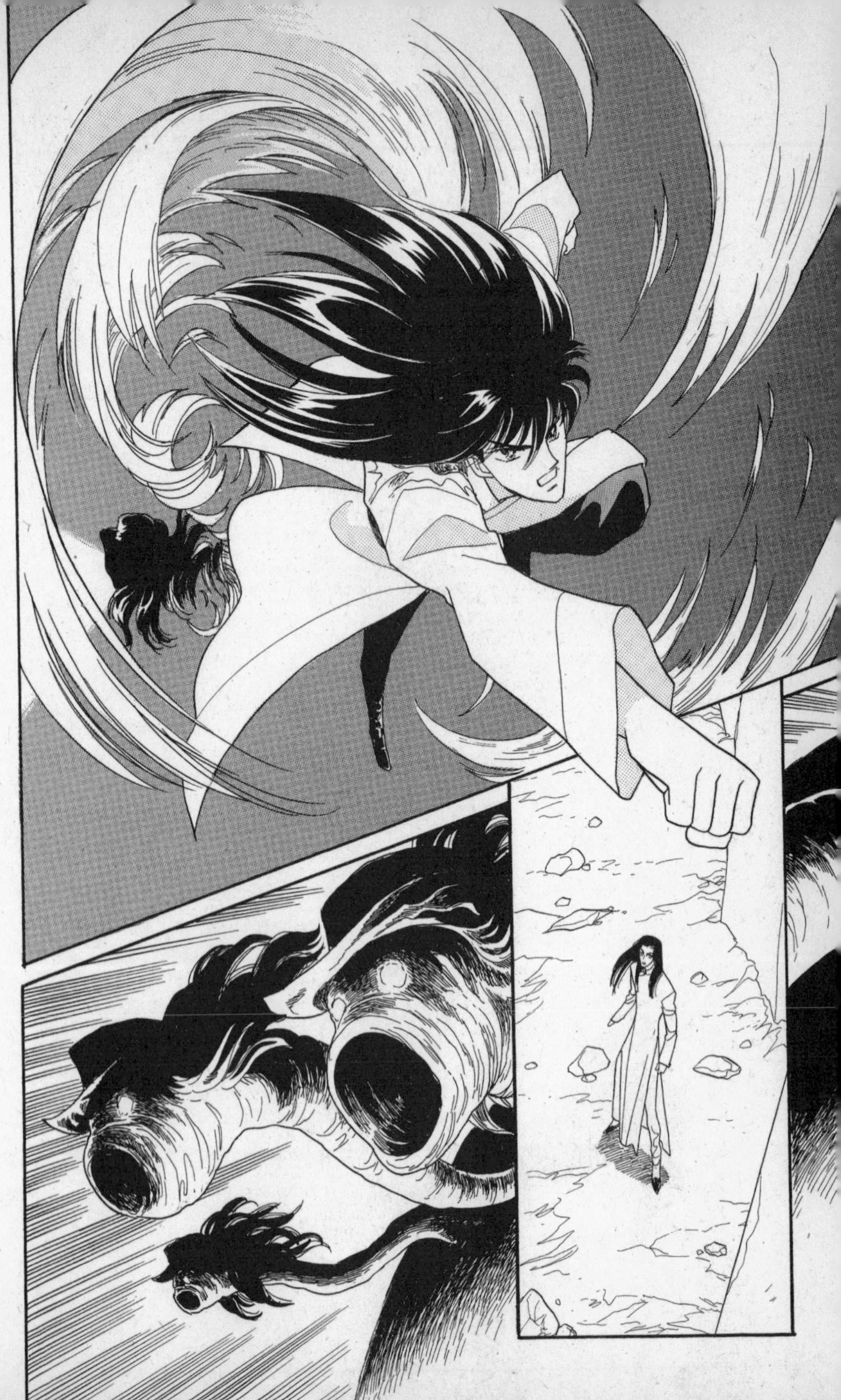

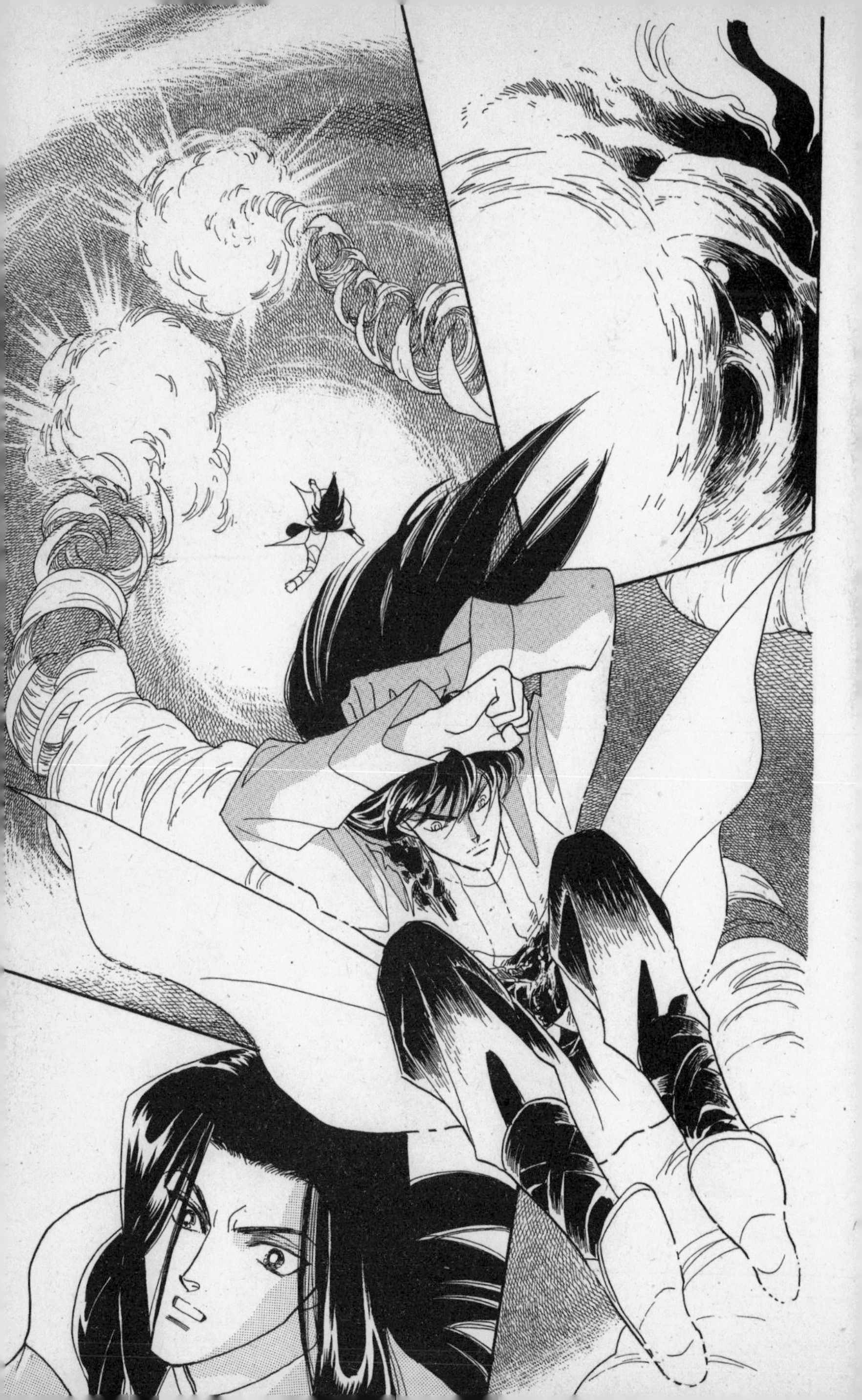

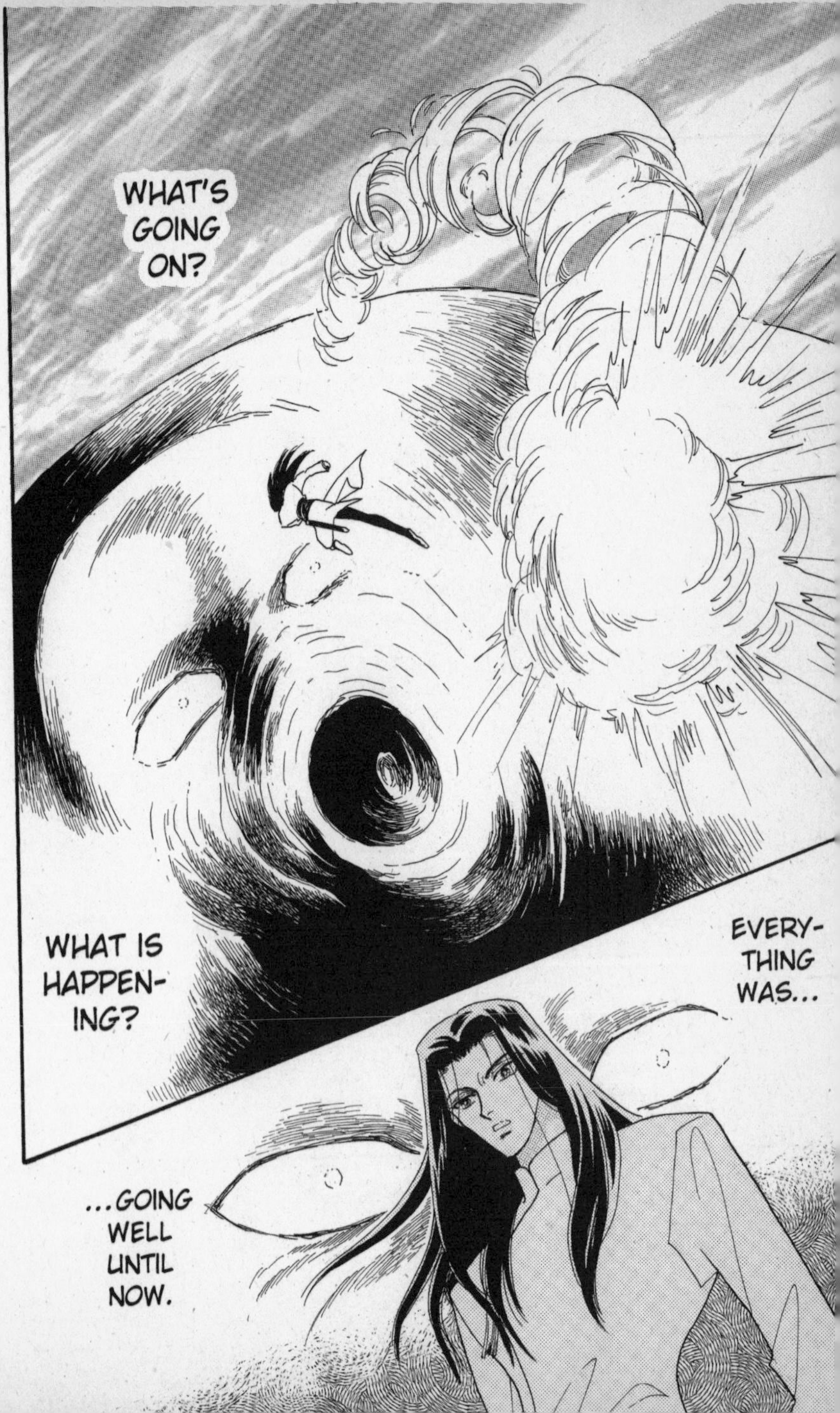
WHAT'S GOING ON?
WHAT IS HAPPEN- ING?
EVERY- THING WAS...
...GOING WELL UNTIL NOW.

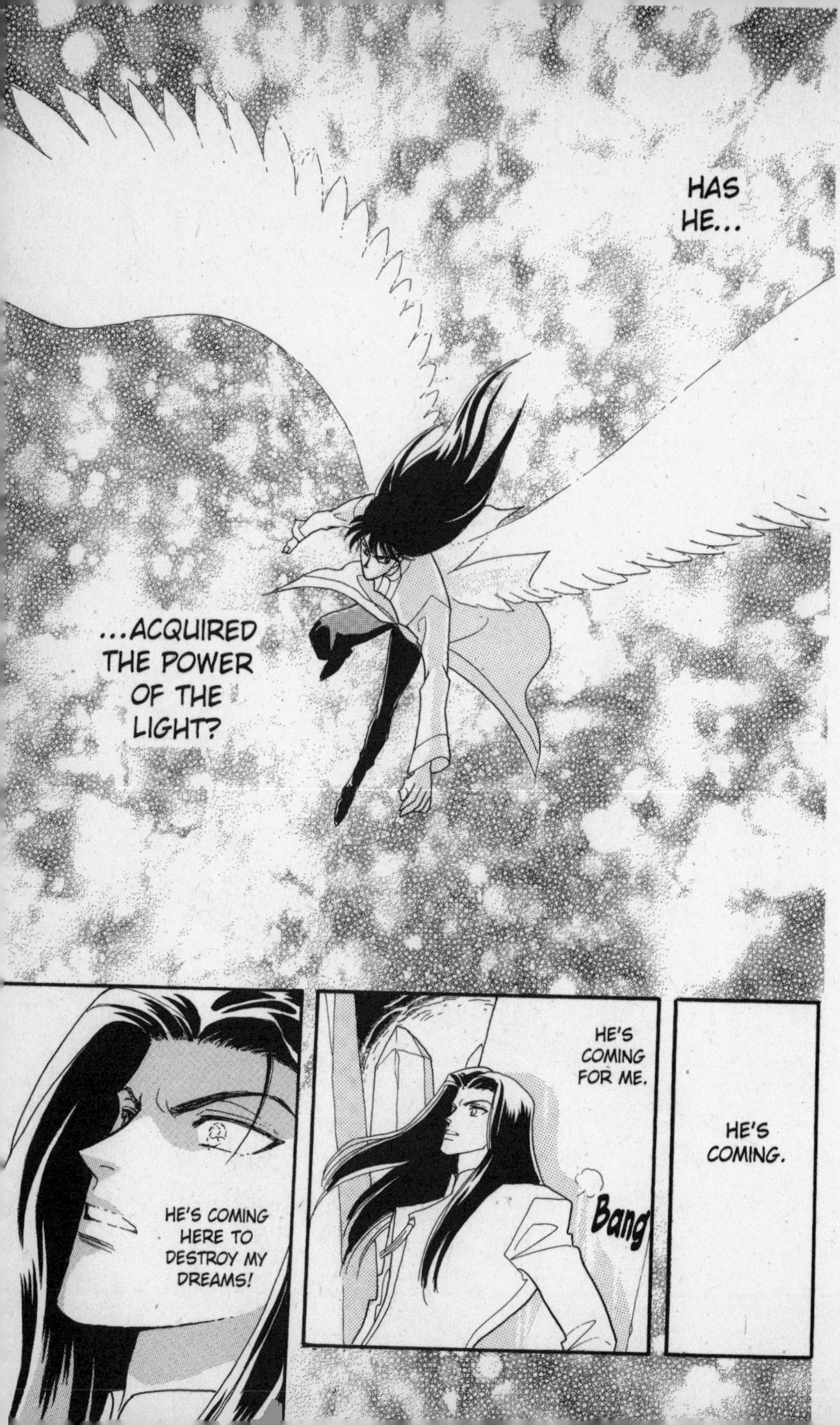
HAS HE...
...ACQUIRED THE POWER OF THE LIGHT?
HE'S COMING.
HE'S COMING FOR ME.
Bang
HE'S COMING HERE TO DESTROY MY DREAMS!

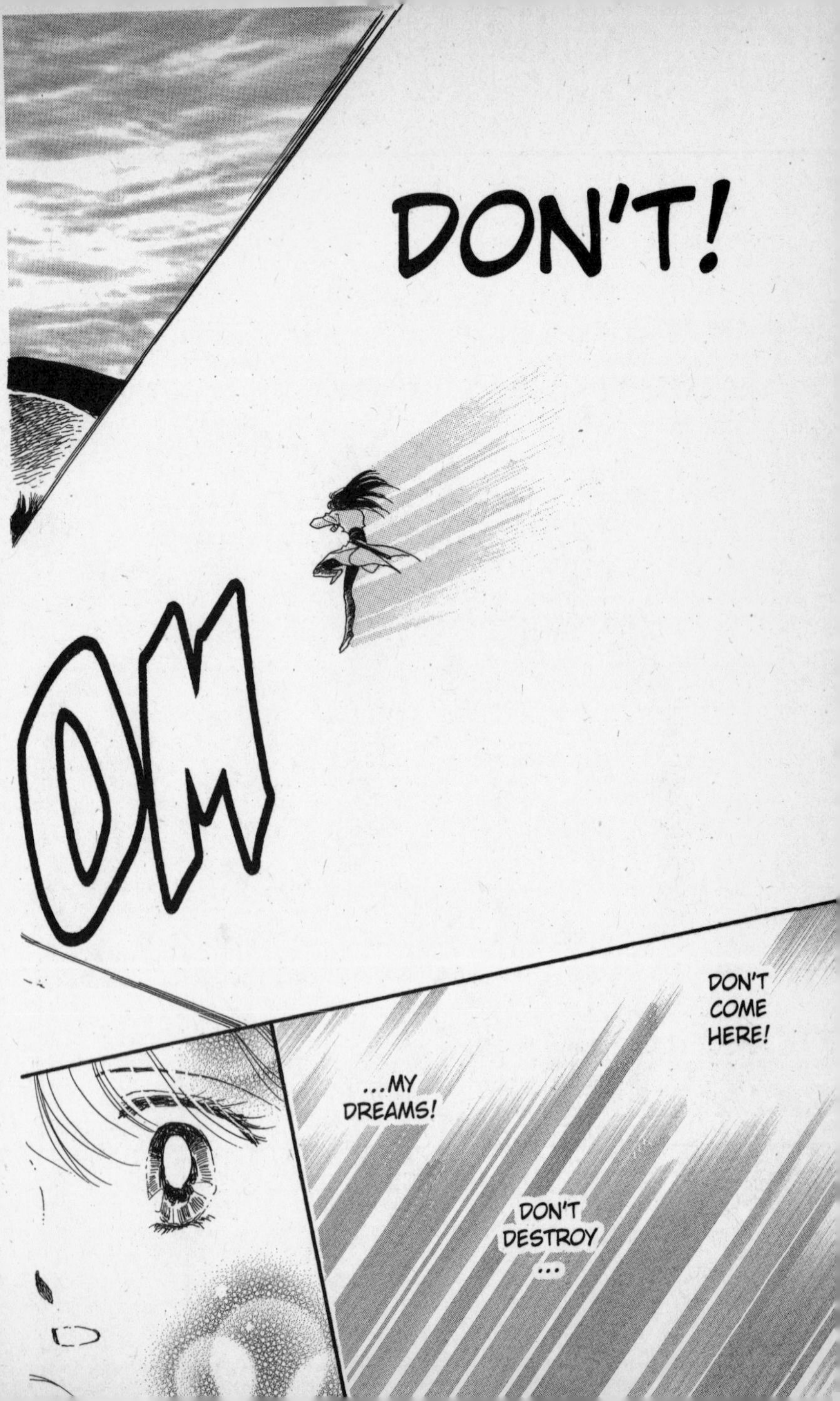
DON'T!
OM
DON'T COME HERE!
DON'T DESTROY ...
...MY DREAMS!

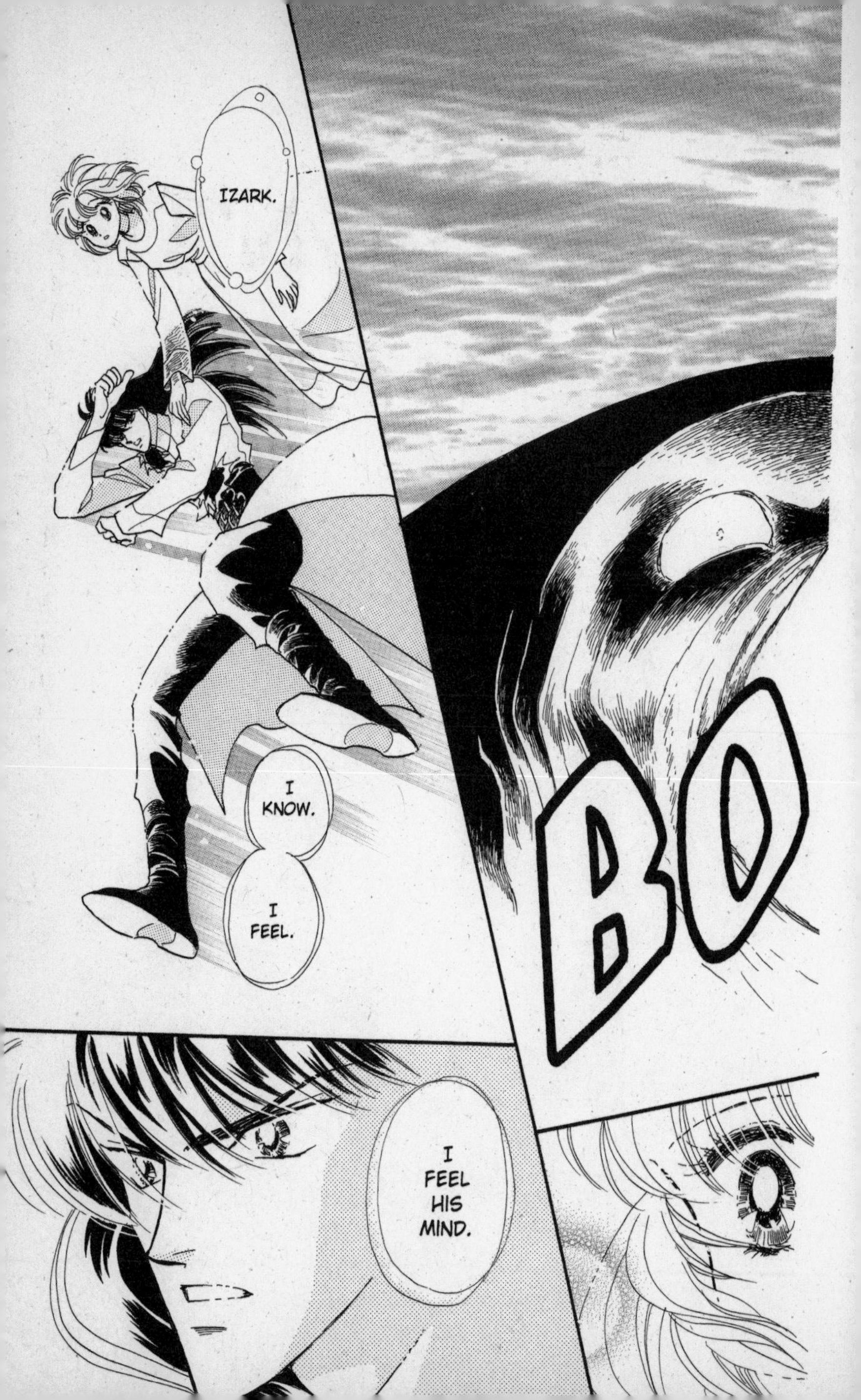
BO
IZARK.
I KNOW.
I FEEL.
I FEEL HIS MIND.

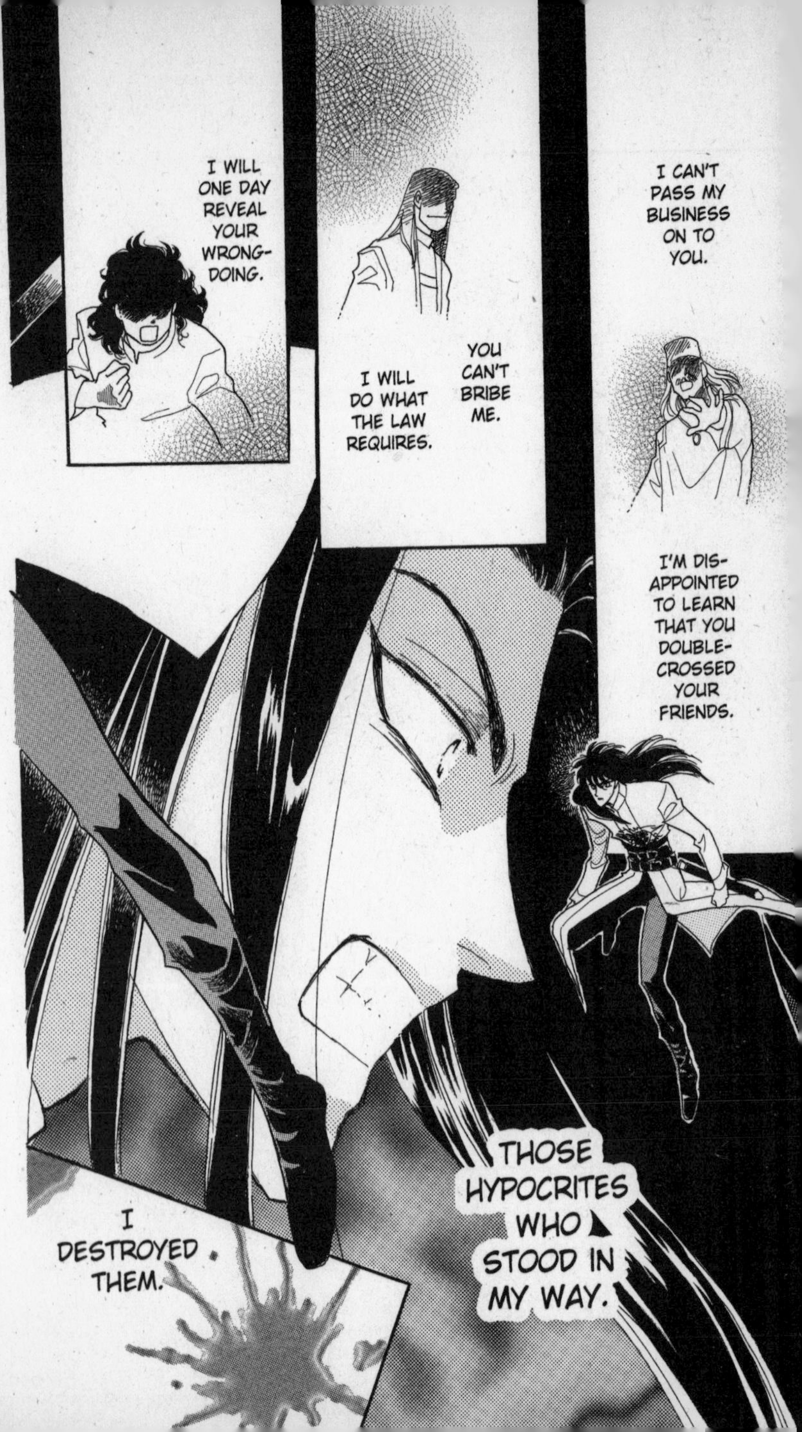
I CAN'T PASS MY BUSINESS ON TO YOU.
YOU CAN'T BRIBE ME.
I WILL DO WHAT THE LAW REQUIRES.
I WILL ONE DAY REVEAL YOUR WRONG-DOING.
I'M DIS-APPOINTED TO LEARN THAT YOU DOUBLE-CROSSED YOUR FRIENDS.
THOSE HYPOCRITES WHO STOOD IN MY WAY.
I DESTROYED THEM.

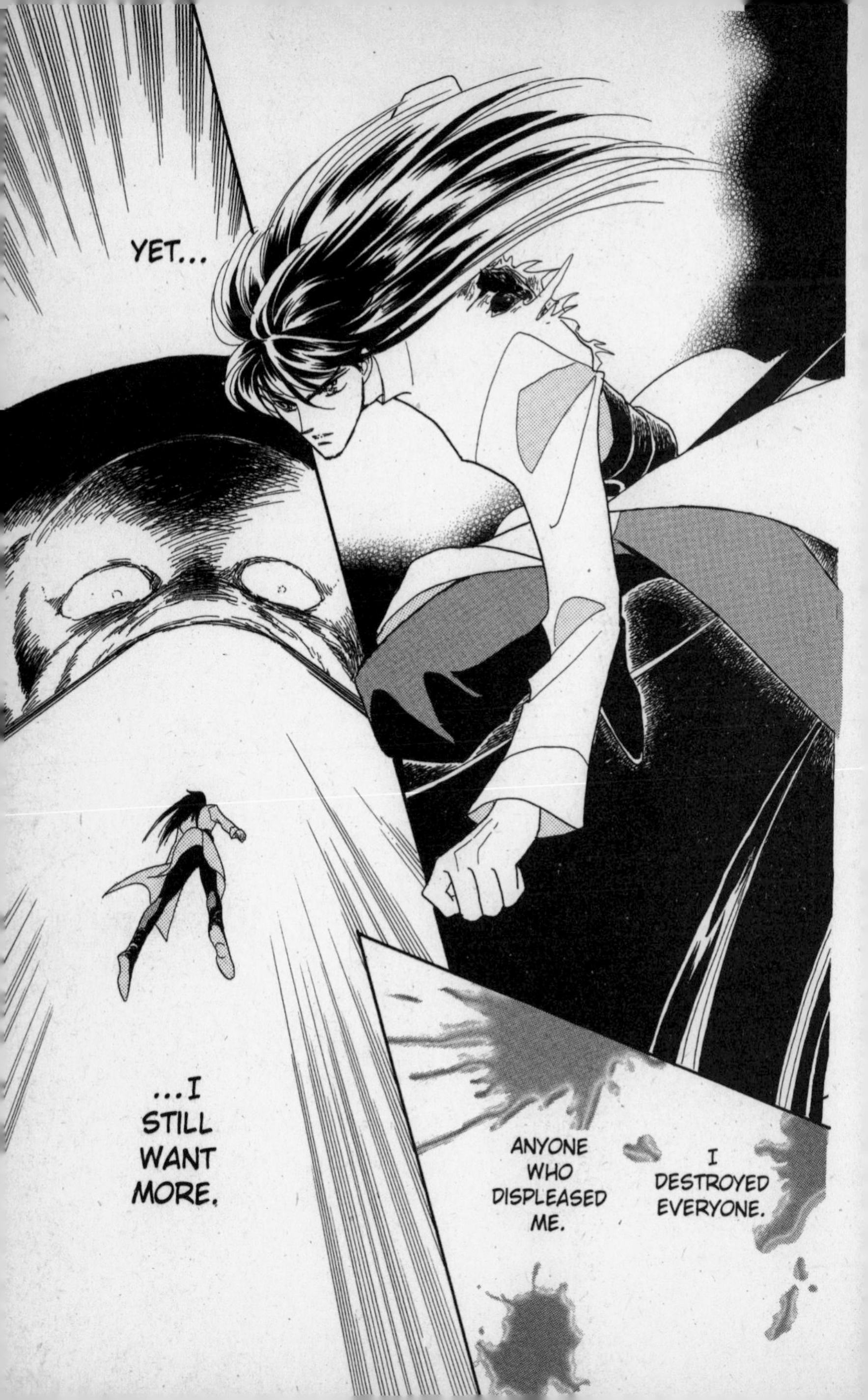
I DESTROYED EVERYONE.
ANYONE WHO DISPLEASED ME.
YET...
...I STILL WANT MORE.

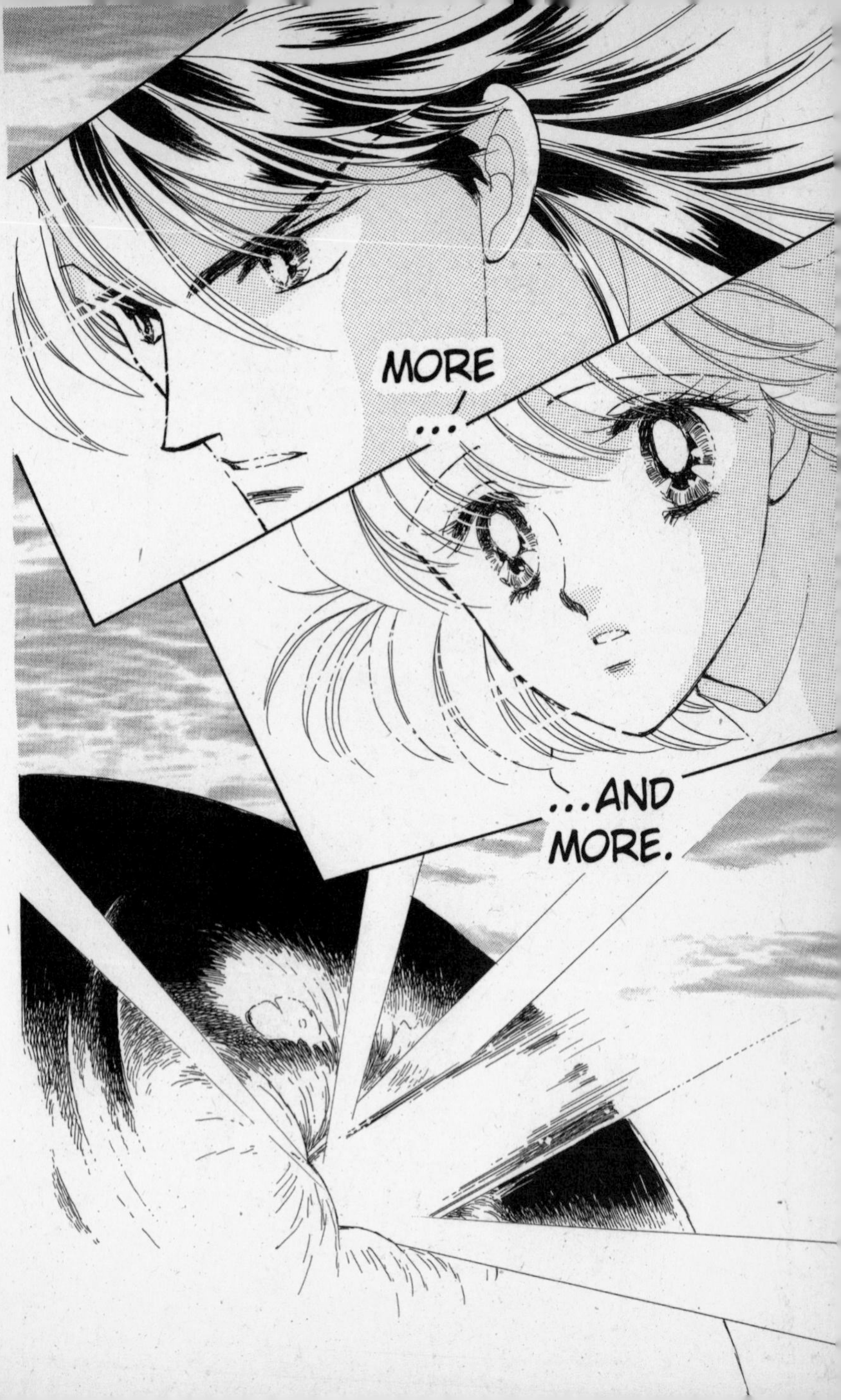
MORE ...
...AND MORE.

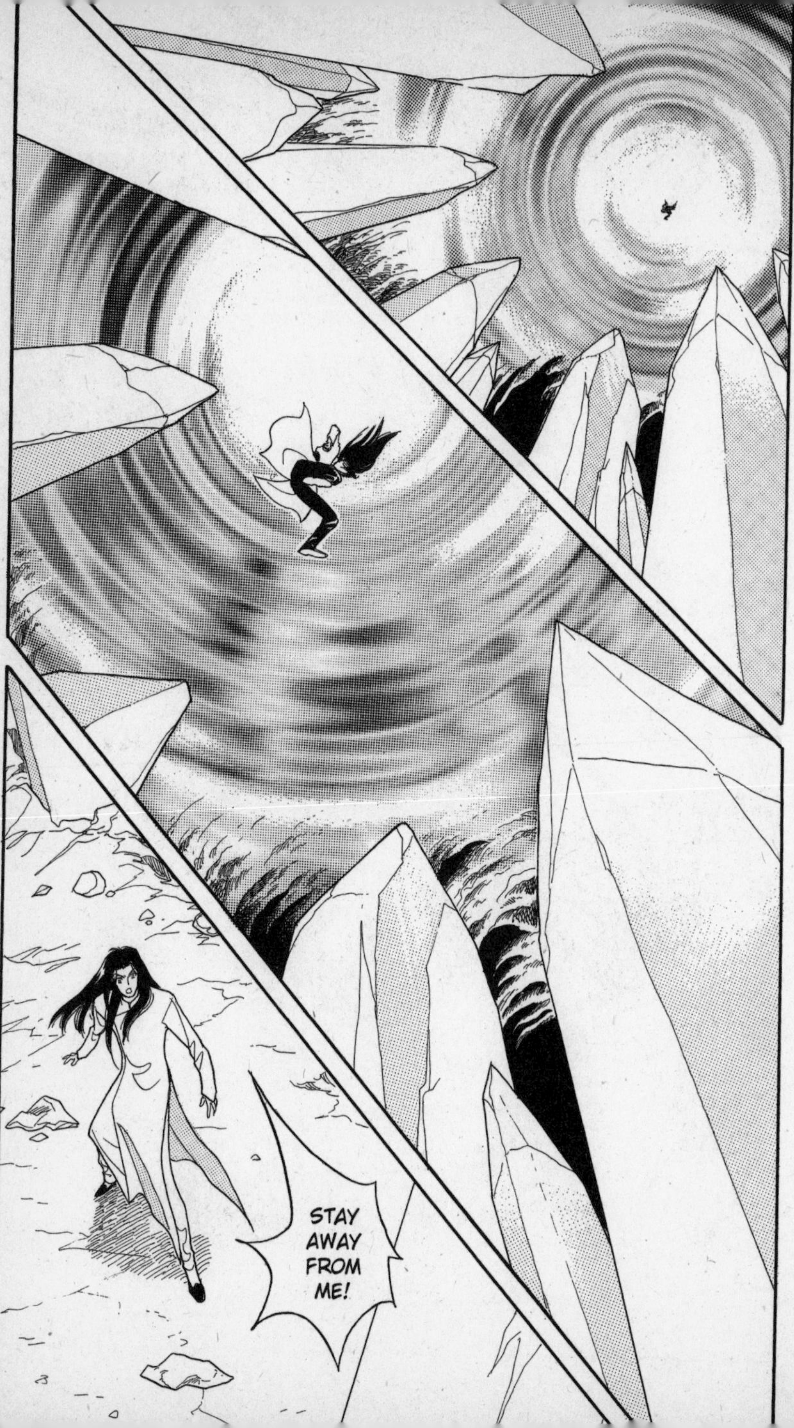
STAY AWAY FROM ME!

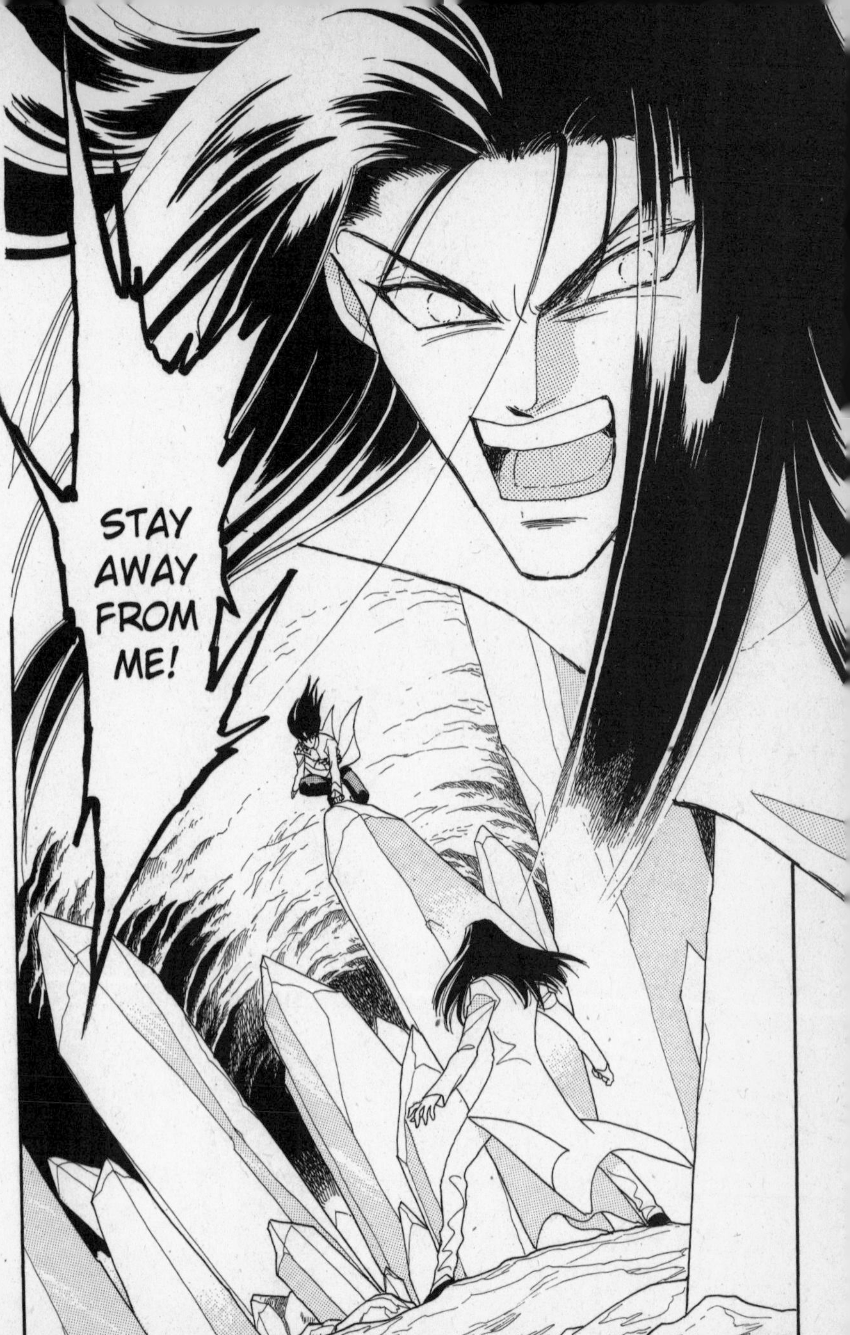
STAY AWAY FROM ME!

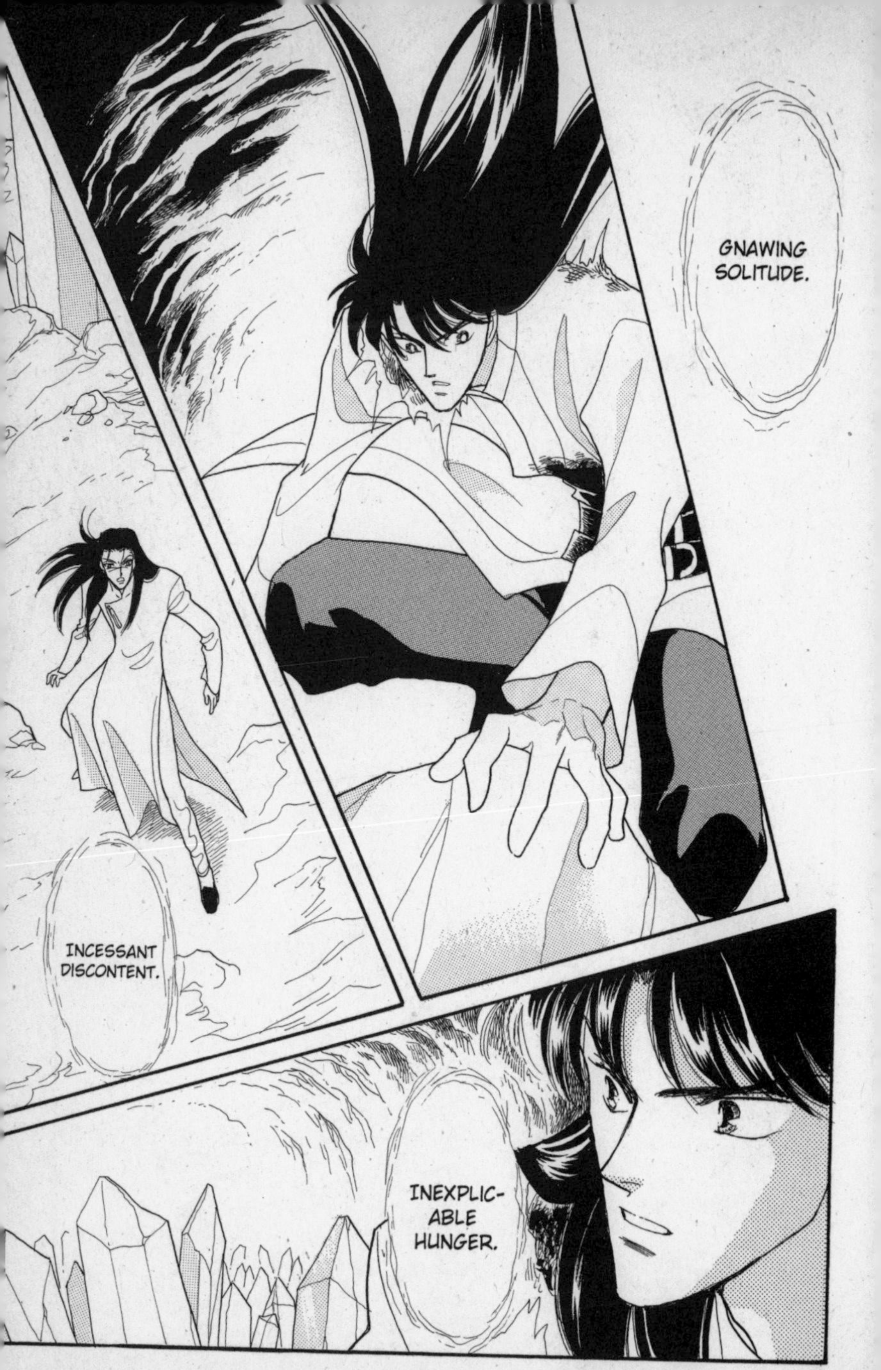
GNAWING SOLITUDE.
INCESSANT DISCONTENT.
INEXPLIC-ABLE HUNGER.

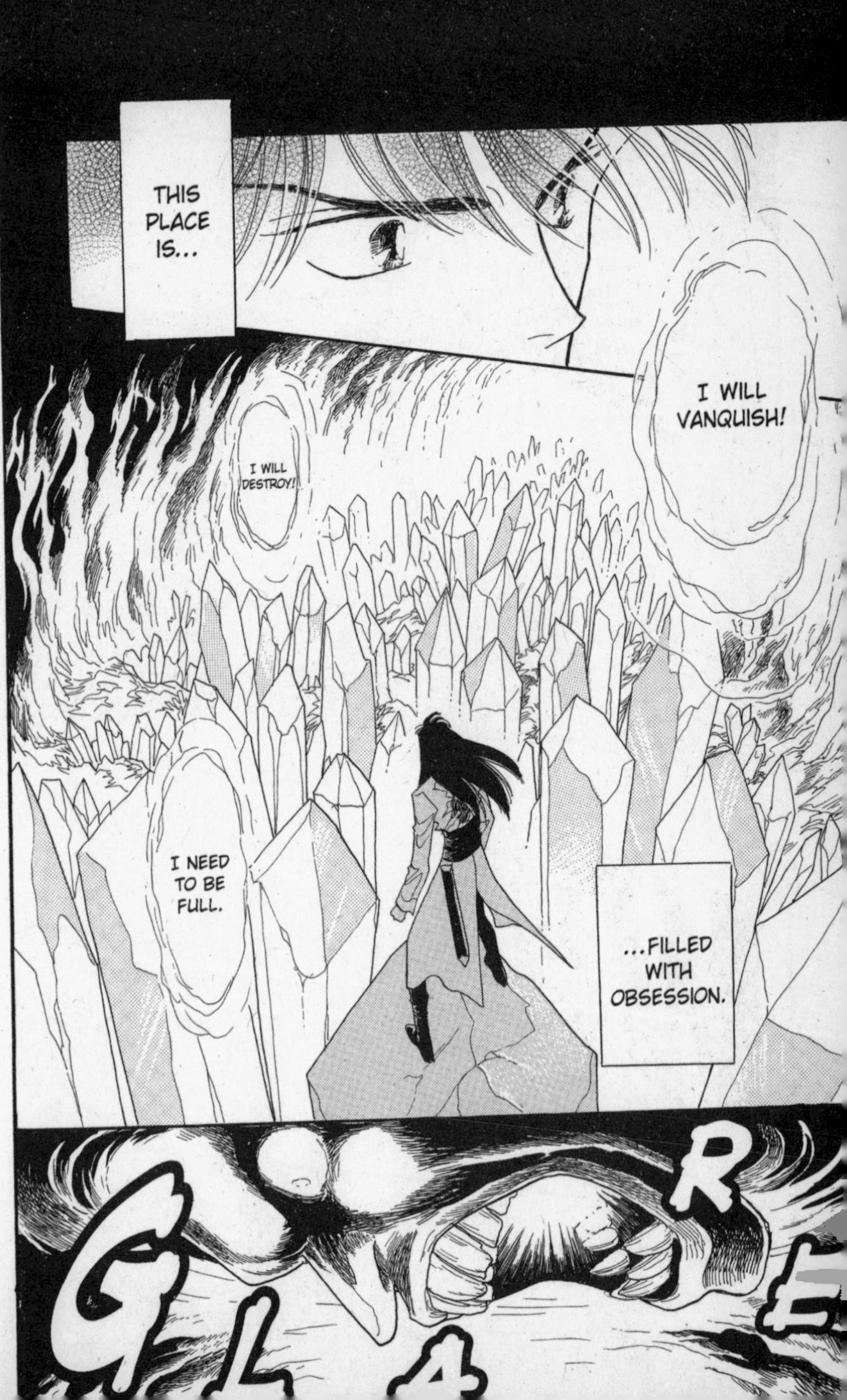
THIS PLACE IS...
I WILL VANQUISH!
I WILL DESTROY!
I NEED TO BE FULL.
...FILLED WITH OBSESSION.
GLARE

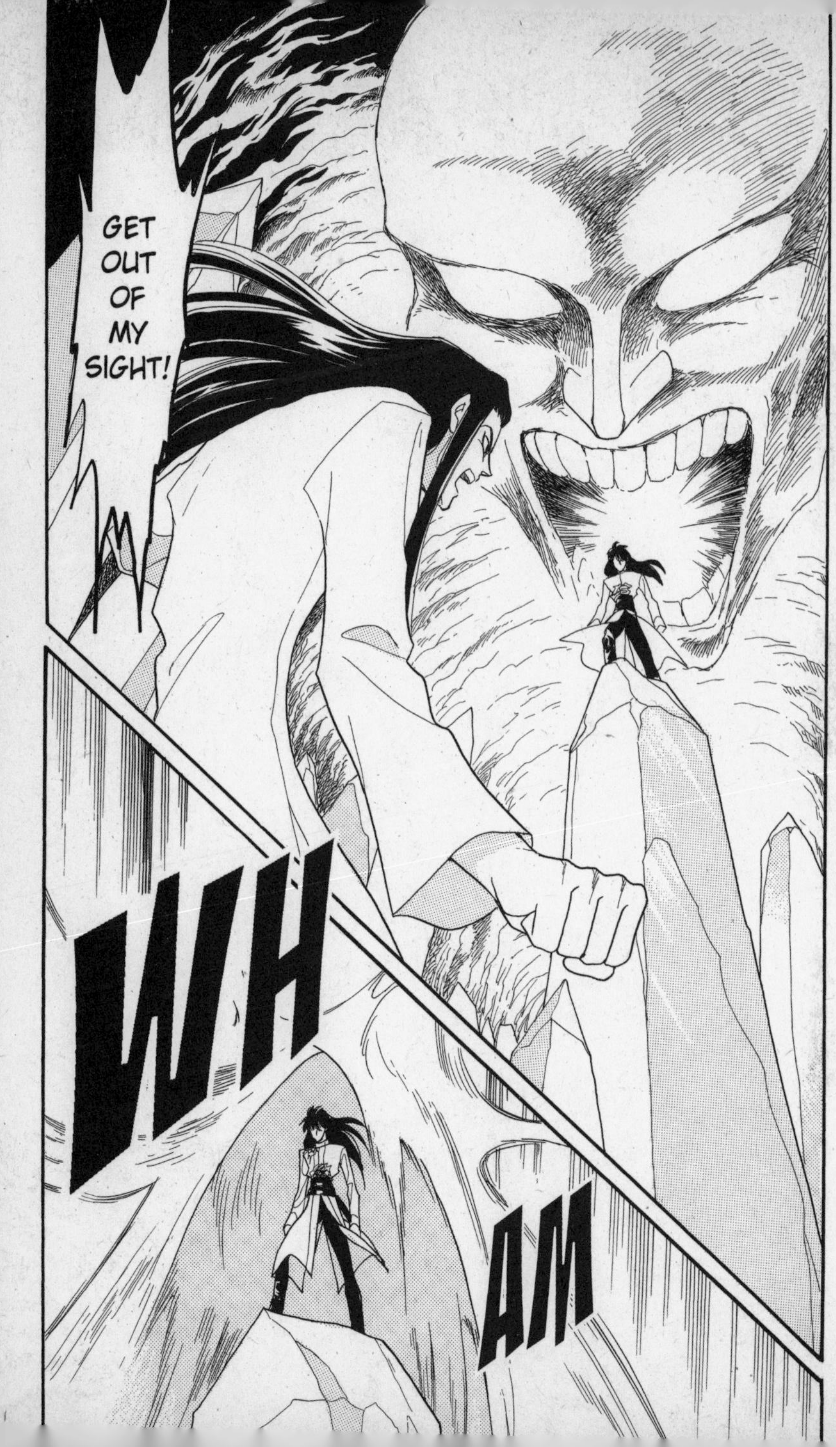
GET OUT OF MY SIGHT!
WH
AM

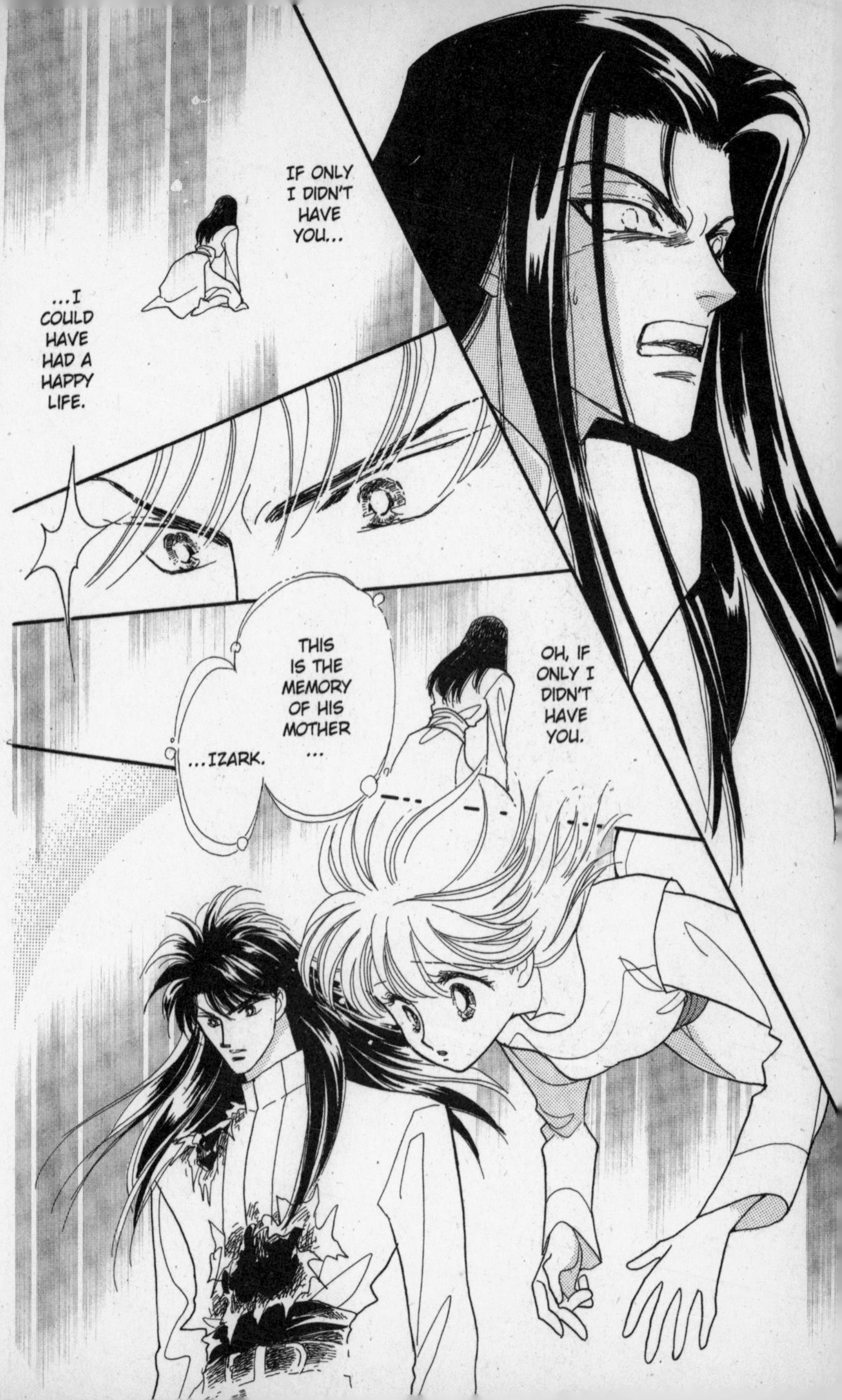
IF ONLY I DIDN'T HAVE YOU...
...I COULD HAVE HAD A HAPPY LIFE.
OH, IF ONLY I DIDN'T HAVE YOU.
THIS IS THE MEMORY OF HIS MOTHER ...
...IZARK.

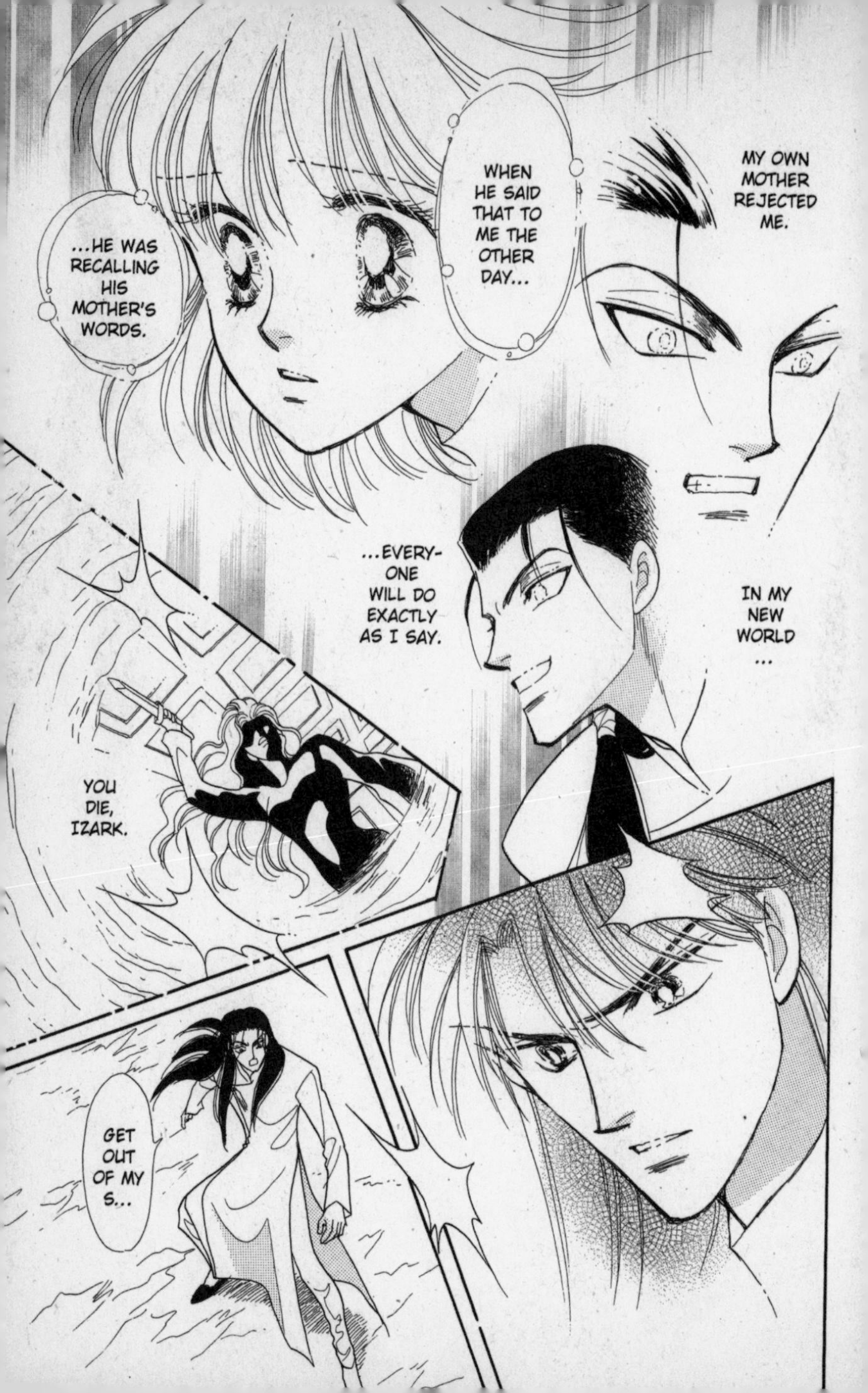
MY OWN MOTHER REJECTED ME.
WHEN HE SAID THAT TO ME THE OTHER DAY...
...HE WAS RECALLING HIS MOTHER'S WORDS.
IN MY NEW WORLD ...
...EVERY-ONE WILL DO EXACTLY AS I SAY.
YOU DIE, IZARK.
GET OUT OF MY S...

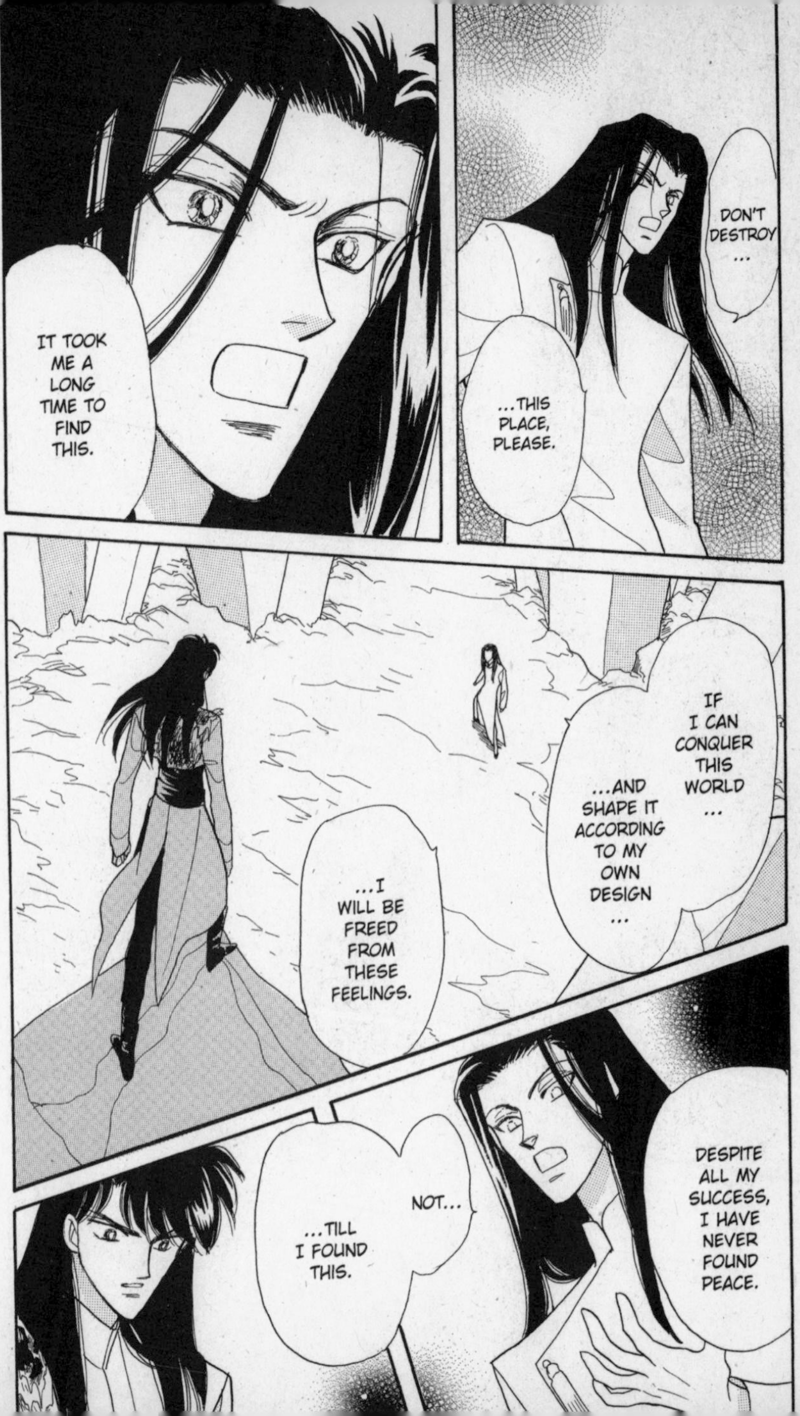
DON'T DESTROY ...
...THIS PLACE, PLEASE.
IT TOOK ME A LONG TIME TO FIND THIS.
IF I CAN CONQUER THIS WORLD ...
...AND SHAPE IT ACCORDING TO MY OWN DESIGN ...
...I WILL BE FREED FROM THESE FEELINGS.
DESPITE ALL MY SUCCESS, I HAVE NEVER FOUND PEACE.
NOT...
...TILL I FOUND THIS.

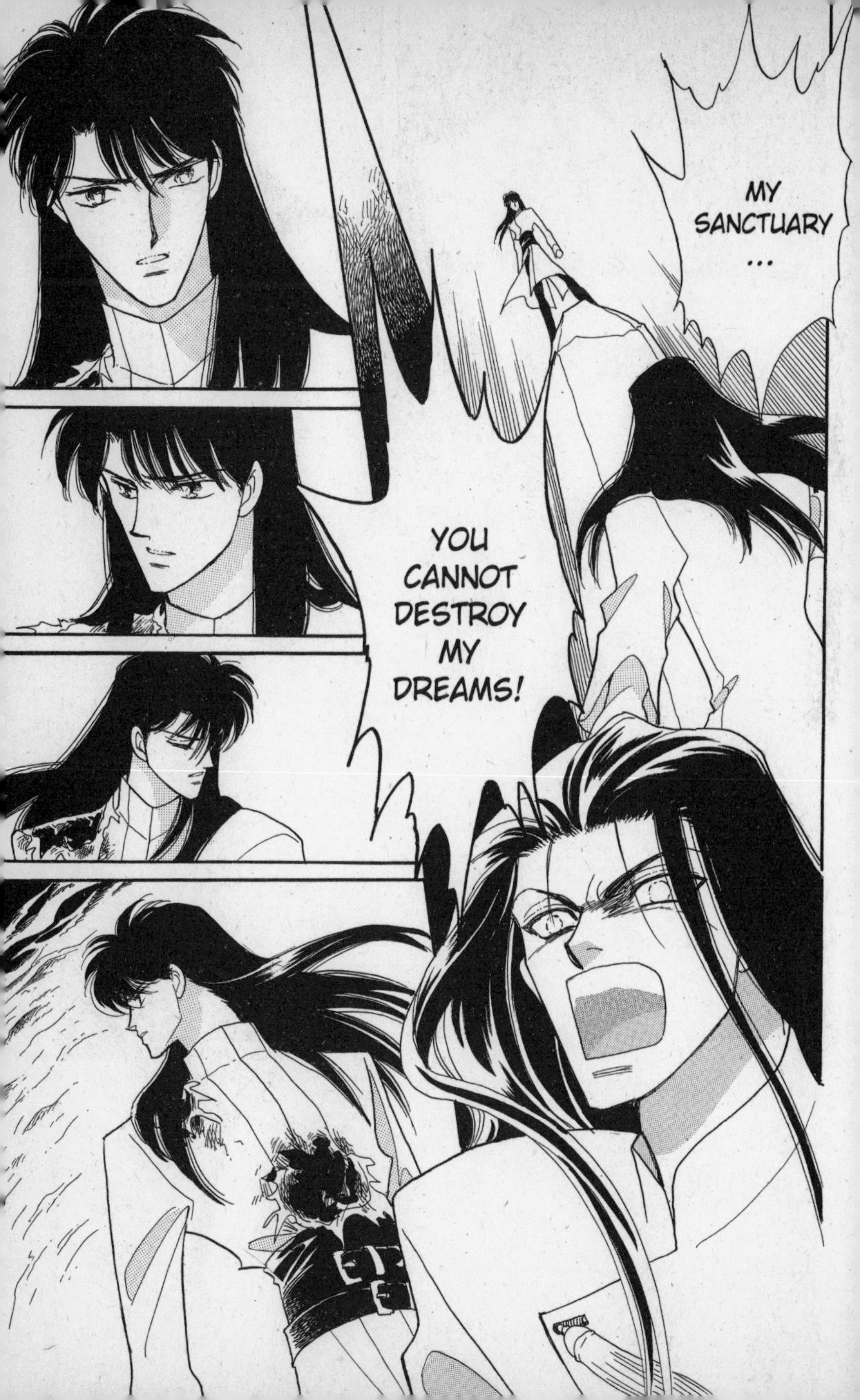
MY SANCTUARY ...
YOU CANNOT DESTROY MY DREAMS!

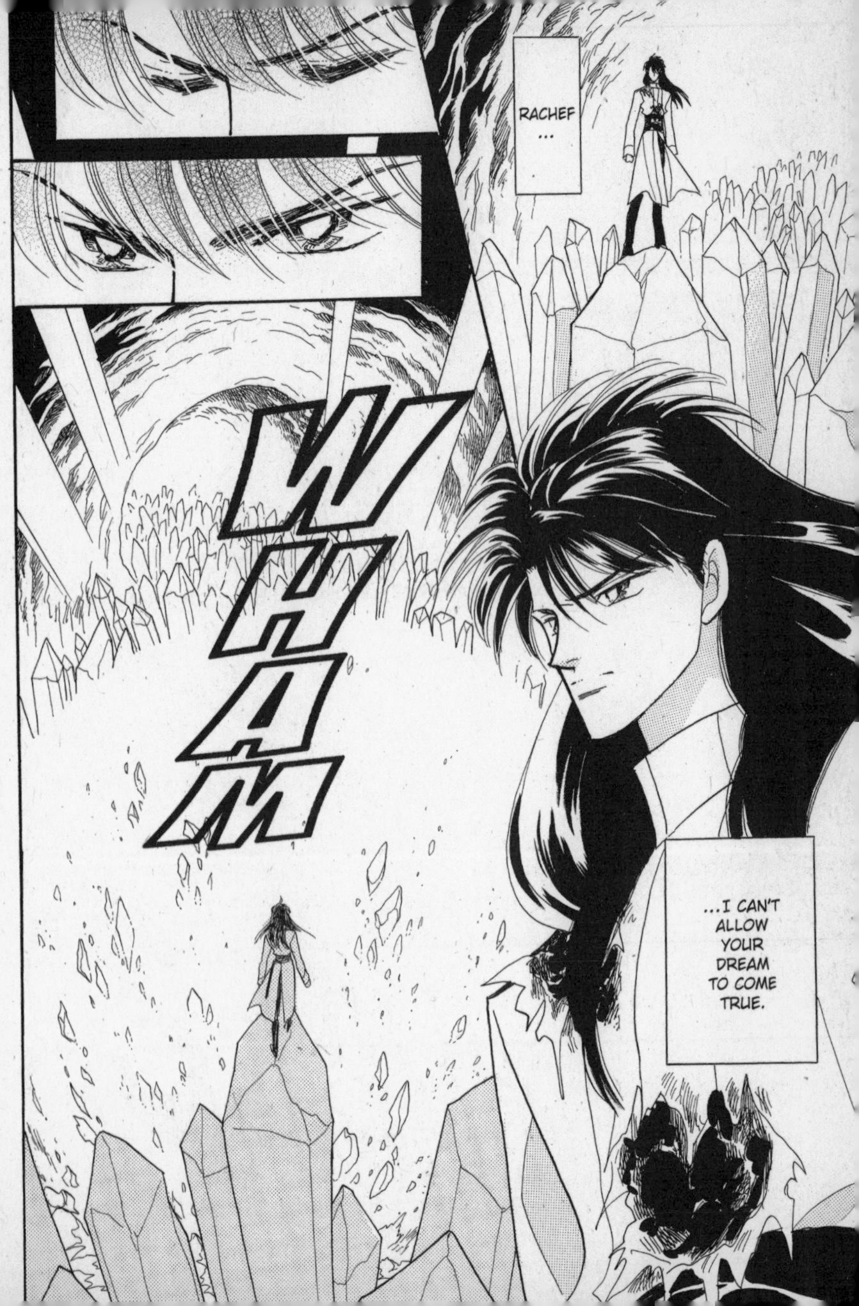
RACHEF...
WHAM
...I CAN'T ALLOW YOUR DREAM TO COME TRUE.

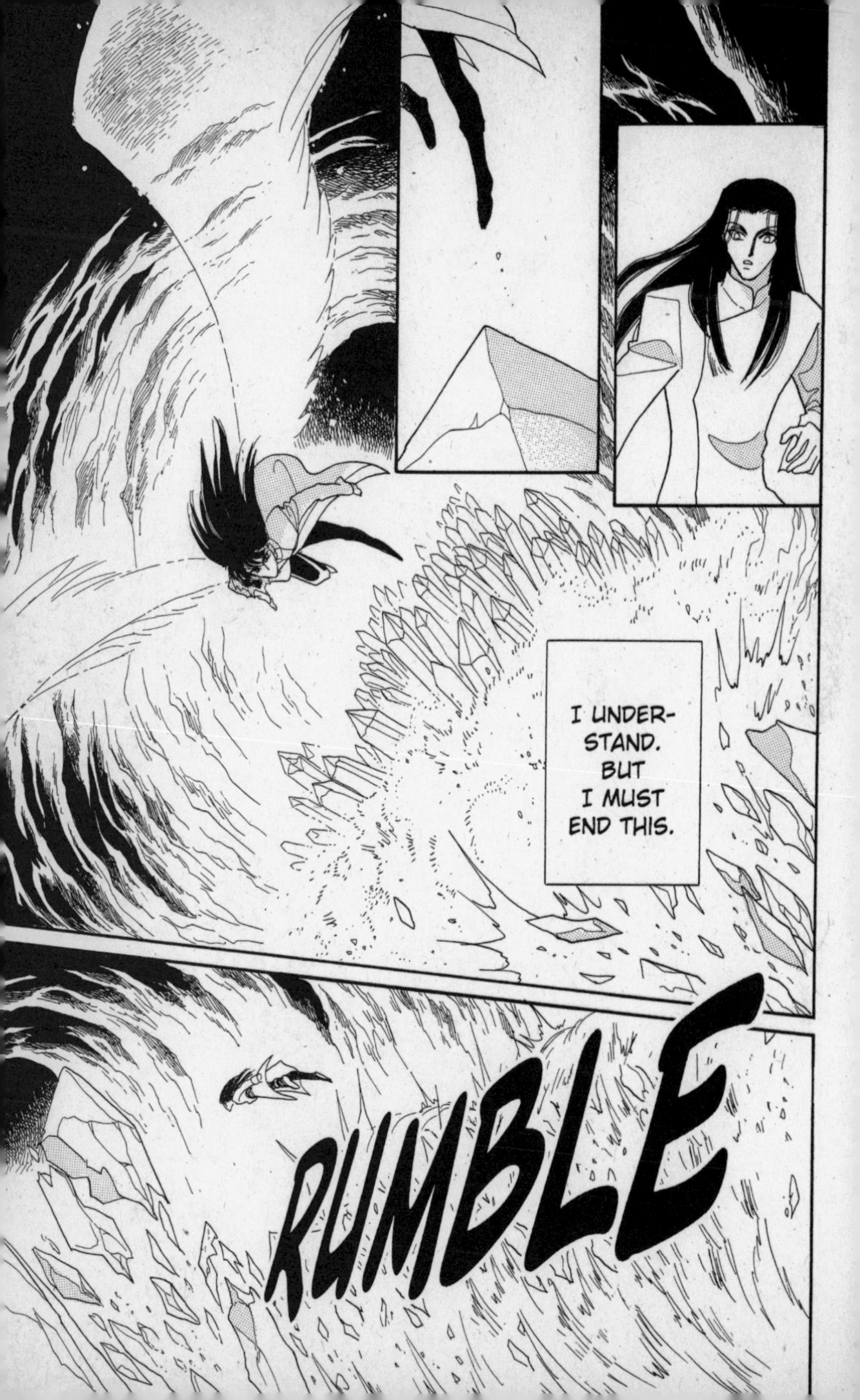
I UNDER-STAND. BUT I MUST END THIS.
RUMBLE

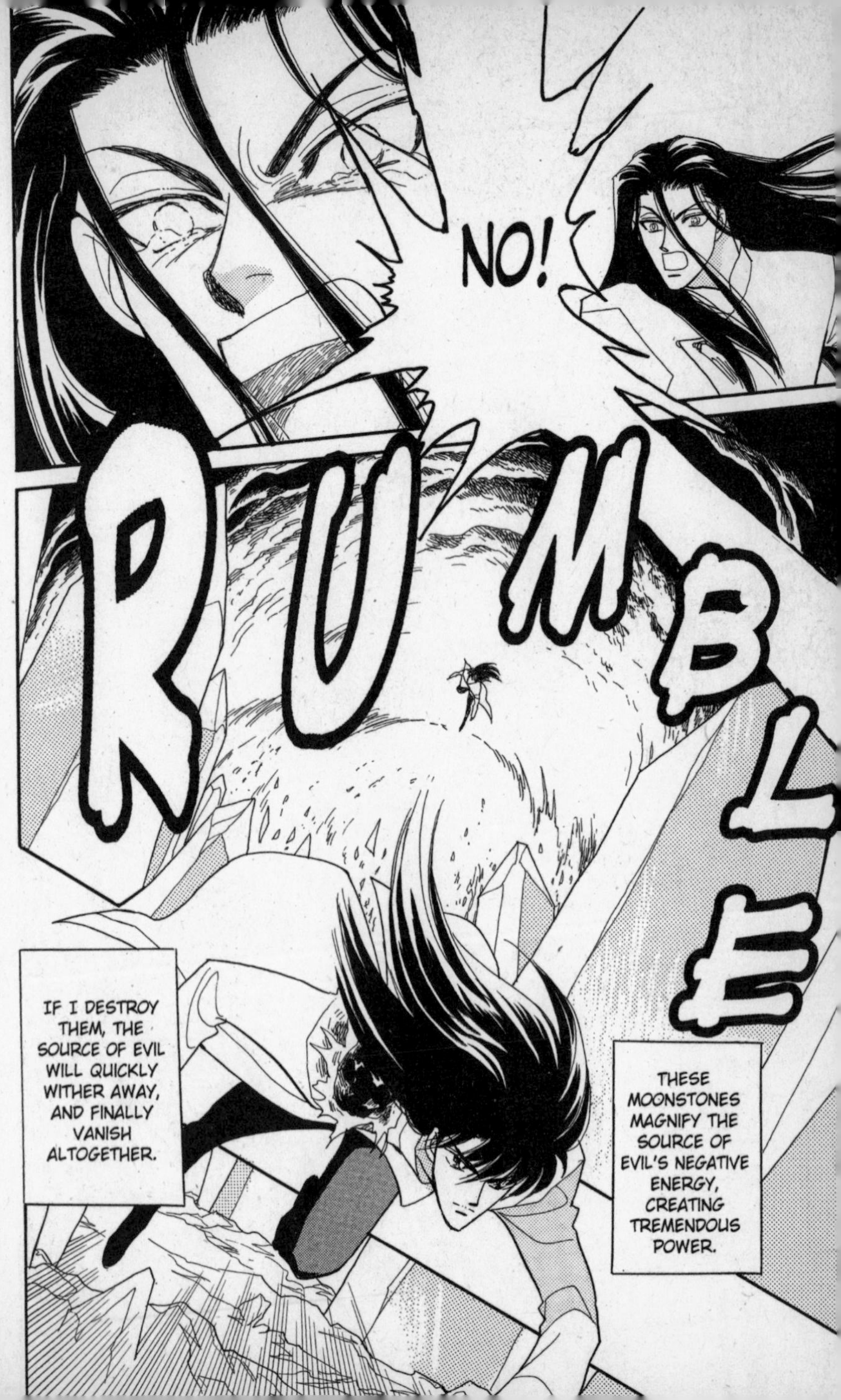
NO!
RUMBLE
THESE MOONSTONES MAGNIFY THE SOURCE OF EVIL'S NEGATIVE ENERGY, CREATING TREMENDOUS POWER.
IF I DESTROY THEM, THE SOURCE OF EVIL WILL QUICKLY WITHER AWAY, AND FINALLY VANISH ALTOGETHER.

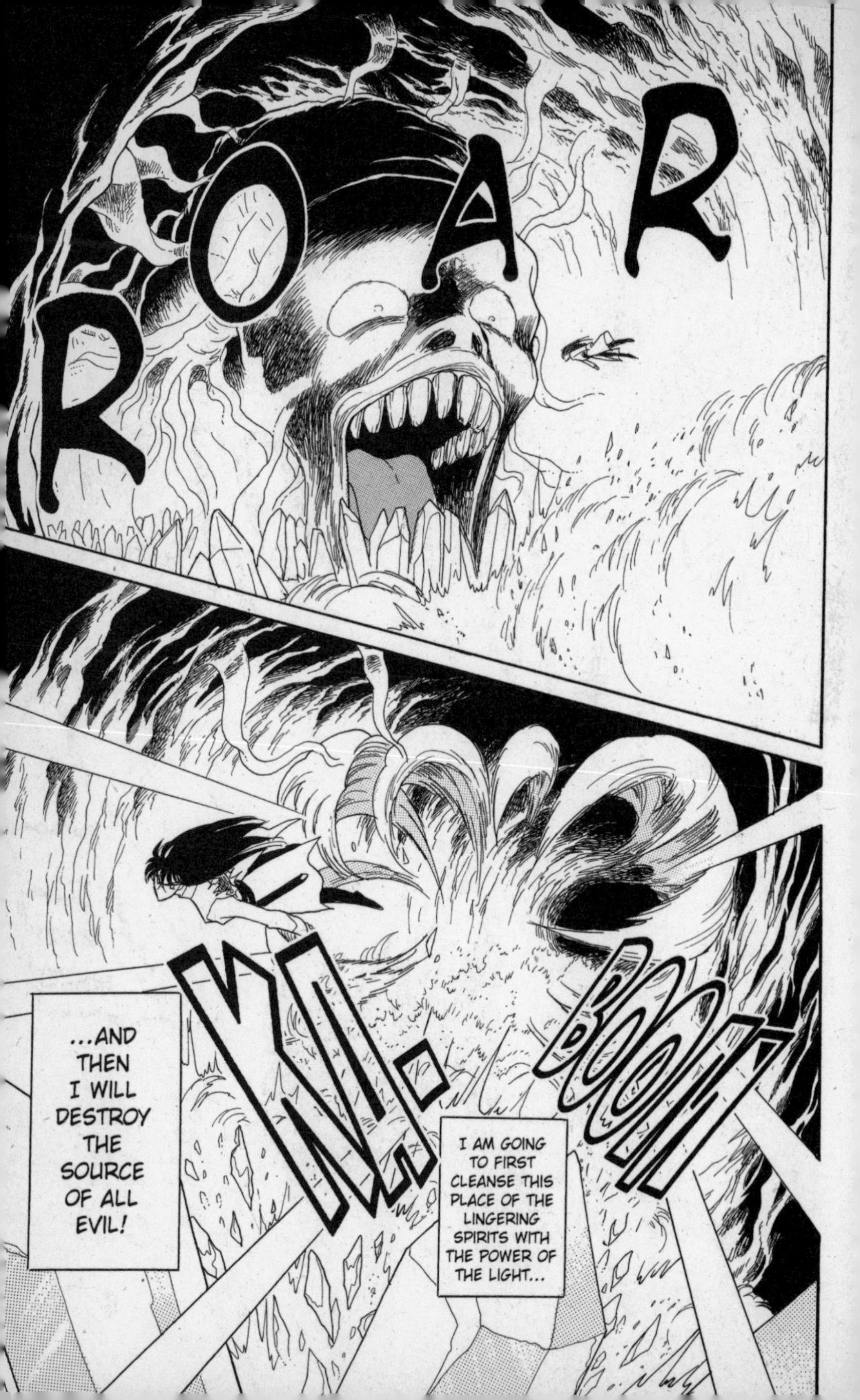
ROAR
BOOM
I AM GOING TO FIRST CLEANSE THIS PLACE OF THE LINGERING SPIRITS WITH THE POWER OF THE LIGHT...
...AND THEN I WILL DESTROY THE SOURCE OF ALL EVIL!

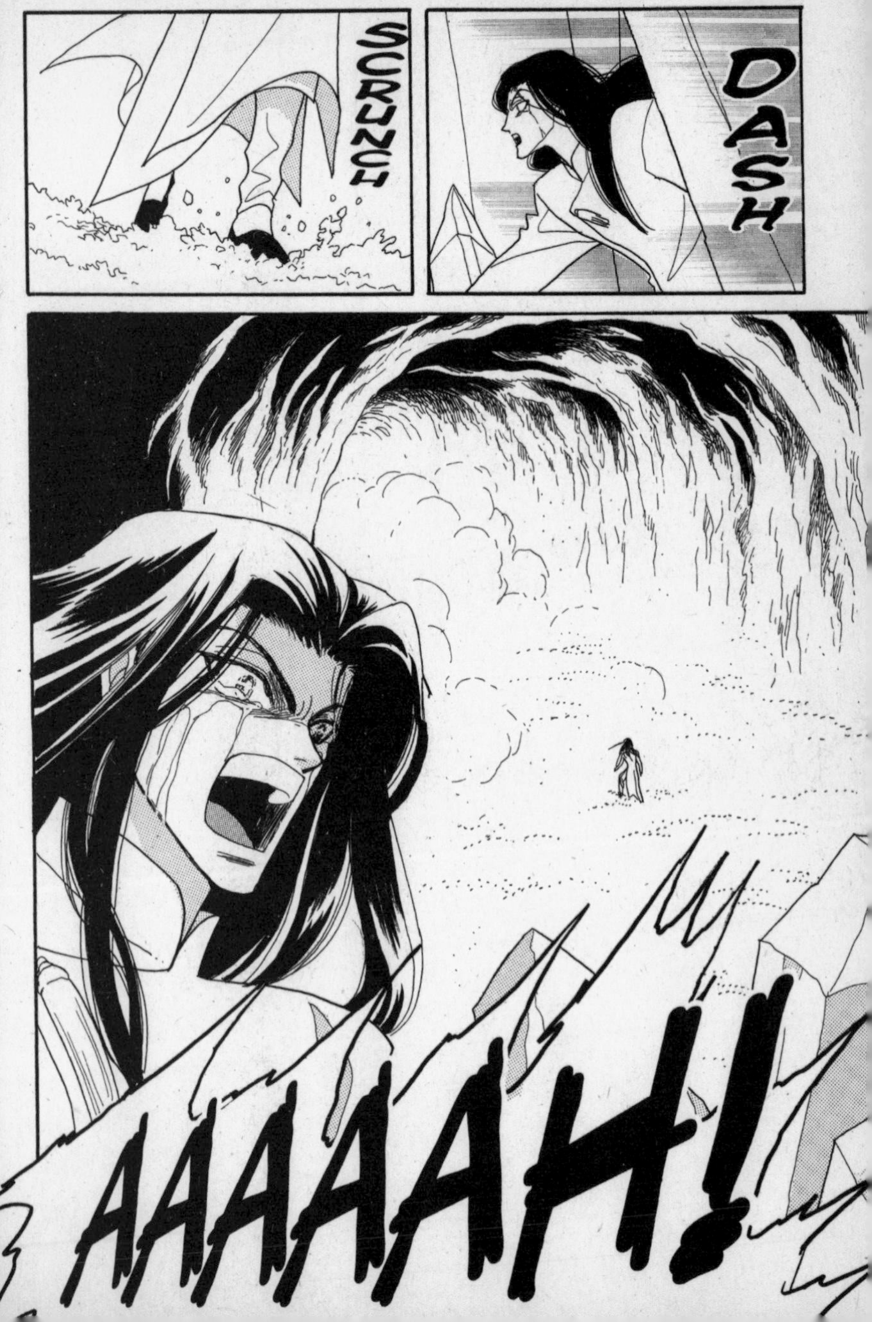
DASH
SCRUNCH
AAAAAH!!

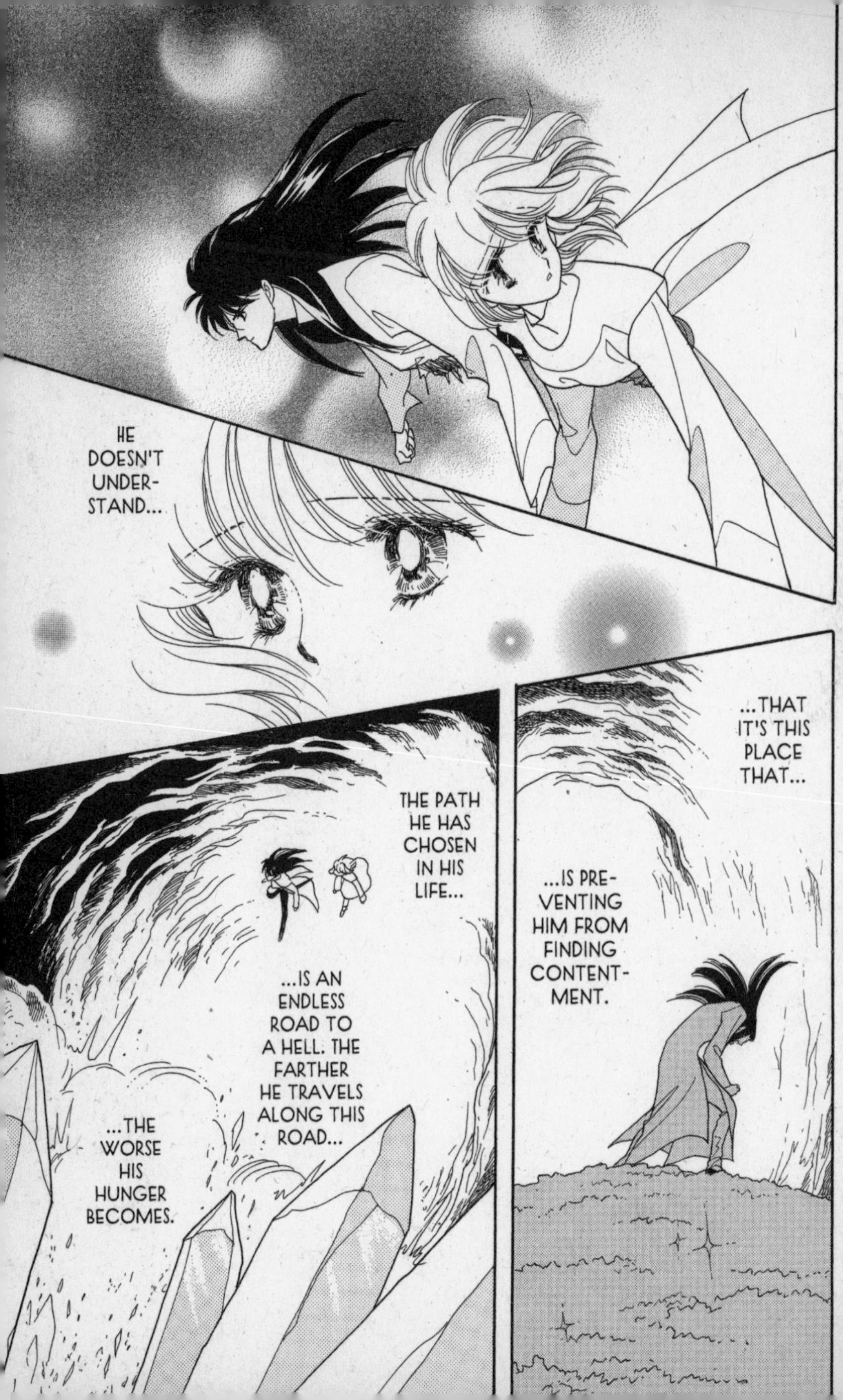
HE DOESN'T UNDERSTAND...
...THAT IT'S THIS PLACE THAT...
...IS PREVENTING HIM FROM FINDING CONTENTMENT.
THE PATH HE HAS CHOSEN IN HIS LIFE...
...IS AN ENDLESS ROAD TO A HELL. THE FARTHER HE TRAVELS ALONG THIS ROAD...
...THE WORSE HIS HUNGER BECOMES.

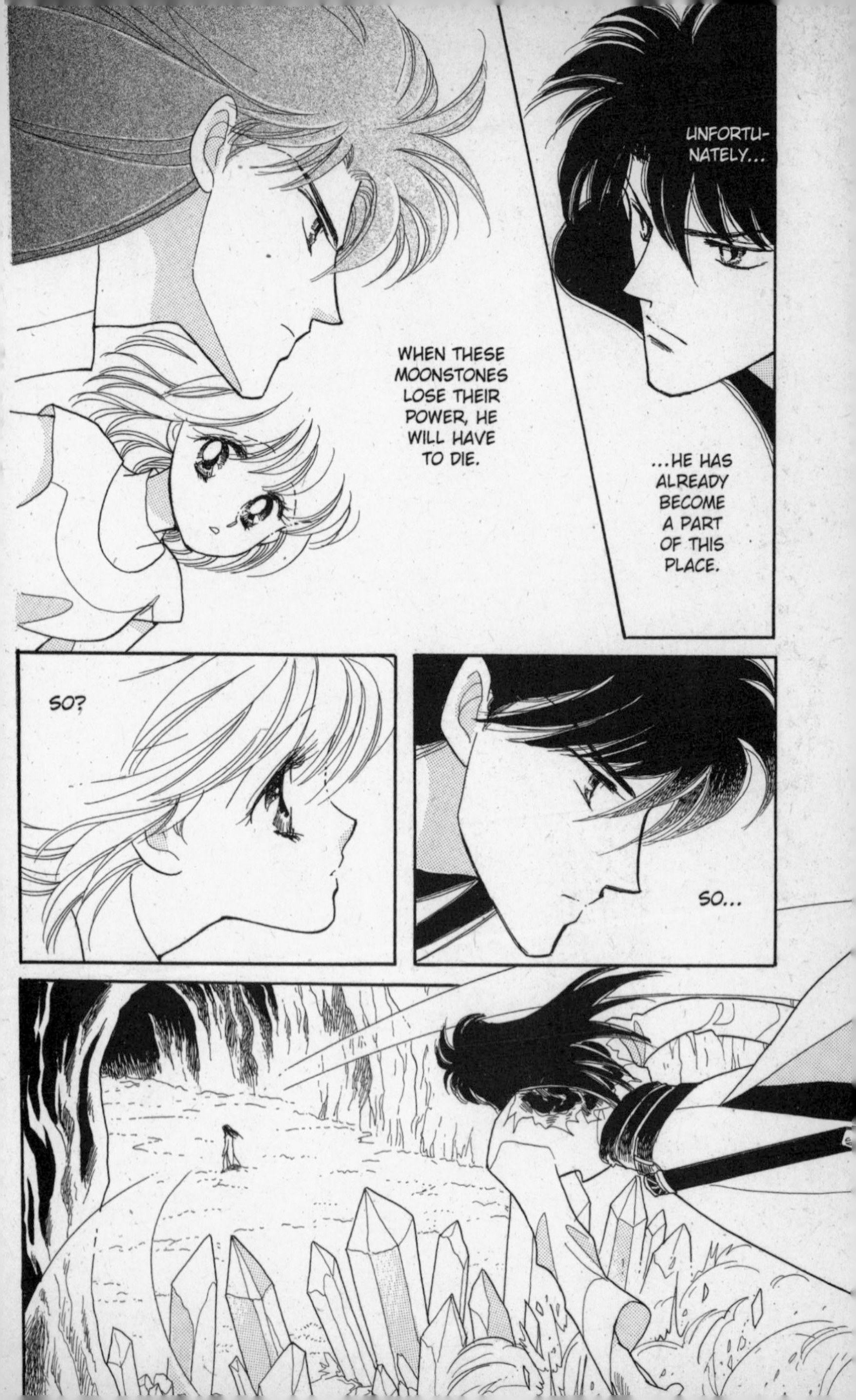
UNFORTU-
NATELY...
...HE HAS ALREADY BECOME A PART OF THIS PLACE.
WHEN THESE MOONSTONES LOSE THEIR POWER, HE WILL HAVE TO DIE.
SO...
SO?

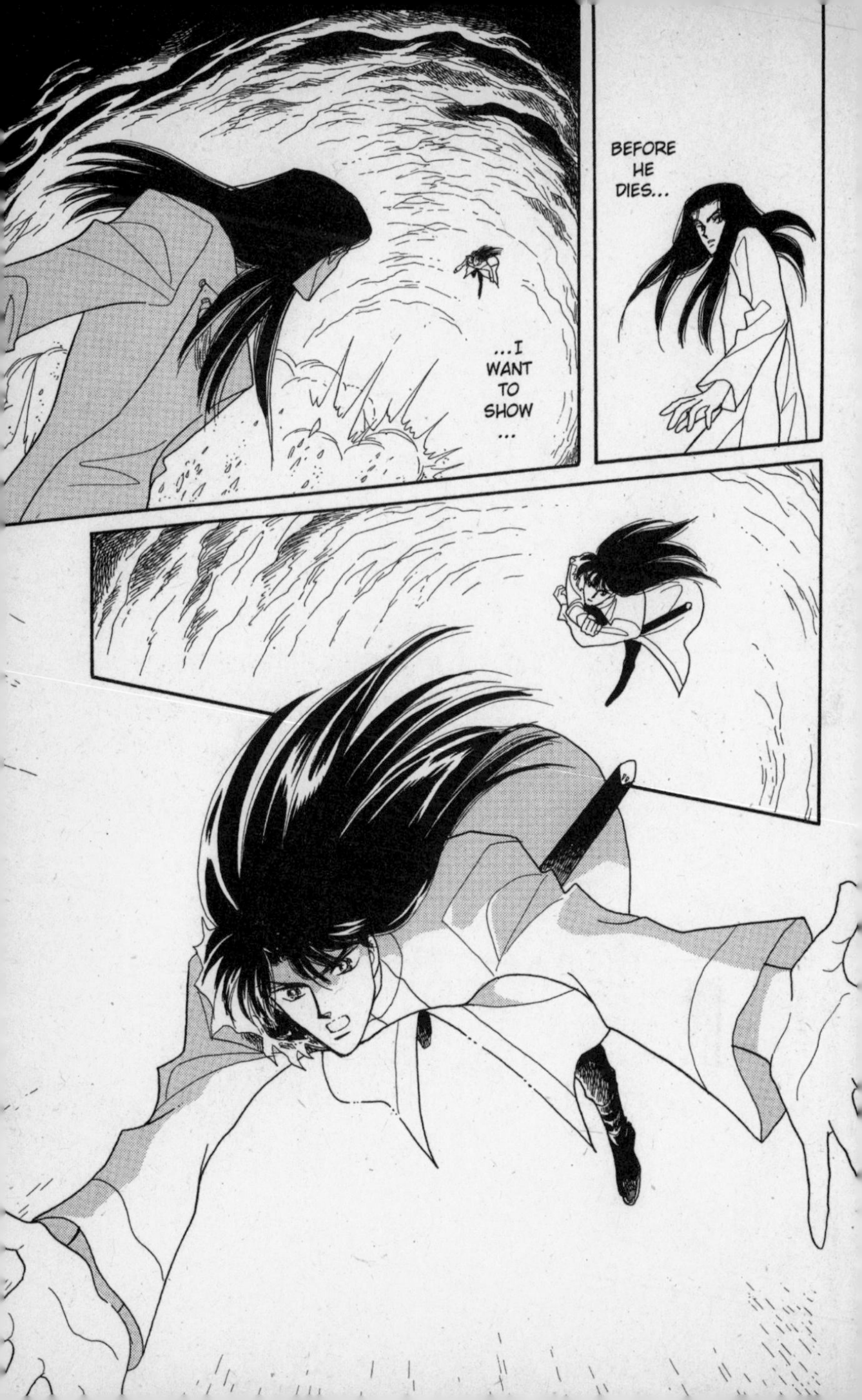
BEFORE HE DIES...
...I WANT TO SHOW ...

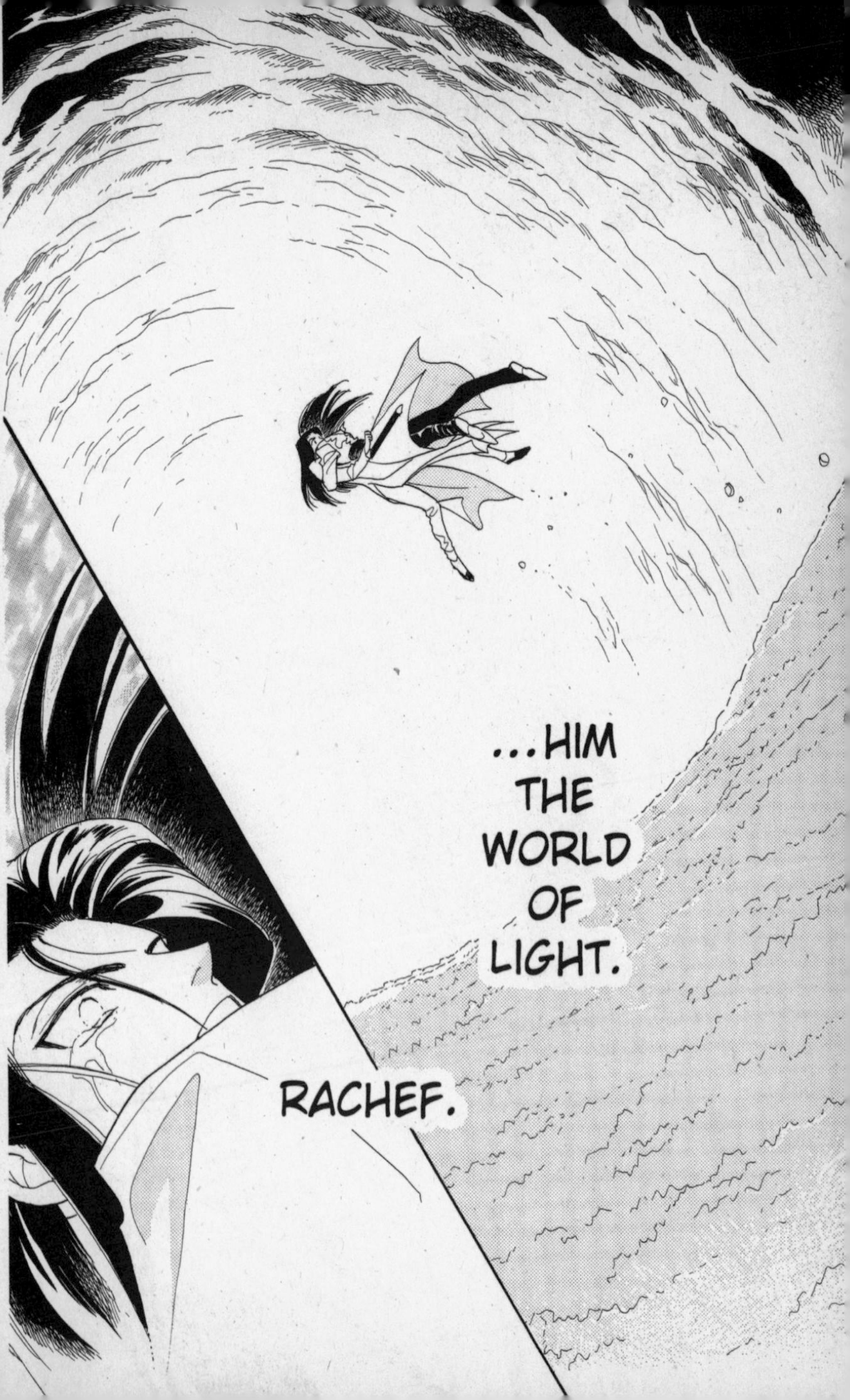
...HIM THE WORLD OF LIGHT.
RACHEF.

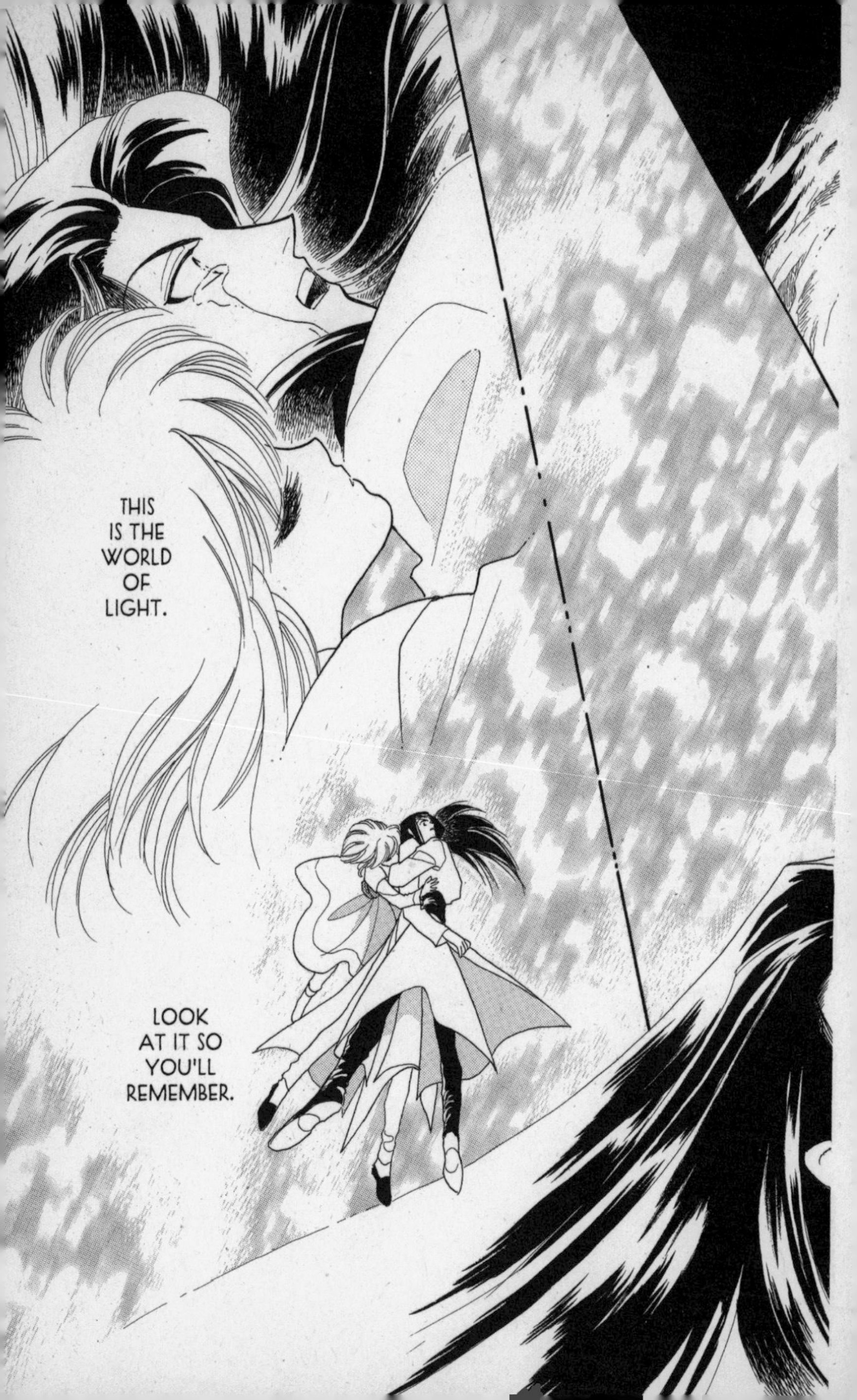
THIS IS THE WORLD OF LIGHT.
LOOK AT IT SO YOU'LL REMEMBER.

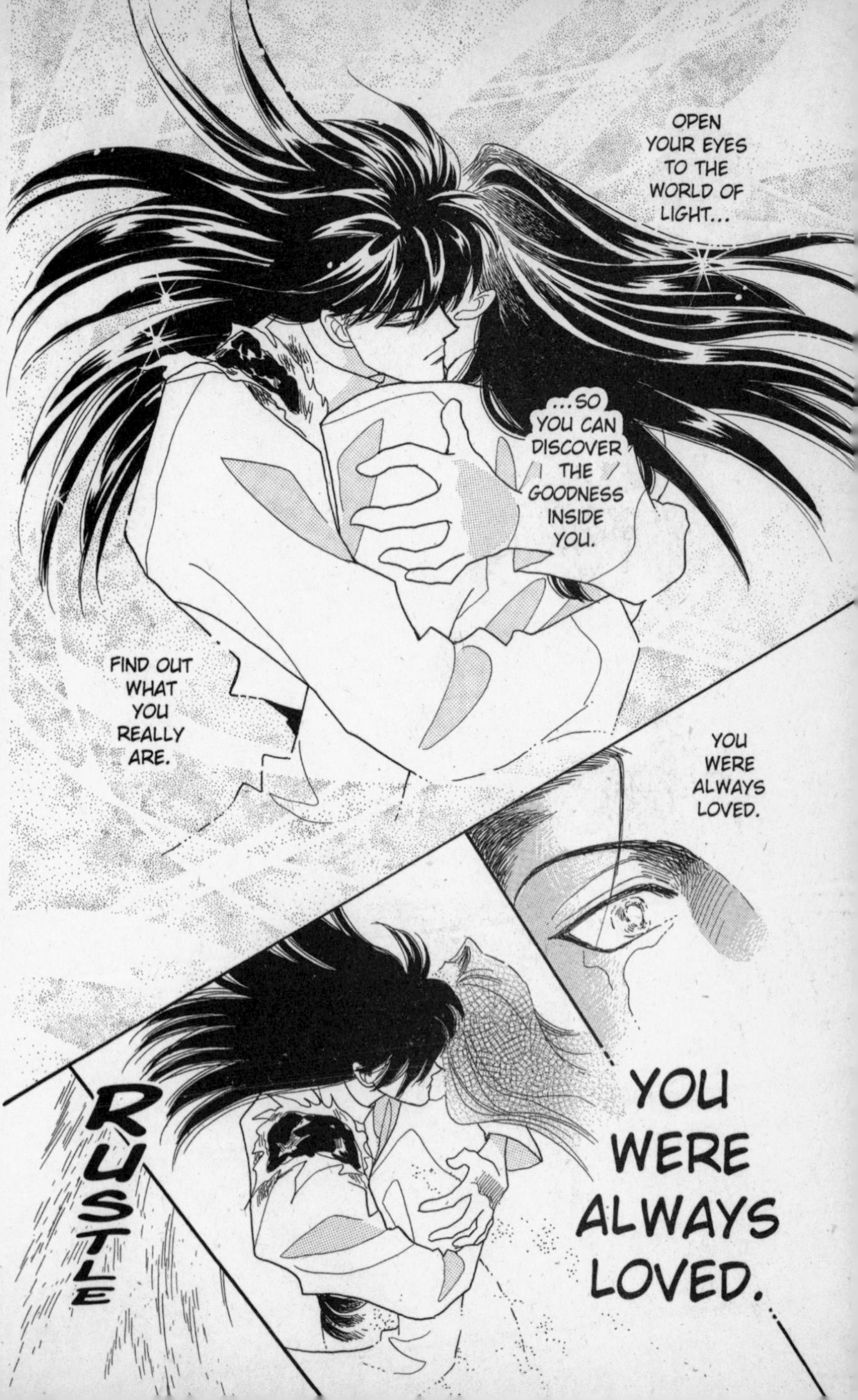
OPEN YOUR EYES TO THE WORLD OF LIGHT...
...SO YOU CAN DISCOVER THE GOODNESS INSIDE YOU.
FIND OUT WHAT YOU REALLY ARE.
YOU WERE ALWAYS LOVED.
YOU WERE ALWAYS LOVED.
RUSTLE

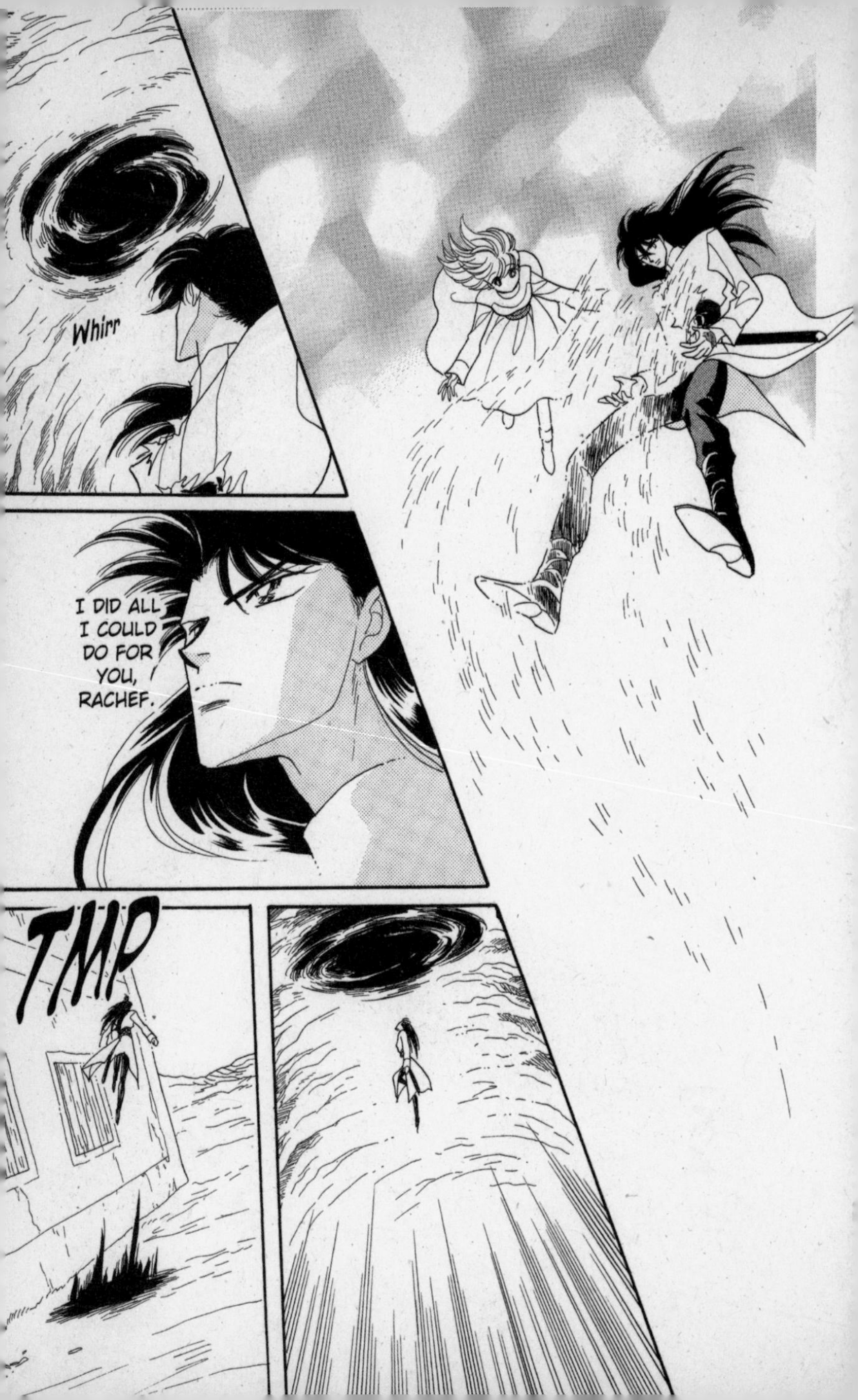
Whirr
I DID ALL I COULD DO FOR YOU, RACHEF.
TMP

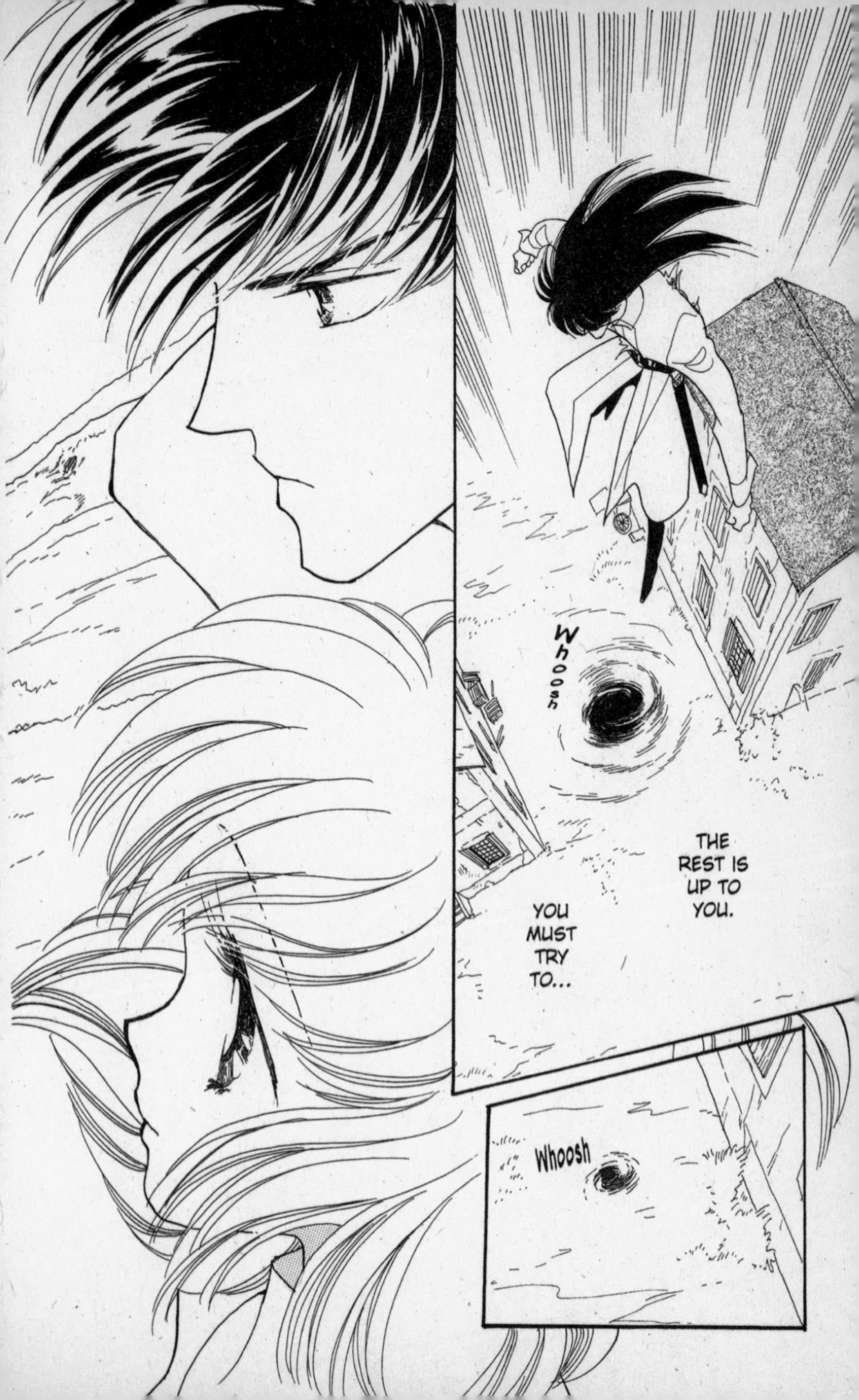
Whoosh
THE REST IS UP TO YOU.
YOU MUST TRY TO...
Whoosh

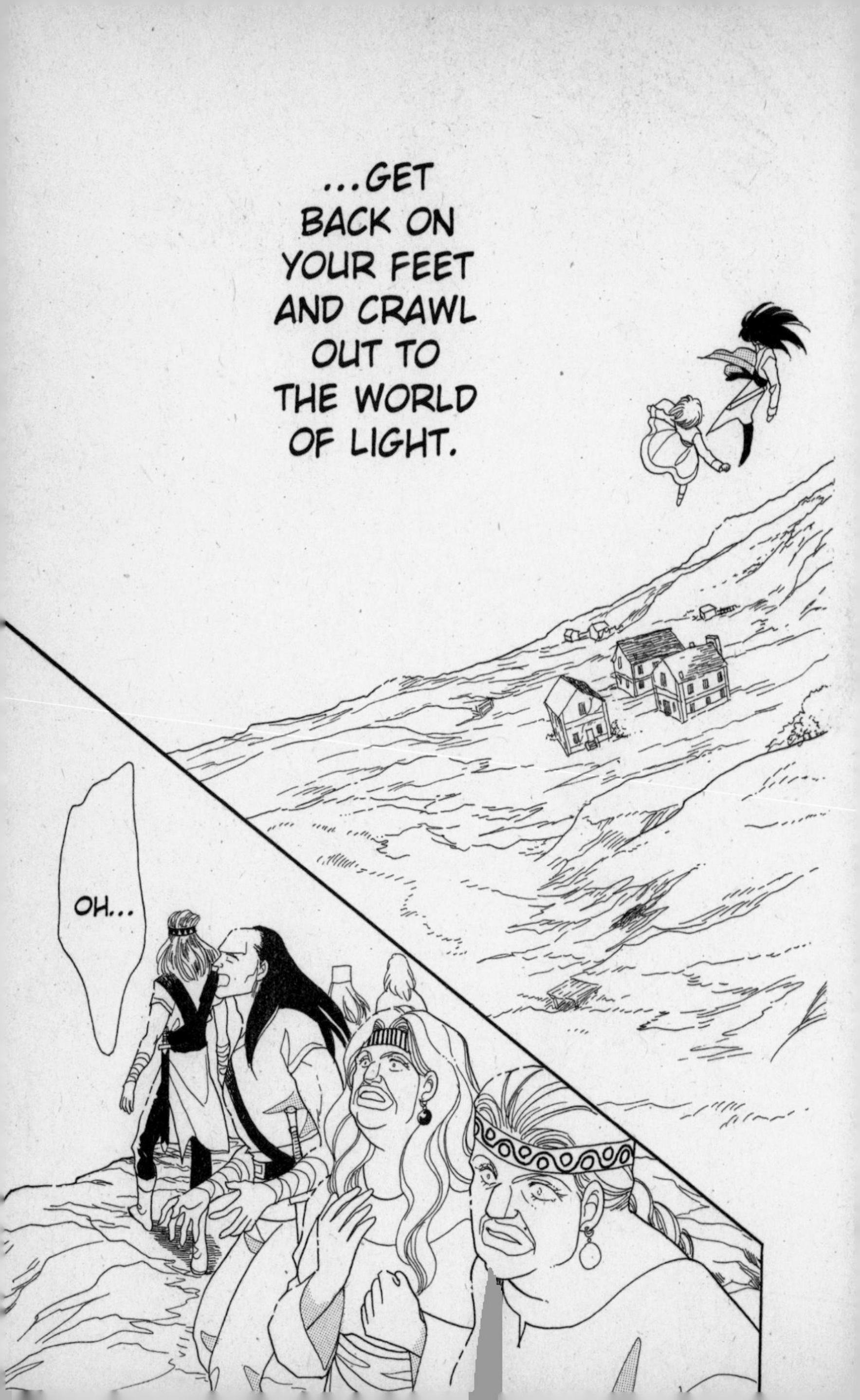
...GET BACK ON YOUR FEET AND CRAWL OUT TO THE WORLD OF LIGHT.
OH...

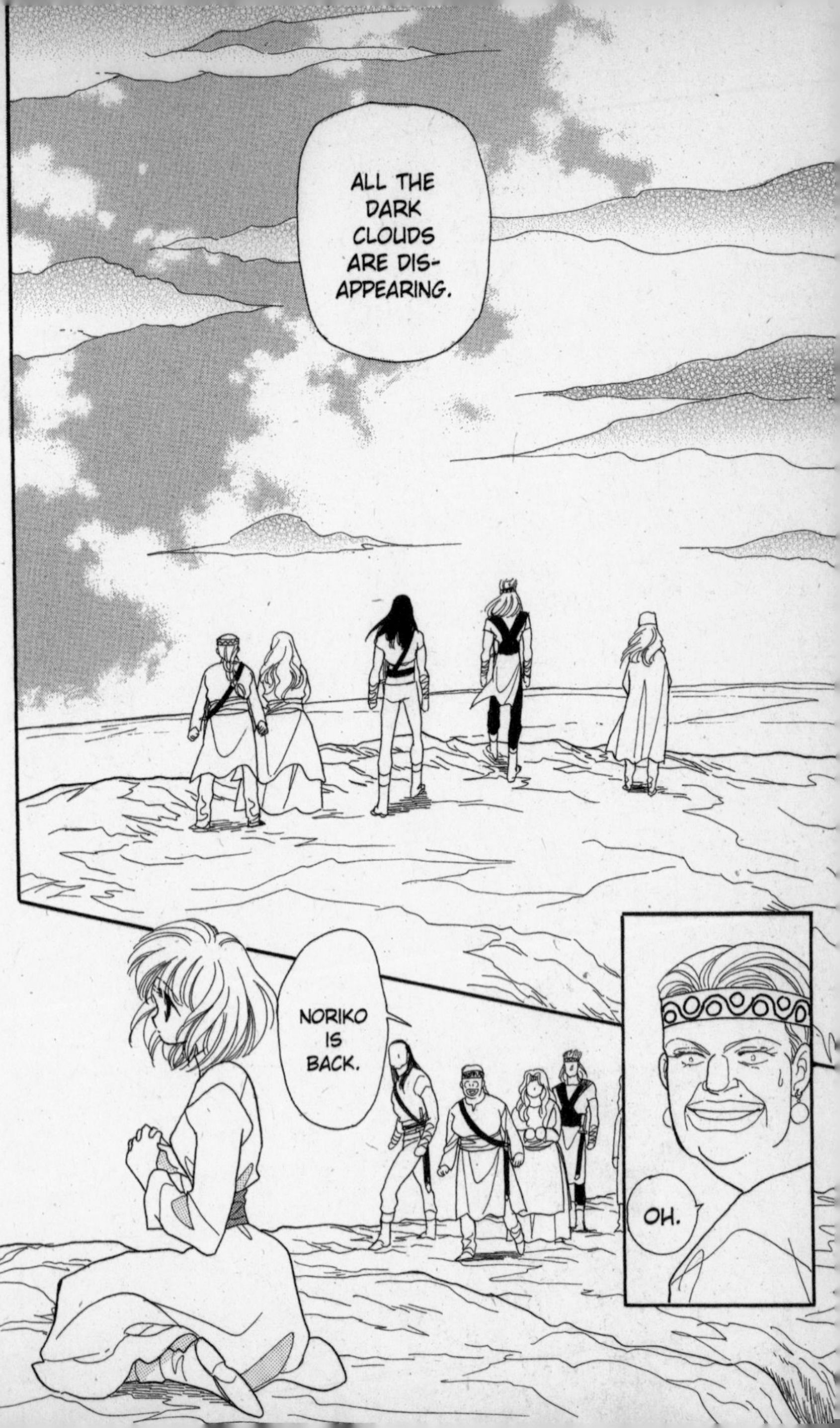
ALL THE DARK CLOUDS ARE DIS-APPEARING.
OH.
NORIKO IS BACK.

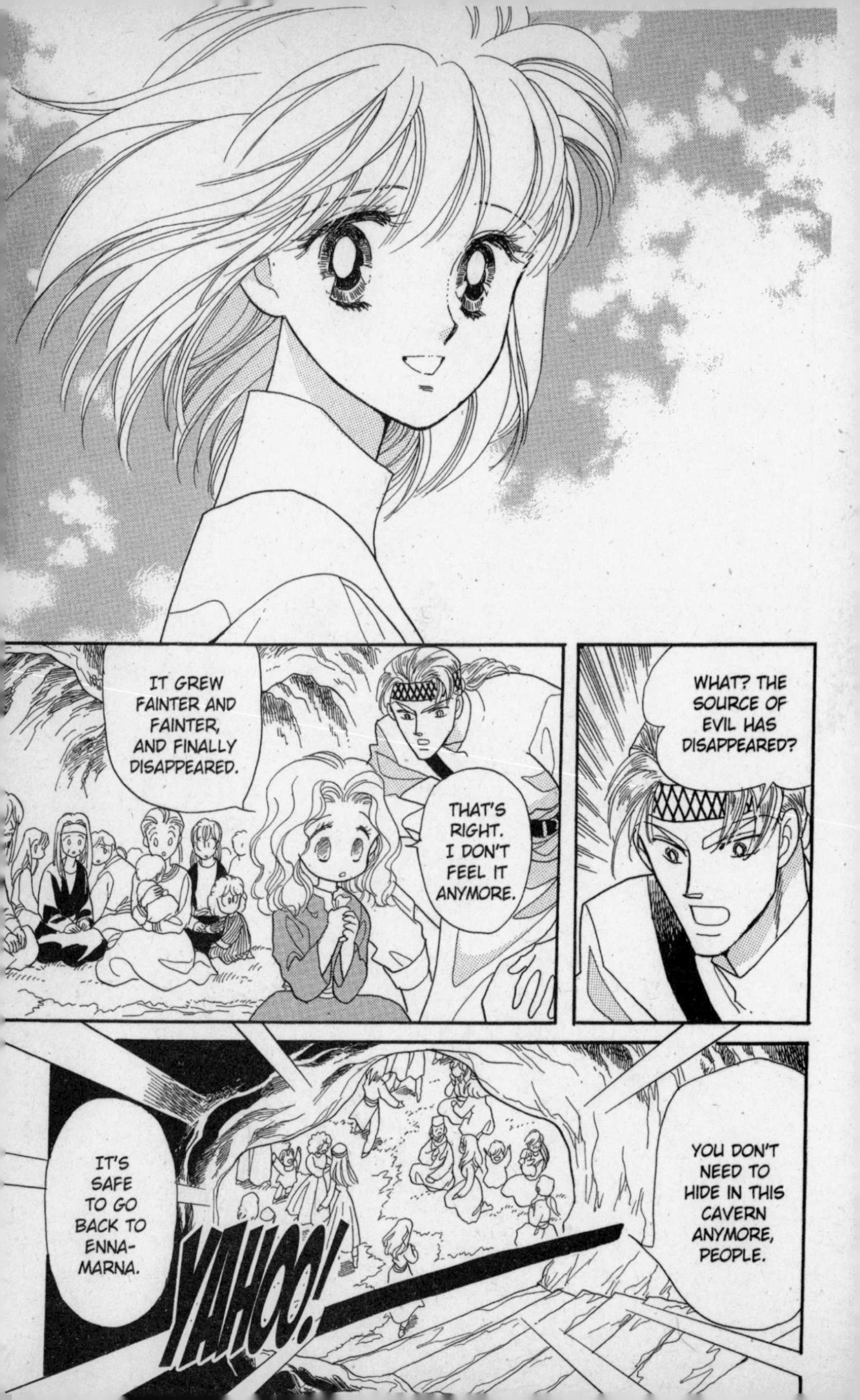
WHAT? THE SOURCE OF EVIL HAS DISAPPEARED?
THAT'S RIGHT. I DON'T FEEL IT ANYMORE.
IT GREW FAINTER AND FAINTER, AND FINALLY DISAPPEARED.
YOU DON'T NEED TO HIDE IN THIS CAVERN ANYMORE, PEOPLE.
IT'S SAFE TO GO BACK TO ENNA-MARNA.
YAHOO!

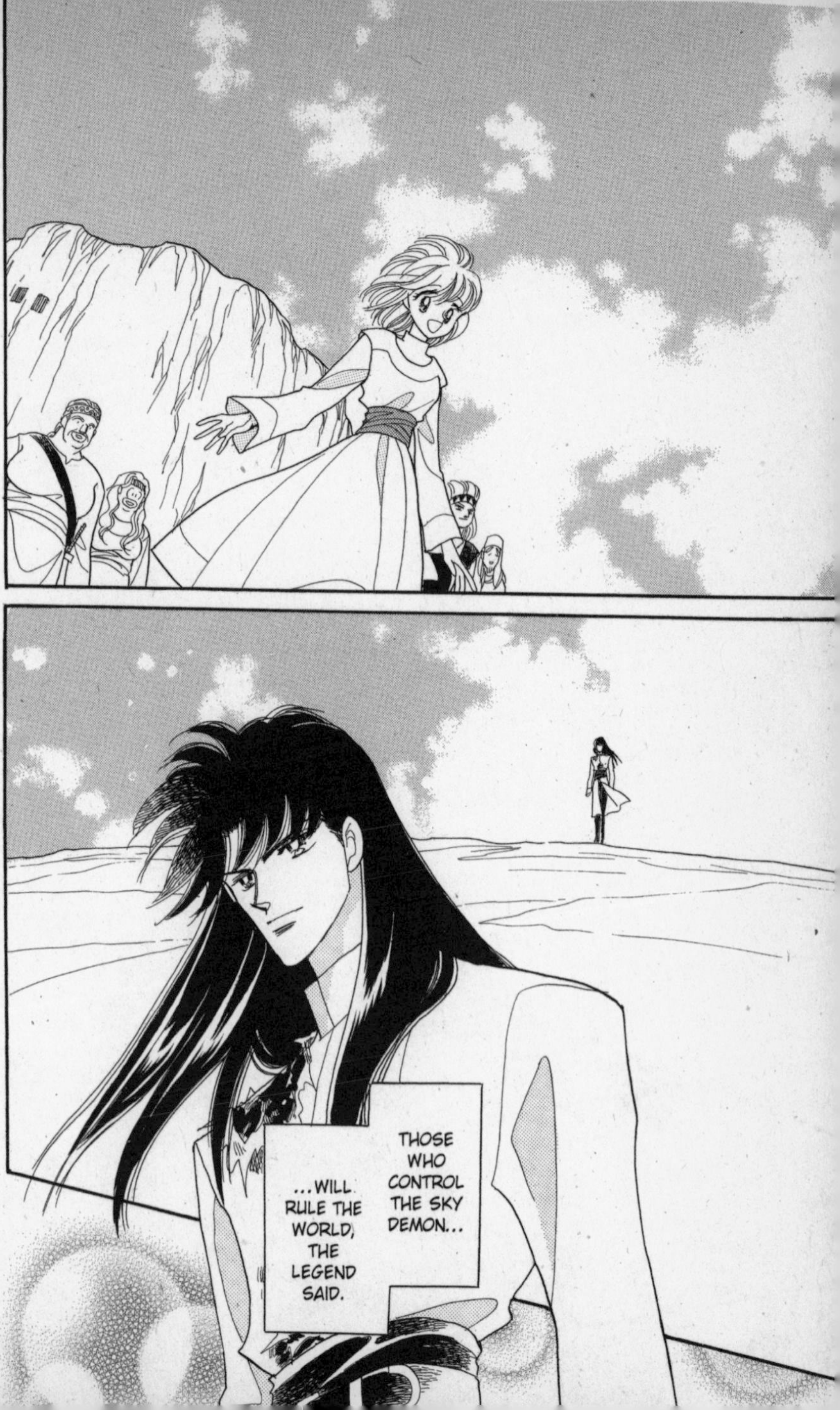
THOSE WHO CONTROL THE SKY DEMON...
...WILL RULE THE WORLD, THE LEGEND SAID.

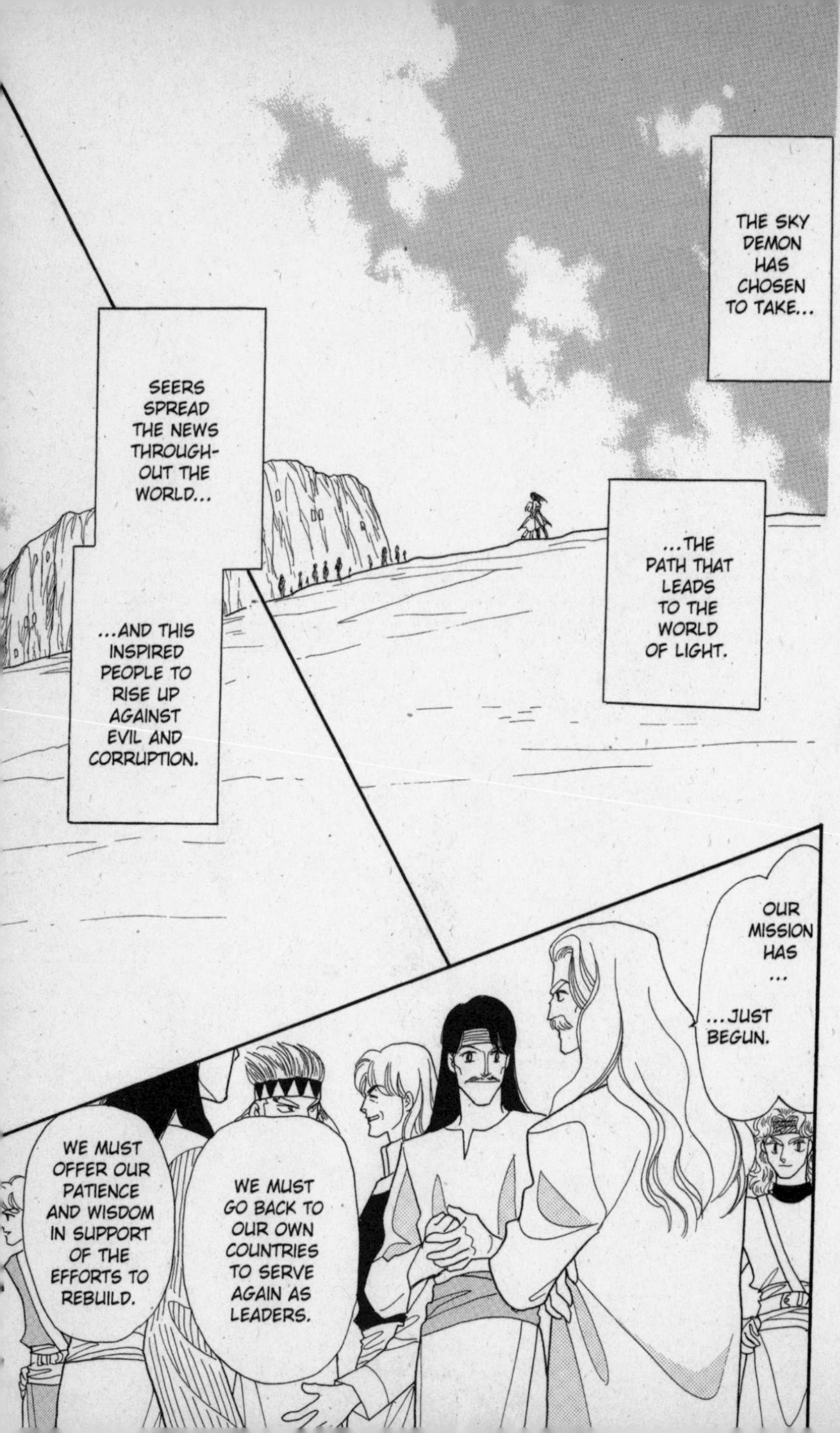
THE SKY DEMON HAS CHOSEN TO TAKE...
...THE PATH THAT LEADS TO THE WORLD OF LIGHT.
SEERS SPREAD THE NEWS THROUGH-OUT THE WORLD...
...AND THIS INSPIRED PEOPLE TO RISE UP AGAINST EVIL AND CORRUPTION.
OUR MISSION HAS...
...JUST BEGUN.
WE MUST GO BACK TO OUR OWN COUNTRIES TO SERVE AGAIN AS LEADERS.
WE MUST OFFER OUR PATIENCE AND WISDOM IN SUPPORT OF THE EFFORTS TO REBUILD.

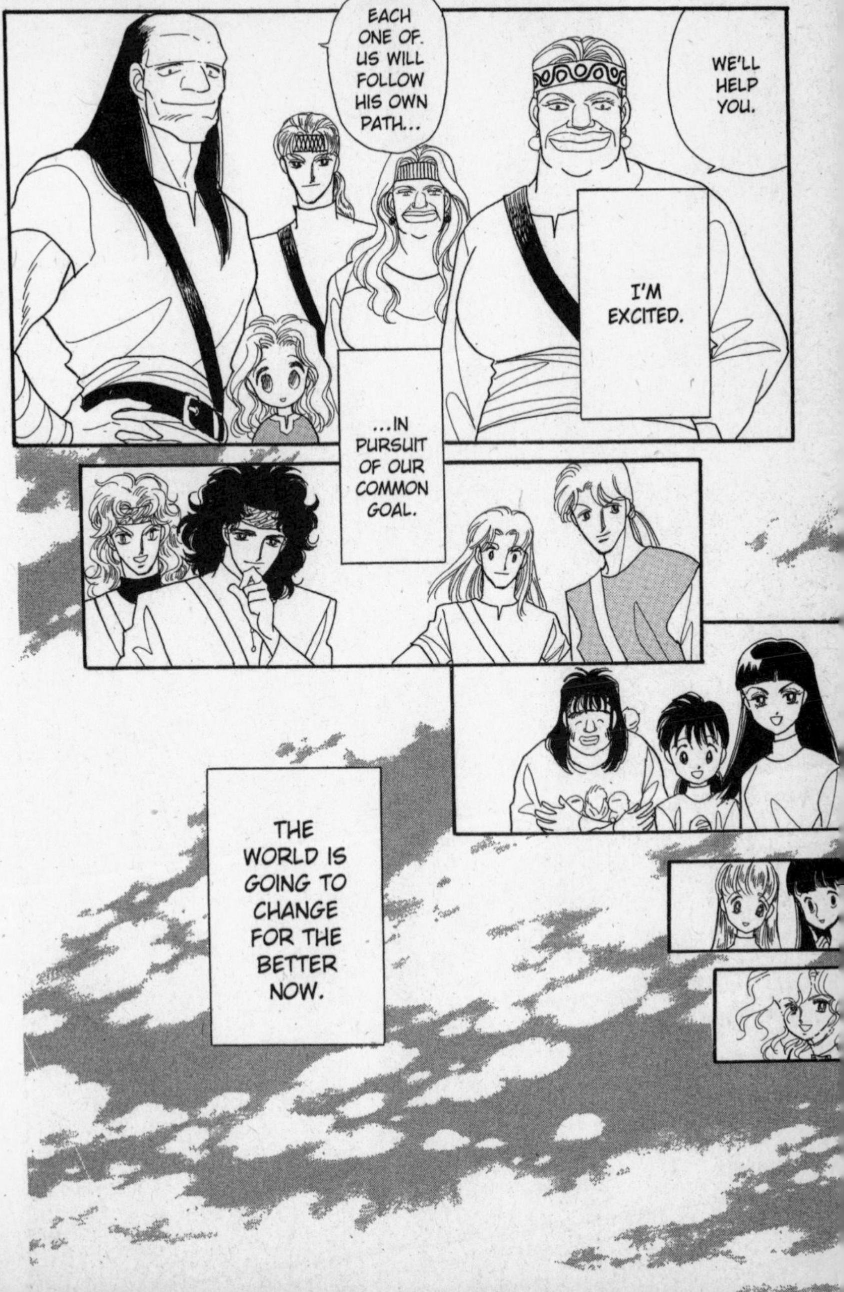
WE'LL HELP YOU.
EACH ONE OF. US WILL FOLLOW HIS OWN PATH...
I'M EXCITED.
...IN PURSUIT OF OUR COMMON GOAL.
THE WORLD IS GOING TO CHANGE FOR THE BETTER NOW.

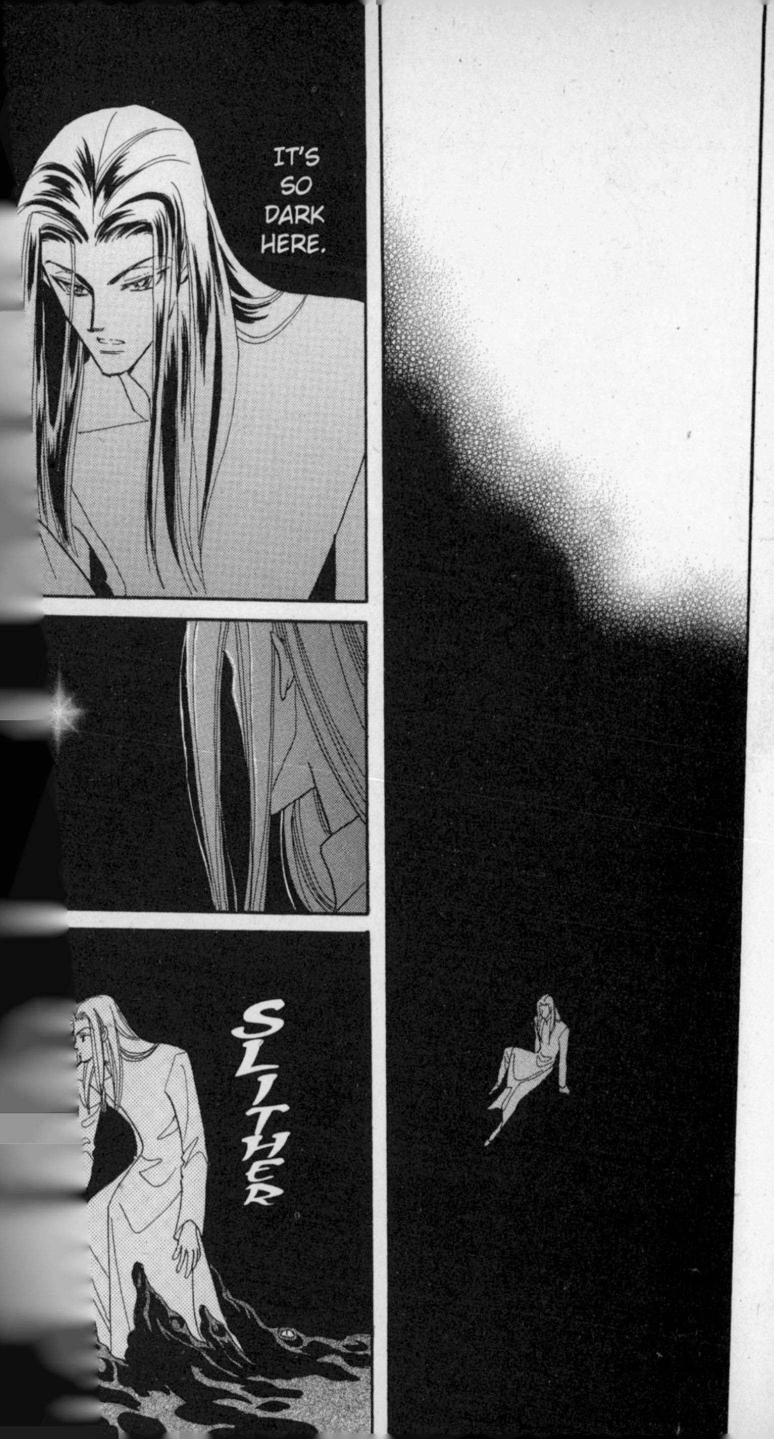
IT'S SO DARK HERE.
SLITHER

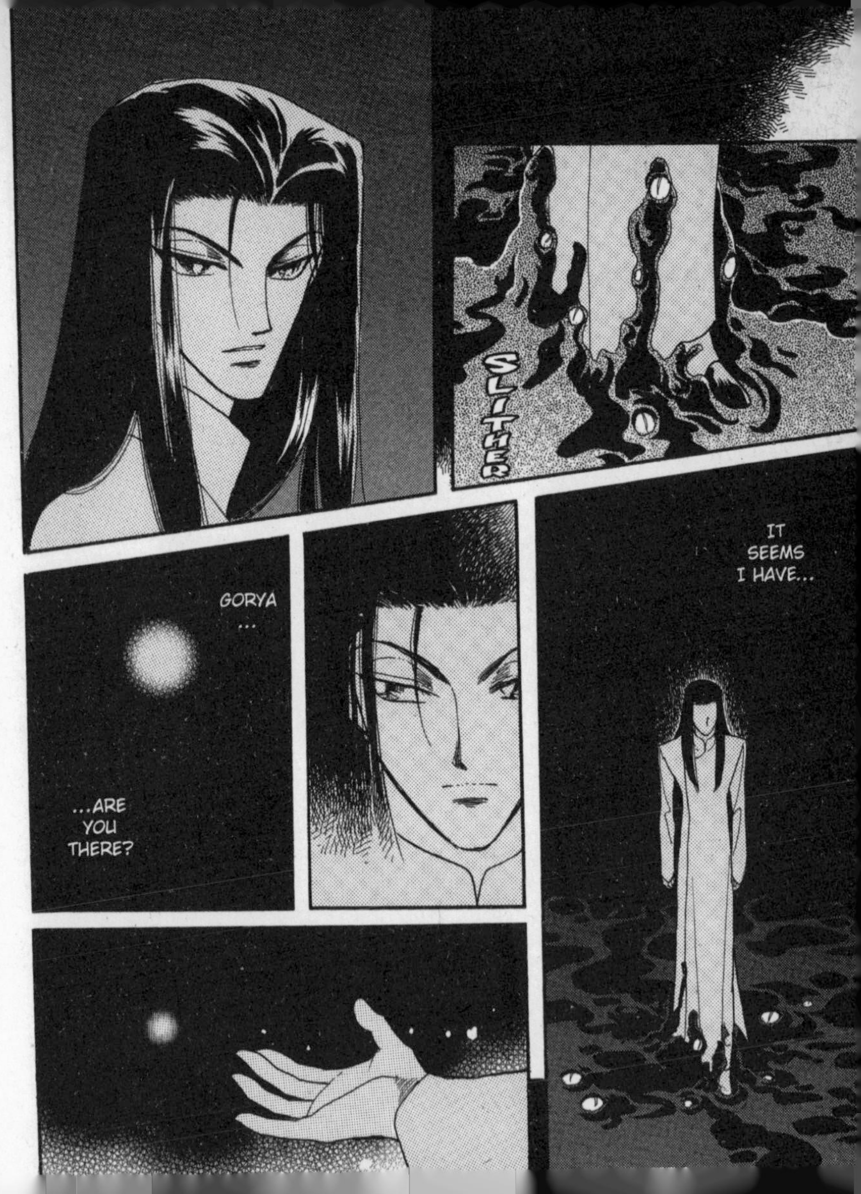
SLITHER
IT SEEMS I HAVE...
GORYA ...
...ARE YOU THERE?

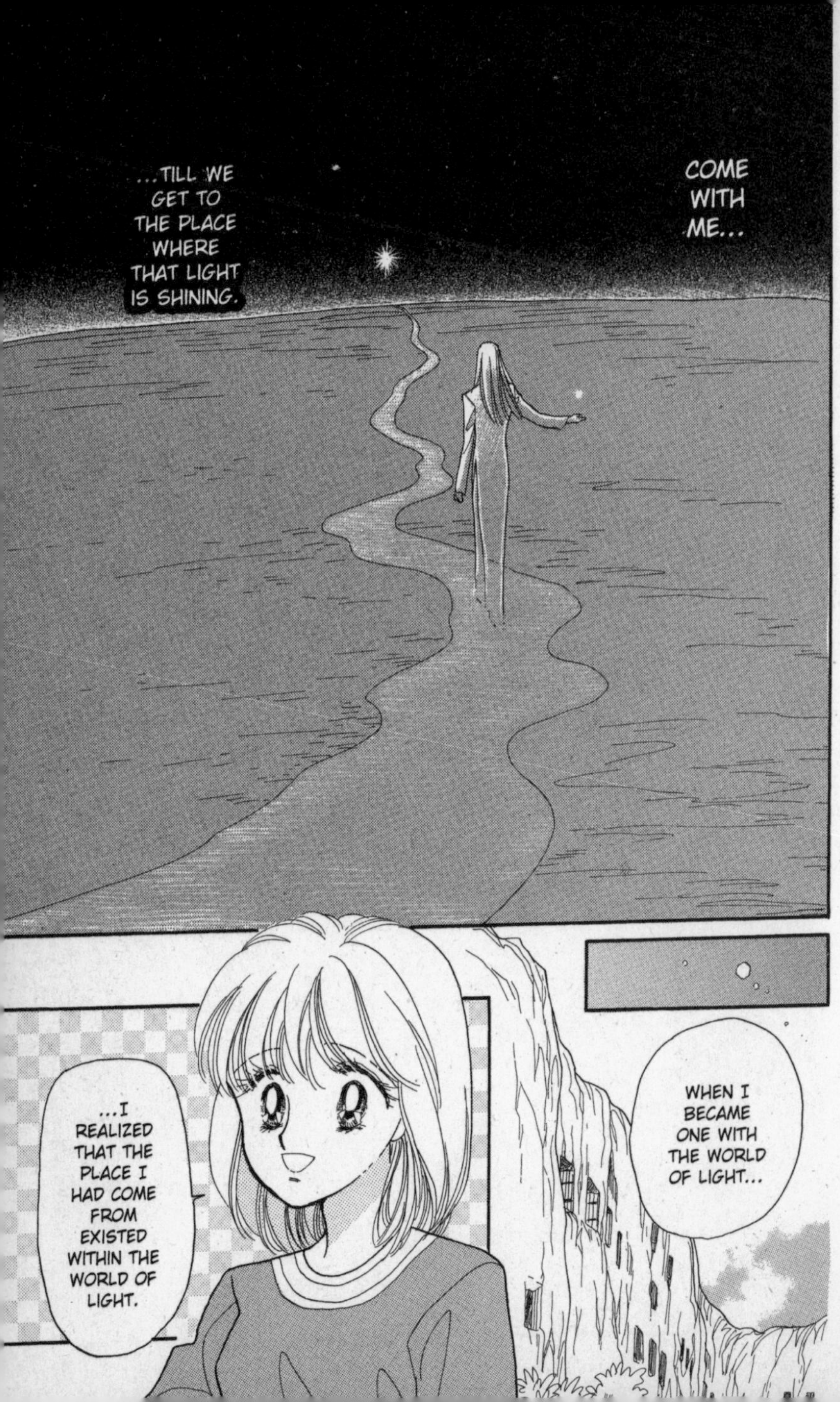
COME WITH ME...
...TILL WE GET TO THE PLACE WHERE THAT LIGHT IS SHINING.
WHEN I BECAME ONE WITH THE WORLD OF LIGHT...
...I REALIZED THAT THE PLACE I HAD COME FROM EXISTED WITHIN THE WORLD OF LIGHT.

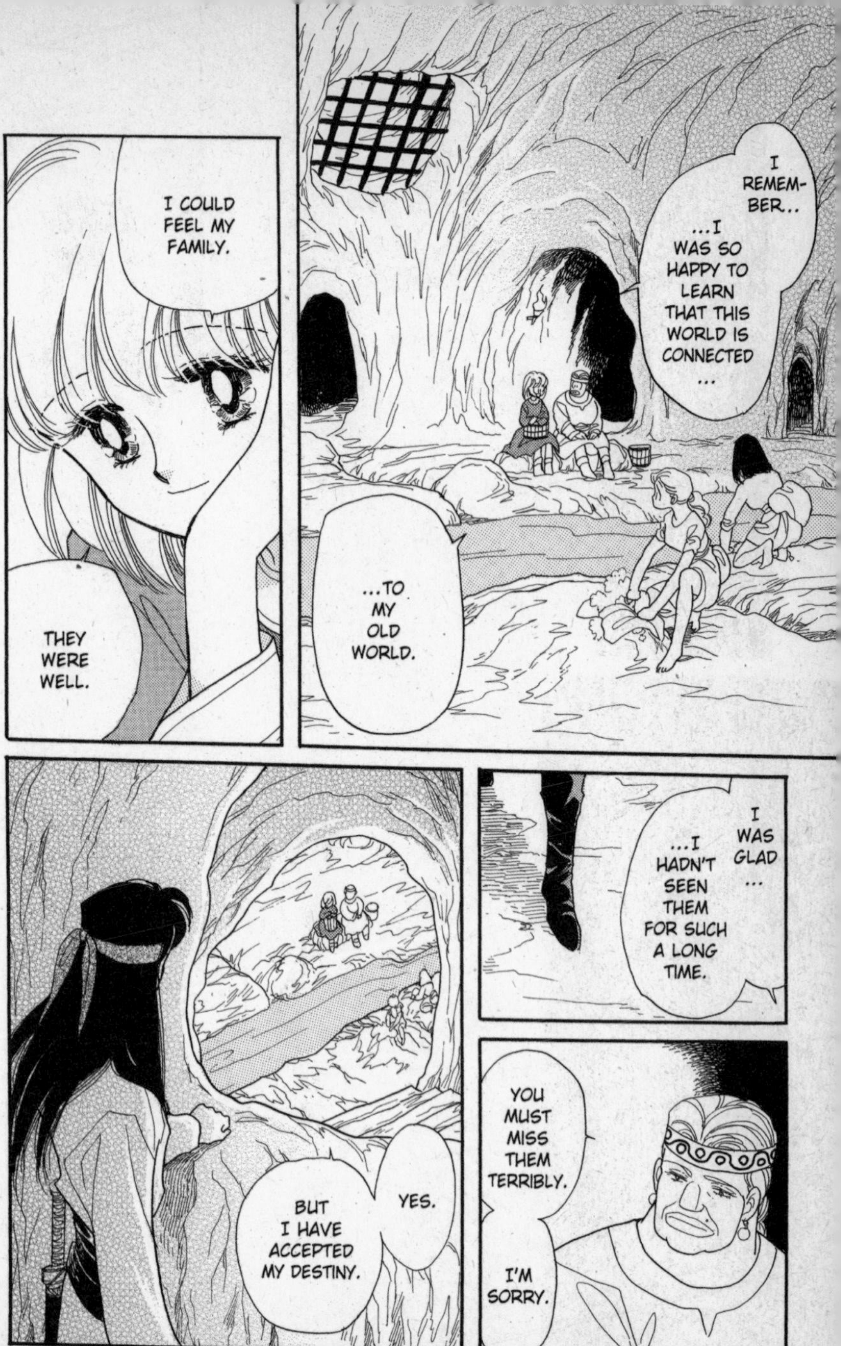
I REMEMBER..
...I WAS SO HAPPY TO LEARN THAT THIS WORLD IS CONNECTED ...
...TO MY OLD WORLD.
I COULD FEEL MY FAMILY.
THEY WERE WELL.
I WAS GLAD ...
...I HADN'T SEEN THEM FOR SUCH A LONG TIME.
YOU MUST MISS THEM TERRIBLY.
I'M SORRY.
YES.
BUT I HAVE ACCEPTED MY DESTINY.

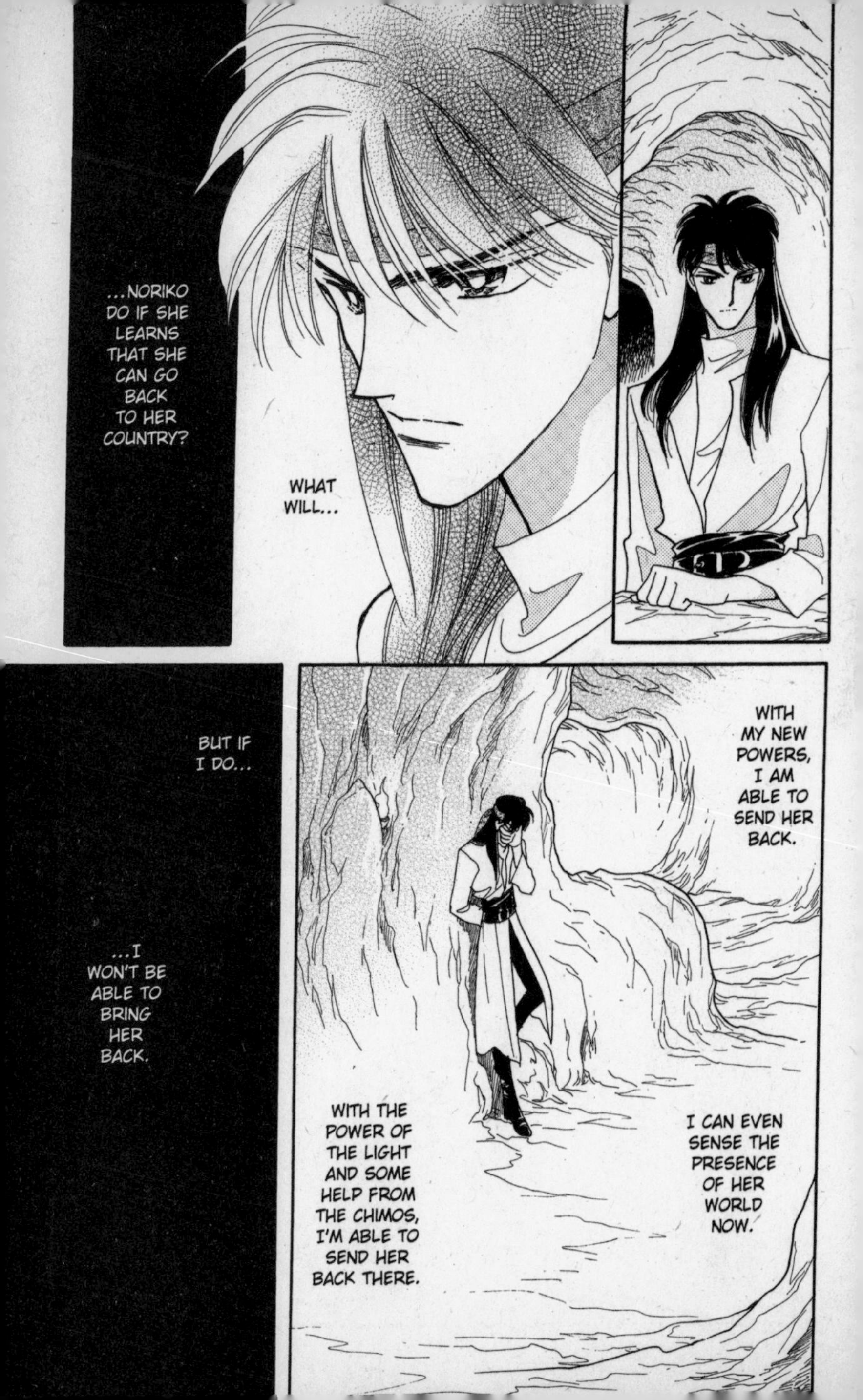
WHAT WILL...
...NORIKO DO IF SHE LEARNS THAT SHE CAN GO BACK TO HER COUNTRY?
WITH MY NEW POWERS, I AM ABLE TO SEND HER BACK.
I CAN EVEN SENSE THE PRESENCE OF HER WORLD NOW.
WITH THE POWER OF THE LIGHT AND SOME HELP FROM THE CHIMOS, I'M ABLE TO SEND HER BACK THERE.
BUT IF I DO...
...I WON'T BE ABLE TO BRING HER BACK.

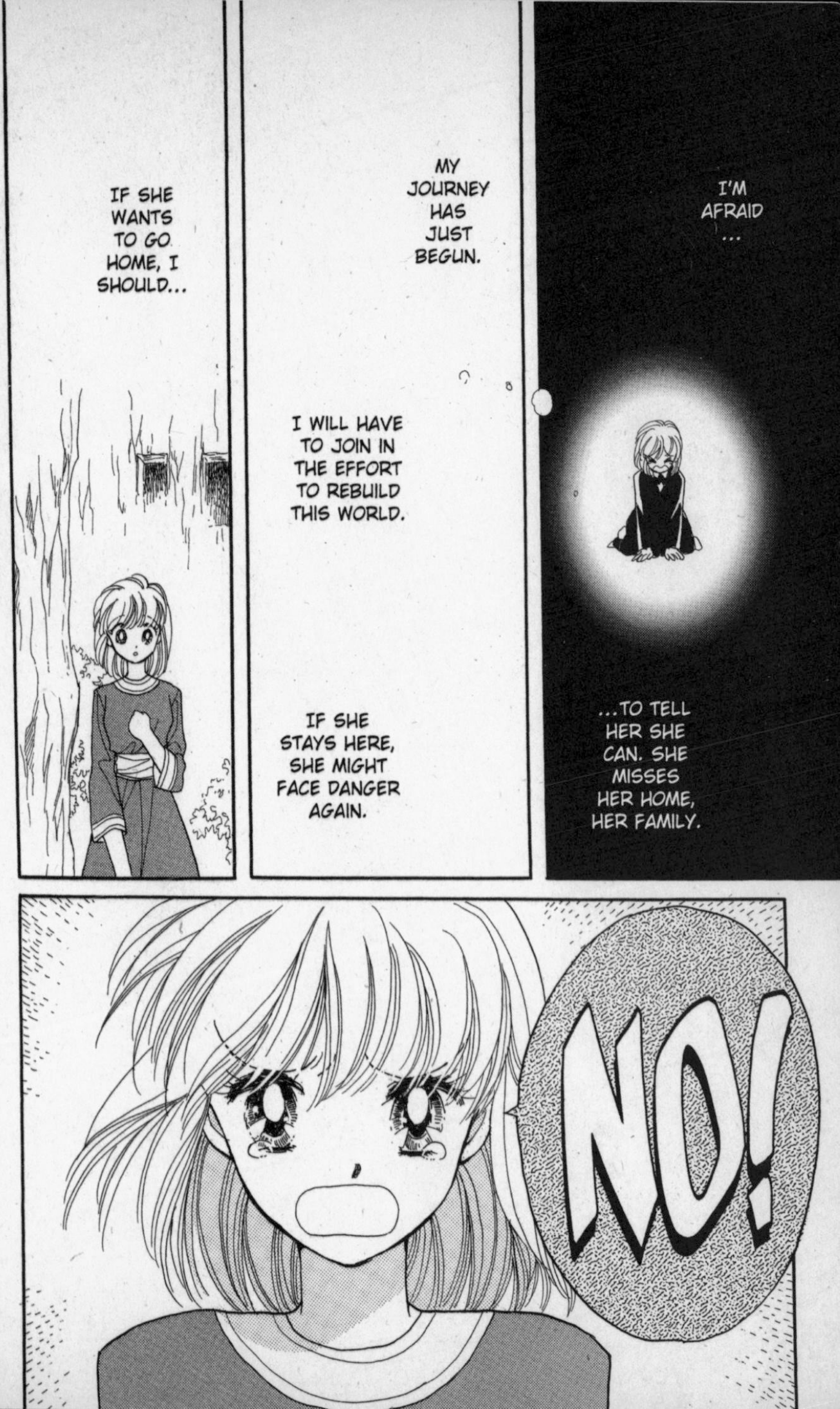
I'M AFRAID ...
...TO TELL HER SHE CAN. SHE MISSES HER HOME, HER FAMILY.
MY JOURNEY HAS JUST BEGUN.
I WILL HAVE TO JOIN IN THE EFFORT TO REBUILD THIS WORLD.
IF SHE STAYS HERE, SHE MIGHT FACE DANGER AGAIN.
IF SHE WANTS TO GO HOME, I SHOULD...
NO!

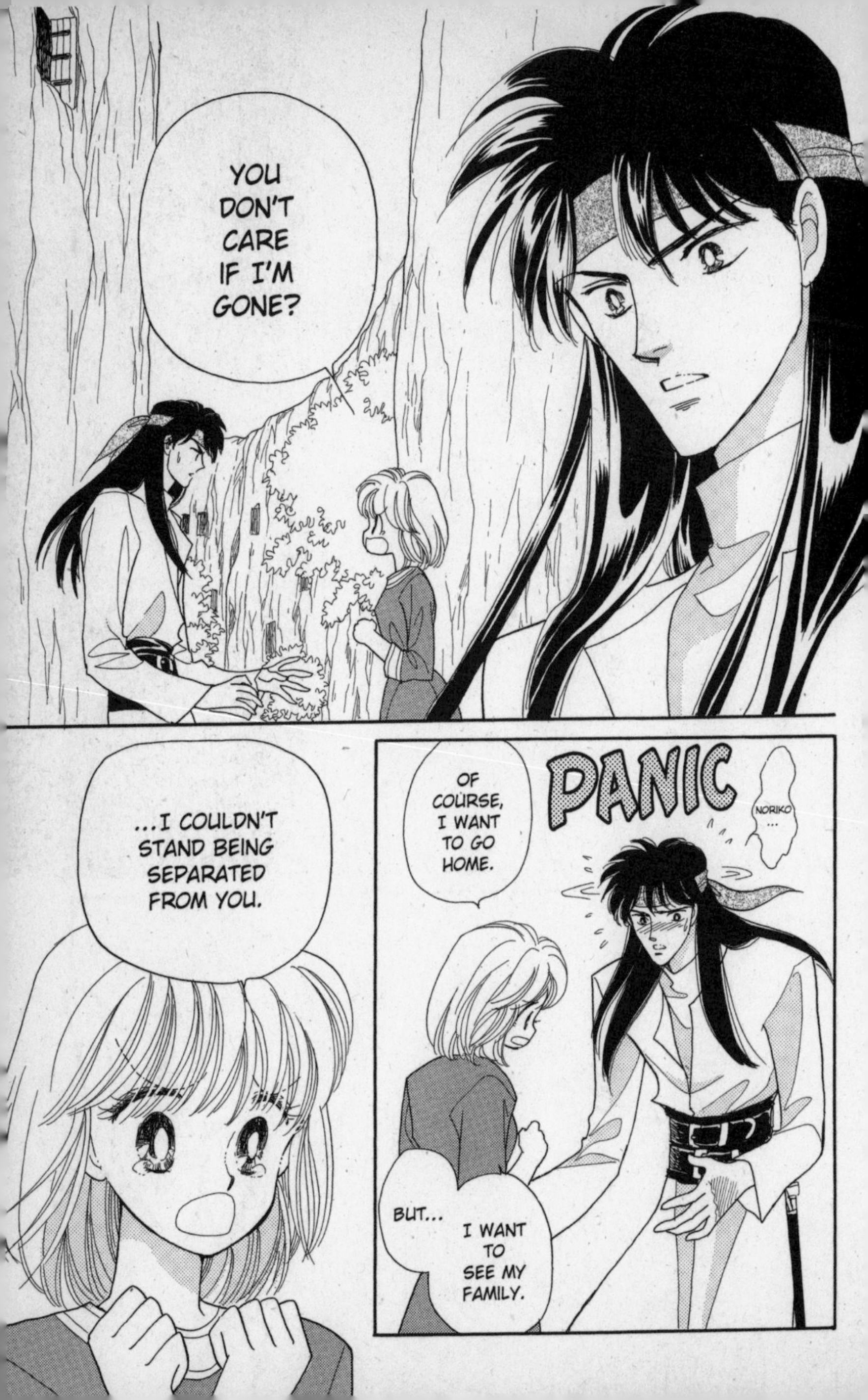
YOU DON'T CARE IF I'M GONE?
PANIC
NORIKO...
OF COURSE, I WANT TO GO HOME.
BUT...
I WANT TO SEE MY FAMILY.
...I COULDN'T STAND BEING SEPARATED FROM YOU.

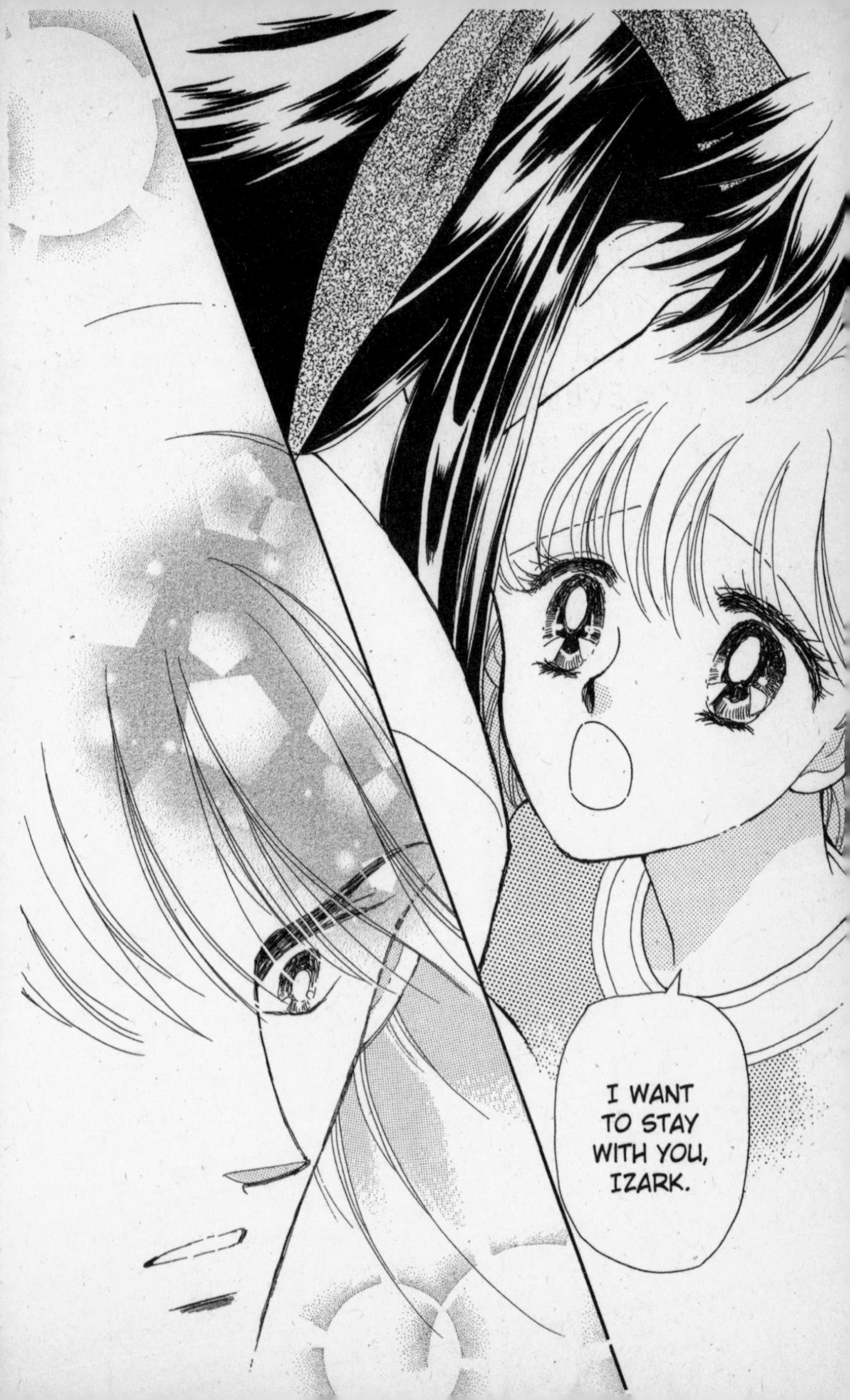
I WANT TO STAY WITH YOU, IZARK.

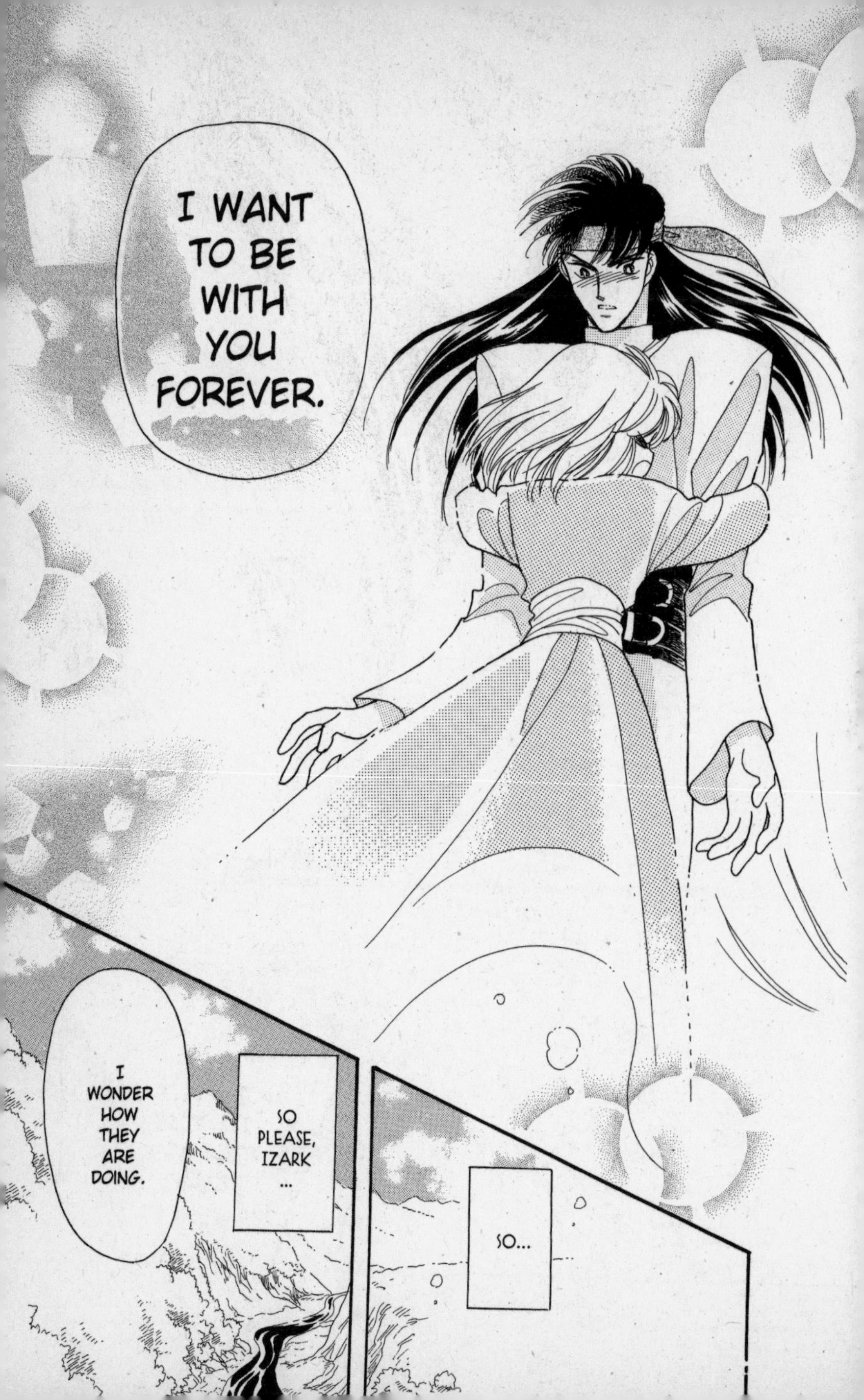
I WANT TO BE WITH YOU FOREVER.
SO...
SO PLEASE, IZARK ...
I WONDER HOW THEY ARE DOING.

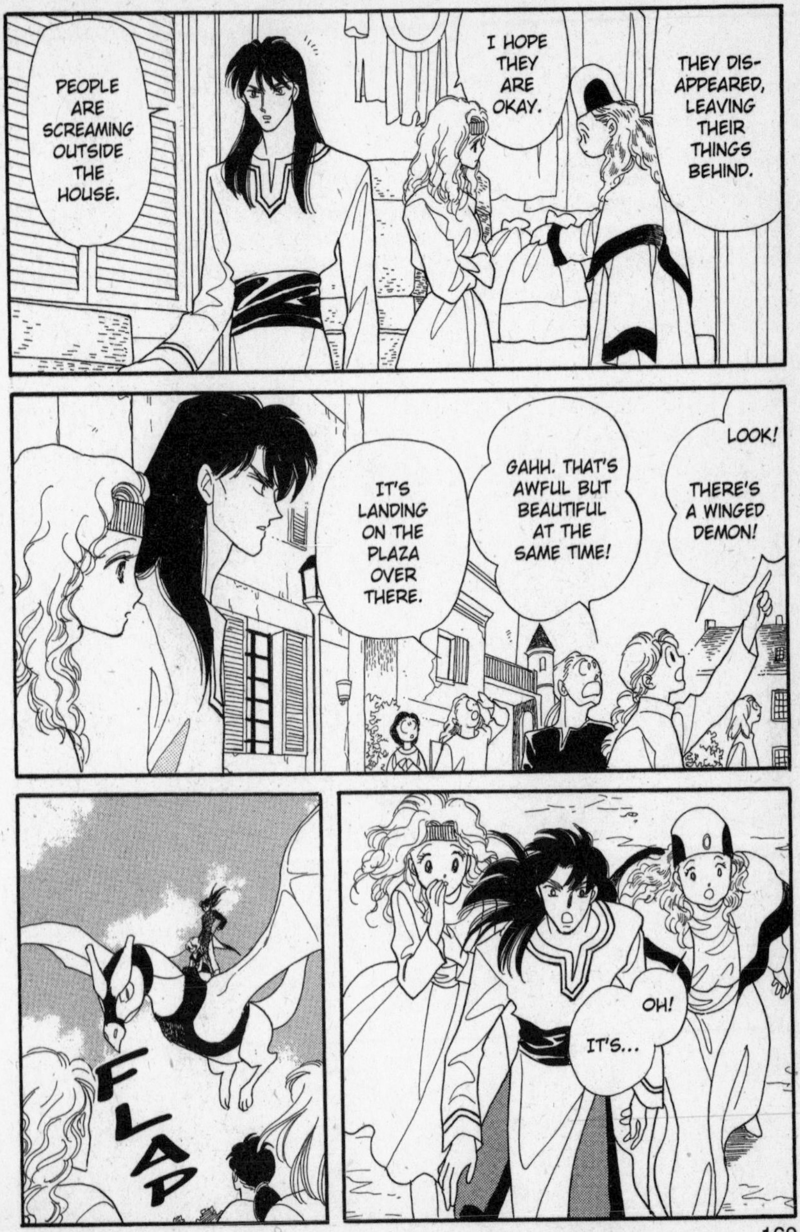
THEY DISAPPEARED, LEAVING THEIR THINGS BEHIND.
I HOPE THEY ARE OKAY.
PEOPLE ARE SCREAMING OUTSIDE THE HOUSE.
LOOK!
THERE'S A WINGED DEMON!
GAHH. THAT'S AWFUL BUT BEAUTIFUL AT THE SAME TIME!
IT'S LANDING ON THE PLAZA OVER THERE.
OH!
IT'S...
FLAP

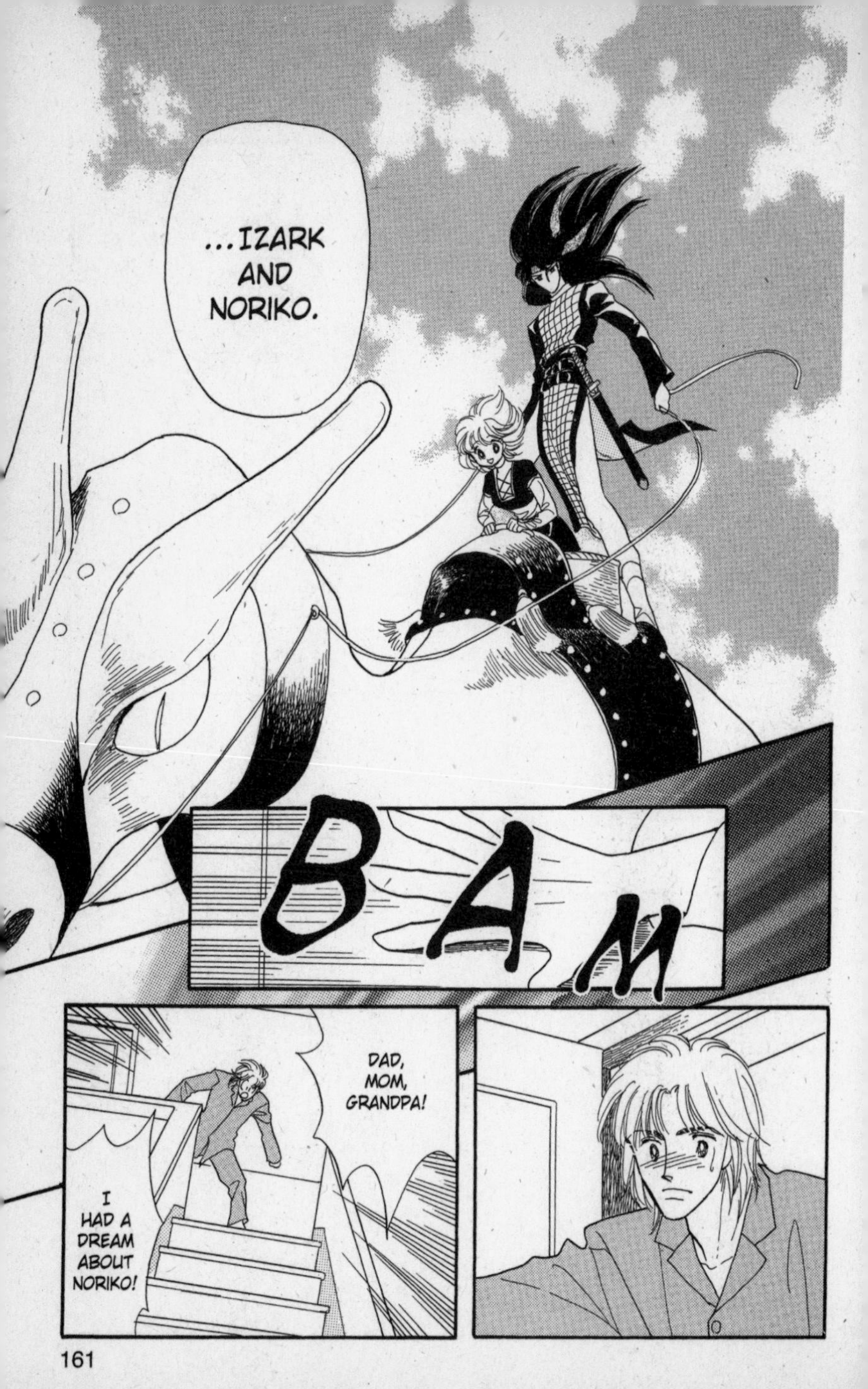
...IZARK AND NORIKO.
BAM
DAD, MOM, GRANDPA!
I HAD A DREAM ABOUT NORIKO!

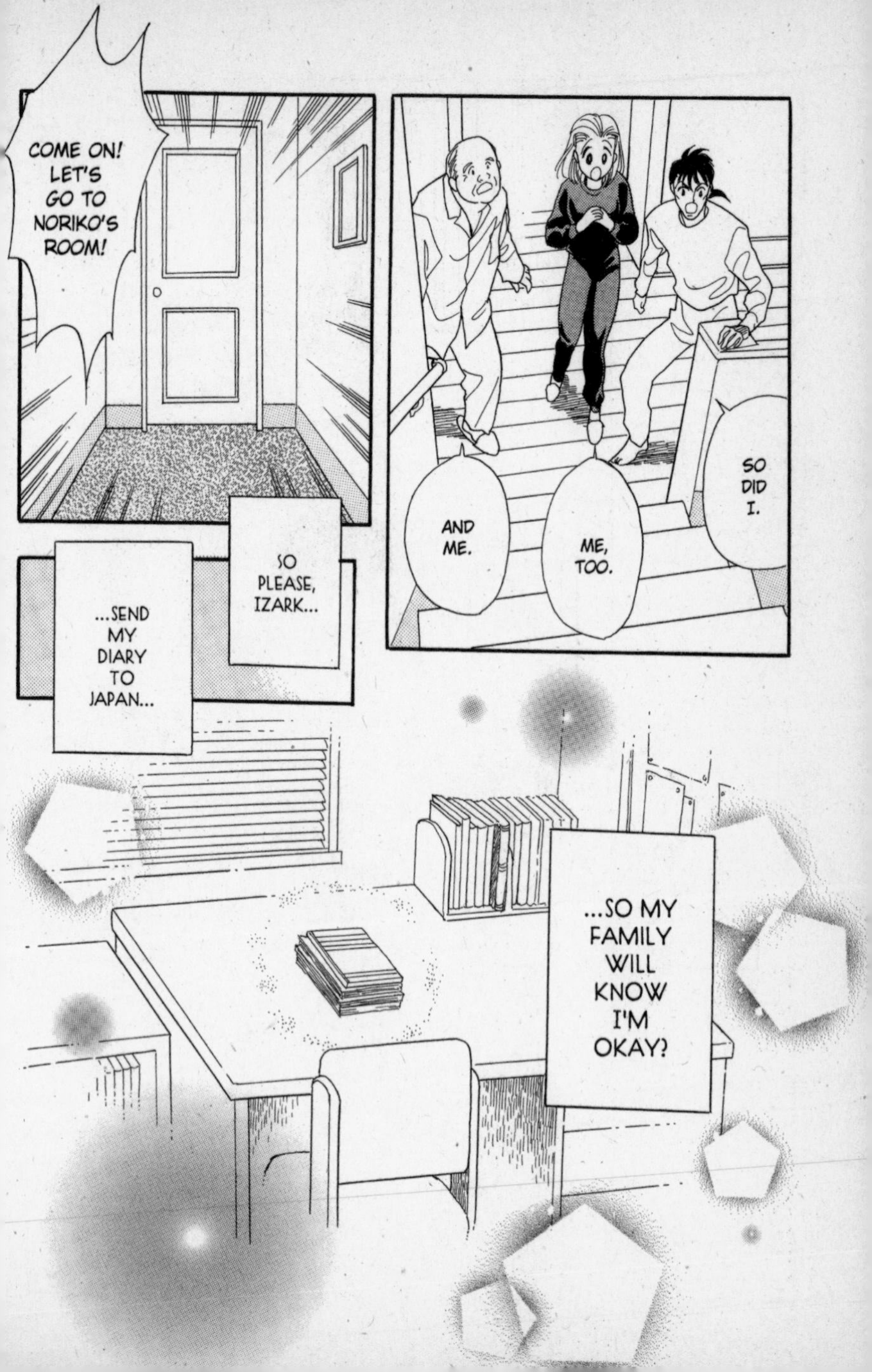
SO DID I.
ME, TOO.
AND ME.
COME ON! LET'S GO TO NORIKO'S ROOM!
SO PLEASE, IZARK...
...SEND MY DIARY TO JAPAN...
...SO MY FAMILY WILL KNOW I'M OKAY?

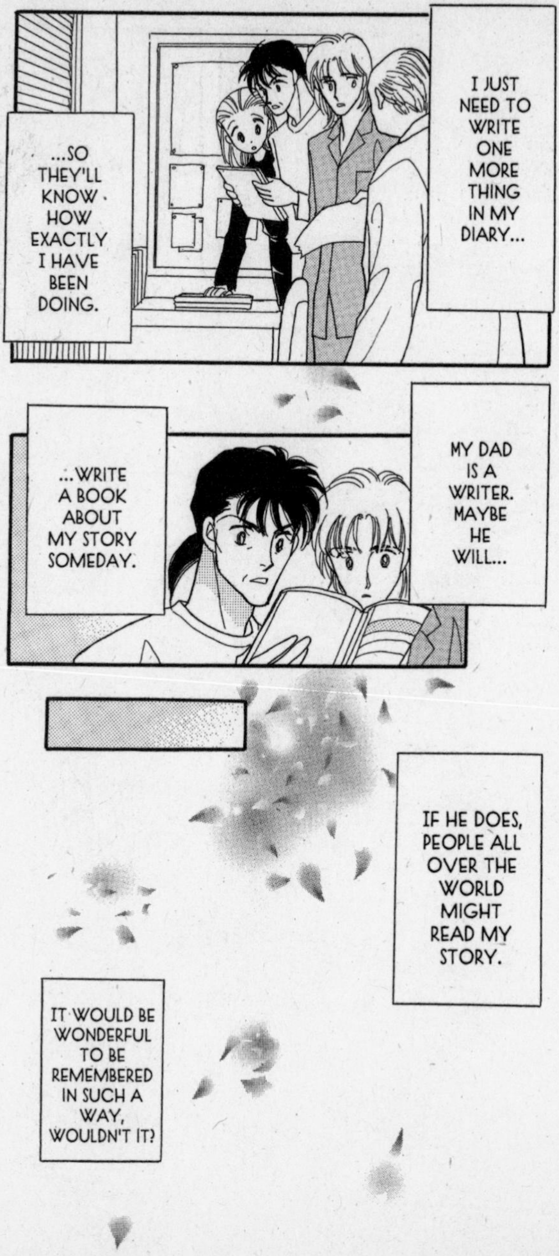
I JUST NEED TO WRITE ONE MORE THING IN MY DIARY...
...SO THEY'LL KNOW HOW EXACTLY I HAVE BEEN DOING.
MY DAD IS A WRITER. MAYBE HE WILL...
...WRITE A BOOK ABOUT MY STORY SOMEDAY.
IF HE DOES, PEOPLE ALL OVER THE WORLD MIGHT READ MY STORY.
IT WOULD BE WONDERFUL TO BE REMEMBERED IN SUCH A WAY, WOULDN'T IT?

From Far Away started in 1991. (It says so in Volume 1.)

The epilogue was printed in January 2003 so the series lasted for 12 years. Wow! Did I spend that many years for only 14 volumes of manga? Hmm...

There have been several hiatuses due to my health problems. The last six volumes or so were published at the rate of one every two months, yet many readers patiently waited for each story to be printed. Without their encouragement, I couldn't have completed the series. I am also deeply grateful to my editors for not abandoning this story despite its delays.

Thank you all very much!

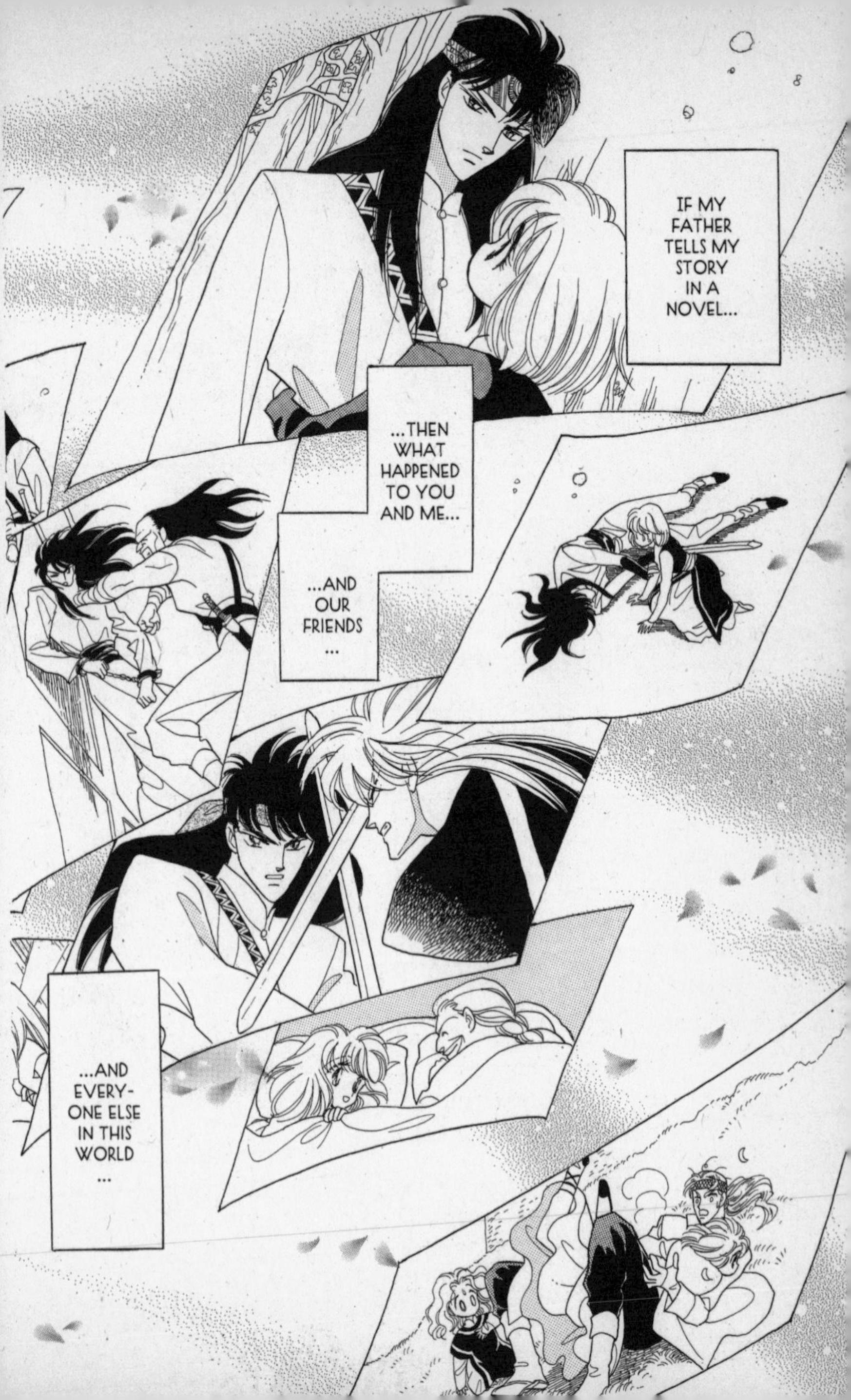
IF MY FATHER TELLS MY STORY IN A NOVEL...
...THEN WHAT HAPPENED TO YOU AND ME...
...AND OUR FRIENDS ...
...AND EVERY-ONE ELSE IN THIS WORLD ...

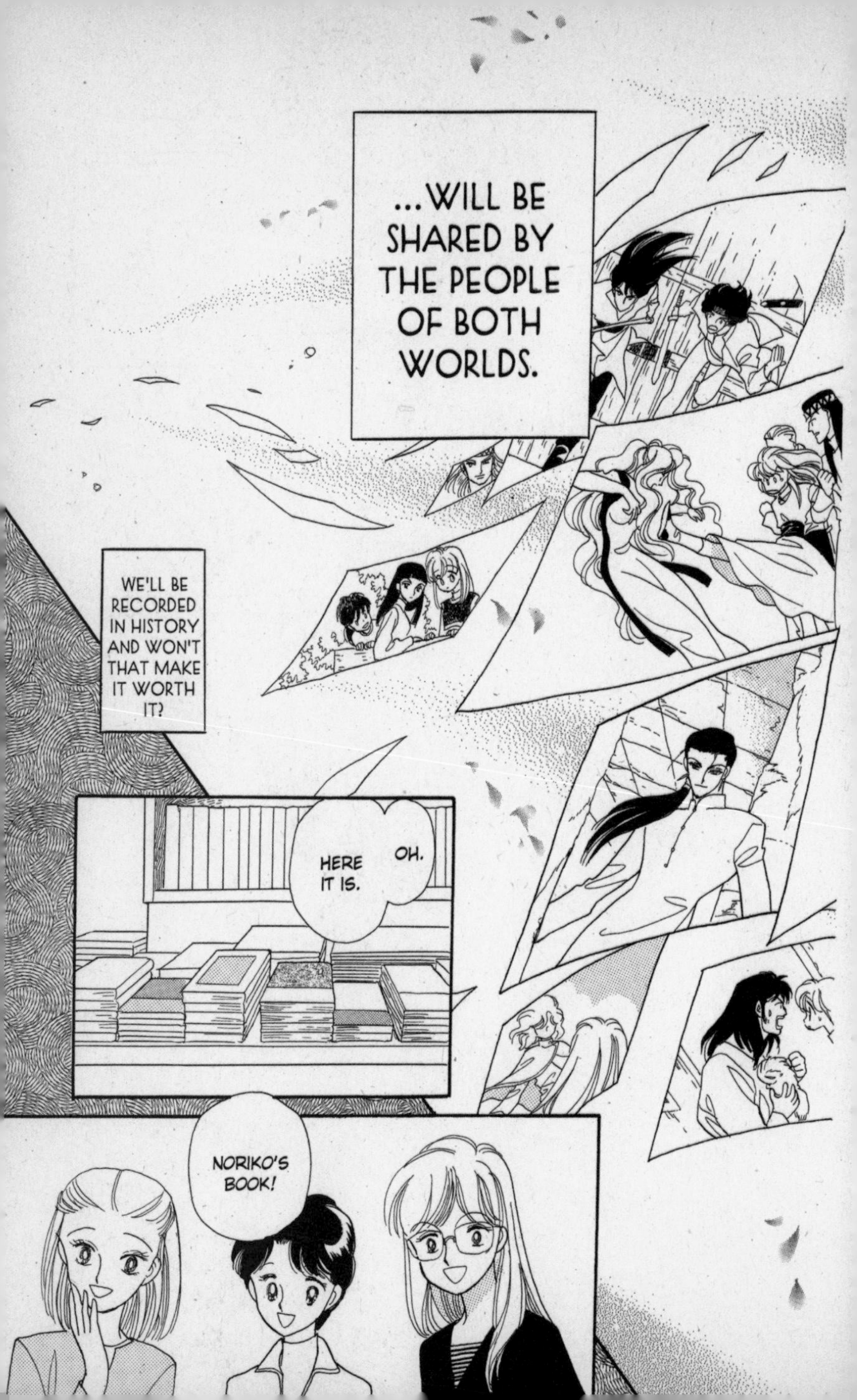
...WILL BE SHARED BY THE PEOPLE OF BOTH WORLDS.
WE'LL BE RECORDED IN HISTORY AND WON'T THAT MAKE IT WORTH IT?
OH.
HERE IT IS.
NORIKO'S BOOK!

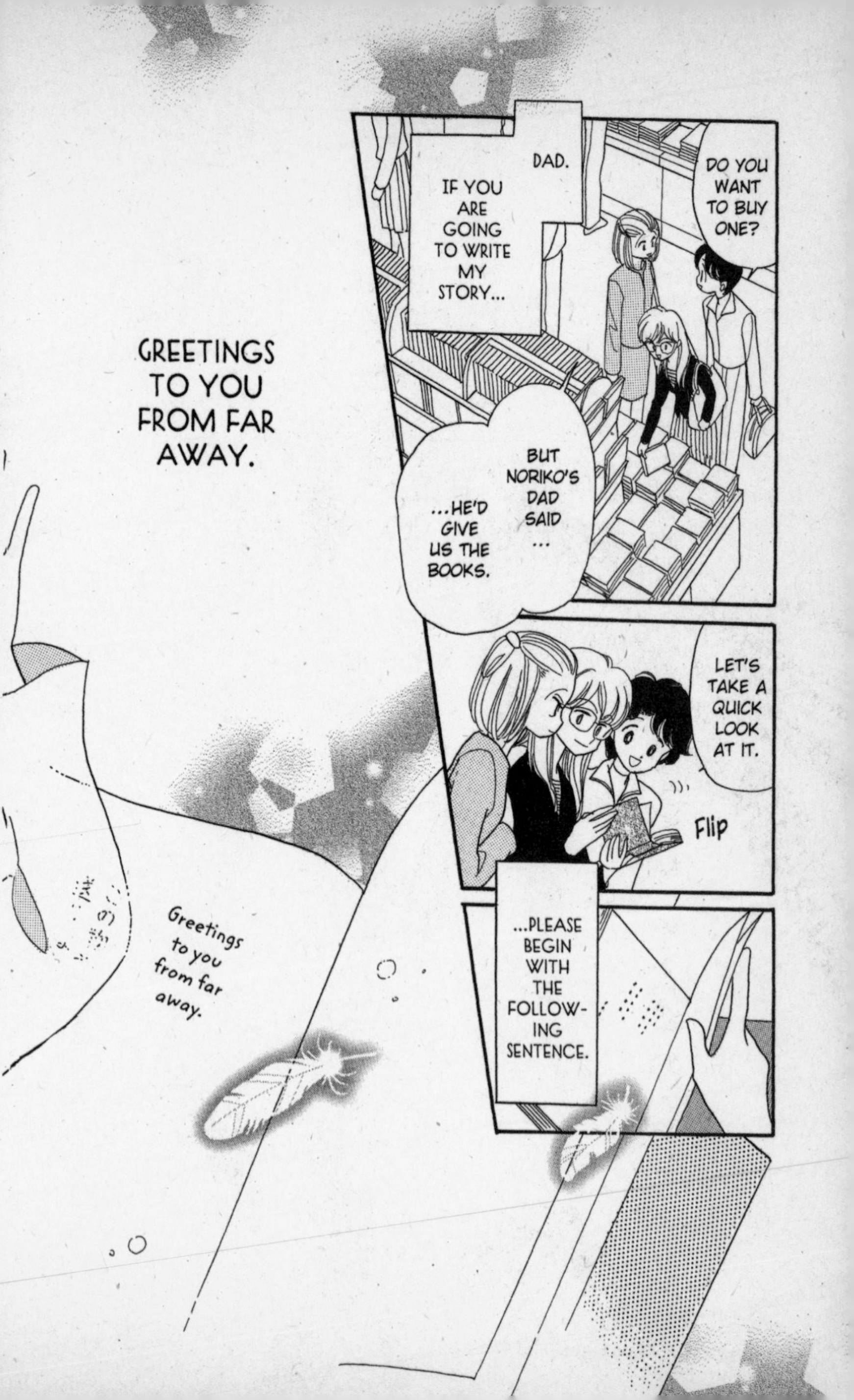
DO YOU WANT TO BUY ONE?
DAD.
IF YOU ARE GOING TO WRITE MY STORY...
BUT NORIKO'S DAD SAID...
...HE'D GIVE US THE BOOKS.
LET'S TAKE A QUICK LOOK AT IT.
Flip
...PLEASE BEGIN WITH THE FOLLOWING SENTENCE.
GREETINGS TO YOU FROM FAR AWAY.
Greetings to you from far away.

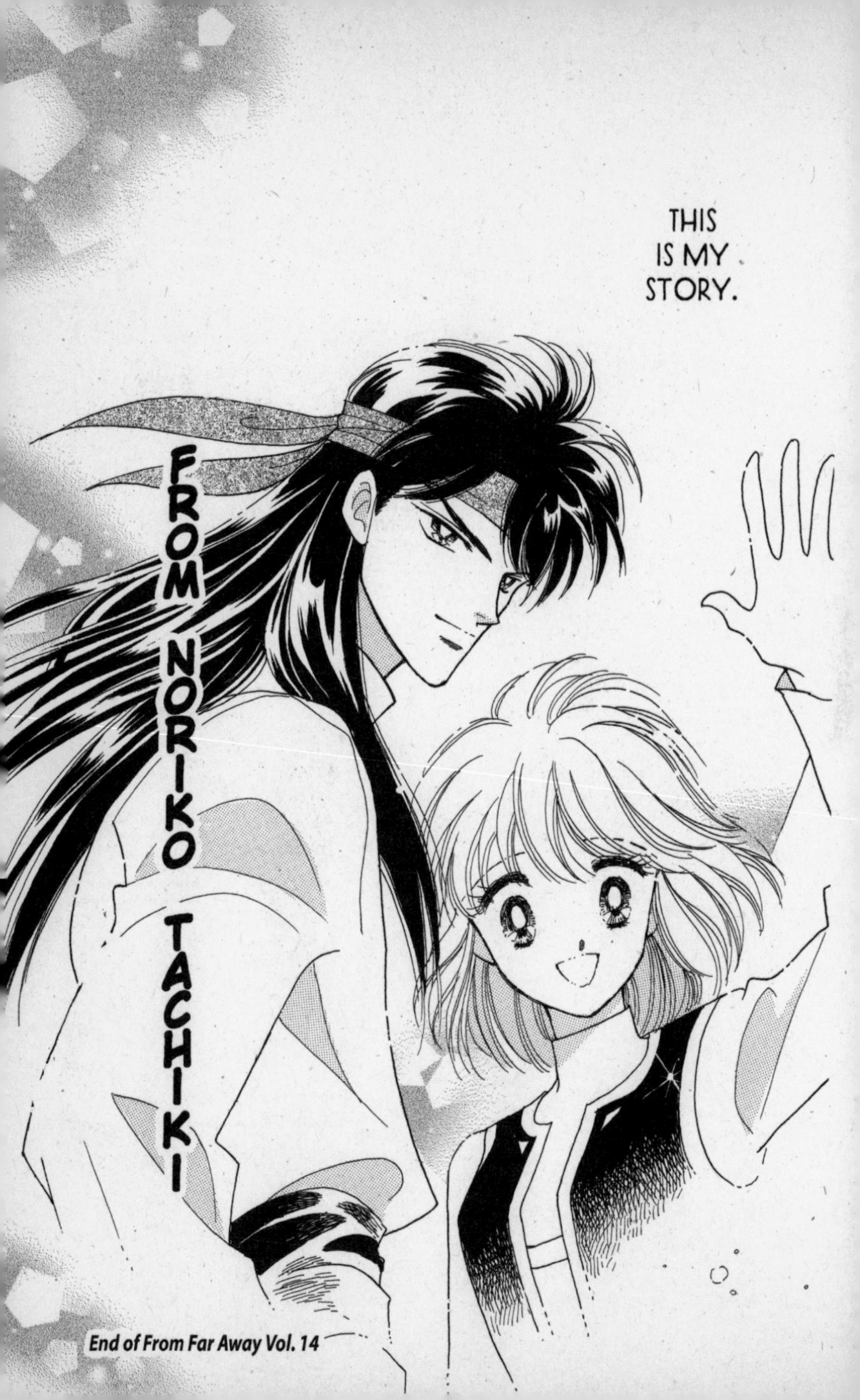
THIS IS MY STORY.
FROM NORIKO TACHIKI

End of From Far Away Vol. 14

彼方(かなた)から

FROM FAR AWAY

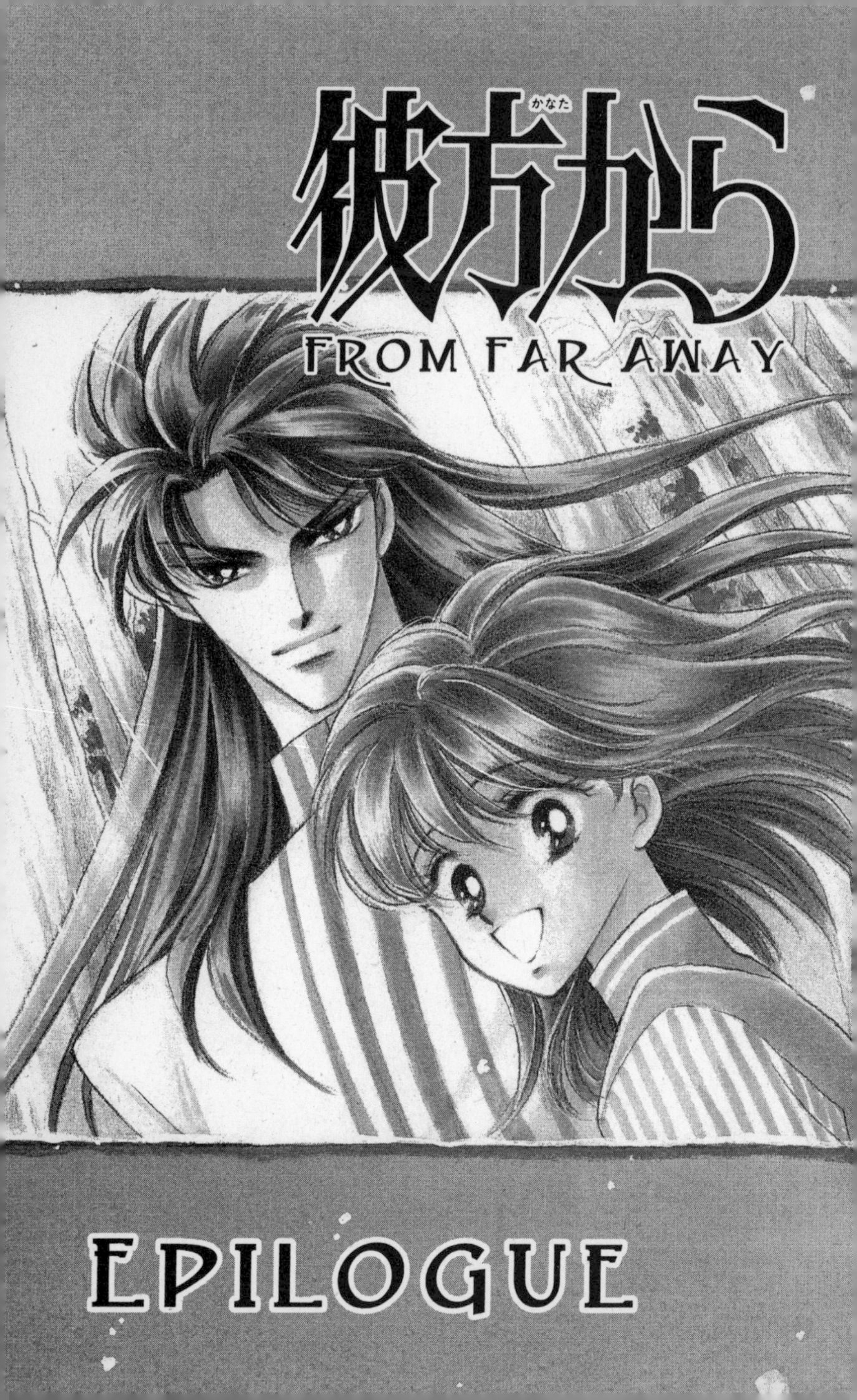

EPILOGUE

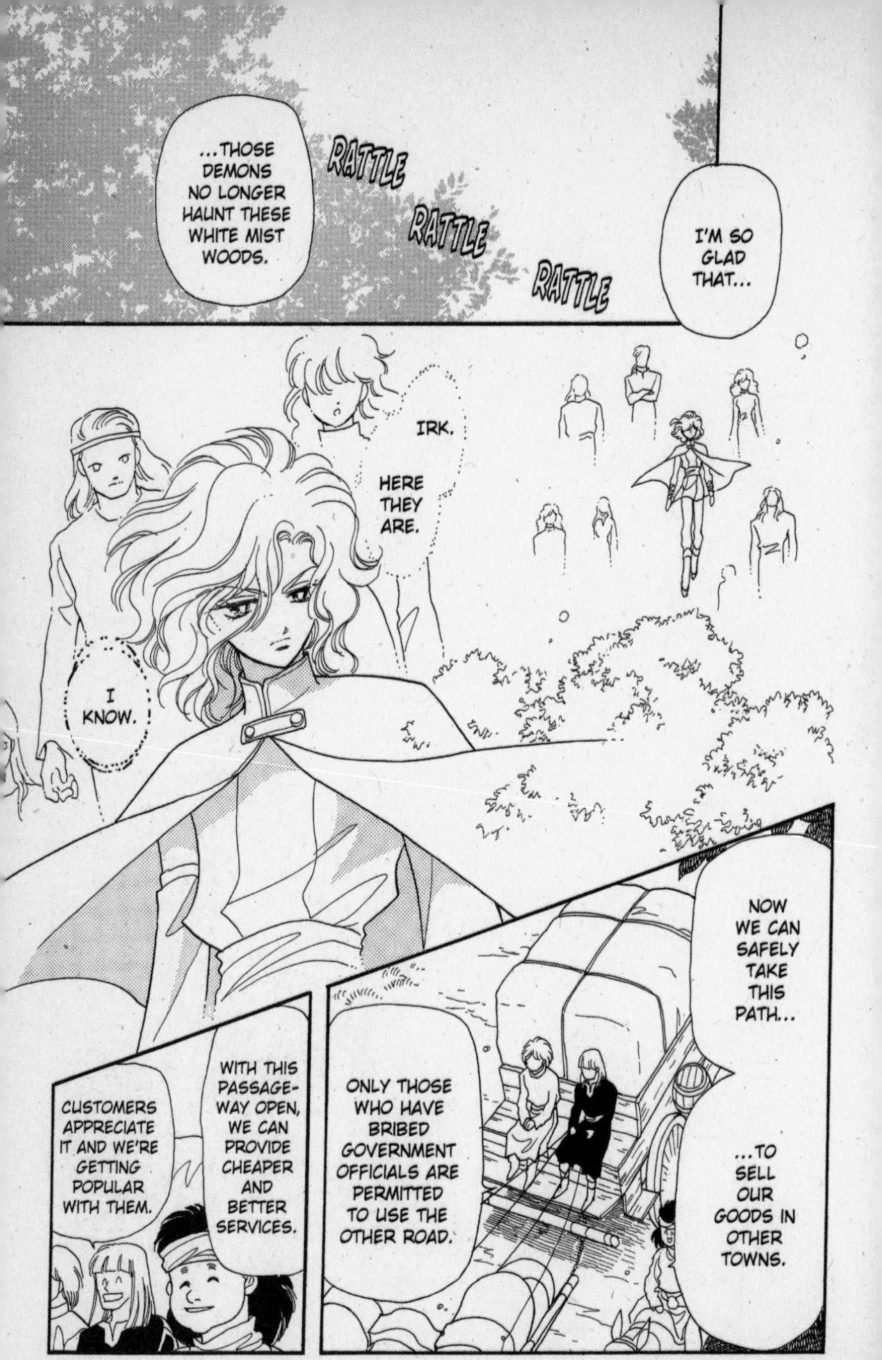
I'M SO GLAD THAT...
RATTLE
RATTLE
RATTLE
...THOSE DEMONS NO LONGER HAUNT THESE WHITE MIST WOODS.
IRK.
HERE THEY ARE.
I KNOW.
NOW WE CAN SAFELY TAKE THIS PATH...
...TO SELL OUR GOODS IN OTHER TOWNS.
ONLY THOSE WHO HAVE BRIBED GOVERNMENT OFFICIALS ARE PERMITTED TO USE THE OTHER ROAD.
WITH THIS PASSAGE-WAY OPEN, WE CAN PROVIDE CHEAPER AND BETTER SERVICES.
CUSTOMERS APPRECIATE IT AND WE'RE GETTING POPULAR WITH THEM.

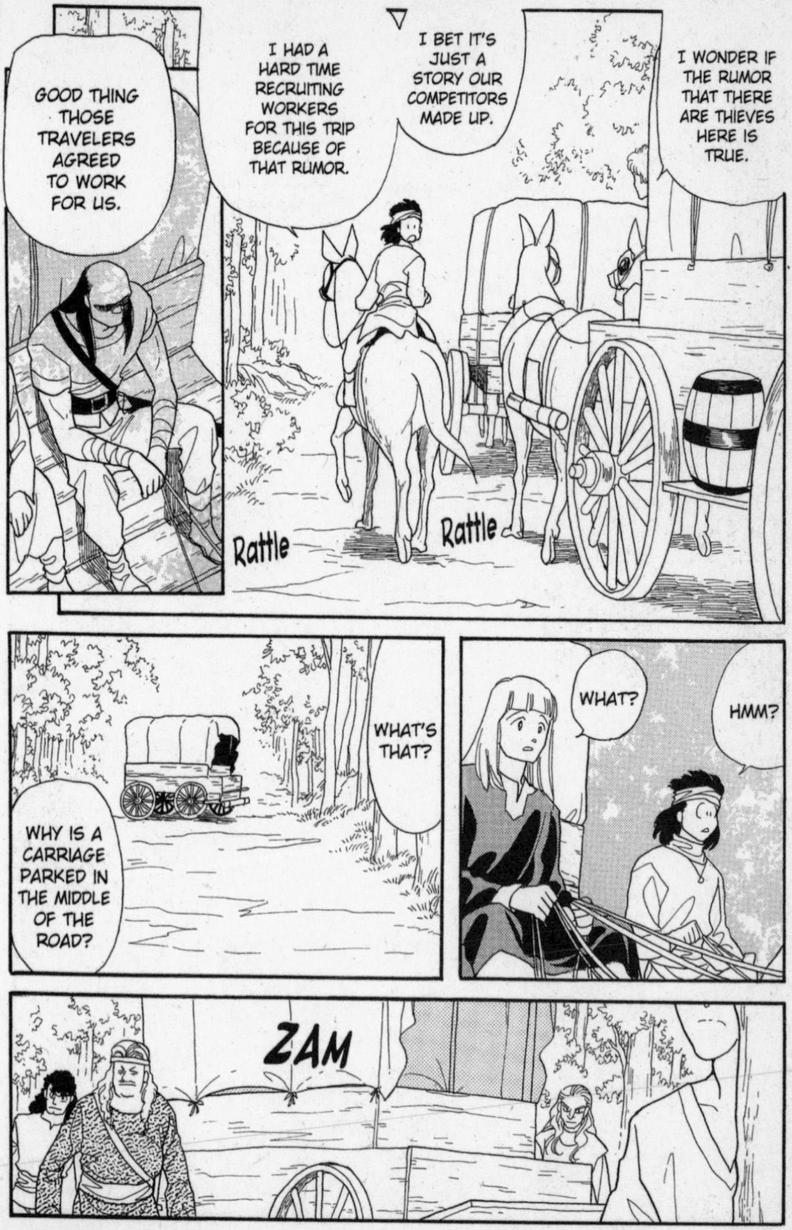
I WONDER IF THE RUMOR THAT THERE ARE THIEVES HERE IS TRUE.
I BET IT'S JUST A STORY OUR COMPETITORS MADE UP.
I HAD A HARD TIME RECRUITING WORKERS FOR THIS TRIP BECAUSE OF THAT RUMOR.
Rattle
Rattle
GOOD THING THOSE TRAVELERS AGREED TO WORK FOR US.
HMM?
WHAT?
WHAT'S THAT?
WHY IS A CARRIAGE PARKED IN THE MIDDLE OF THE ROAD?
ZAM

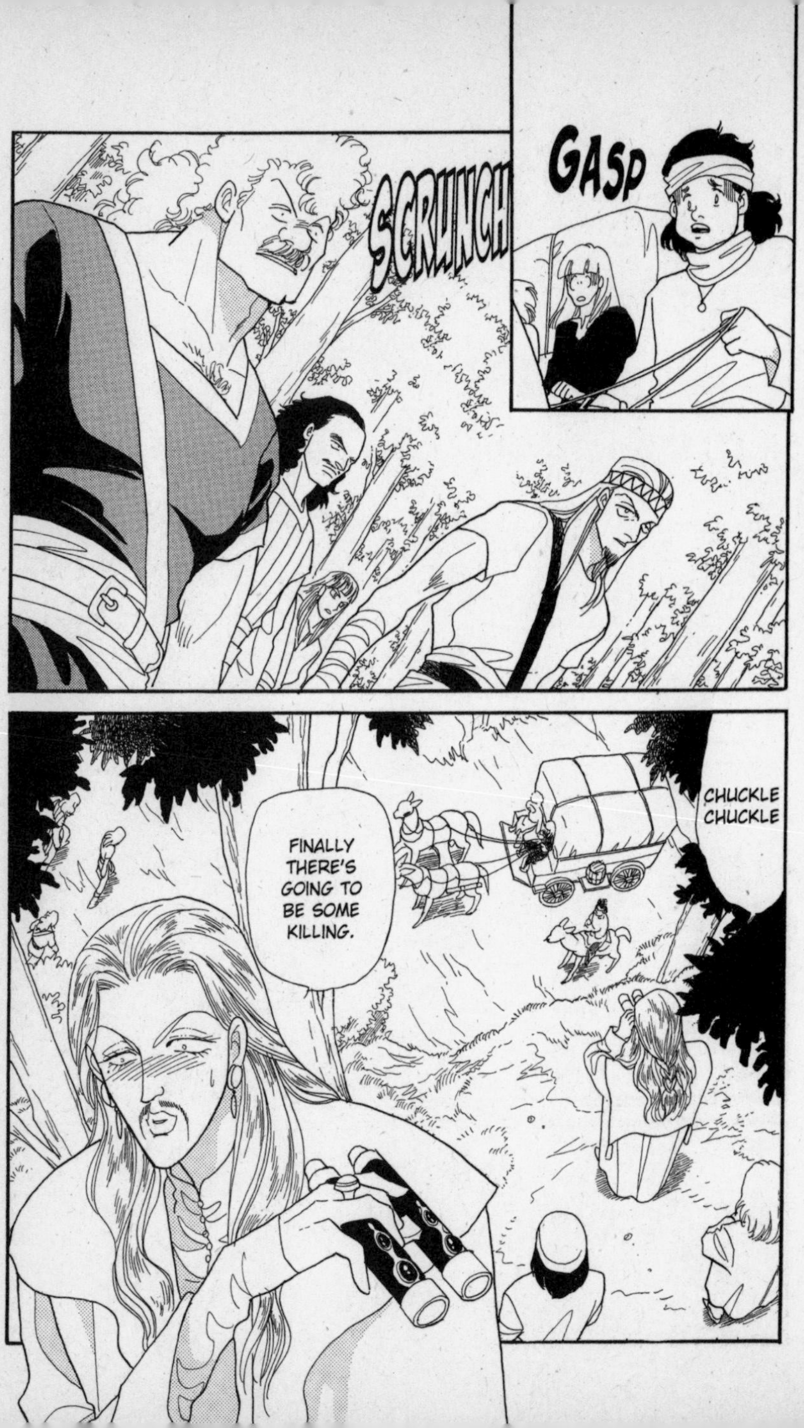
GASP
SCRUNCH
CHUCKLE CHUCKLE
FINALLY THERE'S GOING TO BE SOME KILLING.

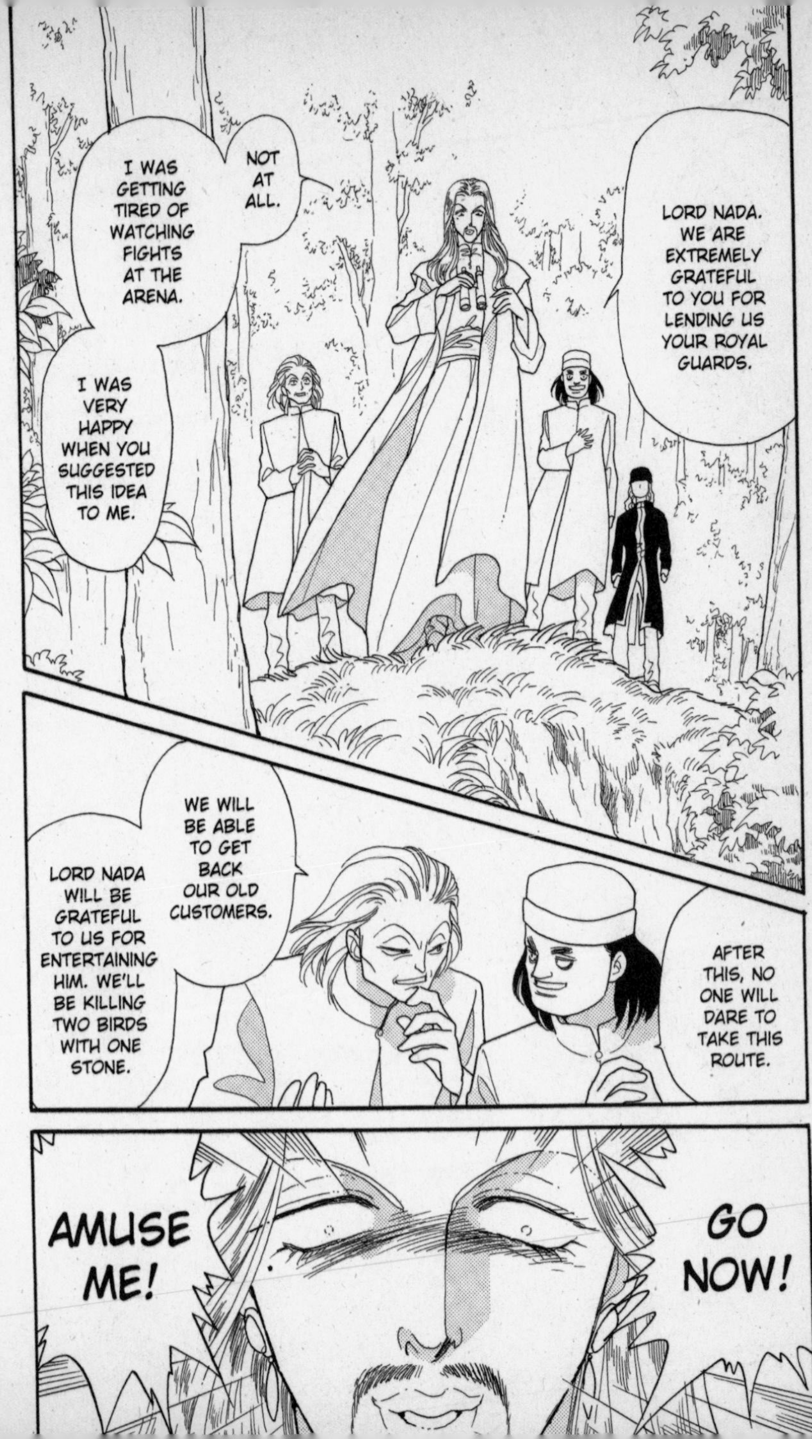
LORD NADA. WE ARE EXTREMELY GRATEFUL TO YOU FOR LENDING US YOUR ROYAL GUARDS.
NOT AT ALL.
I WAS GETTING TIRED OF WATCHING FIGHTS AT THE ARENA.
I WAS VERY HAPPY WHEN YOU SUGGESTED THIS IDEA TO ME.
AFTER THIS, NO ONE WILL DARE TO TAKE THIS ROUTE.
WE WILL BE ABLE TO GET BACK OUR OLD CUSTOMERS.
LORD NADA WILL BE GRATEFUL TO US FOR ENTERTAINING HIM. WE'LL BE KILLING TWO BIRDS WITH ONE STONE.
GO NOW!
AMUSE ME!

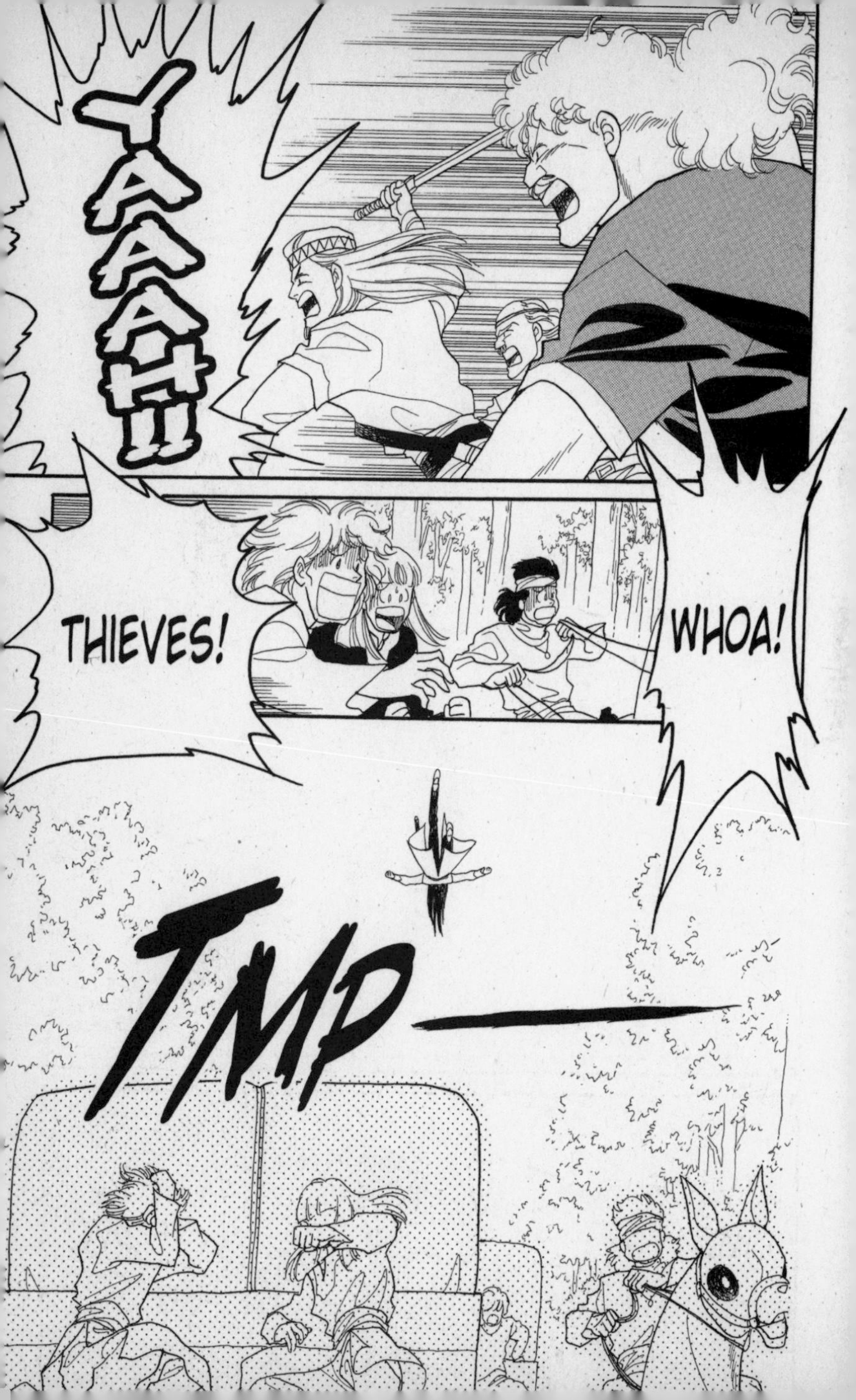
YAAAH!!
WHOA!
THIEVES!
TMP

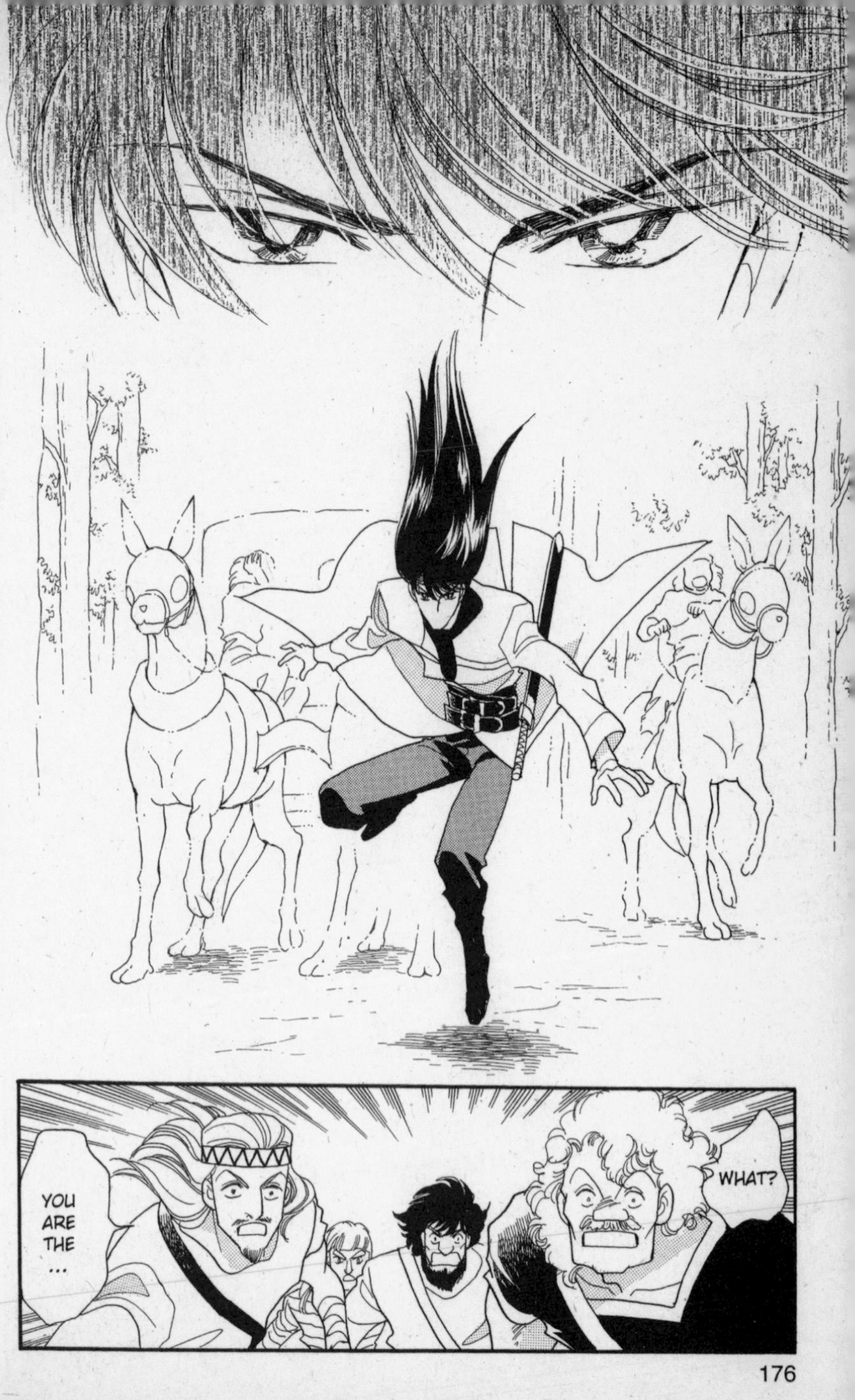
WHAT?
YOU ARE THE ...

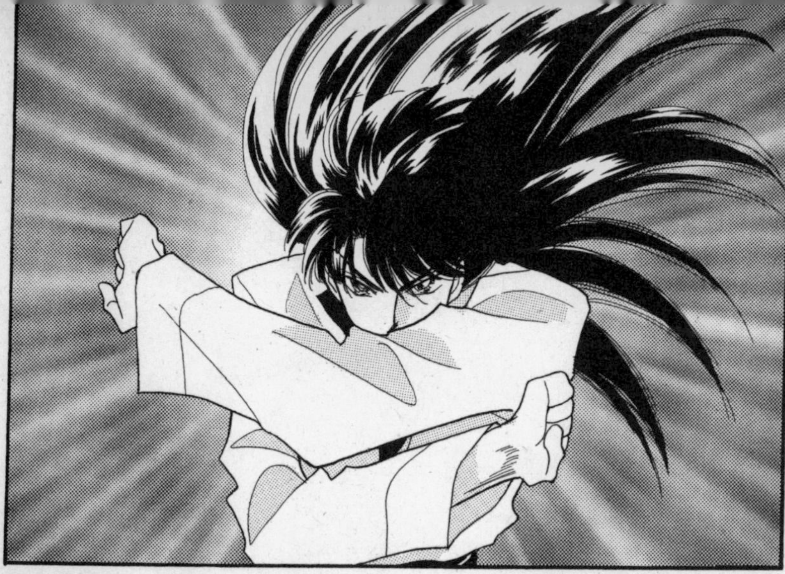

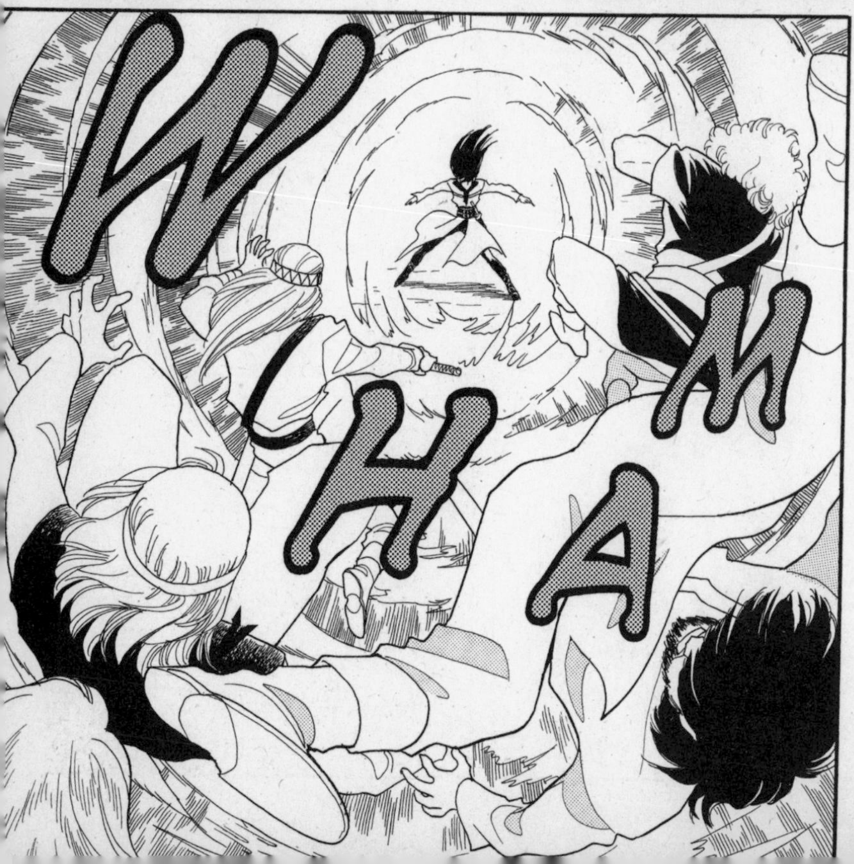
WHAM

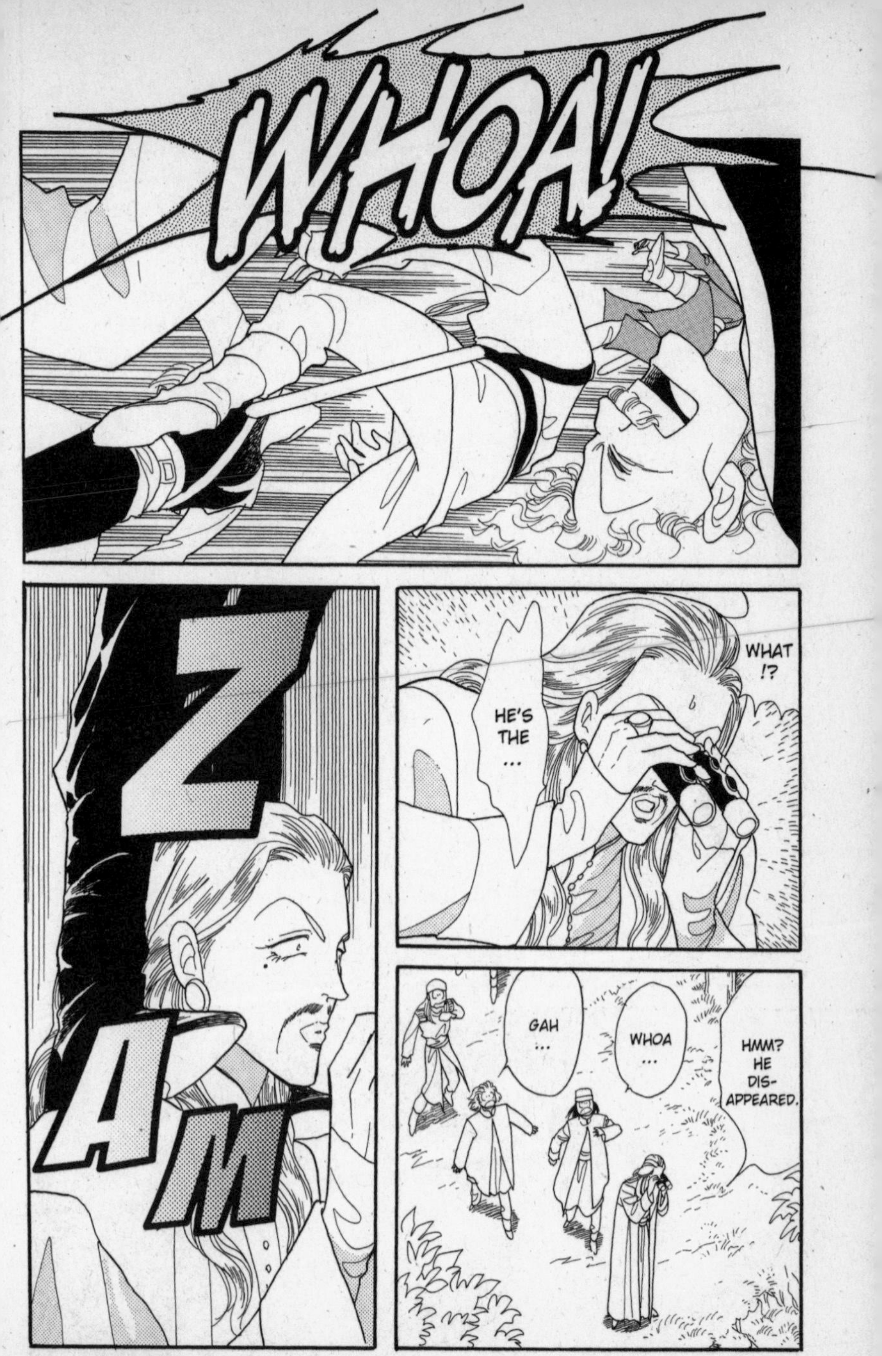
WHOA!
WHAT !?
HE'S THE ...
HMM? HE DIS-APPEARED.
WHOA ...
GAH ...
ZAM

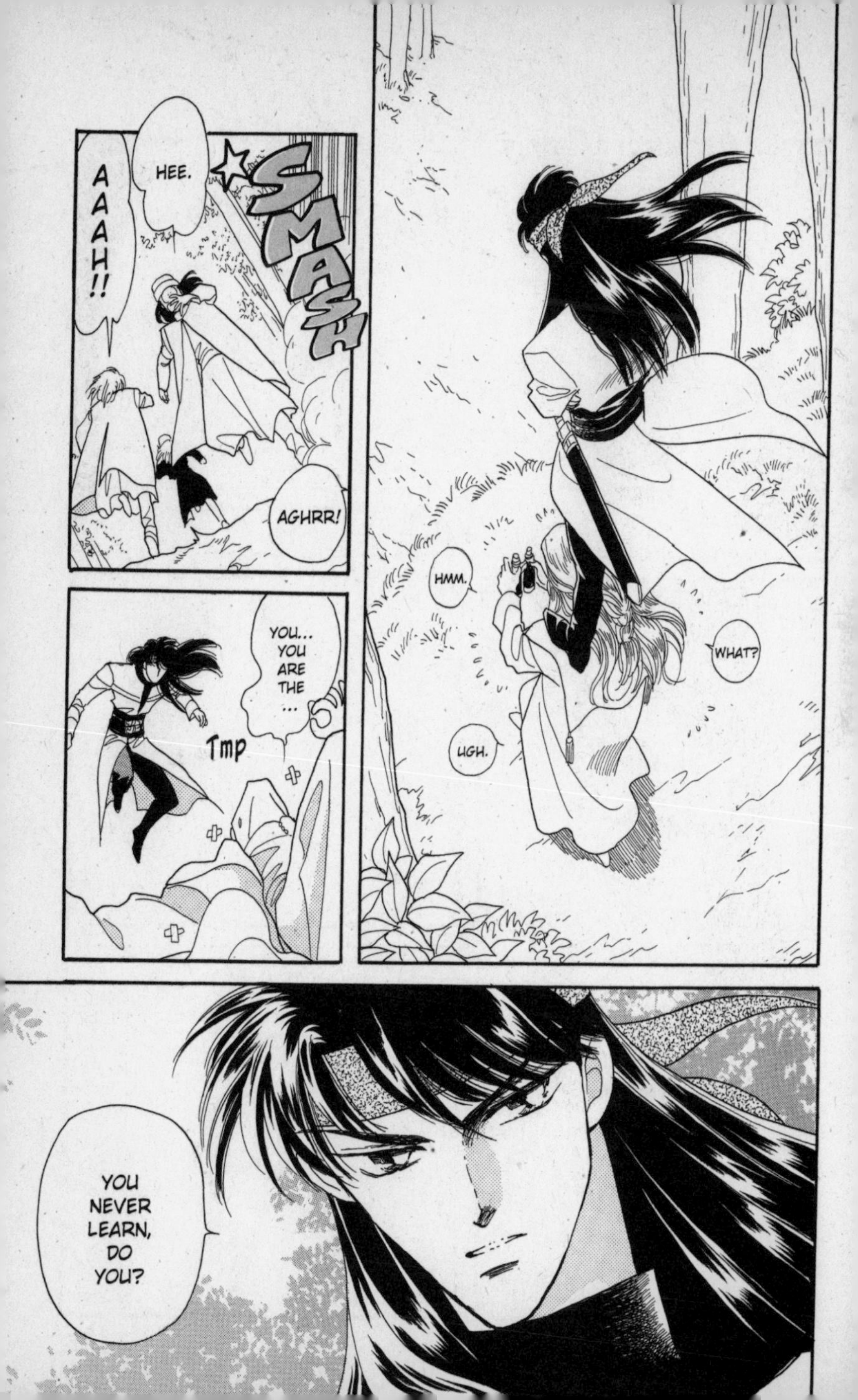
HMM.
WHAT?
UGH.
SMASH
HEE.
AAAH!!
AGHRR!
YOU... YOU ARE THE ...
Tmp
YOU NEVER LEARN, DO YOU?

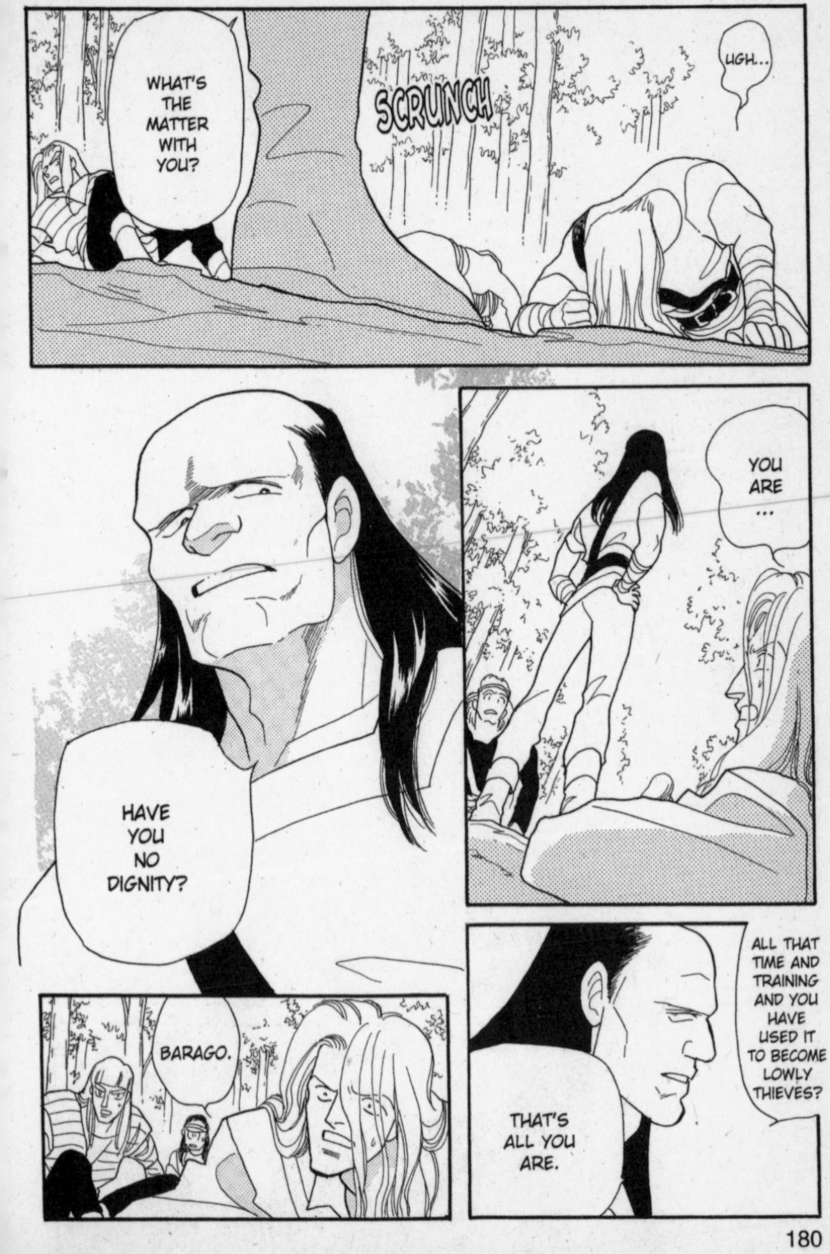
UGH...
SCRUNCH
WHAT'S THE MATTER WITH YOU?
YOU ARE ...
HAVE YOU NO DIGNITY?
ALL THAT TIME AND TRAINING AND YOU HAVE USED IT TO BECOME LOWLY THIEVES?
THAT'S ALL YOU ARE.
BARAGO.

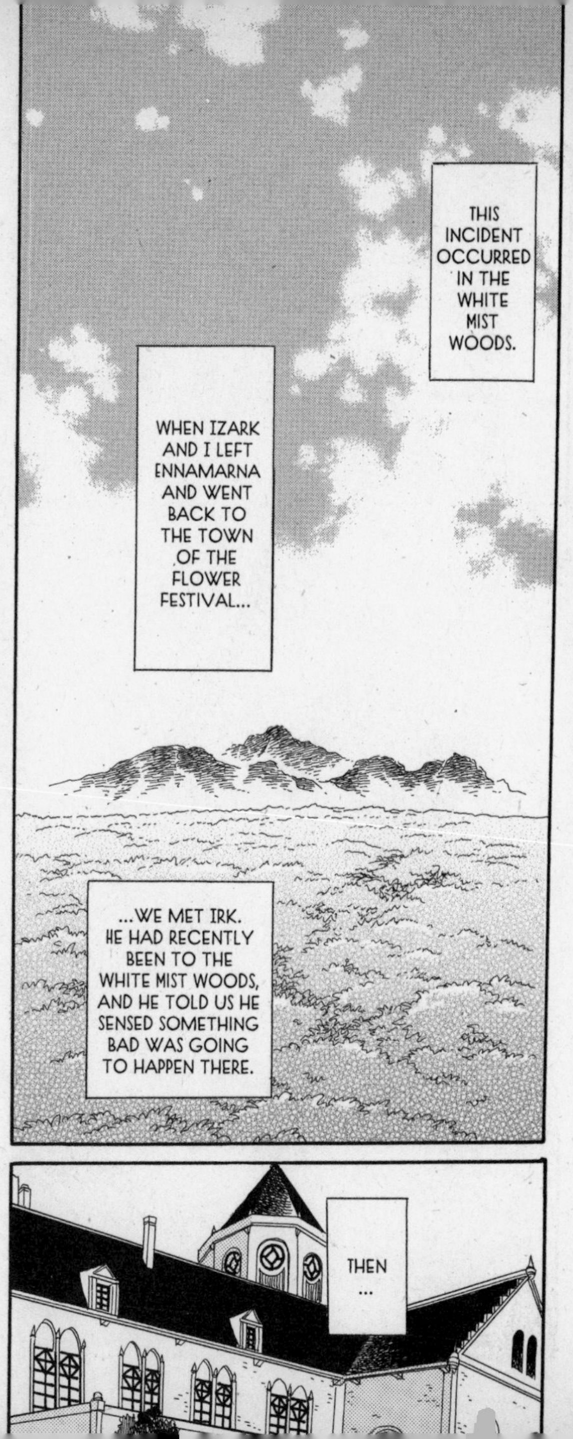
THIS INCIDENT OCCURRED IN THE WHITE MIST WOODS.
WHEN IZARK AND I LEFT ENNAMARNA AND WENT BACK TO THE TOWN OF THE FLOWER FESTIVAL...
...WE MET IRK. HE HAD RECENTLY BEEN TO THE WHITE MIST WOODS, AND HE TOLD US HE SENSED SOMETHING BAD WAS GOING TO HAPPEN THERE.
THEN ...

After the last volume was completed, I realized I wanted to add more episodes. To my surprise, my editor gave me 33 pages to be used for those episodes. The result is this epilogue. It's not easy to fill thirty-three pages. I had to depict each character's life after the last volume keeping in mind the drastic change their world had undergone. It wasn't an easy task, and consequently I'm beginning to ramble a bit.

In the end, I am glad that I had the opportunity to add a little about what will happen to Noriko and Izark in the future.

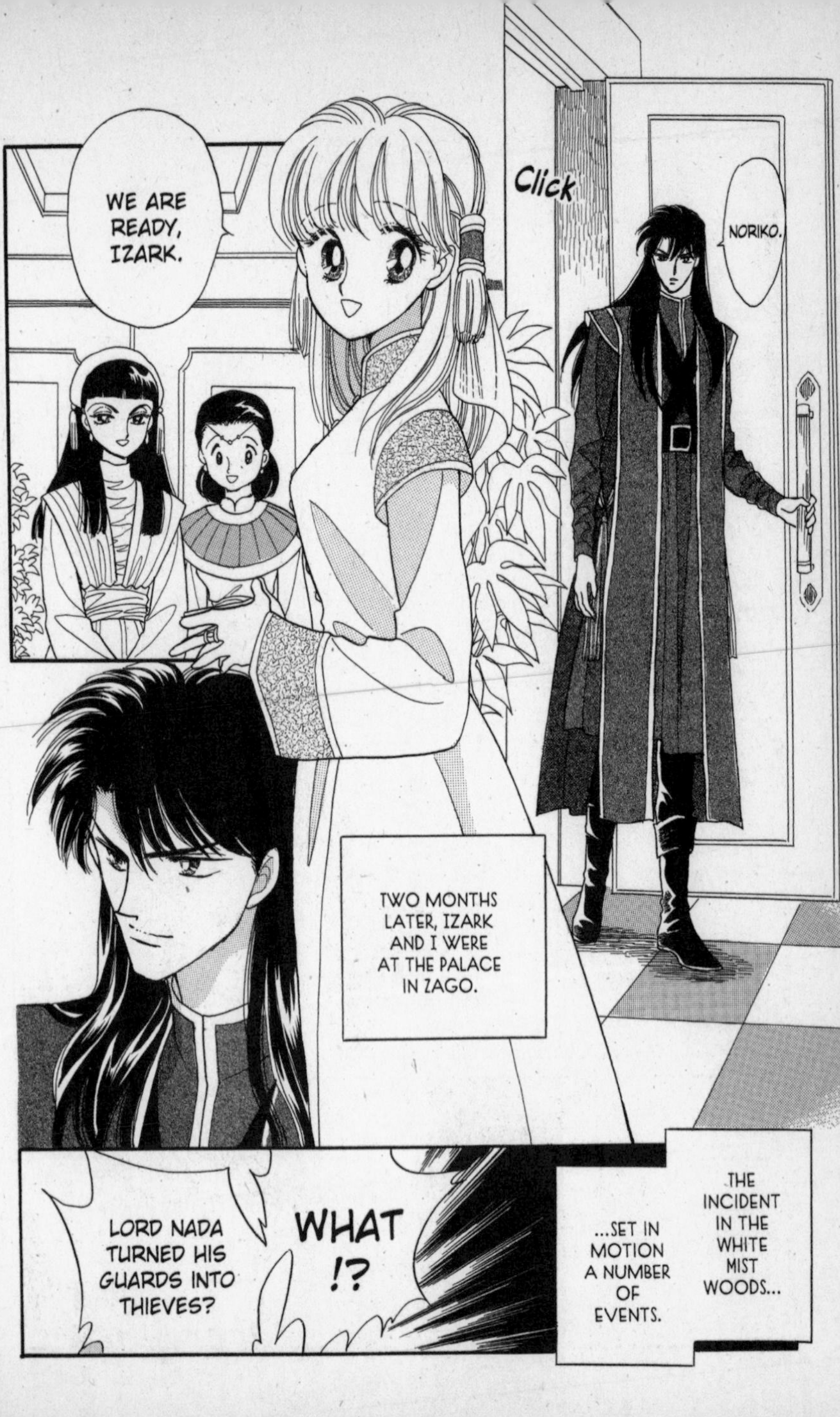
Click
NORIKO.
WE ARE READY, IZARK.
TWO MONTHS LATER, IZARK AND I WERE AT THE PALACE IN ZAGO.
THE INCIDENT IN THE WHITE MIST WOODS...
...SET IN MOTION A NUMBER OF EVENTS.
WHAT !?
LORD NADA TURNED HIS GUARDS INTO THIEVES?

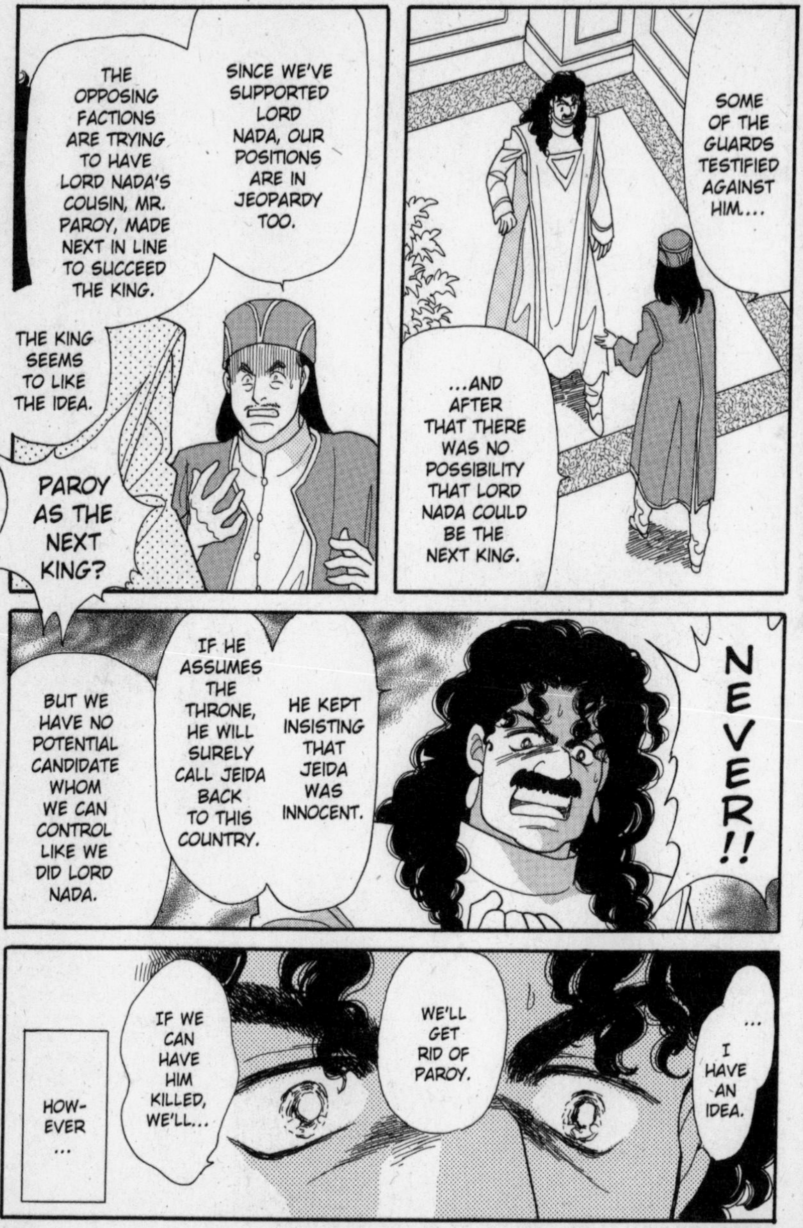
SOME OF THE GUARDS TESTIFIED AGAINST HIM...
...AND AFTER THAT THERE WAS NO POSSIBILITY THAT LORD NADA COULD BE THE NEXT KING.
SINCE WE'VE SUPPORTED LORD NADA, OUR POSITIONS ARE IN JEOPARDY TOO.
THE OPPOSING FACTIONS ARE TRYING TO HAVE LORD NADA'S COUSIN, MR. PAROY, MADE NEXT IN LINE TO SUCCEED THE KING.
THE KING SEEMS TO LIKE THE IDEA.
PAROY AS THE NEXT KING?
NEVER!!
HE KEPT INSISTING THAT JEIDA WAS INNOCENT.
IF HE ASSUMES THE THRONE, HE WILL SURELY CALL JEIDA BACK TO THIS COUNTRY.
BUT WE HAVE NO POTENTIAL CANDIDATE WHOM WE CAN CONTROL LIKE WE DID LORD NADA.
... I HAVE AN IDEA.
WE'LL GET RID OF PAROY.
IF WE CAN HAVE HIM KILLED, WE'LL...
HOW-EVER ...

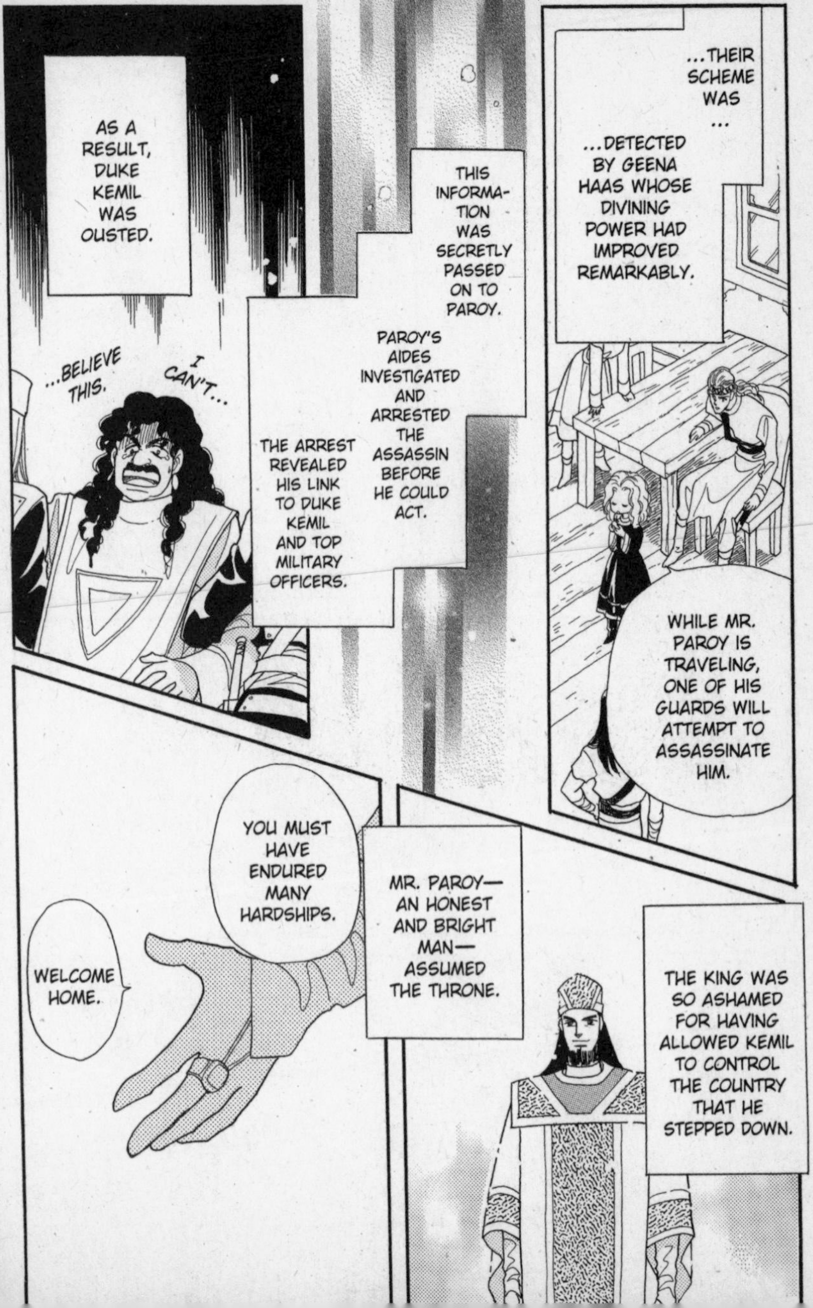
...THEIR SCHEME WAS ...
...DETECTED BY GEENA HAAS WHOSE DIVINING POWER HAD IMPROVED REMARKABLY.
WHILE MR. PAROY IS TRAVELING, ONE OF HIS GUARDS WILL ATTEMPT TO ASSASSINATE HIM.
THIS INFORMATION WAS SECRETLY PASSED ON TO PAROY.
PAROY'S AIDES INVESTIGATED AND ARRESTED THE ASSASSIN BEFORE HE COULD ACT.
THE ARREST REVEALED HIS LINK TO DUKE KEMIL AND TOP MILITARY OFFICERS.
AS A RESULT, DUKE KEMIL WAS OUSTED.
I CAN'T...
...BELIEVE THIS.
THE KING WAS SO ASHAMED FOR HAVING ALLOWED KEMIL TO CONTROL THE COUNTRY THAT HE STEPPED DOWN.
MR. PAROY—AN HONEST AND BRIGHT MAN—ASSUMED THE THRONE.
YOU MUST HAVE ENDURED MANY HARDSHIPS.
WELCOME HOME.

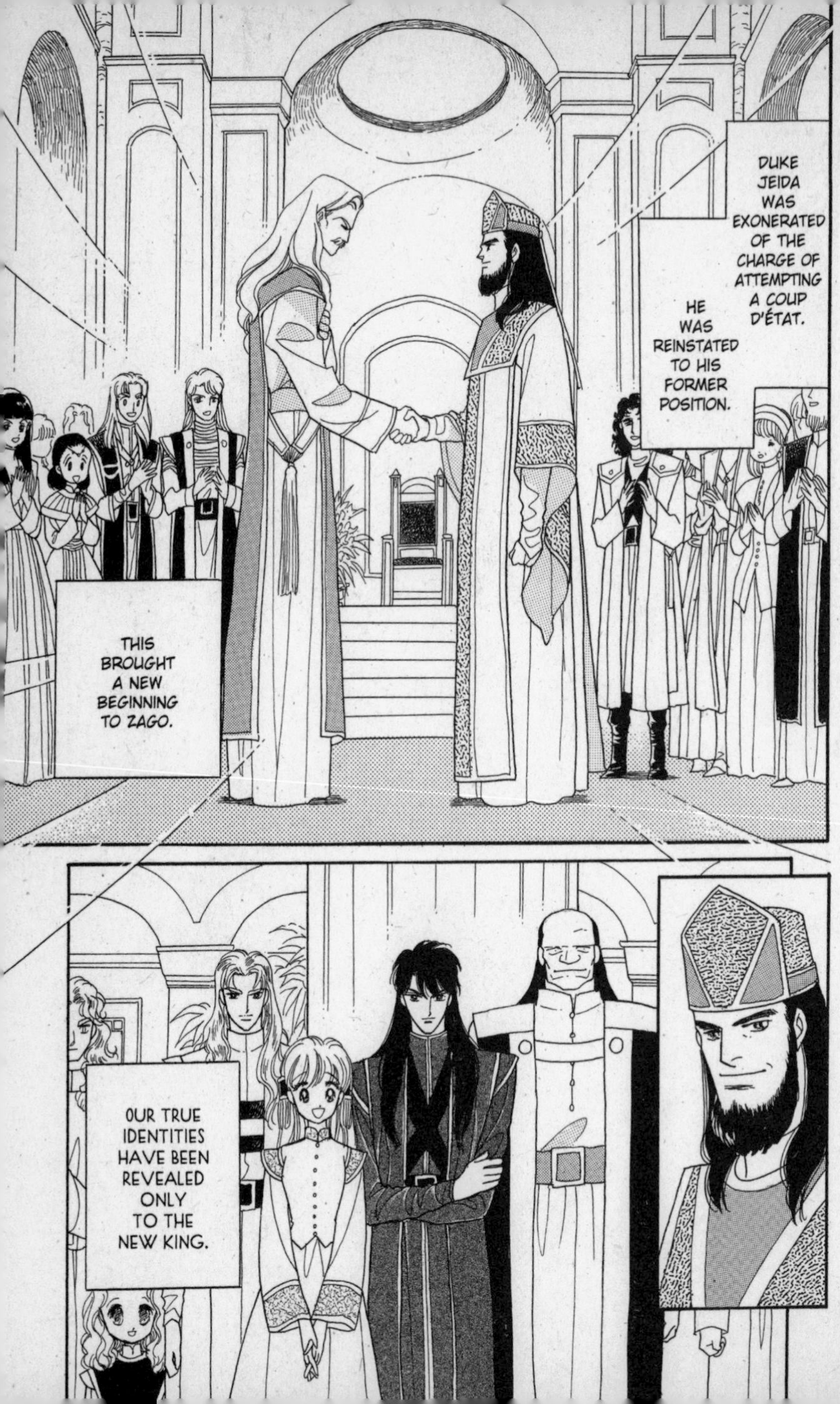
DUKE JEIDA WAS EXONERATED OF THE CHARGE OF ATTEMPTING A COUP D'ÉTAT.
HE WAS REINSTATED TO HIS FORMER POSITION.
THIS BROUGHT A NEW BEGINNING TO ZAGO.
OUR TRUE IDENTITIES HAVE BEEN REVEALED ONLY TO THE NEW KING.

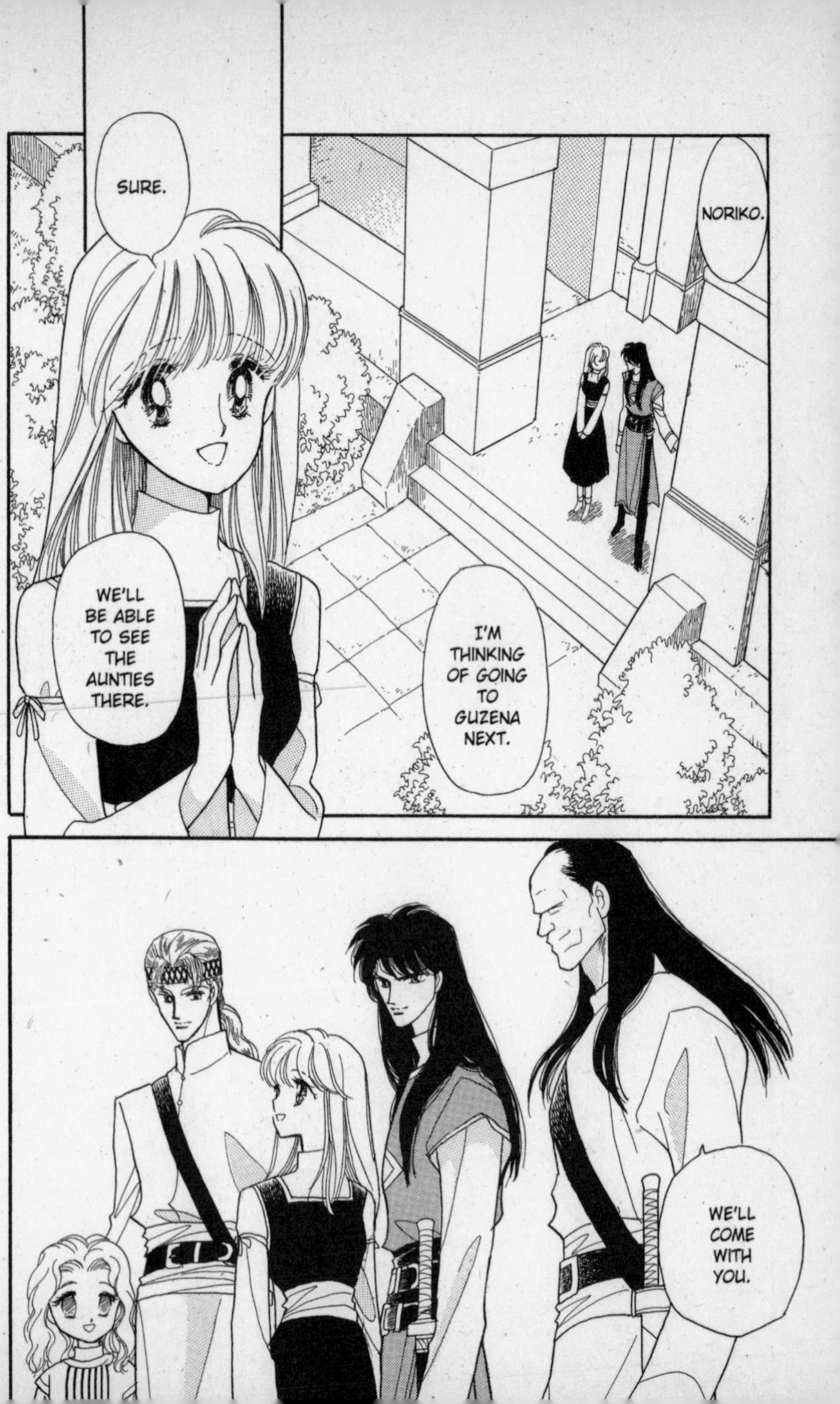
NORIKO.
I'M THINKING OF GOING TO GUZENA NEXT.
SURE.
WE'LL BE ABLE TO SEE THE AUNTIES THERE.
WE'LL COME WITH YOU.

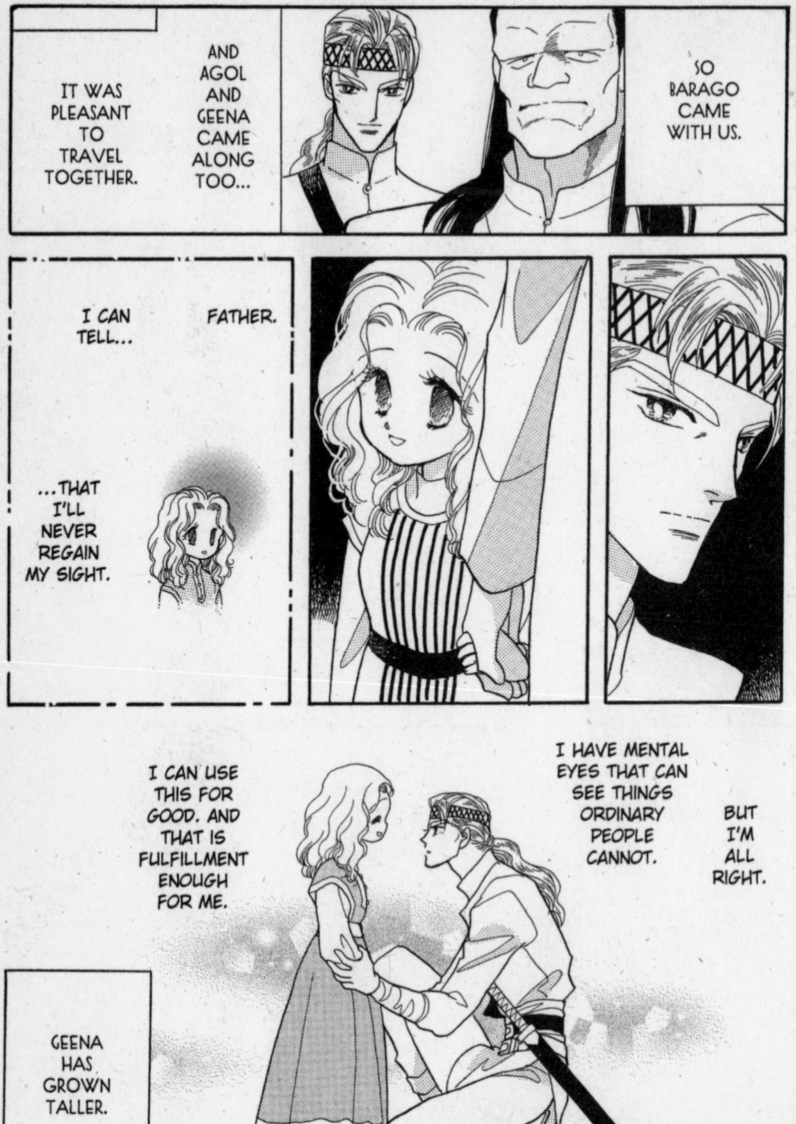
SO BARAGO CAME WITH US.
AND AGOL AND GEENA CAME ALONG TOO...
IT WAS PLEASANT TO TRAVEL TOGETHER.
FATHER.
I CAN TELL...
...THAT I'LL NEVER REGAIN MY SIGHT.
BUT I'M ALL RIGHT.
I HAVE MENTAL EYES THAT CAN SEE THINGS ORDINARY PEOPLE CANNOT.
I CAN USE THIS FOR GOOD. AND THAT IS FULFILLMENT ENOUGH FOR ME.
GEENA HAS GROWN TALLER.

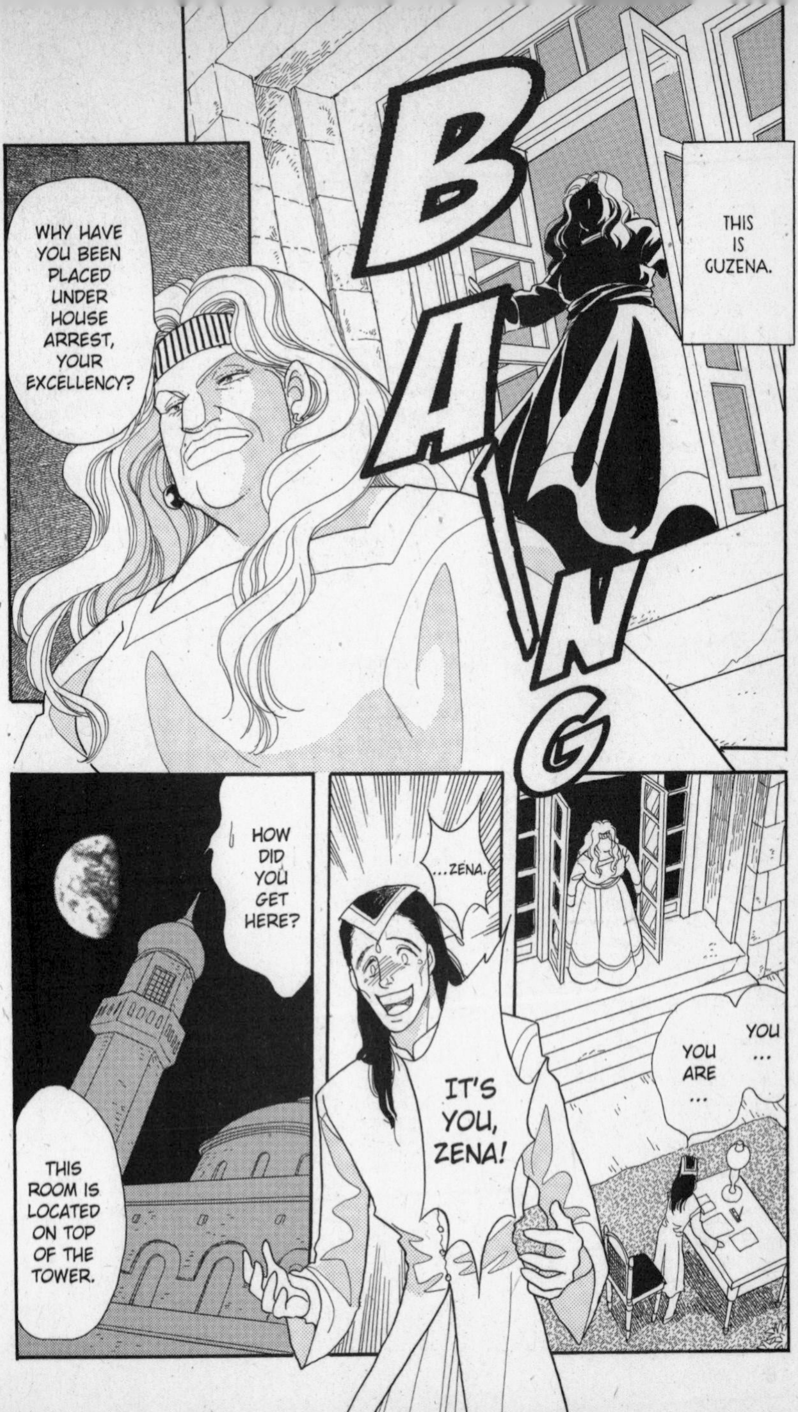
BANG
THIS IS GUZENA.
WHY HAVE YOU BEEN PLACED UNDER HOUSE ARREST, YOUR EXCELLENCY?
YOU ... YOU ARE ...
...ZENA.
IT'S YOU, ZENA!
HOW DID YOU GET HERE?
THIS ROOM IS LOCATED ON TOP OF THE TOWER.

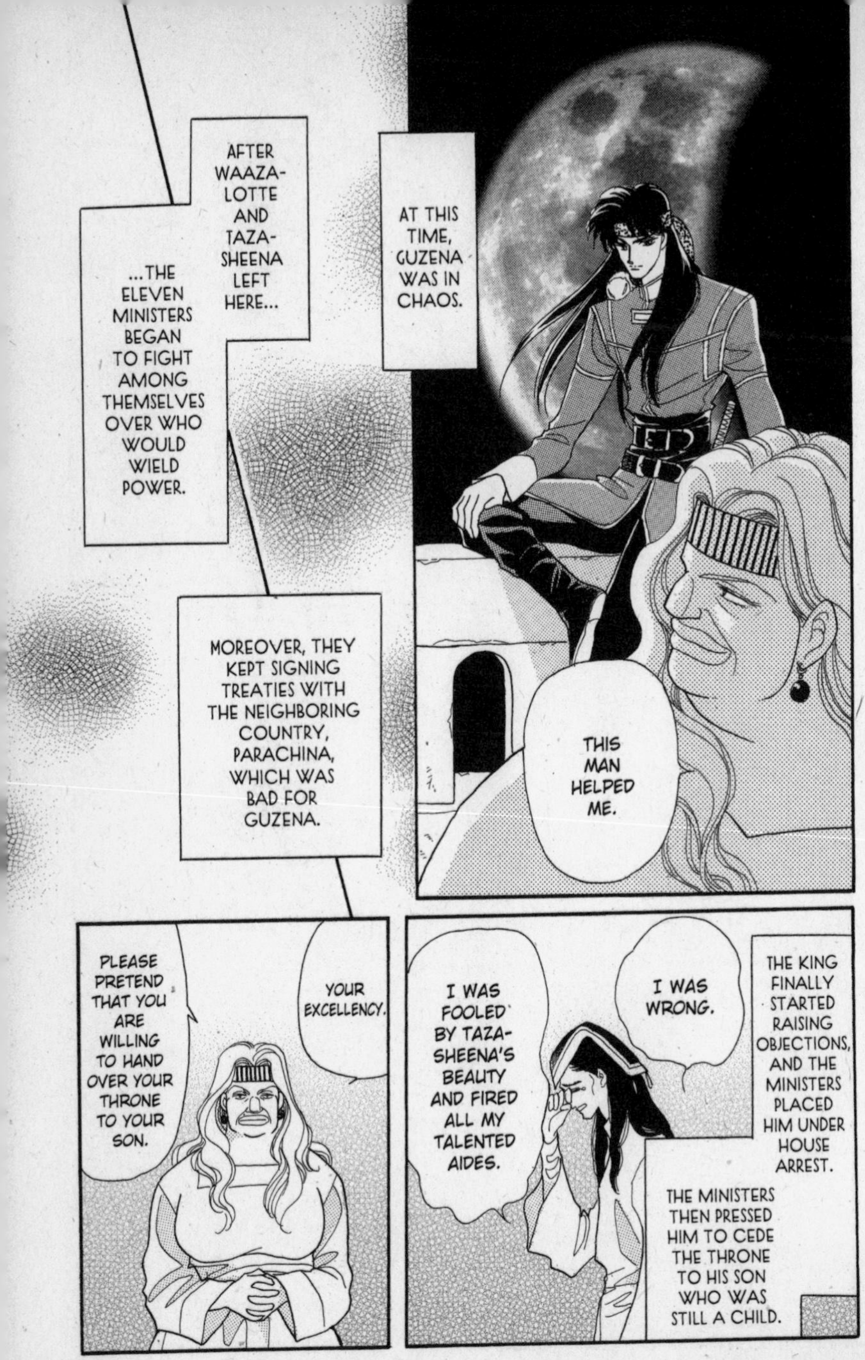
AT THIS TIME, GUZENA WAS IN CHAOS.
AFTER WAAZA-LOTTE AND TAZA-SHEENA LEFT HERE...
...THE ELEVEN MINISTERS BEGAN TO FIGHT AMONG THEMSELVES OVER WHO WOULD WIELD POWER.
MOREOVER, THEY KEPT SIGNING TREATIES WITH THE NEIGHBORING COUNTRY, PARACHINA, WHICH WAS BAD FOR GUZENA.
THIS MAN HELPED ME.
THE KING FINALLY STARTED RAISING OBJECTIONS, AND THE MINISTERS PLACED HIM UNDER HOUSE ARREST.
I WAS WRONG.
I WAS FOOLED BY TAZA-SHEENA'S BEAUTY AND FIRED ALL MY TALENTED AIDES.
THE MINISTERS THEN PRESSED HIM TO CEDE THE THRONE TO HIS SON WHO WAS STILL A CHILD.
YOUR EXCELLENCY.
PLEASE PRETEND THAT YOU ARE WILLING TO HAND OVER YOUR THRONE TO YOUR SON.

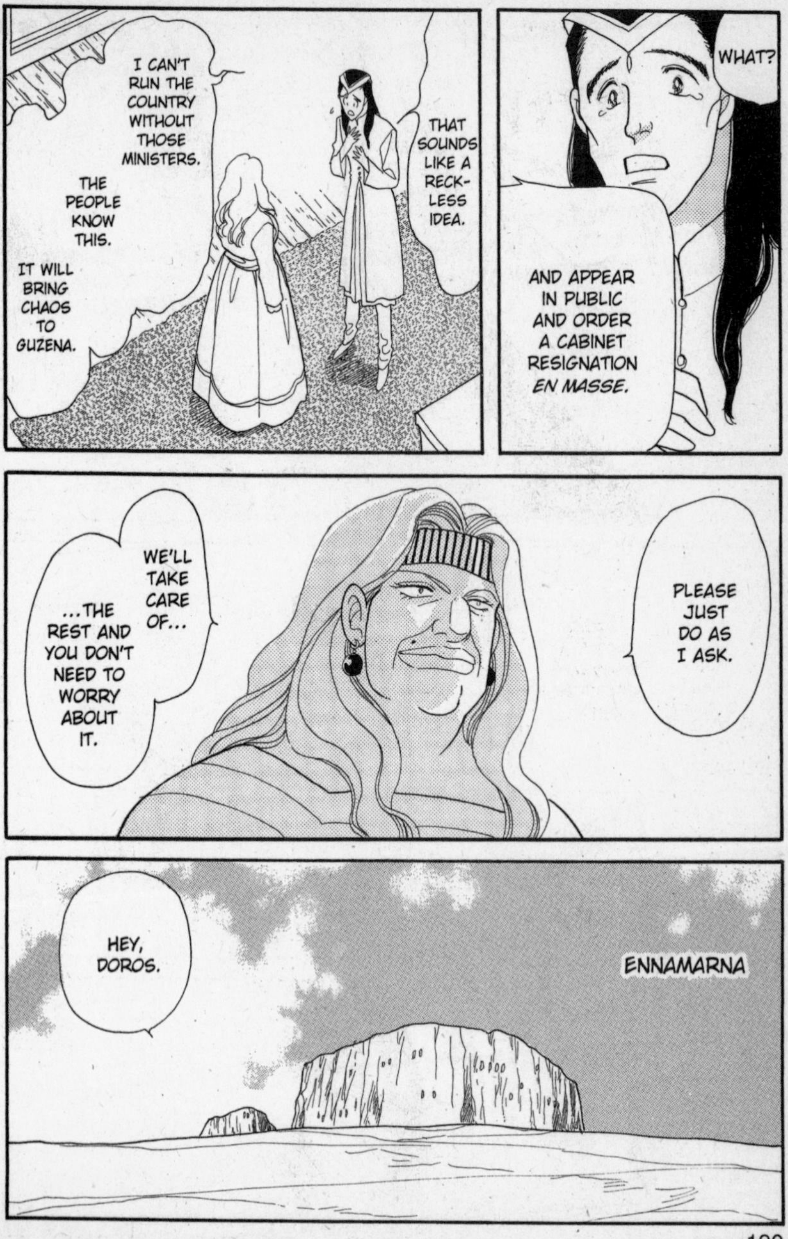
WHAT?
AND APPEAR IN PUBLIC AND ORDER A CABINET RESIGNATION *EN MASSE.*
THAT SOUNDS LIKE A RECK-LESS IDEA.
I CAN'T RUN THE COUNTRY WITHOUT THOSE MINISTERS.
THE PEOPLE KNOW THIS.
IT WILL BRING CHAOS TO GUZENA.
PLEASE JUST DO AS I ASK.
WE'LL TAKE CARE OF...
...THE REST AND YOU DON'T NEED TO WORRY ABOUT IT.
ENNAMARNA
HEY, DOROS.

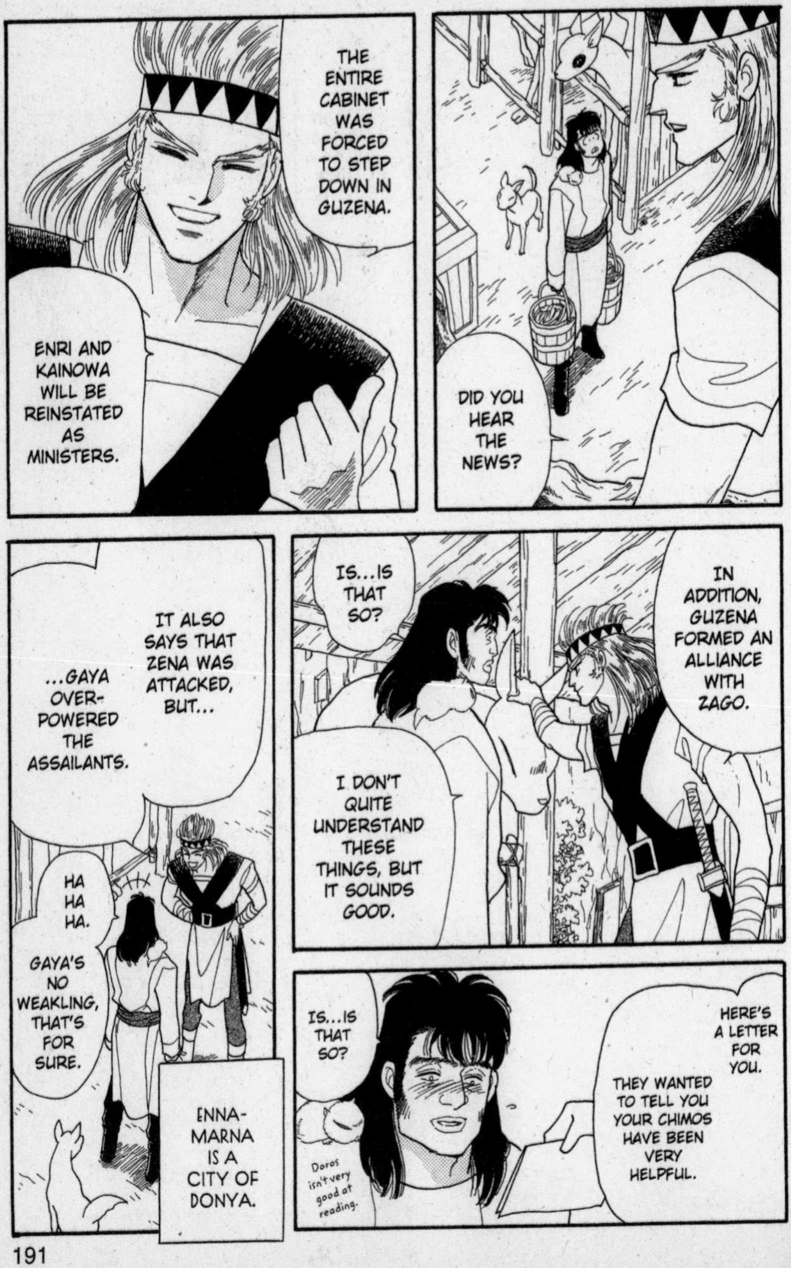
DID YOU HEAR THE NEWS?
THE ENTIRE CABINET WAS FORCED TO STEP DOWN IN GUZENA.
ENRI AND KAINOWA WILL BE REINSTATED AS MINISTERS.
IN ADDITION, GUZENA FORMED AN ALLIANCE WITH ZAGO.
IS...IS THAT SO?
I DON'T QUITE UNDERSTAND THESE THINGS, BUT IT SOUNDS GOOD.
HERE'S A LETTER FOR YOU.
THEY WANTED TO TELL YOU YOUR CHIMOS HAVE BEEN VERY HELPFUL.
IS...IS THAT SO?
Doros isn't very good at reading.
IT ALSO SAYS THAT ZENA WAS ATTACKED, BUT...
...GAYA OVER-POWERED THE ASSAILANTS.
HA HA HA.
GAYA'S NO WEAKLING, THAT'S FOR SURE.
ENNA-MARNA IS A CITY OF DONYA.

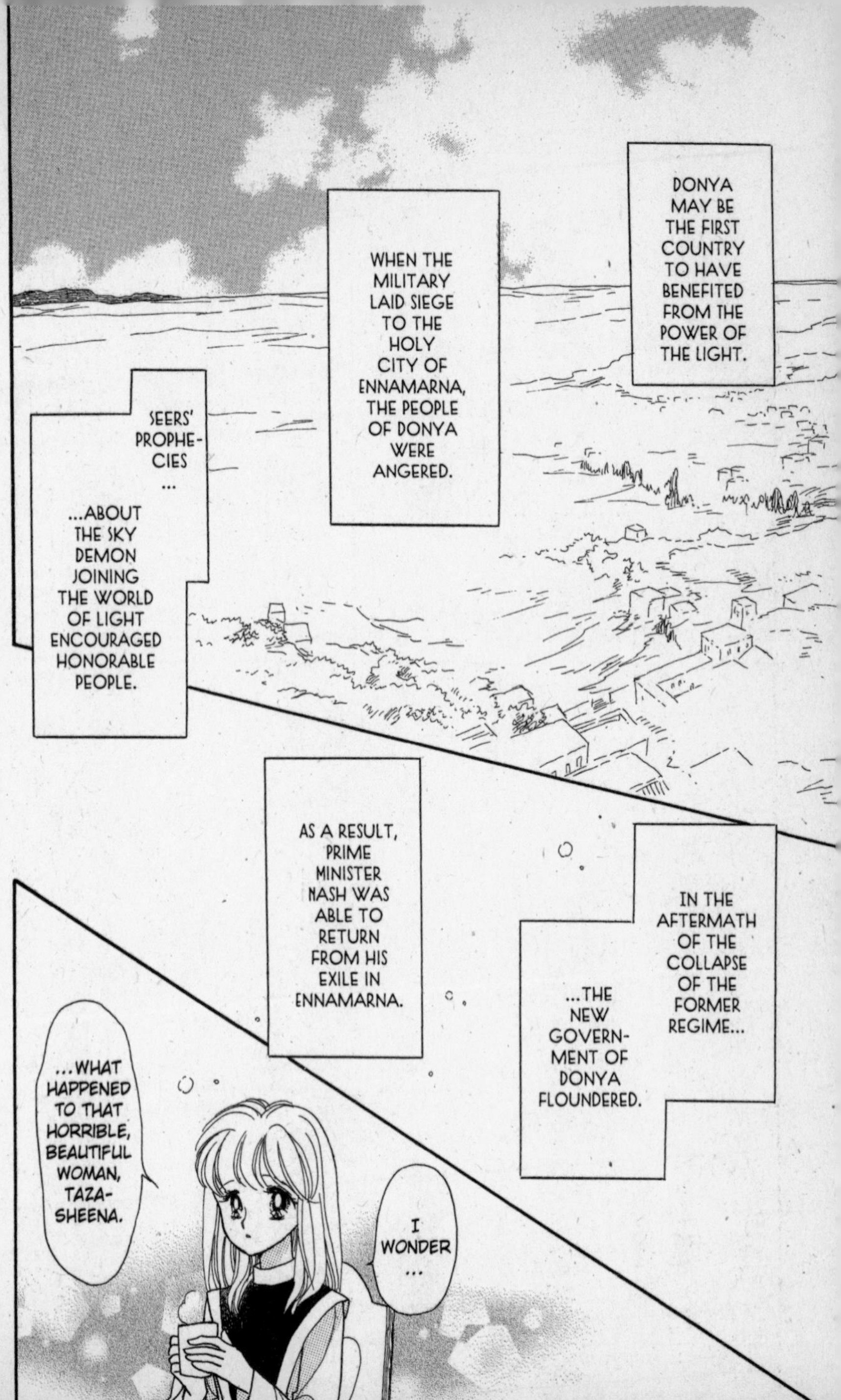
DONYA MAY BE THE FIRST COUNTRY TO HAVE BENEFITED FROM THE POWER OF THE LIGHT.
WHEN THE MILITARY LAID SIEGE TO THE HOLY CITY OF ENNAMARNA, THE PEOPLE OF DONYA WERE ANGERED.
SEERS' PROPHECIES ...
...ABOUT THE SKY DEMON JOINING THE WORLD OF LIGHT ENCOURAGED HONORABLE PEOPLE.
IN THE AFTERMATH OF THE COLLAPSE OF THE FORMER REGIME...
...THE NEW GOVERNMENT OF DONYA FLOUNDERED.
AS A RESULT, PRIME MINISTER NASH WAS ABLE TO RETURN FROM HIS EXILE IN ENNAMARNA.
I WONDER ...
...WHAT HAPPENED TO THAT HORRIBLE, BEAUTIFUL WOMAN, TAZA-SHEENA.

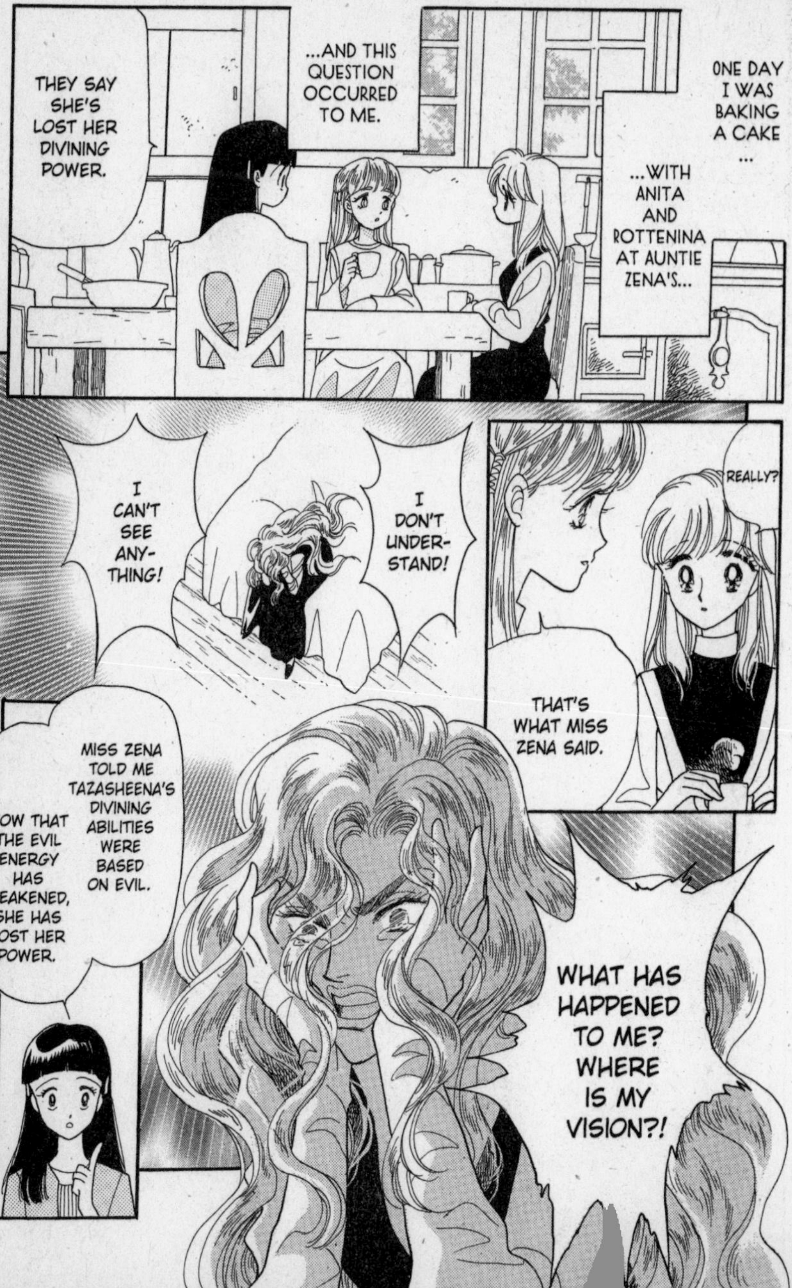
ONE DAY I WAS BAKING A CAKE ...
...WITH ANITA AND ROTTENINA AT AUNTIE ZENA'S...
...AND THIS QUESTION OCCURRED TO ME.
THEY SAY SHE'S LOST HER DIVINING POWER.
REALLY?
THAT'S WHAT MISS ZENA SAID.
I DON'T UNDER-STAND!
I CAN'T SEE ANY-THING!
WHAT HAS HAPPENED TO ME? WHERE IS MY VISION?!
MISS ZENA TOLD ME TAZASHEENA'S DIVINING ABILITIES WERE BASED ON EVIL.
NOW THAT THE EVIL ENERGY HAS WEAKENED, SHE HAS LOST HER POWER.

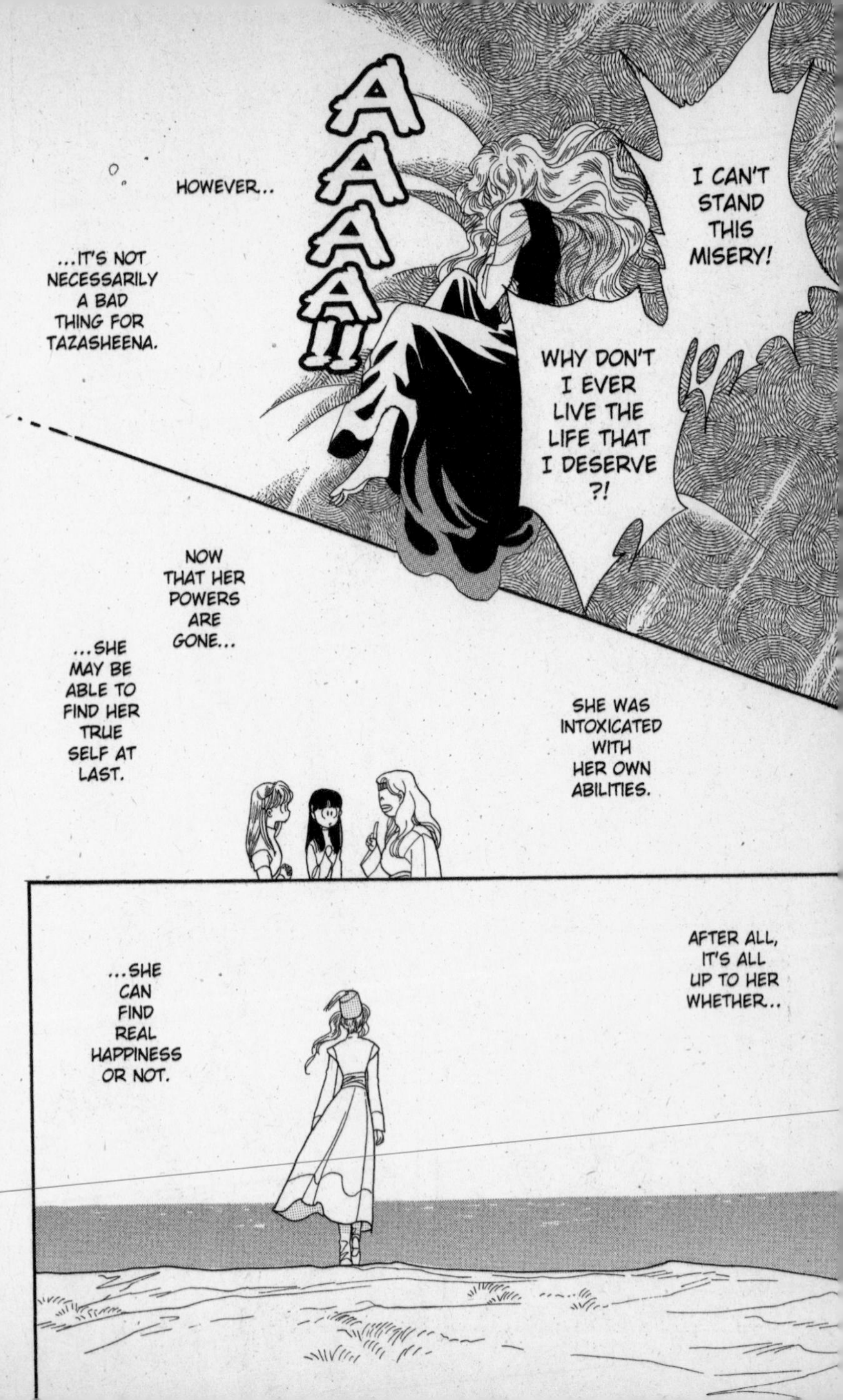
I CAN'T STAND THIS MISERY!
AAAAA!!
WHY DON'T I EVER LIVE THE LIFE THAT I DESERVE?!
HOWEVER...
...IT'S NOT NECESSARILY A BAD THING FOR TAZASHEENA.
SHE WAS INTOXICATED WITH HER OWN ABILITIES.
NOW THAT HER POWERS ARE GONE...
...SHE MAY BE ABLE TO FIND HER TRUE SELF AT LAST.
AFTER ALL, IT'S ALL UP TO HER WHETHER...
...SHE CAN FIND REAL HAPPINESS OR NOT.

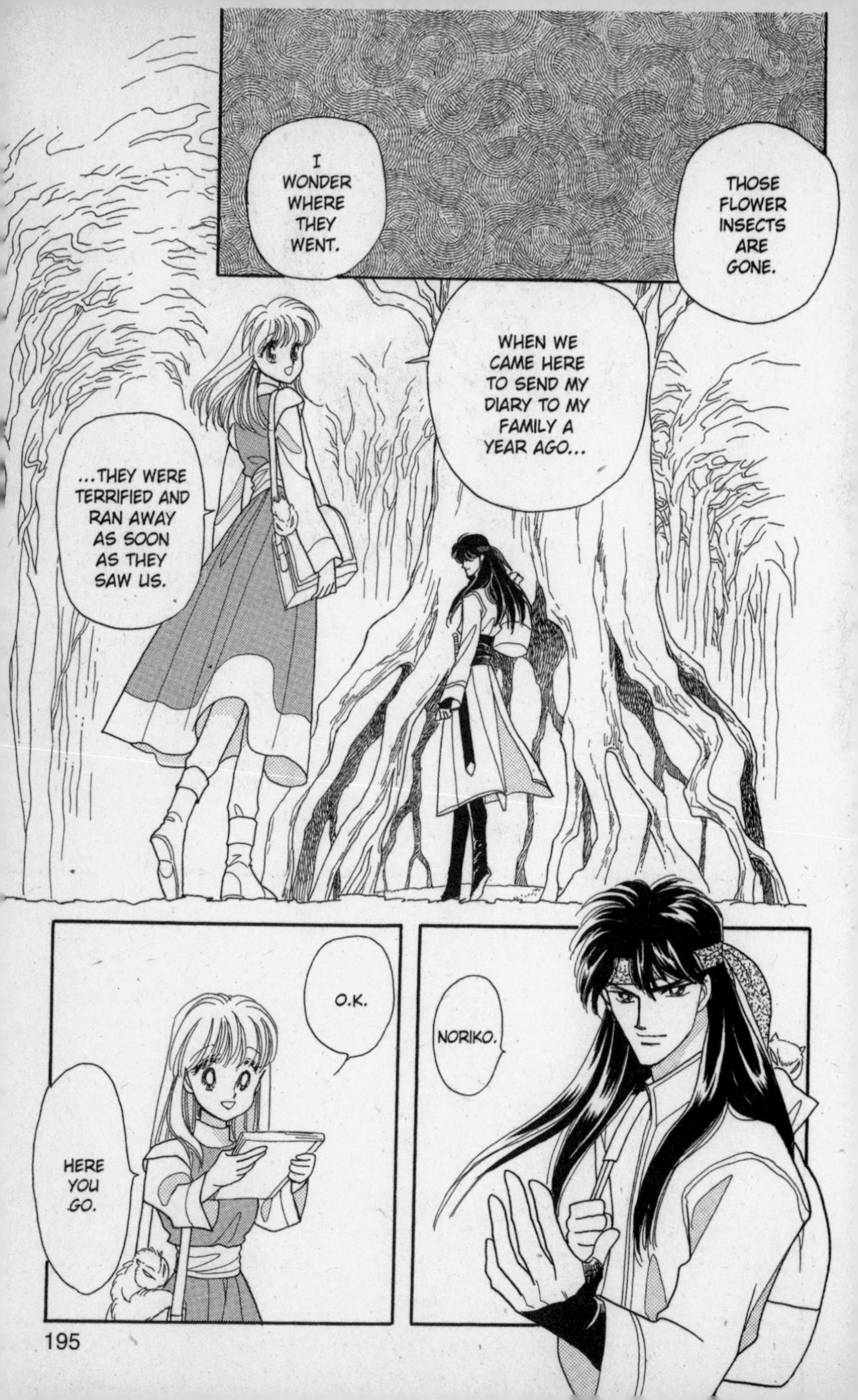
THOSE FLOWER INSECTS ARE GONE.
I WONDER WHERE THEY WENT.
WHEN WE CAME HERE TO SEND MY DIARY TO MY FAMILY A YEAR AGO...
...THEY WERE TERRIFIED AND RAN AWAY AS SOON AS THEY SAW US.
NORIKO.
O.K.
HERE YOU GO.

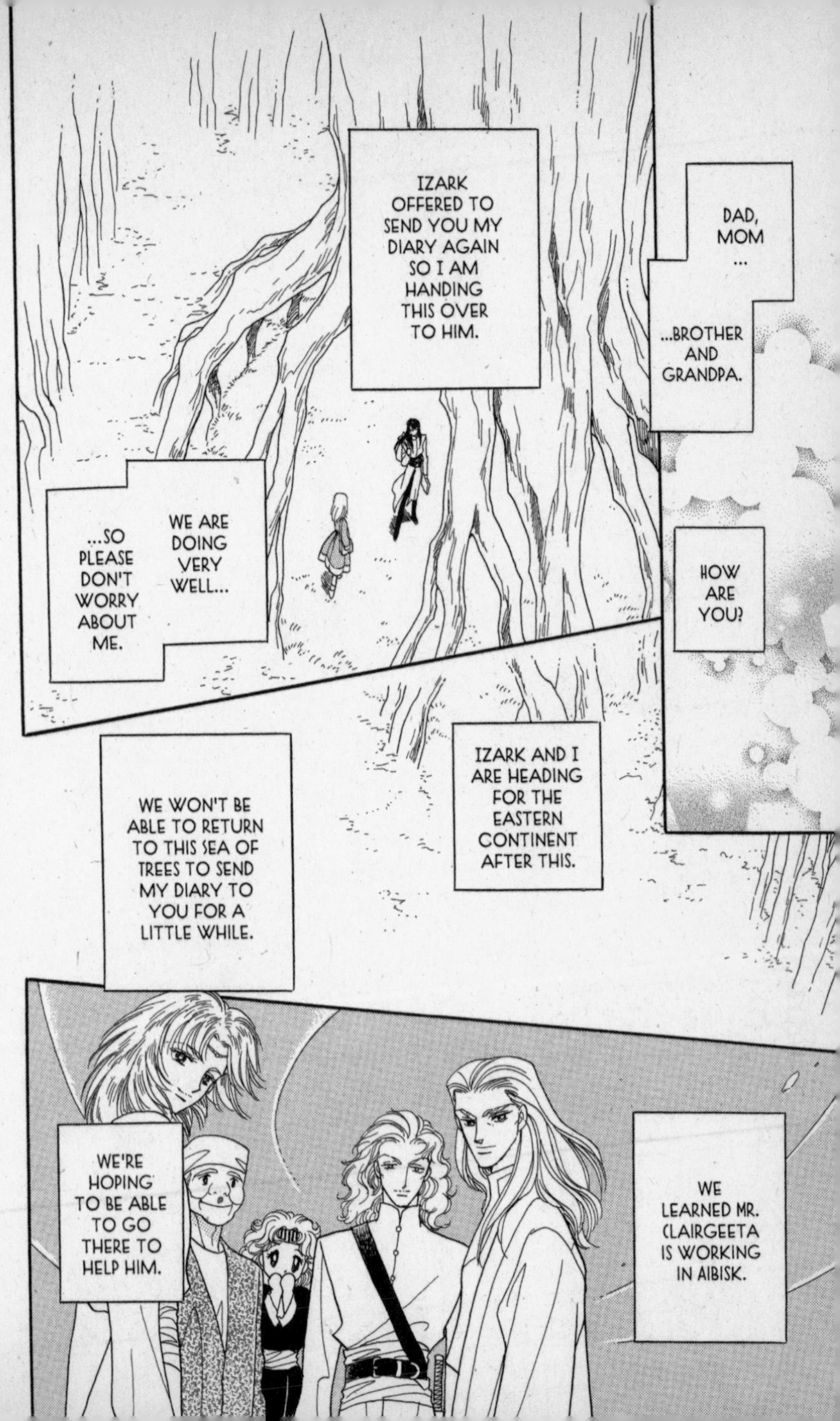
DAD, MOM ...
...BROTHER AND GRANDPA.
HOW ARE YOU?
IZARK OFFERED TO SEND YOU MY DIARY AGAIN SO I AM HANDING THIS OVER TO HIM.
WE ARE DOING VERY WELL...
...SO PLEASE DON'T WORRY ABOUT ME.
IZARK AND I ARE HEADING FOR THE EASTERN CONTINENT AFTER THIS.
WE WON'T BE ABLE TO RETURN TO THIS SEA OF TREES TO SEND MY DIARY TO YOU FOR A LITTLE WHILE.
WE LEARNED MR. CLAIRGEETA IS WORKING IN AIBISK.
WE'RE HOPING TO BE ABLE TO GO THERE TO HELP HIM.

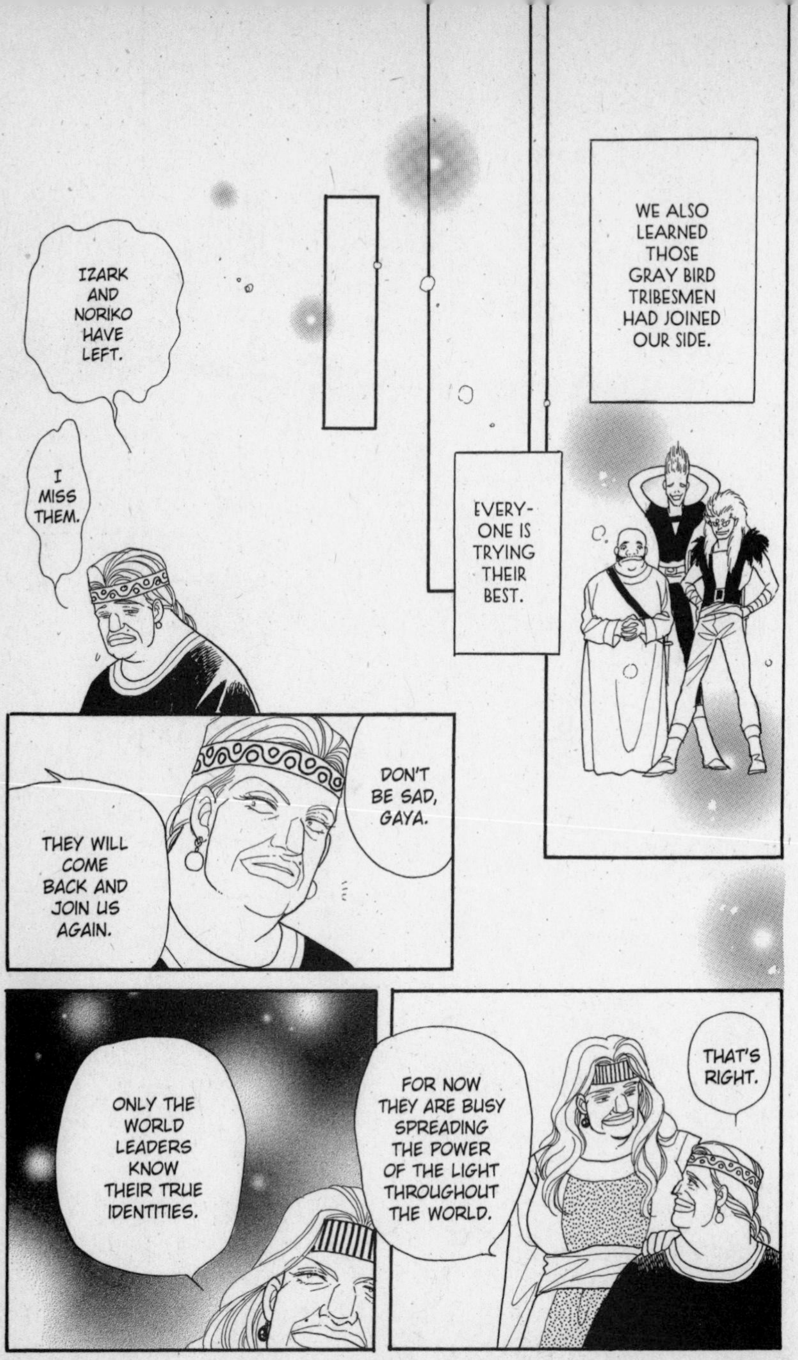

WE ALSO LEARNED THOSE GRAY BIRD TRIBESMEN HAD JOINED OUR SIDE.
EVERY-ONE IS TRYING THEIR BEST.
IZARK AND NORIKO HAVE LEFT.
I MISS THEM.
DON'T BE SAD, GAYA.
THEY WILL COME BACK AND JOIN US AGAIN.
THAT'S RIGHT.
FOR NOW THEY ARE BUSY SPREADING THE POWER OF THE LIGHT THROUGHOUT THE WORLD.
ONLY THE WORLD LEADERS KNOW THEIR TRUE IDENTITIES.

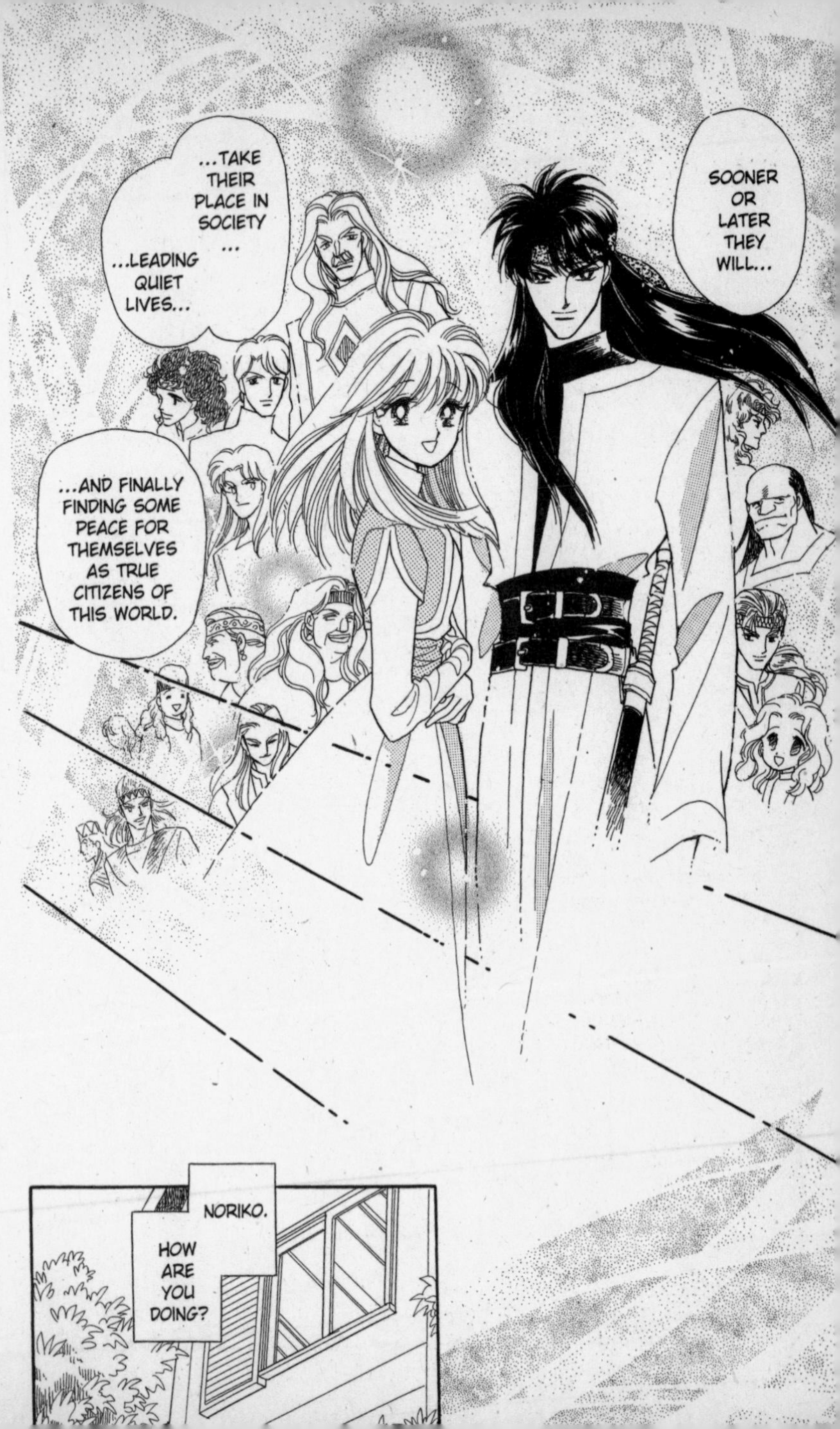
SOONER OR LATER THEY WILL...
...TAKE THEIR PLACE IN SOCIETY...
...LEADING QUIET LIVES...
...AND FINALLY FINDING SOME PEACE FOR THEMSELVES AS TRUE CITIZENS OF THIS WORLD.
NORIKO.
HOW ARE YOU DOING?

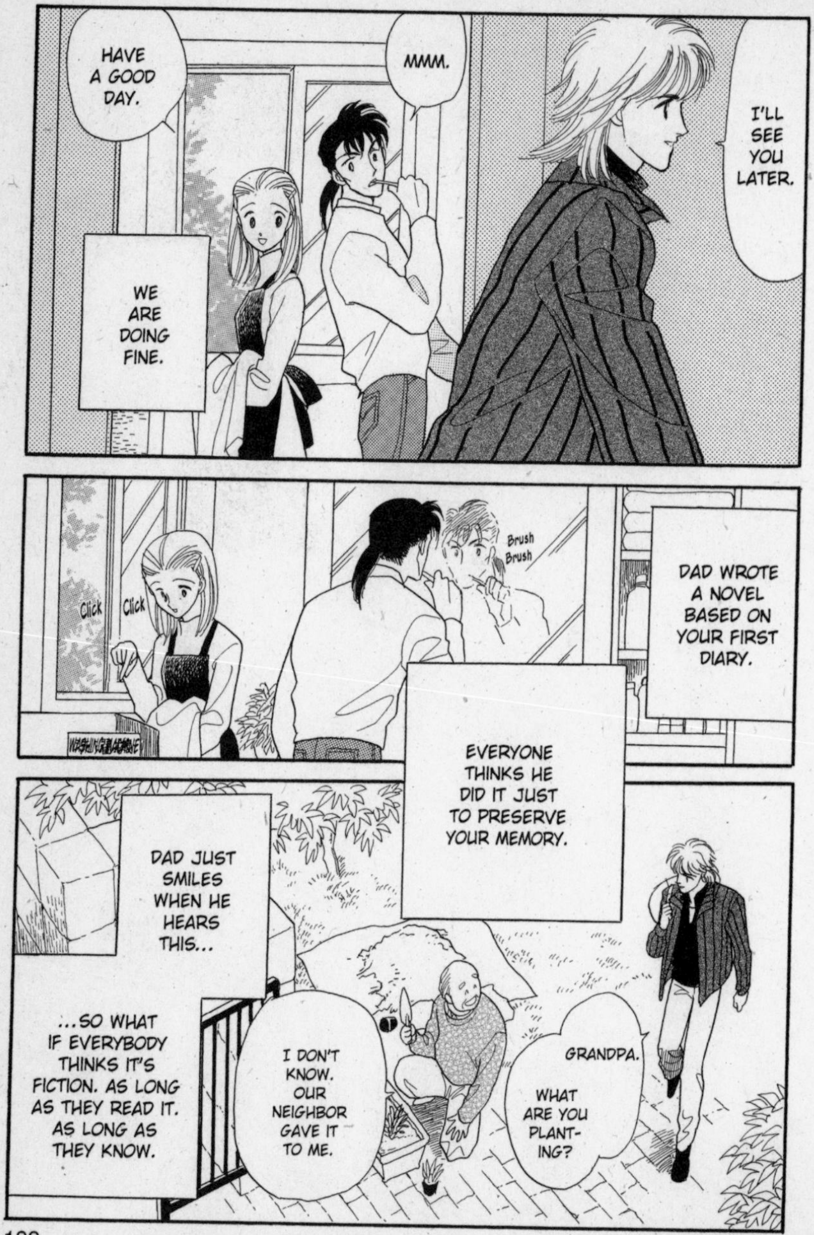
I'LL SEE YOU LATER.
MMM.
HAVE A GOOD DAY.
WE ARE DOING FINE.
DAD WROTE A NOVEL BASED ON YOUR FIRST DIARY.
Brush Brush
Click Click
EVERYONE THINKS HE DID IT JUST TO PRESERVE YOUR MEMORY.
DAD JUST SMILES WHEN HE HEARS THIS...
GRANDPA.
WHAT ARE YOU PLANT-ING?
I DON'T KNOW. OUR NEIGHBOR GAVE IT TO ME.
...SO WHAT IF EVERYBODY THINKS IT'S FICTION. AS LONG AS THEY READ IT. AS LONG AS THEY KNOW.

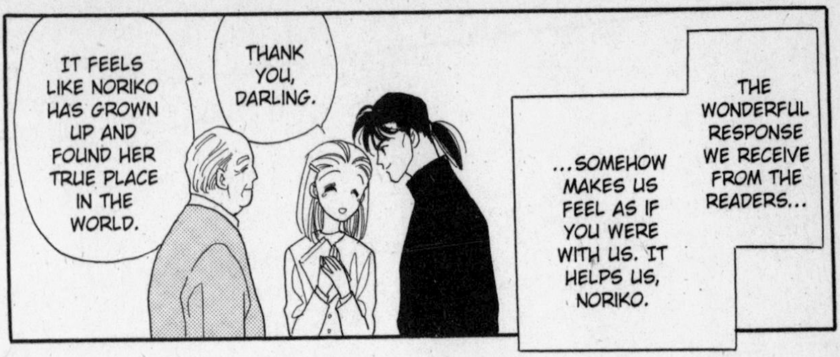
THE WONDERFUL RESPONSE WE RECEIVE FROM THE READERS...
...SOMEHOW MAKES US FEEL AS IF YOU WERE WITH US. IT HELPS US, NORIKO.
THANK YOU, DARLING.
IT FEELS LIKE NORIKO HAS GROWN UP AND FOUND HER TRUE PLACE IN THE WORLD.

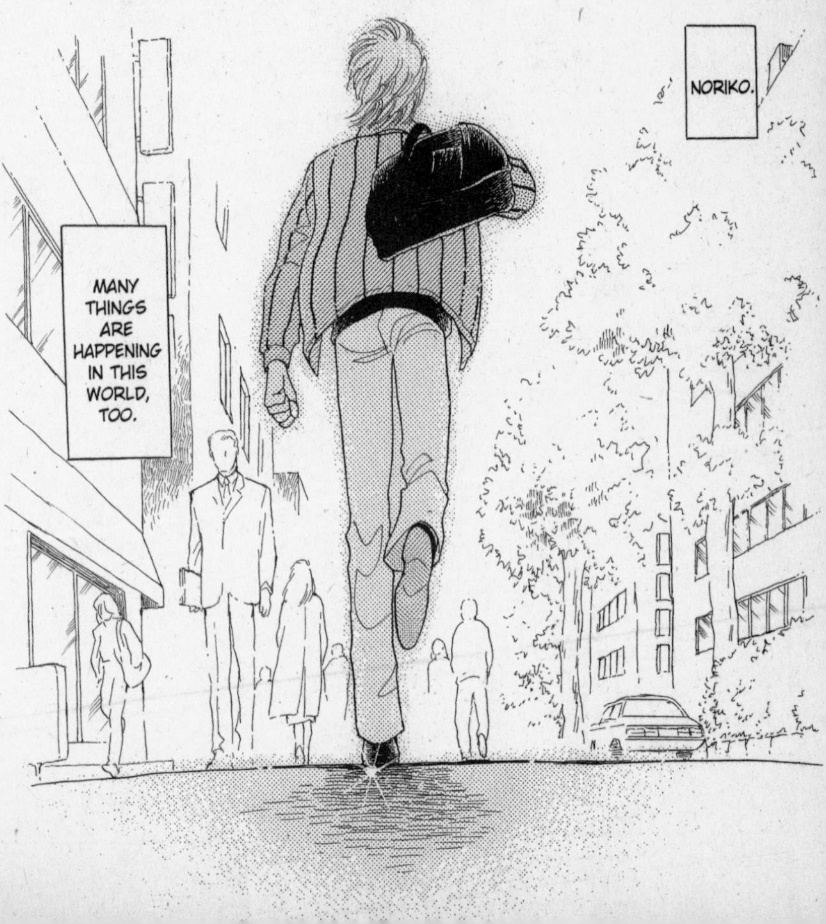
NORIKO.
MANY THINGS ARE HAPPENING IN THIS WORLD, TOO.

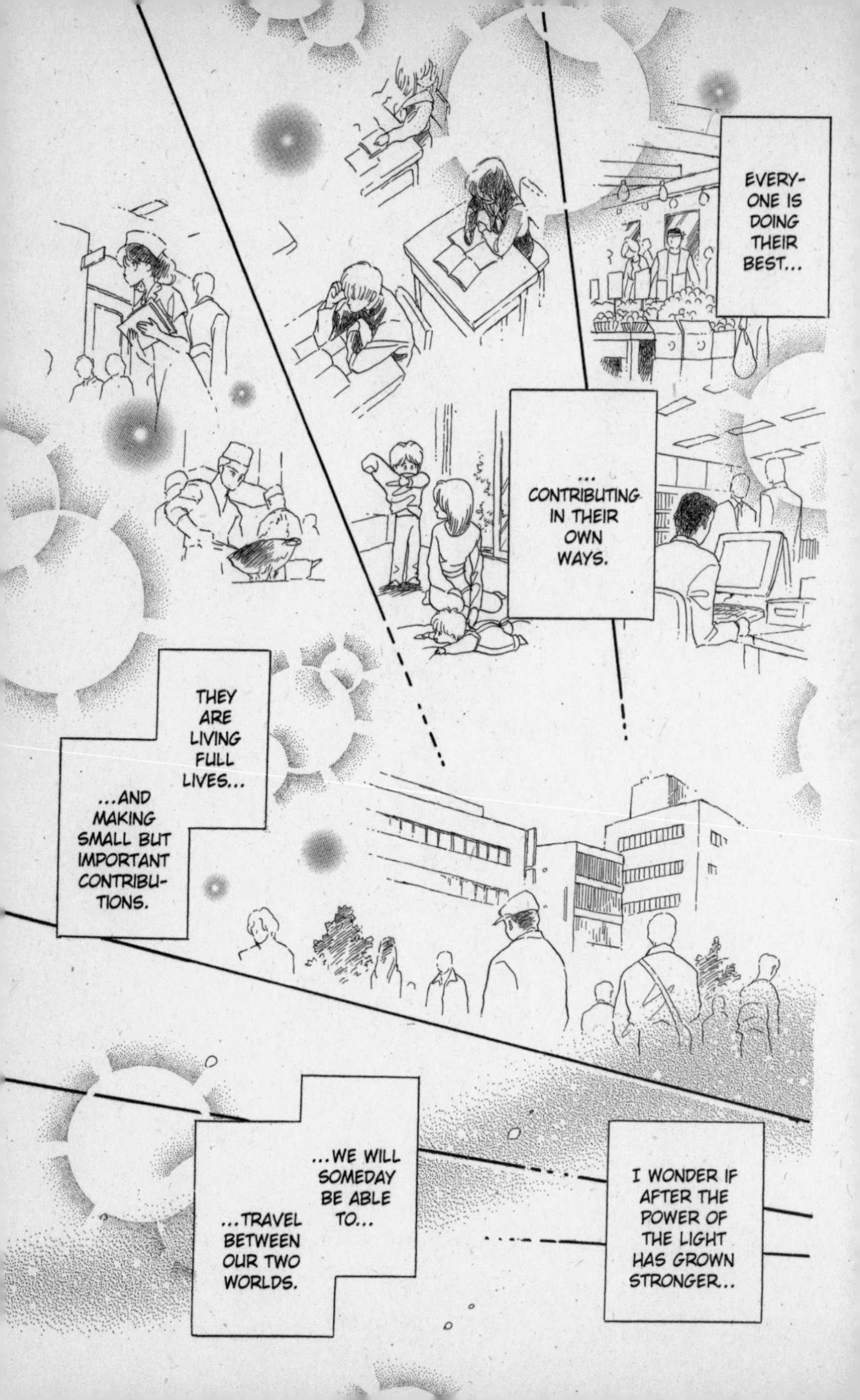
EVERY-ONE IS DOING THEIR BEST...
...CONTRIBUTING IN THEIR OWN WAYS.
THEY ARE LIVING FULL LIVES...
...AND MAKING SMALL BUT IMPORTANT CONTRIBU-TIONS.
I WONDER IF AFTER THE POWER OF THE LIGHT HAS GROWN STRONGER...
...WE WILL SOMEDAY BE ABLE TO...
...TRAVEL BETWEEN OUR TWO WORLDS.

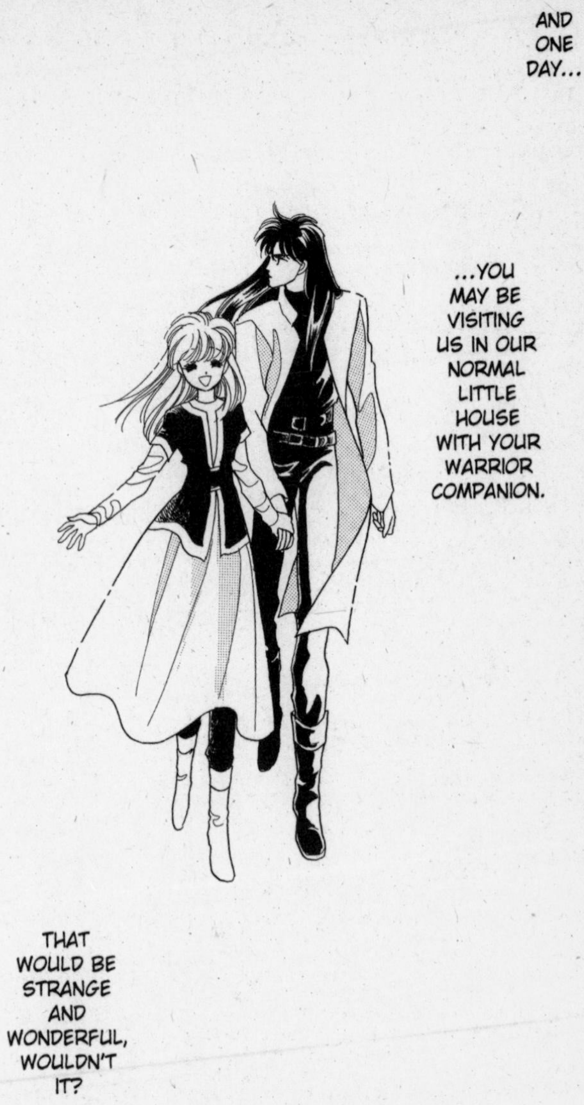
AND ONE DAY...
...YOU MAY BE VISITING US IN OUR NORMAL LITTLE HOUSE WITH YOUR WARRIOR COMPANION.
THAT WOULD BE STRANGE AND WONDERFUL, WOULDN'T IT?

End of Epilogue

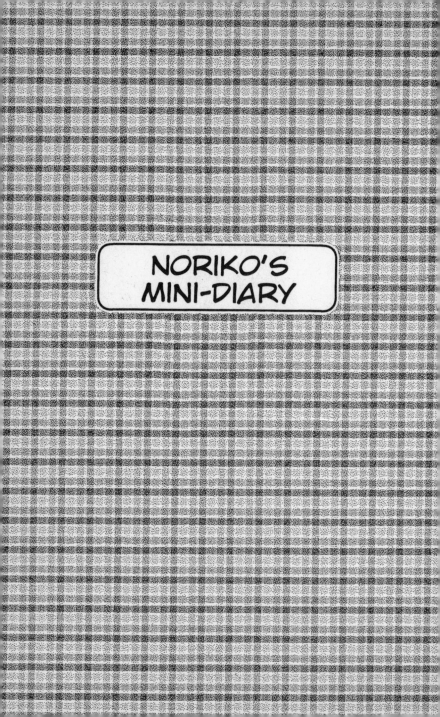

NORIKO'S
MINI-DIARY

NORIKO'S MINI-DIARY: ADDITIONAL EPISODES TO EPILOGUE

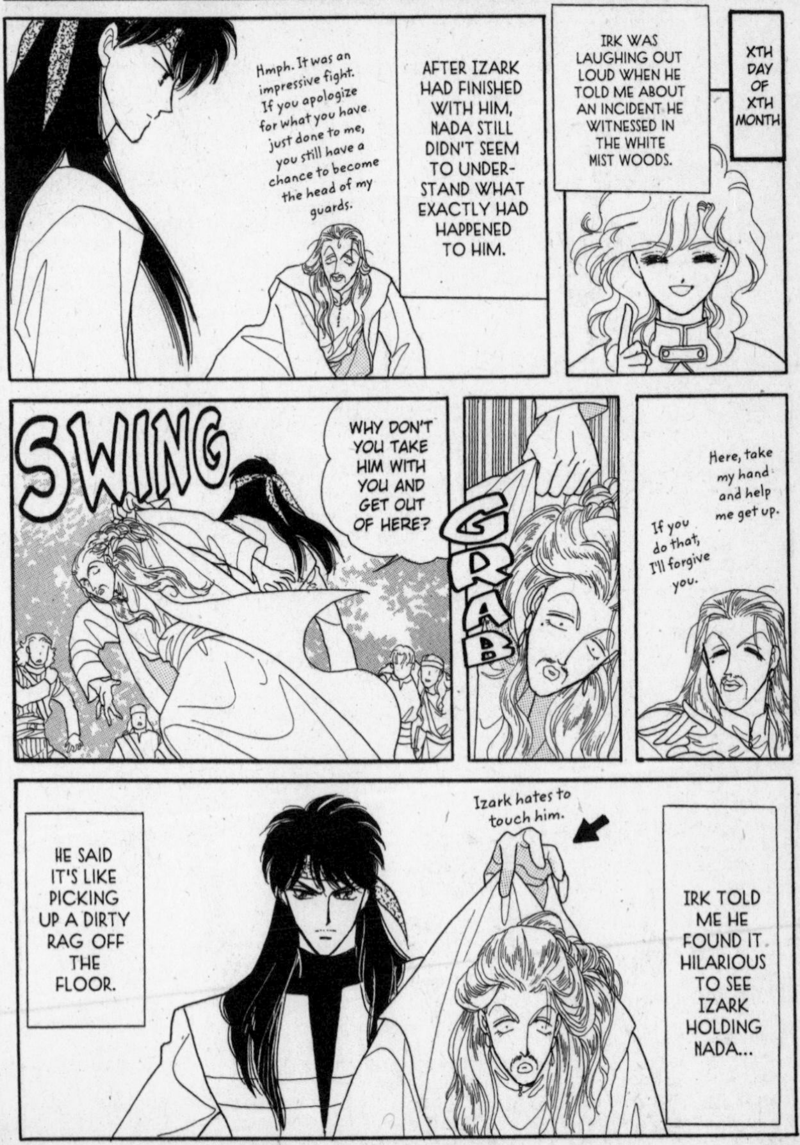
XTH DAY OF XTH MONTH
IRK WAS LAUGHING OUT LOUD WHEN HE TOLD ME ABOUT AN INCIDENT HE WITNESSED IN THE WHITE MIST WOODS.
AFTER IZARK HAD FINISHED WITH HIM, NADA STILL DIDN'T SEEM TO UNDERSTAND WHAT EXACTLY HAD HAPPENED TO HIM.
Hmph. It was an impressive fight. If you apologize for what you have just done to me, you still have a chance to become the head of my guards.
Here, take my hand and help me get up.
If you do that, I'll forgive you.
GRAB
WHY DON'T YOU TAKE HIM WITH YOU AND GET OUT OF HERE?
SWING
IRK TOLD ME HE FOUND IT HILARIOUS TO SEE IZARK HOLDING NADA...
Izark hates to touch him.
HE SAID IT'S LIKE PICKING UP A DIRTY RAG OFF THE FLOOR.

NORIKO'S MINI-DIARY:
ADDITIONAL EPISODES TO EPILOGUE

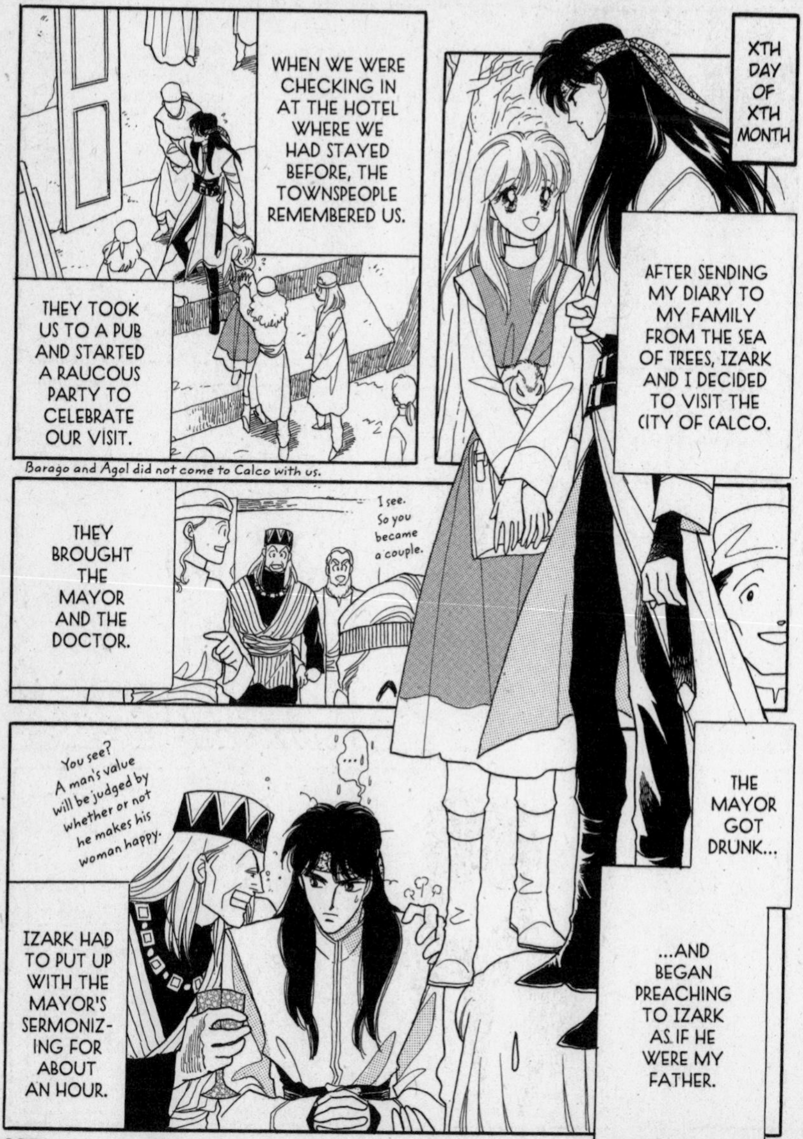
XTH DAY OF XTH MONTH
AFTER SENDING MY DIARY TO MY FAMILY FROM THE SEA OF TREES, IZARK AND I DECIDED TO VISIT THE CITY OF CALCO.
WHEN WE WERE CHECKING IN AT THE HOTEL WHERE WE HAD STAYED BEFORE, THE TOWNSPEOPLE REMEMBERED US.
THEY TOOK US TO A PUB AND STARTED A RAUCOUS PARTY TO CELEBRATE OUR VISIT.
Barago and Agol did not come to Calco with us.
THEY BROUGHT THE MAYOR AND THE DOCTOR.
I see. So you became a couple.
THE MAYOR GOT DRUNK...
...AND BEGAN PREACHING TO IZARK AS IF HE WERE MY FATHER.
...
You see? A man's value will be judged by whether or not he makes his woman happy.
IZARK HAD TO PUT UP WITH THE MAYOR'S SERMONIZING FOR ABOUT AN HOUR.

NORIKO'S MINI-DIARY: ADDITIONAL EPISODES TO EPILOGUE

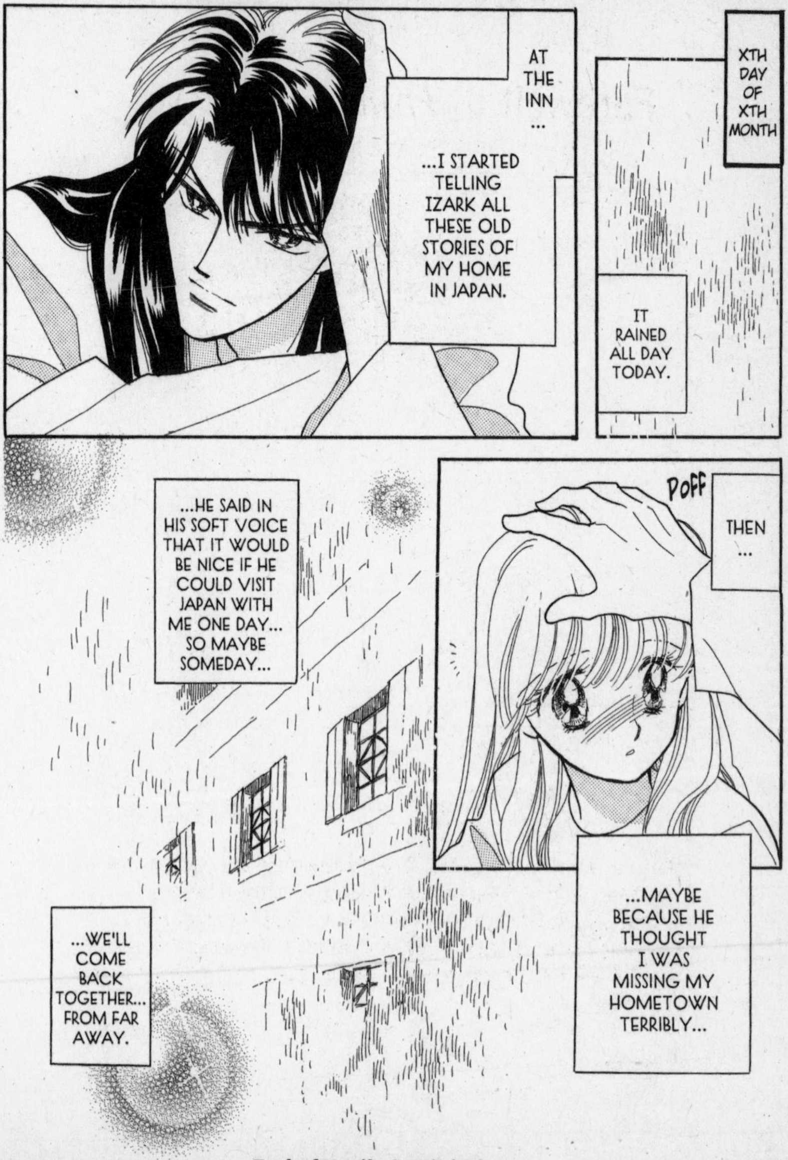
XTH DAY OF XTH MONTH
IT RAINED ALL DAY TODAY.
AT THE INN ...
...I STARTED TELLING IZARK ALL THESE OLD STORIES OF MY HOME IN JAPAN.
THEN ...
POFF
...MAYBE BECAUSE HE THOUGHT I WAS MISSING MY HOMETOWN TERRIBLY...
...HE SAID IN HIS SOFT VOICE THAT IT WOULD BE NICE IF HE COULD VISIT JAPAN WITH ME ONE DAY... SO MAYBE SOMEDAY...
...WE'LL COME BACK TOGETHER... FROM FAR AWAY.

End of Noriko's Mini Diary

The Final Volume

From Far Away™

Farewell to *From Far Away*

Make sure you turn the page to read our goodbye notes, and learn the hopes (and fears) the *From Far Away* team (both past and present) has for our favorite characters. We'll all miss working on this book — it's been a great series and we hope you all enjoyed Kyoko Hikawa's fantasy world as much as we did. Thank you for reading!

The *From Far Away* Team
January, 2007

Farewell to *From Far Away*™

The *From Far Away* team clue you in to their favorite characters – and what they hope happens for them next!

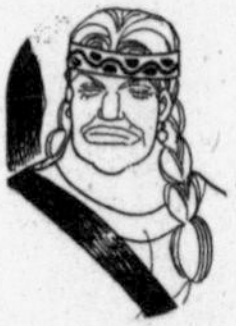

Gaya

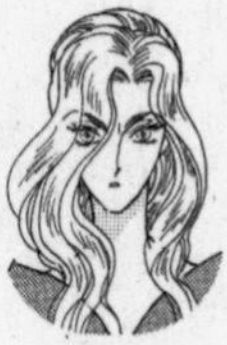

Tazasheena

Gaya is so great. My only hope for her is that she continues to gently lead her people as she does so well. As for Tazasheena, the woman you love to hate, I'd like to see her lose her powers and have no choice but to come to our world and find work on TV as the evil vamp character in a daytime soap opera.

—Trina Robbins, English Adaptation, Vol. 1-9

Noriko and Izark should get married and make babies. Then they can have little kiddies that transform into dragons and spit smoke. Once the little dragons grow up, they can take care of their mommy and daddy. When Noriko and Izark get old and grey, their dragon children can fly them to someplace safe...somewhere VERY Far Away!

—Walden Wong, Touch Up & Lettering, Vol. 1-9

Noriko & Izark

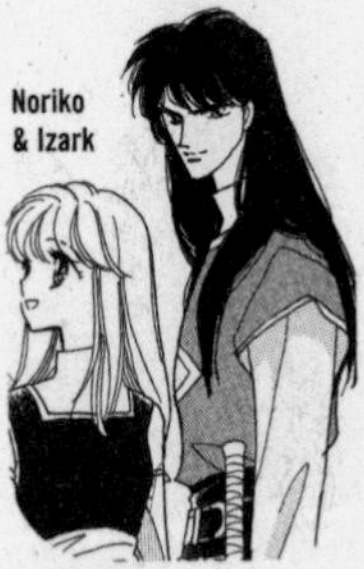

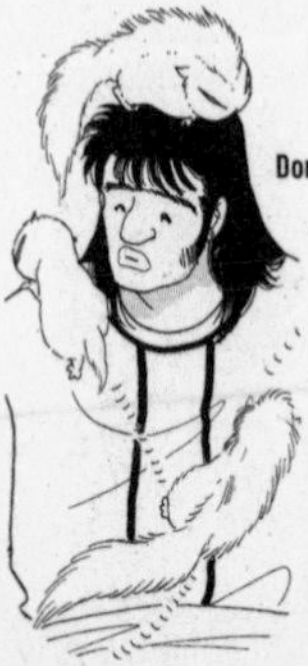

Doros

I always wanted to know more about Doros. What was his past like? Where did he come from? He's a lot like me...the bumbling idiot with a heart of gold! He's a little misguided at first, but he was just hanging out with the wrong crowd. When push comes to shove, he does the right thing (like the time he rescued Noriko). Doros may not be bright, but he's loyal. He deserves a good life with his friends.

—Freeman Wong, Touch Up & Lettering, Vol. 10-14

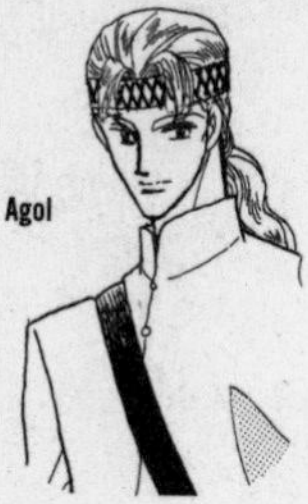

Agol

I'm sad to see From Far Away *end. I was afraid to read the last volume because I feared Noriko might be leaving Izark to go back to her own world. I was so relieved when I found it didn't happen. My favorite character is Izark, of course. He's extremely strong but with such a gentle heart. I loved his shyness and pure love for Noriko. But I also always wanted to know a little more about Agol. He seems like such a potentially romantic figure to me.*

—Yuko Sawada, Translator, Vol. 1-14, English Adaptation, Vol. 10-14

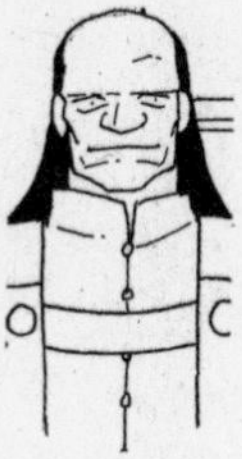

Barago

Right from their first clutch (volume 1, page 30, panel 2), we all knew Noriko would, uh, awaken the ardor of the stoic swordsman. Secretly, I was hoping our young heroine would hook up with Barago. A hero trapped in someone else's story, Barago was always my favorite. Dependable, trustworthy and the ultimate team player, he was really the heart of From Far Away. *He deserves a little love, don't you think?*

—Eric Searleman, Editor, Vol. 1-9

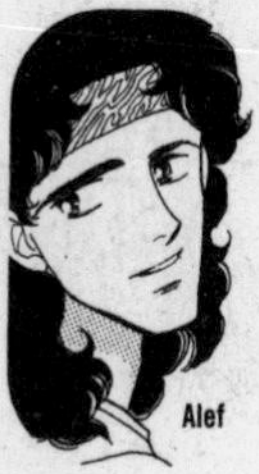

Alef

I'm partial to that career-confused jack-of-all-trades but master-of-none, Alef. He's been a soldier, a bodyguard, a shopkeeper, and even keeps trying to, er, um, manage the entertainment career of the reluctant Izark. He deserves to have his hard work and soul-searching pay off and become the first media mogul in the land, mentoring performers, producing shows, and making a heap of money!

—Joel Enos, Editor, Vol. 8-14

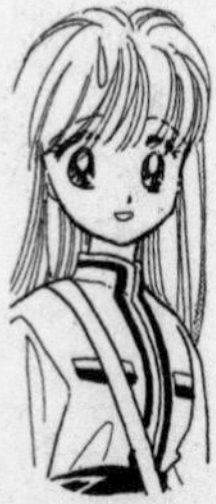

Noriko

I could relate to this schoolgirl-in-another-world heroine in a way that I can't with most others. She's an inspiration to anyone suddenly finding themselves in a Cutie and the Beast type situation. She handles herself with such pluck and down-to-earth practicality that I must assume she is a Virgo. I hope she will get a college degree one day.

—Andrea Rice, Graphic Designer, Vol. 1-14

From Far Away
Vol. 14
Shôjo Edition

Story and Art by
Kyoko Hikawa

Translation & Adaptation/Yuko Sawada
Touch-Up Art & Lettering/Freeman Wong
Cover & Graphic Design/Andrea Rice
Editor/Joel Enos

Managing Editor/Megan Bates
Editorial Director/Elizabeth Kawasaki
Vice President & Editor in Chief/Yumi Hoashi
Sr. Director of Acquisitions/Rika Inouye
Sr. VP of Marketing/Liza Coppola
Exec. VP of Sales & Marketing/John Easum
Publisher/Hyoe Narita

Printed in the U.S.A.

Published by VIZ Media, LLC
P.O. Box 77010
San Francisco, CA 94107

10 9 8 7 6 5 4 3 2 1
First printing, January 2007

www.viz.com

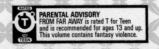

PARENTAL ADVISORY
FROM FAR AWAY is rated T for Teen
and is recommended for ages 13 and up.
This volume contains fantasy violence.

store.viz.com

What happens when the hottest guy in school is a girl?!?

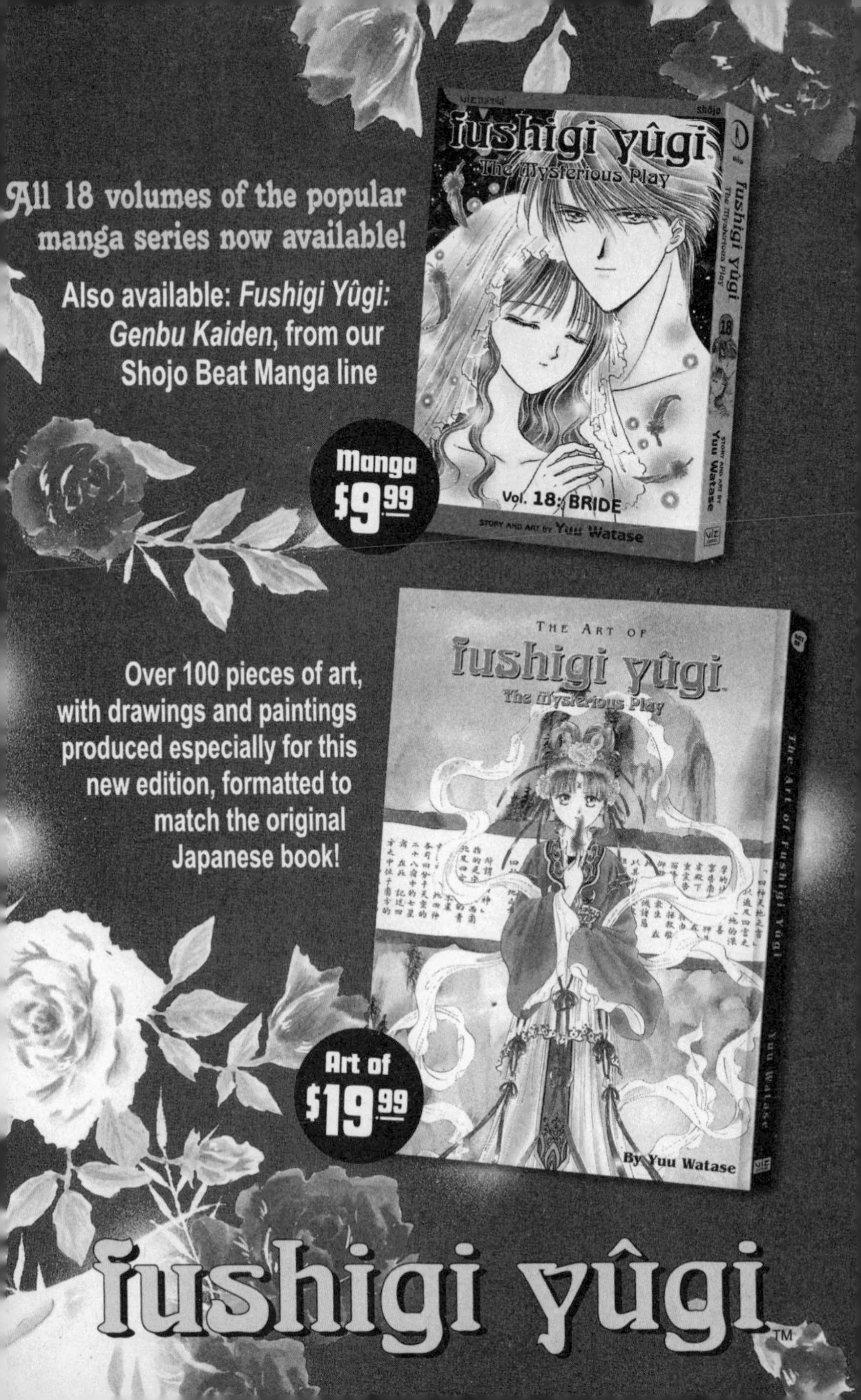
All 18 volumes of the popular manga series now available!
Also available: Fushigi Yûgi: Genbu Kaiden, from our Shojo Beat Manga line
fushigi yûgi
The Mysterious Play
Vol. 18: BRIDE
STORY AND ART BY Yuu Watase
Manga $9.99
Over 100 pieces of art, with drawings and paintings produced especially for this new edition, formatted to match the original Japanese book!
THE ART OF
fushigi yûgi
The Mysterious Play
By Yuu Watase
Art of $19.99
fushigi yûgi™